Anne

OPEN MINDED

JONATHAN LEAR

OPEN MINDED

Working Out the Logic of the Soul

HARVARD UNIVERSITY PRESS

Cambridge, Massachusetts, and London, England

Fifth printing, 1999

First Harvard University Press paperback edition, 1999

Library of Congress Cataloging-in-Publication Data

Lear, Jonathan.
Open minded : working out the logic of the soul / Jonathan Lear.
   p. cm.
Includes index.
ISBN 0–674–45533–9 (cloth)
ISBN 0–674–45534–7 (pbk.)
1. Psychoanalysis and philosophy.   I. Title.
BF175.4.P45L43   1998
150.19′5—dc21   97–41055

Designed by Alyssa Morris

TO SOPHIA LEAR

with love

Contents

❖ THIS DISCUSSION IS NOT ABOUT ANY CHANCE
QUESTION, BUT ABOUT THE WAY
ONE SHOULD LIVE.

Socrates in the *Republic*

❖ IT IS OWING TO THEIR WONDER THAT PEOPLE BOTH NOW
BEGIN AND AT FIRST BEGAN TO PHILOSOPHIZE.

Aristotle, *Metaphysics*

❖ AND WITH THE OLD, INTERMITTENT CADDISHNESS
WHICH REAPPEARED IN HIM WHEN HE WAS NO LONGER
UNHAPPY AND HIS MORAL STANDARDS DROPPED
ACCORDINGLY, HE EXCLAIMED TO HIMSELF: "TO
THINK THAT I'VE WASTED YEARS OF MY LIFE, THAT
I'VE LONGED TO DIE, THAT I'VE EXPERIENCED
MY GREATEST LOVE, FOR A WOMAN WHO
DIDN'T APPEAL TO ME, WHO
WASN'T EVEN MY TYPE!"

Marcel Proust, *In Search of Lost Time*

❖ SHE KNOWS THERE'S NO SUCCESS LIKE FAILURE,
AND THAT FAILURE'S NO SUCCESS AT ALL.

Bob Dylan, "Love minus Zero/No Limit"

CHAPTER 1

Preface: The King and I

❖ I AM ALWAYS DISAPPOINTED WHEN A BOOK LACKS A PREFACE: IT IS LIKE ARRIVING AT SOMEONE'S HOUSE FOR DINNER, AND BEING CONDUCTED STRAIGHT INTO THE DINING-ROOM.

Michael Dummett, *Frege: Philosophy of Language*

From childhood, I was brought into a peculiar ritual which I did not understand. Neither did anyone else. As far as I can remember, it began on the first day of real school, first grade. Leaning against the edge of her desk, the teacher, Mrs. Gilmette, explained that she was going to assign each of us our own desks for the year. She went in alphabetical order, and when she got to me she said, "Are you related to the king?" Obviously, I had no idea what she was talking about. But the idea that I might somehow be related to a king was placed in my mind when I was six years old. Perhaps that single grain of phantasy-sand would have been enough for my imagination to work over and make into a pearl; or perhaps I would have forgotten all about it. I wouldn't know: *every year*, on the first day of school, the teacher would ask if I were related to the king. It is hard to describe the bored fascination this question would arouse. On the one hand, I'd inwardly groan: here we go again. And I'd realize that in the intervening year I had done nothing to find out who this king was. On the other hand, as the years passed, I came to think that the answer to this question had something to do with me. This was my special meaning. It would tell me who I was. But I didn't know what this meaning meant.

As a young man I learned that I was in fact related to a King Lear. My father's uncle Eli was a con man; and in Leavenworth Prison, where he died, the other inmates knew him as "King." According to family lore, my father was on his way to the Plaza Hotel to meet my mother's parents to ask for her hand in marriage when he glimpsed the tabloid headline "Toy-Gun Bandit Arrested!" If the headline-writers had only known, it could have said, "King in Dungeon!" I have often tried to imagine my father—then a young doctor, but from a humble Jewish home—trying to explain to these wealthy, Jewish-proper-Bostonian parents-in-law-to-be that yes, he was related to royalty, but not *quite* in the way they might imagine. This vignette set my mind moving toward crime. Two generations above me, on my father's side, there was a significant strain of sociopathy running through the family. In my father's generation there was enormous worldly success. Perhaps this represented a decline! Perhaps we were descended from a great line of crooks! This made some intuitive sense to me, for I could recognize a touch of larceny in my soul. And then I read Isaac Babel's "The King," in his *Odessa Stories,* a wonderful tale of a Russian-Jewish King of Crime—and for a passing moment I thought I had the answer. My family reputedly comes from Odessa. The King was my great, great . . . grandfather, a Jewish Moriarity, a Karla or Macavity— and from that golden age we have fallen into the bronze. Whether I considered my toy-gun-bandit uncle or my successful television-producer cousin, it was two sides of the same bronze coin. The mantle of truly great criminality had passed out of our family. The Great Violators of established norms were no longer to be found among the Lears. Our only choice now was between petty criminality and vast legitimate success. It didn't seem fair. How had we gone wrong?

Though I have played with this idea for years, and it does have some resonance for me, it has never had that convincing ring of truth. Neither did my first approaches to Shakespeare's King Lear. I know in the center of my soul that I would understand what Cordelia was saying to me and I would love her for it. I also know absolutely that, even were I at the center of that drama, I would find Regan and Goneril's flattery as repellent as I do from the audience. Whatever my many faults, I simply do not have Lear's insecurity and vanity. Try as I might, I couldn't identify with him. This is a shame, because the play moves me deeply: I consider it one of a handful of the very best things a human being has ever made. And yet, I couldn't get from there to *being* King Lear. There things lay fallow for years. None of this was particularly pressing: it was just an occasional fancy which would not allow itself to be completely forgotten.

And then one night, during the time I was in analysis, I woke up with a start and realized I had it: I am Cordelia! I *am* related to the King! He's my father! I love him dearly, and he just doesn't get it. To identify with Cordelia is to want to be blunt, to avoid embellishment, flattery, or hypocrisy—*and to want to be loved for doing just that.* This is not a set of desires which get satisfied often. By and large, people prefer to be flattered. They find it hard to recognize love in a blunt appraisal; and they find it even harder to reciprocate such love. Cordelia's strategy is not the route to massive popularity. Nevertheless, I have no choice: I *am* Cordelia. Why do I tell you this? Because I want to say that there is something dead in the profession of psychoanalysis and something dead in the profession of philosophy—and I want to be loved for saying so. This book is above all a response to a sense of deadness: it is an attempt to bring some life into two activities which lie at the heart of our humanity.

It has crossed my mind to wonder whether it isn't the point of all professions—of medicine and law as much as of philosophy and psychoanalysis—to instill deadness. Of course, the conscious self-image of every profession is that it is there to maintain high standards. And there must be *some* truth in this image. But what does this image cover over? Don't standards themselves impose a kind of rigidity on a practice? Doesn't a professional set of standards enable the profession to forget about standards? That is, it enables the profession to stop thinking critically about how it ought to go on precisely because the standards present themselves as having already answered the question. The profession can then act as though it *already knows* what high standards are. This is a form of deadness. Now for certain forms of professional activity, this is all right. Indeed, it is what we want. We do not want our dentists, for example, to be too creative in their activity. We want there to be a relatively fixed set of norms of dental hygiene, and we want our dentists to adhere to those norms rigidly, over and over again. We want our dentists to be dead!

But philosophy and psychoanalysis are activities which resist professionalization in this sense. Perhaps this is because they share the same fundamental question, posed by Socrates: in what way should one live?[1] In psychoanalysis, the accent is more on the first person singular—How shall *I* live? in philosophy, on the first person plural—How shall *we* go on? But as anyone who has engaged in either activity knows, you cannot investigate I without addressing We, and vice versa. For Socrates, human living consists in living openly with this question. And any fixed set of norms—whether the standards of a profession or the set morality of a culture—presents itself as having already answered the question. That is, the norms try to shut down the question of how to live by giving a packaged answer. Whatever other functions they may have, norms often serve as a defense against living openly with the fundamental question. For Socrates, this is an evasion of life. This is why, for Socrates, the unexamined life is not worth living: it is not a form of living, but a form of deadness. To live openly with the fundamental question is to avoid assuming that there are any fixed answers which are already given. It is, above all, to avoid all forms of "knowingness."

No wonder Socrates was put to death! The citizens of Athens decided by democratic vote that in him and around him there was too much living going on for them to tolerate. The way they put it was that Socrates was corrupting the youth and introducing new gods. That's how living openly looks to a group which is tenaciously clinging to a desiccated form of life. And Socrates, for his part, did nothing to help the Athenians analyze their transference-distortion. Indeed, he seems to have invited and provoked the transference-storm which resulted in his death.

In the calmer worlds of the professions, symbolic murders go on all the time. How many times have I heard distinguished members of the philosophical profession say, for example, that Hegel and Heidegger are "not *really* philosophers"! One well-known professor had on his office door a sign which read, "Just Say No to the History of Philosophy." The psychoanalytic profession, at least in America, is no better. For decades the curriculum committees of institutes affiliated with the American Psychoanalytic Association systematically excluded the work of such creative thinkers as the British psychoanalyst Melanie Klein and the French analyst Jacques Lacan. And the method of exclusion was the same, whether it was occurring in analysis or in philosophy. Some extreme or obscure statement would be pulled out of context, there would be a contemptuous shrugging of shoulders—"What could this possibly mean!" "Isn't that absurd!"—and that one statement or position would be used as an excuse to dismiss the entire corpus of work. Each profession thus worked actively to reassure itself that it was all right, indeed, one *ought*, to remain ignorant. All in the name of maintaining high standards.

And this type of facile dismissal seeps effortlessly into the culture. In countless conversations—at cocktail and dinner parties, not to mention the informal conversations which go on in professional settings, like the grand rounds of a psychiatry department or a conference of historians or philosophers, I will hear someone say, "But, of course, Freud has been completely discredited." There will be a tacit assent of the group, and then it will dawn on me that no one in the group has read a word of Freud. Already knowing that Freud is discredited gives the group permission to know nothing.

Psychoanalysis, Freud said, is an *impossible* profession.[2] So is philosophy. This is not a metaphor or a poetically paradoxical turn of phrase. It is literally true. And the impossibility is ultimately a matter of logic. For *the very idea* of a profession is that of a defensive structure, and it is part of *the very idea* of philosophy and psychoanalysis to be activities which undo such defenses. It is part of the logic of psychoanalysis and philosophy that they are forms of life committed to living openly—with truth, beauty, envy and hate, wonder, awe and dread. The idea of a profession of psychoanalysis or a profession of philosophy is thus a contradiction in terms. Or, to put it bluntly, there is no such idea. Before we began the inquiry, we might have thought we were thinking about something when we tried to think about the profession of psychoanalysis or the profession of philosophy—we might have thought we had an idea in our heads. What we come to recognize is that there is no such idea and there couldn't be such an idea: there is really nothing we are thinking about.

But then, what are the American Psychoanalytic Association and the American Philosophical Association? Attempts to act on an illusion. An illusion, for Freud, is a belief, set of beliefs, or worldview caused by a wish rather than by perception of how the world is. These organizations spring from the wish to hold onto psychoanalysis and philosophy—and from the ensuing belief that one might do so by professionalizing them. I don't intend this as a criticism. Trying to act on an illusion can be among life's satisfying activities—just so long as one doesn't entirely lose one's sense of humor. One discovers philosophical or psychoanalytic activity, and *of course* one wants to try to preserve it and to pass it along. One has bumped into something fundamental, and one cannot bear the idea of its simply disappearing from the human scene. Erotically we strive for the immortality of these deeply valuable activities. And inevitably we face the vicissitudes of dogmatism. Dogma, belief: we want to pass on fundamental truths, and in our attempts to do so truth becomes rigid and dies. The only remedy I have found is to treat this as a comedy rather than a tragedy. At the end of the *Symposium,* Socrates enigmatically suggests that poets should be as good at writing comedy as they are at tragedy. And I suspect he meant that poets ought to be able to tell the same story both ways. (If one tries, as I do in Chapter 3, one *can* read Oedipus as farce.) I suppose one could shed tears that, really, it *is* impossible to preserve and pass on truth. Important insights die. Yet we contribute to that death if we lose the lighthearted sense that, indeed, we are engaged in an impossible profession.

Through a variety of life choices I won't bore you with, I found myself in my twenties in a tenured position at one of the world's great universities, the University of Cambridge. Though I adored being at Cambridge, the fact of tenure caused me anxiety rather than pleasure. And I have thought about that anxiety ever since. In America, the great East Coast universities think of themselves as modeled on Oxford and Cambridge—

but this is really a false-self presentation. In fact they are modeled on Heidelberg. In the German model, the older professor reigns and the younger academics work under him, often in servile submission, hoping that one day they too will be the senior. Tenure is the American-democratic form of a rite of passage which favors seniority. Oxford and Cambridge, by contrast, formed themselves around a phantasy of an ancient Greek ideal of homosexual love. In that world, what is best is to be the beautiful, brilliant young man. The older men, past their bloom, look with nostalgia, delight, admiration, and a touch of envy at their brilliant youngers. Read almost any biography of Keynes, Turing, Wittgenstein, Russell, Ramsey, and you will get some of this flavor.

It is in thinking about my anxiety that I came to realize that the American tenure system is a form of distraction. If I had had to spend the next decade or two worried about whether I would get tenure, I probably would have acted like so many assistant professors, obsessing about getting articles in the right journals, dealing with the issues which were currently fashionable in the profession, wondering what the professors in the department thought of me, and so on. And I might even have been seduced by the profession's self-image that this is all about maintaining high standards. As it was, with tenure out of the way, the only hurdle I seemed to face was the fact of my own death. It didn't seem to be all that far away. And I realized that before I died, I wanted to be in intimate touch with some of the world's great thinkers, with some of the deepest thoughts which humans have encountered. I wanted to think thoughts—and also to write something which mattered to me.

I set out to work my own way through the history of philosophy. I did this by teaching undergraduate courses on thinkers I barely knew—one of the best ways of learning about them—by talking endlessly to colleagues, and by reading voraciously. I wanted to know: in the world of ideas, *where are we?* And what I seemed to discover was not so much an answer to that question, as a mystery in its own right: the very idea of psychology seemed to have gone missing. The most philosophical formulation of this disappearance is expressed by Hegel. For him, the account of human beings in the Western philosophical tradition had become too "abstract," too formal, to yield anything substantive about who we are. If we want to learn anything valuable about the human condition, Hegel argued, philosophy has to become more "concrete." But how can philosophy become more "concrete" without collapsing into an empirical discipline, like anthropology or empirical psychology? Can philosophy become "concrete" without itself disappearing? And if all that is left is, say, empirical psychology, has psychology itself survived? Plato's answer would be "of course not." And he is not alone. Everyone has his or her own version of "If I had a dime for every time . . . , I'd be rich." My version is, ". . . for every time a student came to my office hours and said, 'I tried taking a course in psychology, but it didn't seem to be about *psychology*.'" The students can never clearly articulate their sense of *what* is missing, but they are filled with longing.

This is not in any way meant to criticize the valuable work in cognitive science, neuroscience, statistical research which goes on in the best psychology departments. It is only to say that a certain activity which Plato called "giving a logos of the psyche" has all but disappeared. An everyday way of rendering the Greek is "working out the logic of the soul." In the twentieth century it has become difficult to understand this phrase because the remarkable advances in formal logic since 1879 have so colored our understanding of what logic is. We lose sight of Plato's project, laid out so beautifully in the *Republic,* of giving a *non*formal but rigorous, not-quite-empirical yet not nonempirical account of what it is to be human. Plato, one might say, is working out *the very idea* of what it is to be minded as we are. And he does this in the light of Socrates' exemplification—a life spent showing—that one of the most important truths about us is that we have the capacity to be *open minded:* the capacity to live nondefensively with the question of how to live.

Human life in general is a study of why this capacity is not exercised: why open-mindedness is, for the most part, evaded, diminished, and attacked. Allow me to say something bold and without a shred of argument: one cannot understand the *Republic* until one can see the entire book as organized around the issue of how to avoid despair. Plato's solution is to introduce matter. If we come to understand ourselves as living in a world in which ideas are realized in matter, then we can hold onto the belief that ideas themselves are good, while recognizing that human life in general—whether in individual psychology or in politics—is, by and large, a falling away from those ideas. Matter eventually loses form. Disappointment is built into the very fabric of who we are. But in disappointment there is hope, if not optimism, and thus the avoidance of despair.

I have spent the past twenty years not so much trying to answer the question "What is psychology?" as trying to recover a sense of what the question is. I was led, almost simultaneously, back to Plato and Aristotle, to Freud and psychoanalysis, and to Wittgenstein. It may surprise readers to learn that I consider this as being led in one direction. Of course, that psychoanalysis is a continuation of the Platonic tradition is itself hardly news. In the *Republic,* Plato basically invents psyche-analysis. He divides the psyche into three basic parts—and though Plato comes up with slightly different parts from Freud, the method of division they use is the same. For Plato, the appetitive part, consisting largely of drives for sex and food, is more or less identical with Freud's id. Then there is a narcissistic component, concerned with pride, winning recognition from others, anger, humiliation, and shame. In this way, Plato reveals himself as much more concerned with the vicissitudes of narcissism than Freud was, at least at the beginning of his career. Finally, there is a part concerned with thinking and finding out the truth about the world. And Plato understood, perhaps better than anyone else has ever understood, that even this thoughtful attempt to understand one's world is basically an erotic engagement. It is for love of the world that we try to understand it. Again, Freud came upon this insight later in his career, when he reconceptualized and expanded the sex drive into eros. And he thanked "the divine Plato" for inspiration:

> In its origin, function and relation to sexual love, the eros of the philosopher Plato coincides exactly with the love-force, the libido of psychoanalysis.[3]
>
> . . . what psychoanalysis calls sexuality was by no means identical with the impulsion towards a union of the two sexes or towards producing a pleasurable sensation in the genitals; it had far more resemblance to the all-inclusive and all-embracing love of Plato's *Symposium.*[4]

Plato also invented the first sophisticated object-relations theory. He understood that the human psyche is in dynamic interaction with the cultural-political environment, and that both are fundamentally shaped by the movement of meanings from polis to psyche and back again. He works out one of the most insightful accounts of psychosocial degeneration ever formulated. Contemporary object-relations theorists, if they go back to Plato, will study his account of psychopathology with awe. For Plato, the influence of polis on psyche or of psyche on polis is largely unconscious.[5] And human life is, for the most part, lived in the midst of illusion. In Plato's famous image of the cave, we are, unbeknownst to ourselves, strapped to a wall and forced to watch the projections of images onto the opposite wall which we mistake not only for reality, but for ourselves.[6] We are, on this account, strangers to ourselves. But for Plato as for Freud, there is therapeutic potential in pushing hard at contradictions inherent in the illusions themselves. Every image is *a shadow*, a distortion of something bearing more reality than it. In focusing on the distortion we can painfully and slowly work our way toward what the distortion is a distortion of. Once again Plato plants the hope of avoiding despair.

Plato understands the power and shape of unconscious wishes, which he calls lawless unnecessary desires:

> Those that are awakened in sleep, when the rest of the soul—the rational, gentle, and ruling part—slumbers. Then the beastly and savage part, full of food and drink, casts off sleep and seeks to find a way to gratify itself. You know there is nothing it won't dare to do at such a time, free of all control by shame or reason. It doesn't shrink from trying to have sex with a mother, as it supposes, or with anyone else at all, whether man, god or beast. It will commit any foul murder, and there is no food it refuses to eat. In a word, it omits no act of folly or shamelessness.[7]

These desires are, Plato says, "probably present in everyone." In his diagnosis of tyrannical personality disorder, these lawless appetites come to dominate, turning waking life into a living nightmare and ushering in a disintegration of the soul. This is the first serious theoretical discussion of a person powerless to do anything other than act out his inner life.

Freud may have been more or less aware of these various influences upon him, but there is one thread running between him and Plato of which he was certainly unaware: that he, like Plato, was trying to work out a logic of the psyche. Freud could not see this because his self-image and ego-ideal are those of a working empirical scientist and medical doctor, perhaps one with cultural ambitions. Thus he is not well placed to see that his empirical research is not simply in the service of working out what, as a matter of fact, the human psyche is like, nor simply in the service of treating the psyche, but that it is also working out *what it is to be* a human psyche. So, for example, Freud doesn't just discover the fact of neurotic conflict; he lays before us the inevitable possibility of neurosis built into the very idea of a creature erotically bound to the world by different types of desires. Or, as I argue in Chapter 5, Freud did not just empirically discover the drives; he showed that the idea of drive is required for a minded creature, like us, who is embodied and working in an environment. There must be a place for, as Freud put it, a "demand made upon the mind for work."[8] In this way, Freud offers what I take to be the most textured answer we yet have to one of Socrates' most important "What is it?" questions: what is the human psyche? Freud also shows us, in the most vivid way, what it might be for philosophy to become "concrete."

BUT IF ONE CAN SEE psychoanalysis as placed broadly in the Platonic tradition, what possible relation can there be between Freud and Wittgenstein? After all, Wittgenstein's few explicit remarks about Freud tend to be quite skeptical. For example: "I have been going through Freud's *Interpretation of Dreams* . . . and it has made me think how much this whole way of thinking wants combatting."[9] Wittgenstein is suspicious that there are no real constraints on what it is to get a psychoanalytic interpretation right, and thus that the correct interpretation ends up being anything Freud says it is. I do not intend here to defend Freud against the charge. Rather, I want to point out that if we stick with these explicit criticisms, we remain at the conscious surface. But if we look at what Freud and Wittgenstein *are doing,* we can see deep, unconscious affinities between the two thinkers. Starting with Wittgenstein, the *Philosophical Investigations* is essentially an attempt to work through a certain illusion.

The *Investigations* begins with a myth of origins, Augustine's account of how he entered into language:

> When they (my elders) named some object, and accordingly moved towards something, I saw this and I grasped that the thing was called by the sound they uttered when they meant to point it out . . . Thus, as I heard words repeatedly used in their proper places in various sentences, I gradually learnt to understand what objects they signified; and after I trained my mouth to form these signs, I used them to express my desires.

Wittgenstein's opening comment is:

> These words, it seems to me, give us a particular picture of the essence of human language. It is this: the individual words in language name objects— sentences are combinations of such names. In this picture of language we find the roots of the following idea: Every word has a meaning. This meaning is correlated with the word. It is the object for which the word stands.[10]

For "picture" read illusion. Reading Augustine's account, we find it so plausible and unexceptional that we think we are looking at something *obviously true.* What we do not understand, to put Wittgenstein's insight in psychoanalytic terms, is that we are being persuaded, not by obvious truth, but by the force of our own projective identifications. We are creatures who cannot help but create mythic accounts of how our mind works, of how we hook onto the world, of what reality is really like. We project this imaginative activity onto the world and then mistake it for "the way things really are." In this way, we systematically mistake a bit of ourselves, our imaginative activity, for the world.

This systematic mistaking we tend to call "philosophy." So, for example, we begin with what we might call this *core myth of meaning*—that individual words are names—a myth only implicit in Augustine, made explicit by Wittgenstein; a fantasy so seemingly innocuous that we are unaware that from it flows a theory of mind, meaning, and world. For if words are names, and if names stand for a meaning, then for me to be speaking meaningfully must be for me to have ideas in my mind, the meanings, with which words are correlated. And thus we form a picture of the mind as a container of ideas which gives my words the meaning they have. It is as though the idea could exist independently of the word—just as the word without the idea would be a meaningless sound—and we form the picture of words naming objects in the world by being animated by ideas in the mind. Here is a picture of language hovering between mind and world. It is as though we were separated from the world, trying to talk about it. And from this picture, to give just one example, skeptical questions—"Are we getting the world right? How do we *really* know?"—become inevitable. And we take this inevitability to reflect the human condition: that it is our fate to live in separation from how things *really* are. Wittgenstein brings to conscious awareness that it is not so much our fate to live in separation as our fate to be tempted to create and be seduced by myths of separation. These are illusions we can work through and ultimately live without. In this way, proper philosophical activity is the working-through and undoing of "philosophy." In Freudian terms, remembering comes to replace repeating.

But if this is a Freudian Wittgenstein, we can also identify a Wittgensteinian Freud. As Freud's thinking developed, he came to think of an unconscious meaning less in terms of a particular idea whose content is hidden in another part of the mind and more in terms of an idiosyncratic activity or *form of life* whose meaning we actively keep ourselves from grasping. As Freud put it, "hysterics are undoubtedly imaginative artists, even if they express their phantasies *mimetically* in the main and without considering the intelligibility to other people; the ceremonials and prohibitions of obsessional neurotics drive us to suppose that they have created a private religion of their own."[11] And so when a person acts out a phantasy—for example, when the Rat Man opens the door to his house at night and exposes his penis—he is—how shall I put it?—*showing* more than he can *say*. His activity is meaningful—it expresses a meaning—but he does not understand it. This is one understanding of the unconscious: the meanings we show that we cannot (yet) say. And once Freud saw unconscious meaning in this way, he saw it everywhere:

> When I set myself the task of bringing to light what human beings keep hidden within them, not by the compelling power of hypnosis, but by observing what they say *and what they show*, I thought the task was a harder one than it really is. He that has eyes to see and ears to hear may convince himself that no mortal can keep a secret. If his lips are silent, he chatters with his finger tips; betrayal oozes out of him at every pore.[12]

The aim of psychoanalytic interpretation, then, is to bring the meanings we show (repeat) into the domain of meanings we can say (remember). In this way we gain some freedom with respect to those meanings. (In Chapter 5, I show how the psychoanalytic understanding of interpretation bears a family resemblance to Wittgenstein's own account of how a prelinguistic infant is brought into language.)

This is, *of course*, not to say that Freud really became a behaviorist. (Neither did Wittgenstein.) Freud remained perfectly comfortable with the notion of unconscious meanings which remain entirely within the mind and do not get acted out or expressed in behavior. But even here, the accent of his thinking shifts from the unconscious as a hidden idea or mental *content*, to the unconscious as a peculiar form of mental activity. Twenty-five years after he first published *The Interpretation of Dreams*, Freud felt he had to insert a new footnote, which he placed at the end of his discussion of the dream-work:

> I used at one time to find it extraordinarily difficult to accustom readers to the distinction between the manifest content of dreams and the latent dream-thoughts . . . But now that analysts at least have become reconciled to replacing the manifest dream by the meaning revealed by its interpretation, many of them have become guilty of falling into another confusion which they cling to with equal obstinacy. They seek to find the essence of dreams in their latent content and in so doing they overlook the distinction between latent dream-thoughts and the dream-work. At bottom, dreams are nothing other than a particular *form* of thinking, made possible by the conditions of the state of sleep. It is the *dream-work* which creates that form, and it alone is the essence of dreaming—the explanation of its peculiar nature.[13]

Analysts are making a mistake, Freud warns, if they take themselves to be looking for the hidden *content* of a dream—as though the unconscious were a hidden idea. Rather, the unconscious is a form of mental activity, a form of (mental) life, which systematically escapes conscious notice. In our dreaming, we are showing more than we can (yet) say.

In its own way, this book is itself an attempt to show more than I can say. I am less concerned with trying to persuade the reader of any particular thesis than with showing various ways in which philosophical and psychoanalytic questions might be pursued with a sense of liveliness and openness. But perhaps it is time to let the rest of the book speak for itself.

CHAPTER 2

On Killing Freud (Again)

This essay originally appeared in the New Republic *on December 25, 1995, in response to the Library of Congress' decision to cave in to yet another instance of Freud-bashing. Since I consider this incident to be exemplary of many others, I have left the essay essentially as it was originally published and have made no effort to "bring it up to date."*

In an extraordinary decision, the Library of Congress this week bowed to pressure from angry anti-Freudians and postponed for as long as a year a major exhibition called "Sigmund Freud: Conflict and Culture." According to a front-page story in the *Washington Post*, some library officials blamed the delay on budget problems; but others contended that the real reason was heated criticism of a show which might take a neutral or even favorable view of the father of psychoanalysis. Some fifty psychologists and others, including Gloria Steinem and Oliver Sacks, signed a petition denouncing the proposed exhibit. As Steinem complained to the *Post*, it seemed to "have the attitude of 'He was a genius, but ...' instead of 'He's a very troubled man, and ...'"

Though the library assured them that the exhibit "is not about whether Freudians or Freud critics, of whatever camp, are right or wrong," the critics refused an offer to contribute to the catalog or advise on the show.

Though this was perhaps the most blatant recent episode in the campaign against Freud, it is far from the only one. From *Time* to the *New York Times,* Freud-bashing has gone from an argument to a movement. In just the past few weeks Basic Books has brought out a long-winded tirade with what it no doubt hopes will be the sensational title *Why Freud Was Wrong;* and the *New York Review of Books* has collected some of its already-published broadsides against Freud into a new book.

In many cases, even the images accompanying these indictments seem to convey an extra dimension of hostility. "Is Freud Dead?" *Time* magazine asked on its cover, Thanksgiving week, 1993. Whether or not this was really a question, it was certainly a repetition; for in the spring of 1966, *Time* had asked, "Is God Dead?" From a psychoanalytic point of view, repetitions are as interesting for their differences as for their similarities. With God, *Time* avoided any graven images and simply printed the question in red type against a black background, perhaps out of respect for the recently deceased. For Freud, by contrast, the magazine offered what was ostensibly a photograph of his face, but with his head blown open. One can tell it is *blown* open because what is left of the skull is shaped like a jigsaw puzzle, with several of the missing pieces flying off into space. The viewer can peer inside Freud's head and see: *there is nothing there.*

How can we explain the vehemence of these attacks on a long-dead thinker? There are, I think, three currents running through the culture which contribute to the fashion for Freud-bashing. First, the truly remarkable advances in the development of mind-altering drugs, most notably Prozac, alongside an ever-increasing understanding of the structure of the brain, have fueled speculation that one day soon all forms of talking therapy will be obsolete. Second, consumers increasingly rely on insurance companies and health maintenance organizations, which prefer cheap pharmacology to expensive psychotherapy.

Finally, there is the inevitable backlash against the inflated claims that the psychoanalytic profession made for itself in the 1950s and 1960s, and against its hagiography of Freud. Many reputable scholars now believe (and I agree) that Freud botched some of his most important cases. Certainly a number of his hypotheses are false, his analytic technique can seem flat-footed and intrusive, and in his speculations he was a bit of a cowboy.

It is also true that the American Psychoanalytic Association is a victim of self-inflicted wounds. In the original effort to establish psychoanalysis as a profession in this country, culminating in the 1920s, American analysts insisted that psychoanalytic training be restricted to medical doctors. The major opponent of such a restriction was Freud himself, who argued that this was "virtually equivalent to an attempt at repression." There was nothing about medical training, Freud thought, which peculiarly equipped one to become an analyst; and he suspected the Americans were motivated by the exclusionary interests of a guild. Freud lost: it was the one matter on which the American analysts openly defied the master. In the short run, this allowed the psychoanalytic profession to take advantage of the powerful positive transference which the American public extended to doctors through most of this century. Every profession in its heyday—and psychoanalysis was no exception—tends to be seduced by its own wishful self-image and to make claims for itself that it cannot ultimately sustain. In the longer run, though, psychoanalysis set itself up for revisionist criticism.

Yet, for all that, it also seems to me clear that, at his best, Freud is a deep explorer of the human condition, working in a tradition which goes back to Sophocles and which extends through Plato, Saint Augustine, and Shakespeare to Proust and Nietzsche. What holds this tradition together is its insistence that there are significant meanings for human well-being which are obscured from immediate awareness. Sophoclean tragedy locates another realm of meaning in a divine world which humans can at most glimpse through oracles. In misunderstanding these strange meanings, humans usher in catastrophe.

Freud's achievement, from this perspective, is to locate these meanings fully inside the human world. Humans make meaning, for themselves and for others, of which they have no direct or immediate awareness. People make more meaning than they know what to do with. This is what Freud meant by the unconscious. And whatever valid criticisms can be aimed at him or at the psychoanalytic profession, it is nevertheless true that psychoanalysis is the most sustained and successful attempt to make these obscure meanings intelligible. Since I believe that this other source of meaning is of great importance for human development, I think that psychoanalytic therapy is invaluable for those who can make use of it; but, crazy as this may seem, I also believe that psychoanalysis is crucial for a truly democratic culture to thrive.

TAKE A CLOSER LOOK at the culture of criticism which has come to envelop psychoanalysis. You do not need to be an analyst to notice that more is going on here than a search for truth. Consider, for example, the emotionally charged debate over alleged memories of child abuse. No matter what side an author is on, Freud is blamed for being on the other. Jeffrey Masson, the renegade Freud scholar who believes that child abuse is more widespread than commonly acknowledged, made a name for himself by accusing Freud of suppressing the evidence in order to gain respectability. On the lecture circuit and in books like *The Assault on Truth* and *Against Therapy*, Masson has emerged as the most charismatic of the Freud-bashers, a self-styled defender of women and children against Freud's betrayals of them. Yet his critique of Freud is dependent on a willful misreading.

It is certainly true that at the beginning of his career, Freud hypothesized that hysteria and obsessional neurosis in adulthood were caused by memories of actual seductions in childhood. Because these memories were so upsetting, they were repressed, or kept out of conscious memory, but they still operated in the mind to cause psychological disease. By the fall of 1897, Freud had abandoned this view, which came to be known as the seduction theory. His explanation was that he had become increasingly skeptical that all the reports of childhood seduction—"not excluding my own"—could be straightforward memories. Masson, however, argues that this was merely Freud's attempt to fall into line with the prejudices of his German colleagues and thus to advance his career.

I FIND IT IMPOSSIBLE to read through Freud's writings without coming to the conclusion that it is Masson who is suppressing the evidence in order to advance his career. In fact, Freud never abandoned the idea that abuse of children caused them serious psychological harm, and throughout his career he maintained that it occurred more often than generally acknowledged. In 1917, for instance, twenty years after the abandonment of the seduction theory, Freud wrote: "Phantasies of being seduced are of particular interest, because so often they are not [merely] phantasies but real memories." Even at the very end of his career, in 1938, Freud said that while "the sexual abuse of children by adults" or "their seduction by other children (brothers or sisters) slightly their seniors" "do not apply to all children, . . . they are common enough." It is, therefore, misleading to say that Freud ever abandoned belief in the sexual abuse of children. What he abandoned was blind faith in the idea that alleged memories of abuse are always and everywhere what they purport to be.

Besides, to focus on child abuse is to miss the point. What is really at stake in the abandonment of the seduction theory is not the prevalence of abuse, but the nature of the mind's own activity. In assuming, as he first did, that all purported memories of child abuse were true, Freud was treating the mind as though it were merely a recipient of experience, recording reality in the same passive way a camera does light. Though the mind might be active in keeping certain memories out of conscious awareness, it was otherwise passive. In realizing that one could not take all memory-claims at face value, Freud effectively discovered that the mind is active and imaginative in the organization of its own experience. This is one of the crucial moments in the founding of psychoanalysis.

Of course, there is a tremendous difference—both clinical and moral—between actual and merely imagined child abuse. But from the point of view of the significance of Freud's discovery the whole issue of abuse or its absence, of seduction or its absence, is irrelevant. Once we realize that the human mind is everywhere active and imaginative, then we need to understand the routes of this activity if we are to grasp how the mind works. This is true whether the mind is trying to come to grips with painful reality, reacting to trauma, coping with the everyday, or "just making things up."

Freud called this imaginative activity phantasy, and he argued both that it functions unconsciously and that it plays a powerful role in the organization of a person's experience. This, surely, contains the seeds of a pro-found insight into the human condition; it is the central insight of psy-choanalysis; yet in the heated debate over child abuse, it is largely ig-nored. In fact the discovery of unconscious phantasy does not itself tilt one way or the other in this debate. Freud himself became skeptical about whether all the purported memories of childhood seduction were actual memories—but that is because he took himself to have been overly cred-ulous. One can equally well argue in the opposite direction: precisely be-cause phantasy is a pervasive aspect of mental life, one needs a much more nuanced view of what constitutes real-life seduction. Because phan-tasy is active in parents as well as children, parents do not need to be crudely molesting their children to be seducing them. Ironically, Freud's so-called abandonment of the seduction theory can be used to *widen* the scope of what might be considered real seductions.

The irony is that while those who believe in the prevalence of child-hood seductions attack Freud for abandoning the cause, those who be-lieve that repressed memories of child abuse are overblown blame him for fomenting this excess. Its real origins, though, are in "recovered-memory therapy," an often quackish practice in which so-called therapists actively encourage their clients to "remember" incidents of abuse from childhood. After some initial puzzlement as to what is being asked of them, clients have been only too willing to oblige: inventing the wildest stories of sa-tanic rituals, cannibalism, and other misdemeanors of suburban life.

The consequences of believing these stories have in some cases been devastating. "As I write," Frederick Crews observes in the *New York Review of Books*, "a number of parents and child-care providers are serving long prison terms, and others are awaiting trial, on the basis of therapeutically induced 'memories' of child sexual abuse that never in fact occurred." But instead of giving Freud credit for being the first person to warn us against taking purportedly repressed memories of abuse at face value, Crews con-tinues: "Although the therapists in question are hardly Park Avenue psy-choanalysts, the tradition of Freudian theory and practice unmistakably lies behind their tragic deception of both patients and jurors."

Crews, who is a professor of English at Berkeley and the *éminence grise* of Freud-bashers, acknowledges that his claim will "strike most readers as

21

a slur." But Crews is undeterred. He feels entitled to make this accusation, first, because Freud spent the earliest years of his career searching for repressed memories and, second, because Freud did suggest certain conclusions to his patients. That is, on occasion he took advantage of the charismatic position which people regularly assign to their doctors, teachers, and political leaders and told patients how to think about themselves or what to do—sometimes to their profound detriment. Like most successful slurs, there is truth in each claim.

What is missing is the massive evidence on the other side. No one in the history of psychiatry has more openly questioned the veracity of purported childhood memories than Freud did. No one did more to devise a form of treatment which avoids suggestion. Looking back, I regularly find Freud's clinical interventions too didactic and suggestive. But the very possibility of "looking back" is due to Freud. It was Freud who first set the avoidance of suggestion as a therapeutic ideal—and it is Freud who devised the first therapeutic technique aimed at achieving it. Psychoanalysis distinguishes itself from other forms of talking cure by its rigorous attempt to work out a procedure which genuinely avoids suggestion.

This is of immense importance, for psychoanalysis thus becomes the first therapy which sets *freedom* rather than some specific image of human *happiness* as its goal. Other kinds of therapy posit particular outcomes—increased self-esteem, overcoming depression—and, implicitly or explicitly, give advice about how to get there. Psychoanalysis is the one form of therapy which leaves it to analysands to determine for themselves what their specific goals will be. Indeed, it leaves it to them to determine whether they will have specific goals. Of course, as soon as freedom becomes an ideal, enormous practical problems arise as to how one avoids compromising an analysand's freedom by unwittingly suggesting certain goals or outlooks. But if we can now criticize Freud's actual practice, we can do so largely as a result of technical advances which Freud himself inspired.

One might wonder: Why isn't Freud the hero of both these narratives, rather than the villain? Why doesn't Masson portray Freud as the pioneer who linked memories of child abuse with later psychological harm; why doesn't Crews lionize Freud as the first person to call the veracity of such memories into question? There are rational answers to these questions— in one case that he reversed his position, in the other that even though he reversed himself, he is responsible for a tradition—but neither of them is very satisfying. Rather, an emotional tide has turned, and reasons are used to cover over irrational currents. Part of this phenomenon may be a healthy reversal, a reaction against previous idealizations. But it is also true that Freud is being made a scapegoat, and in the scapegoating process, nuance is abandoned.

TO SEE NUANCE DISAPPEAR, one has only to look at the supposed debate over the scientific standing of psychoanalysis. In a series of books and articles, Professor Adolf Grunbaum of the University of Pittsburgh has argued that psychoanalysis cannot prove the cause-and-effect connections it claims between unconscious motivation and its visible manifestations in ordinary life and in a clinical setting. Grunbaum argues correctly that Freud made genuine causal claims for psychoanalysis; notably, that it cures neurosis. But Grunbaum goes on to argue, much less plausibly, that in a clinical setting psychoanalysis cannot substantiate its claims. It is remarkable how many mainstream publications—*Time,* the *New York Times, The Economist,* to name a few—have fallen all over themselves to give respectful mention to such abstruse work as Grunbaum's. Mere mention of the work lends a cloak of scientific legitimacy to the attack on Freud, while the excellent critiques of Grunbaum's work are ignored.

There is no doubt that the causal claims of psychoanalysis cannot be established in the same way as a causal claim in a hard-core empirical science like experimental physics. But neither can any causal claim of any form of psychology which interprets people's actions on the basis of their motives—including the ordinary psychology of everyday life. We watch a friend get up from her chair and head to the refrigerator: we assume she is hungry and is getting something to eat. We can, if we like, try to confirm this interpretation, but in nothing like the way we confirm something in physics. Of course, we can "test" our hypothesis by asking her what she is doing, and she may correct us, telling us that she is thirsty and getting something to drink. But it's possible that she's not telling us the truth. Indeed, it's possible, though unlikely, that she believes that the refrigerator is capable of sending messages to outer space, which will save the world from catastrophe. We cannot prove that our ordinary interpretation is correct. At best, we can gather more interpretive evidence of the same type to support or revise our hypothesis.

What are we to do—abandon our ordinary practice of interpreting people? If we want to know what caused the outbreak of the Peloponnesian War, why there is a crisis in the Balkans, what were the origins of the Renaissance, how slavery became institutionalized, we turn to history, economics, and other social sciences for answers. No historical account is immune to skeptical challenge; no historical-causal claims can be verified in the same way as a causal claim in physics. But no one suggests giving up on history or the other interpretive sciences.

Meaning is like that. Humans are inherently makers and interpreters of meaning. It is meaning—ideas, desires, beliefs—which causes humans to do the interesting things they do. Yet as soon as one enters the realm of meaningful explanation one has to employ different methods of validating causal claims than one finds in experimental physics. And it is simply a mistake to think that therefore the methods of validation in ordinary psychology or in psychoanalysis must be less precise or fall short of the methods in experimental physics. To see this for yourself, take the following multiple-choice test:

Question: Which is more precise: Henry James, in his ability to describe how a person's action flows from his or her motivations; or a particle accelerator, in its ability to depict the causal interactions of subatomic particles?
Answers:
(a) Henry James
(b) the accelerator
(c) none of the above

You do not have to flip to the end of the article or turn the page upsidedown to learn that the answer is (c). Actually, a better answer is to reject the question as ridiculous. There is no single scale on which one can place both Henry James and a particle accelerator to determine which is more precise. Within the realm of human motivation and its effects, *The Portrait of a Lady* is more precise than a *Peanuts* cartoon; within the realm of measuring atomic movements, some instruments are more precise than others.

If psychoanalysis were to imitate the methods of physical science, it would be useless for interpreting people. Psychoanalysis is an extension of our ordinary psychological ways of interpreting people in terms of their beliefs, desires, hopes, and fears. The extension is important because psychoanalysis attributes to people other forms of motivation—in particular wish and phantasy—which attempt to account for outbreaks of irrationality and other puzzling human behavior. In fact, it is a sign of the success of psychoanalysis as an interpretive science that its causal claims cannot be validated in the same way as those of the physical sciences.

HOW, THEN, MIGHT WE SET appropriate standards of confirmation for causal claims in psychoanalysis? This genuine and important question tends to be brushed aside by the cliché of the analyst telling a patient who disagrees with an interpretation which she is just resisting. The apotheosis of this cliché can be found in Sir Karl Popper's *The Open Society and Its Enemies,* in which Popper argues that psychoanalysis is a pseudoscience because its discoveries cannot be falsified. what counts as evidence is too large and elusive for the total claim of the discipline to be either checked or challenged. Of course, in this broad sense nothing could "falsify" history or economics or our ordinary psychological interpretation of persons, but no one would think of calling these forms of explanation pseudo. And there is something which would count as a global refutation of psychoanalysis: if people always and everywhere acted in rational and transparently explicable ways, one could easily dismiss psychoanalysis as unnecessary rubbish. It is because people often behave in bizarre ways, ways which cause pain to themselves and to others, ways which puzzle even the actors themselves, that psychoanalysis commands our attention.

Unfortunately, there is some truth to the cliché of the analyst unfairly pulling rank on the analysand. Would that there were no such thing as a defensive analyst! Yet I believe that when psychoanalysis is done properly there is no form of clinical intervention—in psychology, psychiatry, or general medicine—which pays greater respect to the individual client or patient. The proper attitude for an analyst is one of profound humility in the face of the infinite complexity of another human being. Because humans are self-interpreting animals, one must always be ready to defer to their explanations of what they mean. And yet, suppose just for the sake of argument that it is true that humans actively keep certain unpleasant meanings away from conscious awareness. Then one might expect that any process which brings those meanings closer to consciousness will be accompanied by a certain resistance. It then becomes an important technical and theoretical problem how to elicit those meanings without falling into the cliché, without provoking a massive outbreak of resistance, and all the while working closely with and maintaining deep respect for the analysand. We need to know in specific detail when and how it is appropriate to cite resistance in a clinical setting, and when it is not. Some of the best recent work in psychoanalytic theory addresses just this issue.

Consider this elementary example: an analysand may come precisely five minutes late every day for his session. For a while, there may be no point in inviting him to speculate about why. Any such question, no matter how gently or tentatively put, might only provoke a storm of protest: "You don't know how busy I am, how many sacrifices I make to get here," and so on. Even if the habitual lateness and the protests are examples of what analysts call resistance, there is one excellent reason not to say anything about it yet: the analysis is for the analysand. Any interpretation which he cannot make use of in his journey of self-understanding is inappropriate, even if the interpretation is accurate. If coming late is a resistance, and if the analyst is sufficiently patient, there will come a time when the analysand will relax enough to become puzzled by his own behavior. He might say, "It's funny, I always seem to come exactly five minutes late," or "I've thought about asking you to start our sessions five minutes late, but I realized I'd only come five minutes later than that." At this point it would be a mistake not to pursue the issue, for a wealth of material may spontaneously emerge: for example, that he wanted to feel that he was in control, that he wanted the analyst to acknowledge him as a serious professional in his own right, and so on. Once these desires are recognized, they can be explored—and sometimes that exploration can make a big difference in how the analysand sees himself and how he goes on to live the rest of his life. Should all of this be avoided because of some flat-footed assumption that the analyst is always pulling rank when she talks about resistance? The problem with the cliché is that it ignores all specifics. It uses the very possibility of invoking resistance to impugn psychoanalysis generally.

What is at stake in all these attacks? If this were merely the attack on one historical figure, Freud, or on one professional group, psychoanalysts, the hubbub would have died down long ago. After all, psychoanalysis nowadays plays a minor role in the mental health professions; Freud is less and less often taught or studied. There is, of course, a certain pleasure to be had in pretending one is bravely attacking a powerful authority when one is in fact participating in a gang-up. But even these charms fade after a while. The real object of attack—for which Freud is only a stalking-horse—is the very idea that humans have unconscious motivation. A battle may be fought over Freud, but the war is over our culture's image of the human soul. Are we to see humans as having depth—as complex psychological organisms who generate layers of meaning which lie beneath the surface of their own understanding? Or are we to take ourselves as transparent to ourselves?

Certainly, the predominant trend in the culture is to treat human existence as straightforward. In the plethora of self-help books, of alternative therapies, diets, and exercise programs, it is assumed that we already know what human happiness is. These programs promise us a shortcut for getting there. And yet we can all imagine someone whose muscle tone is great, who is successful at his job, who "feels good about himself," yet remains a shell of a human being. Breathless articles in the science section of the *New York Times* suggest that the main obstacle to human flourishing is technological. And even this obstacle—in the recent discovery of a gene, or the location of a neuron in the brain, or the synthesis of a new psychopharmacological agent—may soon be put out of the way. Candide is the ideal reader of the "Science Times." Of course, the *Times* did not invent this image of the best of all possible worlds: it is merely the bellwether for a culture which wishes to ignore the complexity, depth, and darkness of human life.

27

❖   ❖   ❖

IT IS DIFFICULT TO MAKE this point without sounding like a Luddite; so let me say explicitly that psychopharmacology and neuropsychiatry have made, and will continue to make, valuable contributions in reducing human suffering. But it is a phantasy to suppose that a chemical or neurological intervention can solve the problems posed in and by human life. That is why it is a mistake to think of psychoanalysis and Prozac as two different means to the same end. The point of psychoanalysis is to help us develop a clearer, yet more flexible and creative, sense of what our ends might be. "How shall we live?" is, for Socrates, the fundamental question of human existence—and the attempt to answer that question is, for him, what makes human life worthwhile. And it is Plato and Shakespeare, Proust, Nietzsche, and, most recently, Freud who complicated the issue by insisting that there are deep currents of meaning, often crosscurrents, running through the human soul which can at best be glimpsed through a glass darkly. This, if anything, is the Western tradition: not a specific set of values, but a belief that the human soul is too deep for there to be any easy answer to the question of how to live.

If one can dismiss Freud as a charlatan, one can not only enjoy the sacrifice of a scapegoat; one can also evade troubling questions about the enigmatic nature of human motivation. Never mind that we are daily surrounded by events—from the assassination of Yitzhak Rabin to the war in Bosnia; from the murder of Nicole Simpson to the public fascination with it; from the government's burning of the Branch Davidian compound to the retaliation bombing in Oklahoma City—that cannot be understood in the terms which are standardly used to explain them. Philosophy, Aristotle said, begins in wonder. Psychoanalysis begins in wonder that the unintelligibility of the events which surround one do not cause more wonder.

❖   ❖   ❖

THERE ARE TWO very different images of what humans must be like if democracy is to be a viable form of government. The prevalent one today treats humans as preference-expressing political atoms, and pays little attention to subatomic structure. Professional pollsters, political scientists, and pundits portray society as an agglomeration of these atoms. The only irrationality they recognize is the failure of these preference-expressing monads to conform to the rules of rational-choice theory. If one thinks that this is the only image of humanity which will sustain democracy, one will tend to view psychoanalysis as suspiciously antidemocratic.

Is there another, more satisfying, image of what humans are like which nevertheless makes it plausible that they should organize themselves and live in democratic societies? If we go back to the birth of democracy, in fifth-century Athens, we see that the flourishing of that democracy coincides precisely with the flowering of one of the world's great literatures: Greek tragedy. This coincidence is not mere coincidence. The tragic theater gave citizens the opportunity to retreat momentarily from the responsibility of making rational decisions for themselves and their society. At the same time, tragedy confronted them emotionally with the fact that they had to make their decisions in a world which was not entirely rational, in which rationality was sometimes violently disrupted, in which rationality itself could be used for irrational ends.

What, after all, is Oedipus' complex? That he killed his father and married his mother misses the point. Patricide and maternal incest are *consequences* of Oedipus' failure, not its source. Oedipus' fundamental mistake lies in his assumption that meaning is transparent to human reason. In horrified response to the Delphic oracle, Oedipus flees the people he (mistakenly) takes to be his parents. En route, he kills his actual father and propels himself into the arms of his mother. It is the classic scene of fulfilling one's fate in the very act of trying to escape it. But this scenario is possible only because Oedipus assumes he understands his situation, that the meaning of the oracle is immediately available to his conscious understanding. That is why he thinks he can respond to the oracle with a straightforward application of practical reason. Oedipus' mistake, in essence, is to ignore unconscious meaning.

For Sophocles, this was a sacrilegious crime, for he took this obscure meaning to flow from a divine source. But it is clear that, in Sophocles's vision, Oedipus attacks the very idea of unconscious meaning. In his angry confrontation with the prophet Tiresias, Oedipus boasts that it was

29

his conscious reasoning, not any power of interpreting obscure meaning, which saved the city from the horrible Sphinx.

> Why, come, tell me, how can you be a true prophet? Why when the versifying hound was here did you not speak some word that could release the citizens? Indeed, her riddle was not one for the first comer to explain! It required prophetic skill, and you were exposed as having no knowledge from the birds or from the gods. No, it was I that came, Oedipus who knew nothing, and put a stop to her; I hit the mark by native wit, not by what I learned from birds.[1]

What was Sophocles' message to the Athenian citizens who flocked to the theater? You ignore the realm of unconscious meaning at your peril. Do so, and Oedipus' fate will be yours. From this perspective, democratic citizens need to maintain a certain humility in the face of meanings which remain opaque to human reason. We need to be wary that what we take to be an exercise of reason will both hide and express an irrationality of which we remain unaware.

In all the recent attacks on Freud, can't one hear echoes of Oedipus' attack on Tiresias? Isn't the attack on Freud itself a repetition and reenactment of Oedipus' complex, less an attack on the father than an attack on the very idea of repressed, unconscious meaning? One indication that this is so—a symptom, if you will—is that none of the attacks on Freud addresses the problems of human existence to which psychoanalysis is a response. From a psychoanalytic perspective, human irrationality is not merely a failure to make a coherent set of choices. Sometimes it is an unintelligible intrusion which overwhelms reason and blows it apart. Sometimes it is method in madness. But how could there be *method* in madness? Even if Freud did botch this case or ambitiously pursue that end, we still need to account for the pervasive manifestations of human irrationality. This is the issue, and it is one which the attacks on Freud ignore.

❖ ❖ ❖

THE REAL QUESTION IS whether, and how, responsible autonomy is possible. In the development of the human self-image from Sophocles to Freud, there has been a shift in the locus of hidden meaning from a divine to the all-too-human realm. At first, it might look as though the recognition of a dark strain running through the human soul might threaten the viability of democratic culture. Certainly, the twentieth-century critiques of Enlightenment optimism, with the corresponding emphasis on human irrationality, also question or even pour scorn on the democratic ideal. It is in this context that Freud comes across as a much more ambiguous figure than he is normally taken to be. In one way, he is the advocate of the unconscious; in another, he is himself filled with Enlightenment optimism that the problems posed by the unconscious can be solved; in yet another, he is wary of the dark side of the human soul and pessimistic about doing much to alleviate psychological pain. He is Tiresias and Oedipus and Sophocles rolled into one.

If, for the moment, we concentrate on the optimism, we see a vision emerge of how one might both take human irrationality seriously and participate in a democratic ideal. If the source of irrationality lies within, rather than outside, the human realm, the possibility opens up of a responsible engagement with it. Psychoanalysis is, in its essence, the attempt to work out just such an engagement. It is a technique which allows dark meanings and irrational motivations to rise to the surface of conscious awareness. They can then be taken into account, they can be influenced by other considerations, and they become less liable to disrupt human life in violent and incomprehensible ways. Critics of psychoanalysis complain that it is a luxury of the few. But from the current perspective, no thinker has made creativity and imagination more democratically available than Freud. This is one of the truly important consequences of locating the unconscious inside the psyche. Creativity is no longer the exclusive preserve of the divinely inspired or the few great poets. From a psychoanalytic point of view, everyone is poetic; everyone dreams in metaphor and generates symbolic meaning in the process of living. Even in their prose, people have unwittingly been speaking poetry all along.

AND THE QUESTION NOW IS: To what poetic use are we going to put Freud? Freud *is* dead. He died in 1939, after an extraordinarily productive and creative life. Beneath the continued attacks upon him, ironically, lies

31

an unwillingness to let him go. It is Freud who taught that only after we accept the actual death of an important person in our lives can we begin to mourn. Only then can he or she take on full symbolic life for us. Obsessing about Freud *the man* is a way of keeping Freud *the meaning* at bay. Freud's meaning, I think, lies in the recognition that humans make more meaning than they grasp, that this meaning can be painful and disruptive, but that humans need not be passive in the face of it. Freud began a process of dealing with unconscious meaning, and it is important not to get stuck on him, like some rigid symptom, either to idolize or to denigrate him. The many attacks on him, even upon psychoanalysis, refuse to recognize that Freud gave birth to a psychoanalytic movement which in myriad ways has moved beyond him. If Freud is alive anywhere, it is in a tradition which in its development of more sensitive techniques, and more sophisticated ways of thinking about unconscious motivation, has rendered some of the particular things Freud thought or did irrelevant. Just as democracy requires the recognition that the king is dead, both as an individual and as an institution, so the democratic recognition that each person is the maker of unconscious, symbolic meaning requires the acceptance of Freud's death. What matters, as Freud himself well understood, is what we are able to do with the meanings we make.

CHAPTER 3

Knowingness and Abandonment: An Oedipus for Our Time

This essay was delivered as a lecture at a conference on psychoanalysis and culture, sponsored by the New York Psychoanalytic Institute on March 15, 1997. The lecture begins with a few of the symptomatic events of that week. It is left as an exercise for the reader to fill in similarly symptomatic events happening at the time of reading this essay.

This conference is not only about what psychoanalysis can contribute to culture, but about what culture can contribute to psychoanalysis. This is a relief. For the psychoanalytic profession has for too long clung to a defense which is, by now, outworn and boring: namely, the stance that psychoanalysis has a special secret to give to culture. For about fifty years, the profession acted out its own identification with Oedipus, pretending to have solved the riddle of the unconscious. This is ironic because this stance is an *exploitation* of the transference—analysts putting themselves forward as possessors of esoteric knowledge—whereas the whole point of analysis is to *analyze* the transference. Analysts portrayed themselves as "already knowing" the secret, whereas what makes analysis special is its unique form of not already knowing. No wonder the culture became suspicious. And analysts, for their part, fell into confusion and frustration that their "message" was not being received with awe, wonder, respect. In retrospect, one can see that this exploitation of the transference had self-defeat built right into it.

Analysis is not essentially a body of esoteric knowledge; it is a peculiar form of mental activity, a peculiar form of speaking and listening, a peculiar form of life. Above all, it involves a certain form of listening: listening to oneself, listening to another. And if we listen to the culture with an analytic ear, we can gain insight both into the culture and into our fundamental psychoanalytic myths. It is in listening to the culture that I have found a way to reinterpret the Oedipus myth, the archaic myth of psychoanalysis.

If one reads the newspapers, follows the news, one can quickly come to see that there is a crisis of knowingness in the culture. I shall begin with the current flap over campaign finance, not because it is fundamental in itself, but because it is happening this week. It is the cultural equivalent of what an analysand brings into a session on any given day. No matter when this conference occurred, there would be something in that week's newspapers which was symptomatic.

In the campaign-finance scandal, one can watch the culture slowly waking up. Before the election, it was virtually only William Safire who had the audacity to intimate a corrupt "Asian connection"; then other journalists joined in as ever more instances of corruption were brought to light; but political commentators are baffled, and somewhat irritated, that—to this date, at least—President Clinton's standing in the polls has not been dented. Of course, that may well change. But so far, Clinton can still stand before the nation and do his bring-us-all-together, focus-on-the-larger-issues shtick; he can even righteously call for campaign-finance reform; and, though he drives Maureen Dowd wild, he can, for the moment at least, get away with it. How come? Basically, the public feels it *already knows* that campaign finance is corrupt. The public attitude so far has been: so what's new? Here we can see how the stance of "already knowing" functions as a defense: if you already know, you do not need to find out. And Clinton is masterful in exploiting this defense. It is often thought that we have *discovered* that Clinton is a bit of a con man, but this cannot be the whole truth. Clinton *presents himself* as a bit of a con man— and this is enormously reassuring. For if *he* is willing to let us know that he's conning us, then, in an odd sort of way, he emerges as trustworthy: we can *count on him* to engage in a bit of sleaze when our backs are turned. And when some bit of sleaze does emerge, the public has a sense of "already knowing" he was up to some such thing. And I suspect the Clinton campaign thought it could get away with its dubious fundraising because it knew that the public "already knew"—and thus wouldn't care.

If this defense is going to collapse, it will be around anxious intimations that we don't "already know." Here are two places where one can see anxiety starting to break through: First, in the idea that this is an *Asian* connection. For beneath the legitimate surface concerns that a foreign country may have been trying to affect electoral outcome, there is the cultural phantasy of the Inscrutable Oriental. And this image has its own *phantastic a priori*: it's built into the very idea of the Inscrutable Oriental that we couldn't possibly "already know" what they are up to. That's what it is to be inscrutable. And that's why Clinton's blanket reassurance—you know me, I'm just an honest con man, trying to get by—can't possibly extend to cover an Asian connection. A priori, we cannot possibly "already know" the inner workings of an Asian connection: this is part of the logic of the inscrutable.[1]

The second moment of anxiety comes in the revelation of an active disruption in the flow of knowledge between the FBI and the White House. FBI agents informed two lower-level members of the National Security Council of an investigation into an Asian connection, but told them not to inform anyone higher up. Here the public cannot possibly assume it "already knows" what is going on: for this is a scenario which dramatizes *not* already knowing. No one can say with any confidence who "already knows" what is going on—indeed, if there is anyone who "already knows." This has to provoke anxiety and fascination that the order of knowingness has been disrupted.

Here I am reminded of that rapidly receding moment of public fascination with Dick Morris' adultery. The moment passed quickly—Morris was able to command a two-million-dollar advance yet not able to sell any books—but, still, it is worth thinking about why there was any moment at all. On its own, the idea that a political consultant holed up in a Washington hotel suite, with his wife tucked safely away in Connecticut, should have an affair with a prostitute is hardly news. It can almost be deduced a priori from the idea of a political consultant. On its own, it is one big yawn. What fascinated press and public was that in this incident there was confusion as to who was already in the know. The prostitute was not merely a prostitute; she was a prostitute keeping a secret diary. Even before her toes dried, the incident was being recorded unbeknownst to a man whose job it is to be in the know. And, of course, the political consultant was keeping his own diary, unbeknownst to the president he was supposedly serving. And the president . . . well, who knows? It seemed as though there were unplumbable depths of broken trusts. And the established order of knowingness was disturbed in countless ways.

NOW WHEN THE ORDER OF KNOWINGNESS is undisturbed—when the culture can rest in its phantasy of "already knowing"—there is a widespread sense of boredom and irritation. One has only to read the political columns in the newspapers leading up to the last election: columnists registered crescendos of frustration that this was a campaign designed so that there should be no surprises.[2] What bothered the commentators, I suspect, was a sense that their boredom was the product of a *successful* campaign.

But if journalists are bored silly by already being in the know, hell hath no fury like journalists who discover they are not. Here is one delicious symptom. In 1995 Random House published *Primary Colors,* a political novel about a southern governor's campaign for president. The novel, whose author was Anonymous, shot to the top of the best-seller list, and there was much fascinated speculation about who Anonymous might be. Anonymous even wrote an essay for the *New York Times Book Review* explaining why he or she had decided to be and to remain anonymous. In the winter of 1996, *New York Magazine* published an article by an English professor at Vassar claiming that, on the basis of linguistic analysis, Anonymous must be the political commentator Joe Klein. Klein energetically denied the charge until the summer, when the *Washington Post* ran a story saying that the handwritten corrections on a galley proof of *Primary Colors* matched Klein's handwriting. He then 'fessed up.

The immediate result was a firestorm of moralizing denunciation in the press. The *New York Times*, for example, deemed it fit to run a major editorial on the subject titled "The Color of Mendacity." Here is a selection from that editorial:

> it is shameless of Mr. Klein to excuse his falsehoods as similar to the protection of confidential sources. "There are times," he said, "when I've had to lie to protect a source, and I put that in this category."
>
> In fact, principled journalists do not lie to protect sources. They rely on constitutional and statutory guarantees of journalistic privilege. Scores of reporters have maintained silence, sometimes to the point of going to jail, and their publications have spent a lot of money to defend the confidentiality guarantee in court. But they do so without lying. To try to stretch a noble doctrine to excuse a duplicitous book-selling scheme is irresponsible and disreputable . . .
>
> Mr. Klein wants his colleagues to view his actions as a diverting and highly profitable whimsy. But he has held a prominent role in his generation of political journalists. For that reason, people interested in preserving the core values of serious journalism have to view his actions and words as corrupt and—if they become an example to others—corrupting.[5]

Strong words. Strong feelings. But they don't altogether make sense. I have no interest in defending Mr. Klein, and there is no doubt that Mr. Klein did not handle the whole situation well, but I find this reaction startling. First, we may want to make it a tautology that "principled journalists do not lie to protect sources," but this pompous moralizing covers over a wealth of complex relations which journalists regularly maintain with the truth. Of course, there are a handful of cases in which a journalist went to court, and even to jail, to protect the confidentiality of a source. But in the world of political journalism, it is a commonplace that not only can politicians, advisers, lobbyists speak to journalists "off the record," but the very fact that they have had "off-the-record" conversations, "deep background" briefings, and so on is itself kept "off the record." As a result, stories regularly appear which look as though they are a general surveying of the political scene when in fact they are a reaction to and outgrowth of a few privileged conversations. This is a form of misleading the reader about sources which everyone knows about and few mind. It is an everyday form of deception which the *New York Times* tolerates, if not encourages.

But, second, when Mr. Klein lied it was not about any journalistic fact, source, or story, but as an expression of his desire to protect his anonymity as the author of a novel. Why should we expect an author who publishes a book anonymously and who writes an essay explaining his desire to protect his privacy to tell the truth when he is asked about his authorship? From what pulpit can one *so clearly* see that the public's right to know, or a journalist's right to a straight answer from a fellow journalist, always trumps the right to privacy? In normal social life, we recognize that if we don't want our friends and neighbors to lie to us, there are certain questions we just don't ask. By and large, we don't ask people how much money they earn or whether they have satisfying sex lives. And there is only one person in the country about whom we feel we have the right to ask whether he is having an affair: the president of the United States. (Incidentally, I have been told that a number of Mr. Klein's friends refrained from asking him whether he was Anonymous because they didn't want to put him in the embarrassing position of having to lie to them.)

Suppose Mr. Klein had added a prefatory remark to his book: "Because I want to protect my privacy I have decided to publish this book anonymously. This has the unfortunate consequence that should you ask me directly about it, I shall have to lie. I am sorry about that, but one solution is: don't ask!" Would *that* have made everything all right? And, implicitly, isn't that what he *did* do, by publishing the book anonymously?

I mention this example because I think that the moral outrage about Joe Klein's lie is serving as a rationalizing defense, hiding emotions that are less well understood. If boredom and irritation accompany the claim to already know, the violation of the presumption to already know is met with moralizing fury. It seems almost as though a taboo has been violated.

Of course, these examples are anecdotal and by themselves prove noth-ing, but if you look around for yourselves I think you will see that other examples abound.[4]

I HOPE ENOUGH HAS BEEN SAID to suggest to you that there is some-thing funny going on with "knowingness" in the culture, something we do not understand very well. With this puzzlement in mind, I think we can go back and read *Oedipus Tyrannus* as the fundamental myth of know-ingness. Before offering an interpretation, I should like to make two pre-liminary remarks.

First, a word of warning. It is a symptom of our age that there is what one might call *the fundamental transference-trap of interpretation*. This mani-fests itself as a sense that, in offering an interpretation, there is no escape from making one of two choices: either one presents oneself as offering the real truth, about Oedipus, say; *or* one says that one's interpretation is one among many good-enough interpretations. On the first choice, one is forced to imitate Oedipus, and pretend to guess and reveal the secret of the text. Shrinking from that absurd fate, one feels compelled to adopt a wishy-washy relativism, and try to put a brave or playful face on it. Must life be so impoverished? Obviously, I think the answer is no. The sense that this is our only choice should show us that we are living in a con-stricted universe of possibilities. The interpretation which follows should be thought of as falling on neither side of this false dichotomy. The point is neither to reveal the hidden secret of Oedipus nor to add one more in-terpretation to the good-enough pile, but to invite one to see something which is right there in the text.

Second, it might help to open up the space of interpretation if we begin, in true oedipal fashion, by killing off Freud's Oedipus. We cannot begin to appreciate the meaning of Oedipus if we continue to think that Oedipus was oedipal.[5] According to Freud, Oedipus acts out unconscious childhood wishes which we all share—to possess one parent and get rid of the other. And the fact that we all have such wishes accounts for the deep resonance the play has for us—according to Freud.[6] The proper response to this reading is embarrassingly simple: there is no evidence for it. Oedipus does kill his father, marry his mother, and have children with her. But none of this can be used to support Freud's reading; these are the facts his account is supposed to explain. Freud needs to show that these events occur *because* Oedipus has oedipal wishes. Not only does Freud make no effort to do so—he simply points to the Oedipus myth—there are in the text no hints of oedipal wishes. Of course, *if* one is already convinced of the oedipal reading of the Oedipus myth, one will see the entire play as providing evidence. And it will seem satisfactory simply to point to the play. However, as soon as one takes one skeptical step backward and asks the question "How do we know that in acting this way Oedipus is acting out *oedipal* phantasies, as opposed to some other phantasy?" one comes to see that the surface evidence of the text points in another direction.

This in no way counts against the psychological reality of the oedipus complex; just the opposite. It is precisely because the oedipal configuration is so prominent in so many that it has been possible for a generation of readers to see Oedipus as oedipal. And it is a virtue of Freud's account that it attempts to explain why the drama continues to move us.

People tend to be at their most parochial when they speculate about the human condition. For it is here that they challenge themselves to wander over all of human being, and in the effort make it clear how incapable they are of doing so. Freud thought he had found something universal about the human condition, and he took it as evidence in favor that the same universal could be found back in Sophocles' play. But Freud assumes that this universal is *psychological*—a configuration of wishes *inside the psyche*—and he here shows himself to be a child of the modern world. For Sophocles, "the human condition" did not point inevitably to the human psyche, but to the objective conditions in which humans had to live. It is the human condition to have to live out a fate. And—at least, from the ancient tragic perspective—fate is part of the basic fabric of the world. It is taken to be as fundamental an aspect of the world as we take gravity to be—only, unlike gravity, fate is impossible to defy. Sophocles was wrong that fate is basic to the world, Freud was wrong that the oedipus complex is a psychological universal, and I do not intend to enter a mug's game of trying to come up with some other candidate for the human condition. Rather, there are certain themes in the Oedipus drama which reverberate with our age, and we would do well to listen to them.

Oedipus is not the king. He is *the tyrant*. This is a crucial distinction. It is reflected in Sophocles' title *Oedipus Tyrannus*, and it is flattened in the Latin translation *Oedipus Rex*, and then in the English *Oedipus the King*. For Oedipus to be king, he and the Theban citizens would have to understand that he is the son and heir of King Laius. His claim to the throne would then *run through his blood*. The actual claim he makes on the throne *runs through his mind*. It is he who solved the riddle of the Sphinx and saved Thebes from disaster. Thebes lacked a king, and they thought there was no heir, so the citizens made Oedipus tyrant by acclamation. The king is dead! Long live the tyrant! For the ancient Greeks, "tyrant" did not only have the negative meaning it has for us today; it also referred to a leader who did not inherit the throne along traditional bloodlines.[7] In the case of Oedipus, the fact that he is tyrant means that he comes as close as was possible in ancient Thebes to being its democratically elected leader. And he gains his position on the basis of his achievements—of *what he does*— rather than on the basis of any given sense of *who he is*. In the modern world, the very idea of an inherited claim to rule has fallen into disrepute—though when one observes the public fascination with JFK Jr. one can see that though the cultural superego disapproves of the *idea*, the impulse is still there. In ancient Thebes, the idea had not been challenged, but Thebes had nevertheless been thrown into a *proto*-modern situation: it had to devise some *other* form of legitimate rule. The riddle of political legitimacy is more puzzling than the riddle of the Sphinx, but Oedipus solves both for the Thebans at one blow: in solving the riddle of the Sphinx, Oedipus becomes Thebes's savior. There is no further question of who should rule.

Oedipus' legitimacy flows from success. Oedipus solidifies his position by marrying the queen and having children by her, but, at bottom, everyone knows that his only real claim on the Thebans is his ability to protect them. And so, when, a generation later, Thebes is struck with miasma, it is only natural that the citizens should turn to him, "the first of men, both in the incidents of life and in dealing with the higher powers" (lines 33–34).[8] Now, the only evidence of divine favor is his practical success. It is not as though prophets have come forward saying the gods have ordained that Oedipus should rule; nor have the oracles been properly consulted to determine whether it is a good idea for Oedipus to marry the queen and assume the throne. In effect, the Thebans have taken practical success to be a sign of divine favor. They *think* there are two conditions which make Oedipus first among men—worldly success and divine favor—but there is only one. Should Oedipus start to flub the incidents of life, there is no way he could say, "Well, yes, but I'm *still* first in dealing with the higher powers."

Oedipus is clearer about this than are the citizens of Thebes. When he gets into a quarrel with the prophet Tiresias, he says angrily:

> Why, come tell me, how can you be a true prophet? Why when the versifying hound was here did you not speak some word that could release the citizens? Indeed, her riddle was not one for the first comer to explain! It required prophetic skill, and you were exposed as having no knowledge from the birds or from the gods. No, it was I that came, Oedipus who knew nothing, and put a stop to her; *I hit the mark by native wit, not by what I learned from birds.* (390–398; emphasis added)

Oedipus takes his success with the Sphinx to rest entirely on his ability to think things through. He accepts the responsibility as well as the praise: for Oedipus, his triumph has sprung full-grown from his own mind. But if his mind is the source of his legitimacy, that inevitably puts him in a delicate position, for he has nothing else to fall back on other than his own resources. So when the citizens of Thebes make this plea, "Best of living men, raise up the polis!" (49), there is an implicit "or else." Oedipus' position rests on his ability to deliver Thebans from harm. Much has been made of Oedipus' steadfast determination to solve the riddle of the miasma, as though it reveals his strength of character—and it may well do so. But it is also true that if he cannot do so, he has little other claim on them.

More than any other figure in the ancient world, Oedipus is the self-made man. At birth he is abandoned by his parents, given to a shepherd to be exposed to die on a mountain. Later he abandons what he (mistakenly) takes to be his natural family, social position, and inherited claim to the throne in Corinth, and, through solving the Sphinx's riddle, he thinks his way into a new family, new social position, new throne. The very first word of the play reveals how far Oedipus thinks his mind can go in creating the world around him. "Children!" Oedipus addresses the suppliants assembled in front of the palace. Oedipus has made them into his "children" by becoming tyrant of Thebes; he has made the polis into his family. From Sophocles' perspective, of course, this is outrageous impiety: the family is part of the natural order, a sacred unit, and it is hubristic idiocy to assume one can simply make one, like an artifact. But looking back from this perspective, Oedipus looks like an intimation of postmodernity, refusing to take any category, even the family, as simply given. The bitter irony, of course, is that, unbeknownst to him or the Thebans, these *are* his "children," the polis *is* his family: Oedipus ought to be recognized as the king, the blood ruler, not merely as the tyrant he and the citizens take him to be. As it is, Oedipus, with some plausibility, takes himself to have got where he is by the clever use of human reason.

Oedipus also displays a "knowingness" eerily reminiscent of contemporary culture's demand to already know. When Oedipus asks a question, he takes himself to know the answer. So, for example, when Oedipus asks his "children" why they have come, and they describe the miasma which has overcome the city, he says, "I am not ignorant of the desires with which you have come; yes, I know that you are all sick" (59–61). He expected their plea and has already sent his brother-in-law, Creon, to Delphi to consult the oracle. But there is a sickness in this "knowingness": reason is being used to jump ahead to a conclusion, as though there is too much anxiety involved in simply asking a question and waiting for the world to answer. On the few occasions when someone challenges Oedipus' claim to already know—the prophet Tiresias, Creon, and the Messenger—Oedipus explodes with anger and suspicion.

Consider the dustup with Tiresias. Creon returns with the message that the murderer of Laius is alive and well in Thebes, and that until he is found and expelled, there will be pollution in the city. A practical task has now been set. The prophet has been summoned for help, but he will not speak.

"You will find it easier to bear your fate and I mine," he says to Oedipus, "if you do as I say" (320–321). A puzzling remark; but instead of following the advice or inquiring into its meaning, Oedipus explodes. There is, for Oedipus, no imaginative space to envisage the situation as anything other than a practical problem; and, as they say, if you're not part of the solution, you're part of the problem. Tiresias is blocking his way, refusing to let him "knowingly" leap to a practical conclusion. Oedipus interprets it as an aggressive act and strikes a retaliatory blow: "I am so angry that I will leave unsaid nothing of what I understand!" (345). In other words, anger breaks down Oedipus' inhibition—and what pours forth is a paranoid delusion that Tiresias himself had a hand in the murder and then conspired with Creon, for mercenary reasons, to blame Oedipus. Nothing could be more absurd than to charge this otherworldly prophet with such crass and mundane motives, but Oedipus finds his own phantastic way of leaping to this conclusion anyway. *Inside* Oedipus' phantasy, the charge looks reasonable: so not only can Oedipus feel righteous in his anger; he can also attack the challenge to his claim to already know.[9]

But whatever Oedipus *says* about his *reason* for anger, what he *puts on display* is the same movement of soul which led him to kill his father. Laius blocked his physical path to Thebes, Tiresias blocks his mental path to a conclusion, and in each case Oedipus strikes a retaliatory blow. In his attack on Tiresias, Oedipus *acts out* the murder of his father even as he inquires into it. On each of these occasions, he is under so much pressure to get to his conclusion that there is no time to grasp the full meaning of what he is doing.

Here we can see one way in which the determination to know can be used to obscure any possibility of finding out. Oedipus does not have to inquire into Tiresias' silence, because he already knows. And what he purportedly knows is that Tiresias is a fraud. There is no room within this delusion to see Tiresias as a vehicle of a meaning he doesn't yet grasp, no room for the possibility that the world is different from what he takes it to be. The delusion turns Tiresias into a "crafty beggar, who has sight only when it comes to profit" (388): it paints him not only with base, but with *mundane* motives. The space of inquiry has collapsed, it has imploded into one point: that which Oedipus, in his "knowingness," takes himself already to know. And there is no place for a challenge to Oedipus' "reasonableness" to take hold. Oedipus admits as much himself. Creon pleads with Oedipus to hear him out, and to think about how unreasonable the conspiracy charge laid against him is. Oedipus responds: "I am a poor listener to you, for I have found you to be a bitter enemy to me" (545). Because he has already "figured out" that Creon is part of the conspiracy, Oedipus doesn't have to listen to what he says.

Even when he isn't angry, there is a flatness in his reasoning. With the Sphinx, Oedipus may have "hit the mark by native wit," but he didn't understand it. He treats the Sphinx's riddle as a straightforward puzzle—though one in which the stakes are very high (as though it were set by an archvillain)—ignoring any sacred dimension or oracular meaning which would require interpretation. And he therefore fails to see that if "human" is the solution to the riddle, *he is not part of the solution*. The Sphinx had famously asked: "What walks on four legs in the morning, two legs in the afternoon, and three legs in the evening?" But Oedipus walked on three legs in the morning (because his legs were pinned together), limped in the afternoon, and walked on four legs in the evening (blind, he is led by his daughter Antigone). Oedipus is someone who can jump to the conclusion of a riddle and *still* not get it. If he grasped the riddle's irony, he would recognize that he is a perversion of "human."

Consider Oedipus' own account of how he got to Thebes. As he explains to his wife, Iocaste, Oedipus was brought up in Corinth, the son of King Polybus and Merope. He was "the greatest of citizens" until this chance occurrence: at a dinner party a drunk told him he was not his father's child.

> *I was riled, and for that day scarcely controlled myself;* and on the next I went to my mother and my father and questioned them; and they made the man who had let slip the word pay dearly for the insult. So far as concerned them I was comforted, but *still this continued to vex me, since it constantly recurred to me.* Without the knowledge of my mother and my father I went to Pytho, and Phoebus *sent me away cheated* of what I had come for, but came out with other things terrible and sad for my unhappy self, saying that I was destined to lie with my mother, and to show to mortals a brood they could not bear to look on, and I should be the murderer of my father who had begotten me.

> *When I heard this, I left the land of Corinth,* henceforth making out its position by the stars, and *went where I could never see accomplished the shameful predictions of my cruel oracles.* And I will tell you the truth, lady! When I was walking near this meeting of three roads, I was met by a herald and a man riding in a wagon, such as you describe; and the leader and the old man himself tried to drive me from the road by force. In anger I struck the driver, the man who was trying to turn me back; and when the old man saw it, he waited till I was passing his chariot and struck me right on the head with his double-pointed goad. Yet he paid the penalty with interest; in a word, this hand struck him with a stick, and he rolled backwards right out of the wagon, and I killed them all. But if this foreigner had any tie with Laius, who could be more miserable, and who more hateful to the gods, than I. (779–816; emphasis added)

In other words, Oedipus goes to Delphi because he is troubled by remarks impugning his parentage, but as soon as he hears the oracle he treats it as a simple fact that Polybus and Merope are his parents.

I have daydreamed about meeting Oedipus on the road from Delphi to Thebes. Somehow I am able to avoid his blows, and I get to ask him this question: "Given that you went to Delphi because you were troubled by a remark that Polybus wasn't really your father, why do you respond to the oracle by fleeing Corinth?" Oedipus can give no coherent answer. If he wasn't troubled about who his father was, he had no reason to go to the Delphic oracle; if he was troubled, he shouldn't simply have assumed that Polybus was his father. Note that his acts are incoherent not only from *our* point of view; they are incoherent from what would be *his* point of view, if only he could focus on the problem. Oedipus is suffering *reflexive breakdown:* he cannot give a coherent account of what he is doing. But he can't focus on the breakdown—and thus remains unconscious of it—because he is too busy thinking. He assumes he *already knows* what the problem is; the only issue is how to avoid it. What he misses completely is the thought that his "knowingness" lies at the heart of his troubles: what he doesn't know is that he doesn't know.

When Oedipus hears the oracle, he has no reason to move in any direction at all. But he assumes he already knows the geography of his sorrow: where in physical space his troubles are located and where he can get away from them. Oedipus decides to flee Corinth as a strategy for evading the or-

why do you remind me of that ancient grief?" (1033). He calls it "a dreadful brand of shame that I had from my cradle" (1035). And he is indeed *branded*: as the Messenger explains to him, "it was from that occurrence that you got the name you bear" (1036). All Oedipus had to do was to think about the meaning of his name, wonder why anyone would have named him *that* and looked down at his feet. He would have been en route to discovering who he was.

Instead Oedipus displays a stunning lack of curiosity. He is able to go through life with a name which describes an all-too-suspicious wound without pursuing the thought that the meaning of the name might have something to do with him. That is, he uses the naming function of names defensively, to ignore the meaning of his name. Suppose your name were Abandoned Smith. Would you be able to get through life treating your name as just a name, without a serious wonder whether it had descriptive import for you? And when Oedipus, as a young man on the run, arrives in Thebes, he is remarkably incurious about the missing king. Oedipus marries Iocaste, assumes the throne, has four children with her, and raises them to young adulthood. Only then, when the polis is struck with miasma and the Delphic oracle says that Laius' murderer is in the state and must be expelled, does Oedipus seriously inquire into the fate of his predecessor (102–131). "How long is it now since Laius . . . vanished from sight by a deadly stroke?" he asks (558–560). Does it make sense that Oedipus should be asking this question about twenty years after the event?[14]

If there is evidence in the text of Oedipus' phantasies, they are not oedipal, but phantasies of lowly birth. Oedipus is worried that the drunk's taunt is true, that his mother *did* have sexual relations with a slave—that he is the offspring and *that* is why he was abandoned. When Iocaste begs Oedipus to cease his inquiries, he responds, "Do not worry! Even if I prove to be the offspring of three generations of slaves, you will not be shown to be lowborn!" (1062–63). And as she rushes from the stage, Oedipus interprets this as a flight from the recognition of his base origins. "Leave her to take pride in her noble family!" he says bitterly (1070)—and he defiantly concludes (1076–85):

> May whatever burst forth! Even if it is lowly, I desire to learn my origin; but she, for she is proud in woman's fashion, is perhaps ashamed of my low birth. But I regard myself as child of good fortune, and shall not be dishonored. She is my mother; and the months that are my kin have determined my smallness and my greatness. With such a parent, I could never turn out another kind of person, so as not to learn what was my birth.

In the same breath in which he vows to uncover the circumstances of his birth, he declares that, *really,* he is the child of fortune. On the surface, he is saying that fortune has made him into the kind of person who must find out the truth. But just below the surface is the claim that he owes his real identity to fortune—she is the true mother—so anything he might find out about his biological mother could only have secondary significance. The claim to already know pervades the search to find out.

Oedipus takes the same "knowing" stance with respect to the oracles. As soon as he hears an oracle, he assumes he already knows what it means. So, when Creon comes back from Delphi, he treats the oracle merely as information for practical reason to take into account. This is just the way he treated his own oracle: if he is fated to kill his father, he'd better steer clear of Corinth. Indeed, Oedipus takes the oracle to have "cheated" him, because it did not directly answer his question. And in response Oedipus tries to use his own practical reason to "cheat" his fate. Of course, from Sophocles' point of view, all of this is outrageous impiety: oracles are vehicles of sacred meaning, which are necessarily opaque to human reason. For Oedipus, by contrast, the sacred is treated as a simple extension of the domain of practical reason. The oracle is treated like a hot tip from a very good source.

Oedipus is living a life which denies the possibility of tragedy. He cannot recognize any dimension of meaning other than the one he already knows. It's fine, he thinks, to consult oracles and prophets if they can give useful advice; otherwise they're worse than useless. His way of life *shows* that he does not take seriously the idea that there may be meaning opaque to human understanding. He even says as much.

When he hears the news of Polybus' death from old age, he says to Iocaste: "Ah, ah, lady, why should one look to the prophetic hearth of Pytho, or to the birds that shriek above us, according to whose message I was to kill my father? . . . Polybus lies in Hades, and with him have gone the oracles that were with us, now worth nothing" (963–972). Of course, from a religious perspective, this news could not possibly count against the oracle: it would have to signify that the oracle was somehow not understood and required further interpretation. Oedipus draws the opposite lesson: that there is no point to the activity of interpretation. No sooner does he hear the news than he already knows its significance. In short, Oedipus' confidence in his powers of practical reason shields him from recognition of another realm meaning—and, thus, Oedipus cannot recognize the possibility of tragedy until he is overwhelmed by it.

It has sometimes been claimed that Oedipus is the first philosopher: because of his determination to find out the truth, because of his reliance on human reason in his pursuit, and because he abjures mysticism and obscurantism.[15] But this misses the point. Philosophy, Aristotle says, begins in wonder, or awe. If so, Oedipus cannot get started: he is too busy figuring things out to have any such experience. He is too busy thinking to experience the terror of abandonment, the awe of fate. One may well ask: is that why Oedipus is thinking so hard? Philosophy becomes impossible because the originating act of wonder is too terrible. What takes its place is ersatz: a thin "pragmatism" which purports to offer a solution to any problem. Within this pragmatic outlook, every problem does look solvable. Even the miasma can be attacked "by careful thought" (67). The joker in this deck is that in seeing the miasma as a practical problem, Oedipus remains blind to its divine meaning. Oedipus' practical reason can solve every problem, because it cannot see the problems it cannot solve. They are so meaningless, they cannot even be formulated: thus even dismissal becomes impossible.[16] Oedipus is not the first philosopher; he is the first ersatz-philosopher.

FOR SOPHOCLES, the point of this tragedy is to beat the audience into submission. The strategy is simple. In the Sophoclean universe there are only two possibilities: *either* one relies rigidly on human reason *or* one submits to a divine realm. In neither position is there room for philosophy, that peculiarly thoughtful response to awe. Before the catharsis, awe is impossible because, like Oedipus, one "already knows"; in the catharsis, one experiences awe, but submission is built in. The tragedy is meant to terrify us out of self-confidence and into religiosity.

It's an emotional one-two punch. First, the audience is softened up with pity. We can feel compassion for Oedipus because he is *so* human: we can see ourselves reflected in his puffed-up self-importance. But pity also requires a sense of distance. We can see the absurdity in Oedipus' movement of thought, in a way which he cannot. That is one reason why an audience is able to take pleasure in watching a tragedy performed on-stage. On the face of it, one might wonder why anybody would want to see the portrayal of human disaster. One reason may be that humans simply enjoy watching dramas of other people being destroyed; but there is also a deeper reason. When we pity Oedipus, we can indulge the illusion that we know how things *really* are. It is *Oedipus,* not we, who is stuck with the partial and distorted perspective. Being in the audience, it is as though we are looking on the world from an absolute perspective.

Then comes the second punch. There comes a moment when we recognize that our pity rests on illusion, the illusion that we know absolutely. But we don't. On this occasion we may well be right that Oedipus is making some disastrous mistakes in his thinking and in his emotional life, but overall we are not fundamentally better off than he is. We each must rely on our own sense of what is reasonable and unreasonable. We can, of course, test our views against those of others, but, then, so can Oedipus! There is always the possibility that our "tests" are as distorted as the views we are trying to test. Of course, this does not mean that anything goes, that one test is as good or as bad as another; nor does it mean that there are no practical steps we can take to test our thoughts and emotions. But it does mean we have to give up the illusion of an absolutely independent perspective from which to check how well our reasoning is going—and this should encourage a certain humility. The luxurious sense of distance required for pity vanishes. And fear becomes real. Precisely because of our humanity, we too may bring down catastrophe.

But there is a crucial difference between the Athenian audience for whom this play was written and ourselves: catharsis has become impossible. The Athenian audience was able to experience what Aristotle called "a catharsis through pity and fear." Tragic fear purged the narcissistic temptation to make inflated claims for humanity, but *only* because the audience had a well-worn path of retreat—to religious awe. For fifth-century Athenians, tragic consciousness consisted in the recognition that humans lived their lives in the intersection of two realms of meaning, one human, the other divine and opaque. These divine meanings had profound, sometimes catastrophic, consequences for humans, but these meanings were all but humanly incomprehensible.[17] In other words, tragic consciousness takes human life to be powerfully affected by unconscious meaning. For the Greeks those meanings were part of the basic order of the universe—the gods were on Olympus, fate was embedded in the natural order. Formally, this is the same structure as Freud's topographical model, though Freud continues a tradition which begins with Plato of placing this other realm of meaning inside the human psyche. What the Greek poets took to be the castrations and devourings of the gods, Plato took to be artistic representations of lawless, unconscious desires. But this is a difference which makes all the difference.

Catharsis was possible for the Athenian audience because there is relief in submission. Oedipus was abandoned by his parents, but he and his audience were surrounded by the gods. And there is profound comfort in being able to move almost automatically from hubristic overconfidence in human "knowingness" into humble religious submission. But for us that path is blocked. There is no obvious retreat from "knowingness," for there is nothing clear to submit to. We have been abandoned by our parents *and abandoned by the gods.* Since the Enlightenment, modernity has constituted itself around the idea that there are no categories which are simply given—that even the most basic categories like fate, family, nation must be legitimated before the tribunal of human reason, and cannot simply be handed down as part of the basic moral order of the universe. There seem to be no fixed categories which are simply handed down from beyond. There seem to be no meanings to our lives, no values, which are exempt from our critical scrutiny. This is what Nietzsche meant when he had his madman proclaim that God is dead.[18] How can there be relief when everything is up to us? We seem thus to be trapped in the Oedipal position of "knowingness," with no place to go.

That is one reason, I suspect, we hold on to "knowingness" in spite of our boredom and irritation with it: the "alternative," if there is one, is nameless. This, I think, is one of the more profound reasons that Freud-bashing has recently become so popular in our culture. Of course there are other reasons, some of them good ones: a reaction against a previous hagiography of Freud and inflated claims for psychoanalysis; the demand for cheaper and more biochemical forms of treatment; and so on. But it is striking that none of the Freud-bashers tries to give an account of the fundamental human phenomenon to which all of psychoanalysis is a response: the fact of motivated irrationality. Humans regularly behave in ways they do not well understand, which cause pain to themselves and others, which violate their best understanding of what they want and what they care about. And yet, for all of that, there is, as Shakespeare put it, method in their madness. These behavings are not simply meaningless intrusions into ordinary life: they express some motivational state, they have a "logic" of their own. Once you recognize the phenomenon of motivated irrationality, you are committed to there being some form of unconscious meaning. This is a fact which is recognized by Plato and Aristotle, by Augustine, Shakespeare, Proust, and Nietzsche. Freud's originality lies only in the systematic ways he worked out this fundamental idea.

Freud-bashers act as though once they have killed Freud, they have no further problem: as though there were no such thing as unconscious meaning which needs to be accounted for. In this way, Freud-bashers are like latter-day Oedipuses, blind to the realm of unconscious meaning, confident that any real human problem can be both posed and solved by the transparent use of practical reason. We can, as Oedipus put it, "hit the mark by native wit," not by what we learn from the birds. In short, Freud-bashing retraces Oedipus' steps, partaking of a manic, Enlightenment defense which does not even acknowledge the problem which psychoanalysis sets out to address.

But this manic defense is collapsing even as I speak. The movement from modern to postmodern consciousness can, I think, be seen as a recreation of the oedipal drama, but without any fixed dénouement. Modernity constituted itself with a manic, oedipal defense: even though the gods have left, human reason can take their place. The human mind can create and legitimate all it needs or should want. That is, in response to abandonment, Enlightenment consciousness abandons itself to thinking. One might view the postmodern consciousness as originating in the collapse of this defense. No matter how strident the Freud-bashers, no matter how insistently the culture clings to its "knowingness" and its boredom, oedipal confidence is breaking up before our eyes. Of course, one response to this collapse is pathetic, not tragic: the attempted flight back to premodern, fundamentalist forms of religious engagement. Another response is the playful, even mischievous, breaking up of traditional forms which one finds in so much postmodern literature, art, and philosophy. Tragedy begins with the recognition that neither response will work for long: that flight is not possible, that breaking up past orthodoxy is itself a defense which will eventually collapse. It is in such intimations that ancient Oedipus, Oedipus the tyrant, still has the power to reverberate deeply in our souls.

CHAPTER 4

An Interpretation
of Transference

THE SOCRATIC INHERITANCE

"The unexamined life," Socrates famously said, "is not worth living." By now it is almost commonplace to view Socrates as the ancestor of psychoanalytic method. After all, he fashioned a method of cross-examination, designed to elicit conflicts which had hitherto remained unconscious inside the interlocutor. Like the cathartic method, this inquiry was meant to be therapeutic. His was not an abstract inquiry into, say, the nature of piety, but a practical attempt to help the "analysand" live a better life. For Socrates, "How shall I live?" is the fundamental question confronting each person; his peculiar form of examination was intended to help a person to answer it well. That is why Socrates had his own fundamental rule: state only what you believe. The "analysand" was not allowed to try out a debating position, but had to bring his own commitments to the inquiry. If the inquiry led to contradiction, it was not the reductio of an abstract position with no putative owner, but of the "analysand's" own commitments.[1] That is also why Socrates, like a contemporary psychoanalyst, disavowed knowledge of how the "analysand" should answer the fundamental question. The point of Socratic examination was to help people to be able to ask and answer the question for themselves.

Socrates does, then, have a claim to be recognized as an ancestor. But before we let this family romance proceed further, it is worth noting that this Socratic dictum was among his last words. They were uttered in his own defense, while on trial, charged with introducing new gods and corrupting the youth. His defense was not a success, at least by any standard measure: he was found guilty, sentenced to death, and executed. It is easy enough to blame the Athenian demos for this outrage; but is it not also an indictment of Socrates' therapeutic method?[2] His cross-examination was meant to make people better, but it provoked the demos to act out its murderous impulses. Whatever else one might want to say about the death of Socrates, one must admit that it represents, in the short run at least, a psychotherapeutic disaster.

Socrates' mistake, it seems in retrospect, was to ignore transference. He thought one could go up to anyone in the marketplace and begin a cross-examination. The only effort he made to determine the current psychic state of the "analysand" was to elicit his (conscious or preconscious) beliefs. He acted as though the meaning of his activity would be transparent to others, and he thus provoked a transference storm. He argued, for instance, that it is better to suffer injustice than to be unjust, but he seemed oblivious to the fact that in the marketplace of fifth-century Athens, such an argument would be experienced as an unjust attack. What to Socrates seemed like helping a person continue the inquiry into how to live, seemed to his accusers to be introducing new gods and corrupting the youth. These are very different perspectives on the same activity, and Socrates seems to have lacked a systematic understanding how that gap could be possible. Before we go further in claiming Socrates as our ancestor, we ought to recognize that the concept of transference, fundamental to psychoanalytic method, is one that Socrates, to the peril of all concerned, did not have.

Platonic Revisions

Plato is well known for his defense of Socrates and his condemnation of Athenian democracy, but there is implicit in his work both a recognition of Socrates' therapeutic failure and a revision of the theory of the psyche to accommodate it.[3] Curiously, these revisions bear a family resemblance to developments in psychoanalysis during its first forty years. One suspects that both theories were coming up against and responding to something fundamental in the human psyche. For Socrates, like Freud, began with an essentially cathartic method. He did not have an account of a structured psyche; so while a person may have conflicting beliefs, and thus experience conflict *within* the psyche, there was, for Socrates, no room for conflict of the psyche with itself.[4] Overcoming conflict could, for him, only be a matter of eliciting and expelling false belief. For Socrates, the psyche was little more than a container.

Plato can be credited with the invention of psyche-analysis, at least in the sense of being the first to give a systematic account of a structured psyche. He does this against a background assumption that the human psyche has a characteristic activity: to create a meaningful world in which to live. The members of a community constitute themselves in the creation and maintenance of a social-cultural-political world, the polis. Humans, Plato says, are polis animals. The polis provides the only environment fit for human habitation. That is one reason Socrates refuses to flee Athens, with all its faults: life outside its boundaries would, for him, be meaningless. Indeed, the polis, for Plato, has a deeper claim on humans: they are dependent on it for the very constitution of their psyches. Humans are born with a capacity to internalize cultural influences. That is why Plato spends so much time discussing the stories which mothers and nurses should be allowed to tell children, the art which should be allowed in the polis, the content of children's education. At stake are the shape and content of the human psyche. In maturity, humans raise families, work at their jobs, engage in civic life; all the while they are externalizing the cultural influences they had previously internalized. The social-cultural world is the joint externalization of the psyches of those who live within it. This cultural habitat is an enlargement and reflection of the structure of the psyches of the historically significant actors. That is why, Plato thinks, that in studying the structure of the polis we can discover the structure of the psyche "writ large." In studying the world it inhabits, the psyche will find itself reflected back to itself in its own characteristic activity.

58

Plato thus invented the first systematic object-relations theory: a dynamic theory of the relations between psyche and the world it inhabits. Plato thought he was living in a sick society—after all, Athens had just put to death its best citizen—and, given his dynamic theory, he knew this sickness had to be traced back to the psyche. Following the basic faultlines he saw in the polis, Plato devised a structural theory of the psyche. The psyche, he thought, is divided into three parts: appetite, characterized by its basic desires for food and sex; a narcissistic component, which Plato called "spirit," concerned with pride, honor, and anger; and reason, which desires knowledge. These parts are distinguished not only by their distinctive types of desires but also by the possibility for each part to enter into fundamental forms of intrapsychic conflict with the others. Plato even devised a theory of pathological character types which were the manifestations of typical forms of intrapsychic conflict. So, for example, oligarchical character disorder was the outcome of appetite's dominating the other parts and creating a division within itself, whereby certain appetites were encouraged and others were forcibly held down. The oligarchical personality would tend to create an oligarchical society which was itself divided between the rich and the repressed poor. It was a sign, though, of oligarchy's being a pathological structure that an oligarch could not entirely succeed at his characteristic activity, and would produce only a conflicted structure which would eventually collapse of its own contradictions.

Pathology of character, Plato knew, had to be reflected in pathology of outlook. The tyrant, for example, thinks he is living the best life even though he is living the worst. In general, people are trying to answer the question "How shall I live?" as best they can; since they are doing such a poor job, their methods of inquiry must be distorted. Plato devised a theory of illusion to explain these distorted perspectives. In his famous metaphor of the cave, people are bound at certain levels, exposed only to distorted images which they mistake for reality. The cave is often taken to offer but a bleak prospect for human life, but I think it is the most optimistic metaphor in Western philosophy. Although our experience may be permeated by distorted images, they are ultimately distortions of something real. Moreover, every distorted form of experience has within itself its own conflicts. That is, even from inside a distorted perspective, one can get a glimmer that one is not seeing things as they are. If one were to pursue these conflicts, painful though that would be, one would eventually work through them, and end up better off—at a higher level in the cave.

Only the philosopher, who Plato thinks is also a psyche-analyst, is able to work through the contradictions at each level of experience, and so only he can ascend out of the cave and see reality clearly. Having done that, Plato has his "Socrates" argue that it is the philosopher's obligation to descend back into the cave and help educate and govern his fellow citizens. This will be an unpleasant task for the philosopher: it will take time for his eyes to get used to the dark and to the illusory world his fellow citizens mistake for reality. But in requiring the philosopher to go back down into the cave, the Socrates of the *Republic* is issuing a prescription which the historical Socrates ignored. In the *Republic,* Plato recommends that the philosopher-ruler tell the citizens a "noble falsehood." This is a dense issue, but one point Plato is making is psychological: if one wishes to communicate with people whose lives are dominated by illusion, one must speak the language of the illusory world in which they live. The noble falsehood is Plato's attempt to say something he believes to be true, but in a story form he thinks his hearers can grasp. The translation into a fiction converts a truth into a falsehood, but, for Plato, this is as close as this illusory level of experience can get to truth.

THE RECOGNITION OF TRANSFERENCE

In the story I wish to tell, Plato's reflection on the therapeutic disaster of Socratic method led to the recognition of the phenomenon of transference and to the development of its theory. For transference, I believe, is just the psyche's characteristic activity of creating a meaningful world in which to live. This characteristic must be understood against a background of a structured psyche, vulnerable to myriad forms of internal conflicts, dependent on prior internalizations for its structure and content, and regularly dominated by phantasy.

In my analytic work, I have often had the experience of entering, or being drawn into, a world—a world endowed with its own peculiar meanings and structures. I expect many analysts have had this experience; and the question I should like to address here is: what content can be given to such an experience?

This is not a question which the early Freud can pursue, because he assumes the world is already endowed with its own meanings. In the *Studies on Hysteria*, he introduces the idea of transference as a "false connection." A woman in analysis experiences, to her dismay, a desire that Freud give her a kiss. It turns out that she has previously experienced and repressed such a desire, directed toward another man. As Freud explains:

> The content of the wish had appeared first of all in the patient's consciousness without any memories of the surrounding circumstances which would have assigned it to a past time. This wish which was present was then, owing to the compulsion to associate which was dominant in her consciousness, linked to my person, with which the patient was legitimately concerned; and, as the result of this *mésalliance*—which I describe as a "false connection"—the same affect was provoked which had forced the patient long before to repudiate this forbidden wish.[5]

Transference, on this interpretation, is the unconscious movement of the target of desire across space and time. Having been directed at a significant person in her past, the desire unconsciously shifts direction onto another person in her present. What makes this a *false* connection, for Freud, is that a desire which would have been appropriately directed toward her former would-be lover is merely reenacted with her current doctor. Similarly, in his case study of Dora, Freud speaks of transference phenomena as "new editions or facsimiles of impulses and phantasies which are aroused and made conscious during the progress of the analysis, but they have this peculiarity, which is characteristic for their species, that they replace some earlier person by the person of the physician."[6] On this conception of transference, emotions, desires, phantasies are faxed across a given world and reemerge in the analytic situation, unconscious that they are facsimiles. This is Freud's *Archimedean assumption*: if one holds the world constant, one will see psychological contents traveling across it.

Here, then, is the bare bones of the traditional conception of transference; and it is remarkable how little psychoanalytic understanding is needed to formulate it. The idea that wishes and emotions are transferred or carried over from a previous situation to the analytic situation is there in the *Studies on Hysteria,* before Freud had any detailed grasp of the workings of unconscious mental processes. All Freud needed to formulate this conception of transference was the idea of the repression of forbidden psychological contents and the return of the repressed in the analytic situation. On this interpretation, one can see transference in terms of an empiricist model of learning: the analysand is expecting the future to be like the past. The extra fillip which Freud adds, on this picture, is that the anticipated future is along the lines of a repressed and rejected past. As Freud came to understand archaic mental functioning, he revised and elaborated this conception of transference. These revisions make room for a more psychoanalytically informed conception of transference.

INTRAPSYCHIC TRANSFERENCE

Freud begins to grapple with the nature of unconscious mental processes in *The Interpretation of Dreams,* and he there introduces the idea of transference as an *intra*psychic phenomenon.[7] Freud wants to explain how dreams use day residues and other preconscious ideas to disguise and express an unconscious wish. Because the wish cannot directly enter consciousness, it *transfers* its intensity onto an idea which is already preconscious and thereby gets itself "covered" by it. One might say that, in Freud's view, it is because the wish cannot transfer *itself* from unconscious to conscious that it transfers intensity instead. Freud uses the concept of psychic energy,[8] but the point I wish to emphasize can be made without it. Our conscious thoughts, dreams, daydreams, are linked by webs of associations to unconscious wishes and phantasies. The conscious thought, dream, or daydream becomes a representative of the unconscious wish or phantasy, and its use, even within conscious experience, has to change.[9] There is no reason why this day residue would be occurring in dreams (daydreams or actings out) other than that it is doing duty for the unconscious wish. "Covering," then, is not mere intensification; it is the covering *over* of one idea by another. The conscious idea has been made into *a covering:* an outer shell, an artifact of the unconscious idea. The conscious idea now has a new meaning as a result of its links to the unconscious. It has been endowed with unconscious significance, both in the sense that it now expresses unconscious ideas and in the sense that this very fact must remain hidden.

These intrapsychic transferences tend to be idiosyncratic. Freud was a master at showing how a chance occurrence during the day—for example, seeing a botanical monograph in a store window—can be endowed with deep unconscious significance. The idea of a monograph will become embedded in a web of associations of which the subject is unaware. Such an embedding will by nature be peculiar. The embedding depends on a chance encounter with the monograph at a time when a certain set of issues were psychologically prominent for this person. It must also somehow "fit in with" the loose associations of archaic mental functioning. That is, it enters a web of associations whose formation depends on a history of chance encounters and loose associations. However common some of the basic problems of human existence may be—helplessness, entrance into the social-sexual world—they acquire their meaning for each person through a web of associations which is idiosyncratic through and through. This embedding is made even more complex and idiosyncratic by condensation. Because of the fluidity of archaic associations, a single idea or image may do duty for a wealth of conflicts, wishes, phantasies. The idea will typically be woven into overlapping webs of associations, so the idea of a one-to-one relation between a covering and a covered idea is only a first approximation.[10]

Throughout *The Interpretation of Dreams,* Freud resists the idea that the meaning of a dream can be given by a simple decoding of symbols into meanings. Instead, he insists we do not really understand the meaning of a dream until we understand its location in a entire network of wishes, prohibitions, and associations. This is one manifestation of Freud's *psychological holism:* the full meaning of any particular dream is revealed by its place in the whole web of wishes, desires, and other psychological forces. So, to understand that dream fully, we must understand the (mal)functioning psyche which produced it. In practice, no analysis can explicitly be spent unpacking one dream; conversely, it would not be unusual for an analysis to keep coming back to one or two key dreams and to endow them with ever more richness and complexity. To understand more about the whole is to understand more about the dreams which are embedded in it.

The lesson of intrapsychic transference is that psychological holism must include the unconscious.[11] Any conscious thought will typically be embedded in a wealth of associations which will endow that thought with meanings which are at once unconscious and idiosyncratic. We do not fully understand the meaning of any conscious thought until we understand the myriad ways in which this thought is functioning as a "covering" for unconscious mental forces. It is these transferences which come to light in an analysis. As we listen to analysands' associations over the years, we become increasingly aware that though analysands are adept at speaking a shared natural language, in our case English, each is at the same time speaking an idiolect with its own special meanings and resonances. One of the tasks of analysis is to help analysands become consciously aware of the peculiar meanings with which they endow their words.[12]

When Freud introduced the conception of intrapsychic transference, he had not yet formulated the structural theory, but the idea can be readily extended to accommodate it. For, as we find regularly in analysis, a superego voice is serving as a "covering" for an archaic wish or fury. I regularly hear analysands, referring to themselves in the second and third persons, say something like, "[First name], you ass, just shut up: you're such a jerk." Clearly, this is an attempt to repress or "cover over" an emerging wish or fury, but it is also a "covering" in the sense of being the conscious representative of the repressed. The superego voice, as Freud saw, draws its harsh intensity from the id; and the intensity is reciprocal and dynamic. There would be no need for a harsh superego voice if there were not an intense wish or fury to hold down. One might thus say that there is intrapsychic transference between a person's id and superego. Although the superego's task is to repress the id, in that very role it becomes the id's covering: its artifact and representative. "The superego," says Freud, "is always close to the id and *can act as its representative* vis-à-vis the ego."[13]

The significance of intrapsychic transference is that consciousness in general serves as a covering for the unconscious: it has been made over into an artifact and representative of unconscious wishes, phantasies, and furies.

FROM INTRAPSYCHIC TRANSFERENCE
TO INTERPSYCHIC TRANSFERENCE

If people endow their words and thoughts with idiosyncratic and unconscious meanings, those meanings must resonate in their daily lives. There is, at the very least, an important relation between *intra*psychic and *inter*psychic transference.[14] As a first approximation, take a classic, if simplified, example: an infantile wish for an incestuous relation may be transferred onto the thought of having an affair with one's analyst. The conscious thought, one might say, has been made over into an artifact, a covering. This is intrapsychic transference, which might be revealed in a dream; but it also might be revealed interpsychically as an experienced erotic desire for one's analyst. Might transference, as it emerges in analysis, be an attempt to turn the analyst into an artifact, a covering? In the throes of a powerful parental transference, it seems to the analysand as though the analyst is speaking with a critical voice, a voice with which the superego usually speaks intrapsychically. Just as the superego serves as a "covering" for a powerful unconscious phantasy, so it seems that the analysand attempts to make the analyst into the statue of the Commendatore. In the interpsychic transference, the analysand seems to be attempting to endow the analyst with peculiar, unconscious meaning.

In Freud's later writings on transference, he seems to move toward such a view. The accent of his writings shifts from transference as a transfer (across a given world) to transference as a repetition. The cost of keeping something out of consciousness, Freud says, is that one acts it out unconsciously. Repetition is the return of the repressed, in unconscious form. This reenactment is inescapable in the transference: "As long as the patient is in treatment, he cannot escape from his compulsion to repeat: in the end we understand that this is his way of remembering." The peculiar form of "remembering" is a form not of recollection, but of memorialization. It is an enactment designed to make the present into an artifact of the past, consciousness into an artifact of the unconscious. In its most general sense, the aim of the enactment is to endow the world with comprehensible meaning. As Freud says, transference is a repetition "not only onto the doctor, but onto all other aspects of the current situation."[15] In the transference, the psyche is engaged in its characteristic activity of trying to create a meaningful world in which to live.

One's view of this activity can be obscured by holding too fast to the idea of transference as a repetition. To see something as a repetition is to see it as "the same thing again"; but to understand transference we need to maintain a certain flexibility in the ways we count. Consider, by way of analogy, the soldier, doctor, or shoemaker of Plato's Athens. From one perspective, each person in his profession was engaged in the same characteristic tasks over and over again. From another perspective, each person was living one characteristic type of life and making his contribution to maintenance of the social world. In a healthy polis, Plato said, each person will "do his own thing," perform the *one* task for which he is best suited. And if, like Plato, one sees the continued existence of the social world as dependent on people's performing their distinctive social roles, one will tend to view these roles less as repeated than as *enduring*.[16]

THE CREATION OF A POLIS

Before we can understand what transference within the context of an individual's analysis is, we need to reflect on our joint contributions to the creation and maintenance of the social world. Consider, to begin with, the Athenian polis. On the one hand, it is a psychological creation: who counts as a citizen, and who as a slave, who is inside it and who is barbarian, how property is allocated and justice meted out, where and how the boundaries are delineated—all of this reflects the interests, needs, concerns, and outlooks of the participants. On the other hand, it is not just a psychological state or a mere projection. Athens is a creation, an artifact, and it gains a certain independence from the shifting psychological states of its inhabitants. Athens was a real invention, as is the United States. Yet the continued existence of these social worlds depends on the enduring willingness of its citizens to defend their boundaries, to go through the rituals which lend peculiar meaning to being an Athenian or American, to pay for their characteristic activities. Watching the demise of the Soviet

Union, we see what happens when there is a collective disinvestiture or decathexis: the polis falls apart and loses meaning.[17] Although the polis is dependent on our enduring commitment, and although it reflects our collective psychic activity, it is not just psychology. Rather, we have created an environment which our psyches can, for better or worse, inhabit.

Consider physical artifacts. It is obvious that, say, the houses we build reflect our interests and concerns, our judgment and taste. Yet though they manifest our psychological states, they achieve a quasi-independent status. A house is at once permeated with our psychology and free-standing. Nor do our meaning-endowing activities require physical construction. A prison may be turned into a museum, a concentration camp sanctified as a church, a set of buildings turned into a university, though little or nothing is done to the physical structures. These transformations usually require certain rituals as well as a shared commitment to use the structures in different ways. In general, social institutions—law, medicine, the university, the corporation, art—reflect our interests and depend on our enduring commitments, but they cannot be reduced to our psychological states. These institutions are artifacts, and they help to constitute a social world, a polis, in which we locate ourselves.[18]

The distinction between subjective and objective can be used to make myriad contrasts, but when psychologists or psychoanalysts speak of someone's being able to perceive reality undistorted by phantasy, or of establishing "mature object relations," the reality they are speaking of is social reality. Confusion arises only if one both takes the social world to be objective and, as an Archimedean, implicitly assumes that all psychic activity must be subjective. In his discussion of transitional phenomena, for example, Winnicott used the term "transitional" to designate this form of experience because he conceived of it as en route from subjective experience to experience of an objective world.[19] He saw the psyche's activity in the creation of transitional spaces, and he *also* saw that the boundaries between inside and outside, subjective and objective, are blurred. These are two observations, but if one is an Archimedean, there will be a tendency to lump them together and assume that as boundaries become sharper, the psyche's activity will be located on only one side: inside the psyche.

Winnicott asks where cultural experience is located, and he notes that there are certain forms, for example certain religious experiences, where boundaries do seem to blur. But I wonder if the question of location has to be puzzling to him because he recognizes, on the one hand, that culture is permeated with psyche, but he assumes, on the other, that the world is not. Once one allows that the psyche informs the social world, it becomes easier to say where cultural experience is located. Some of it may be transitional;[20] but some cultural experience is of a world we create and inhabit. Cultural experience, Winnicott says, is an extension of the idea of play; but he is not able to say in what this extension consists. Roughly speaking, the extension consists in the fact that in play we are playing at creating a world, whereas in cultural activity we are *attempting* in earnest to do so. We are at least *trying* to have our psychological activity move out across the boundary of our psyches and inform the world.[21] If one is an Archimedean, there will be a tendency to interpret this activity as projection. Of course, projection is always possible. But when we judge, say, a house to be graceful we need not be projecting grace onto a house (though we can do that too): we may be recognizing grace which has been built into the house.

I am going to suggest that there is something real about the social-cultural world which transference, as it becomes manifest in analysis, lacks. There are many factors which contribute to the reality of the social world, but, in broad outline, they can be divided into two categories: first, the social world is intersubjectively accessible; second, it provides a space in which people can live. It is the first hallmark, intersubjectivity, at least in a moderately strong form, which I shall argue transference in analysis lacks, so it is worth delineating a few of its features. A social world is open to reflection, to debate, to testing in thought and action, and to the possibility of consensual endorsement. A polis, like Athens or the United States, depends on the willingness of its citizens to defend its boundaries from outside incursions, but the polis can also be tested in thought and debate. The question of whether Athens or the United States should be a slave society is one which was tested inside the boundaries of each polis. Here it is worth noting both the power of a question to shape a world and a classic defense against it. The question "Is a slave naturally inferior?"

and the attempt to answer it shaped the course of American history. A slave culture can generally not survive the insight that the difference between slave and citizen is purely accidental. Thus the importance, for the institution of slavery, of stories which portray slaves as innately inferior; and the threat of reflective questioning. A classic way to defend against challenge is what I shall call *the barbarian defense:* put the challenge on the outside, treat it as the attack of a barbarian outsider who does not understand. In the United States, the barbarian defense—which Yankees do not understand—was overcome by force. But the most insidious challenge is when the barbarian defense crumbles and there is a realization *inside the culture* that there is no innate difference between slave and citizen. There is no obvious way that slave culture can survive this internal reflective questioning.

Winnicott suggests that it is religious experience in adult life which bears closest resemblance to the transitional experiences of childhood. But there is nevertheless an asymmetry. With the myriad transitional phenomena of childhood, the parents instinctively understand that they are not to ask whether the object is found or created, whether the play is a game or real. All such questions are species of the genus "Is this subjective or is it objective?", which Winnicott recognized was the great solvent of transitional space. But shared religious experience is in this way more like the rest of shared cultural experience than it is like the transitional phenomena of childhood: it is always open to the question of its reality. To take an example Winnicott mentions, the question as to the meaning and reality of transubstantiation shaped Western civilization.

In general, a social-cultural world is always vulnerable to reflective questioning inside the culture. There is a permanent possibility of bringing the meaning of an activity to consciousness and of questioning its validity.

THE CREATION OF AN IDIOPOLIS

The dynamics of intrapsychic transference reveal that even when a person participates in shared cultural activities, those activities will tend also to have an idiosyncratic, unconscious meaning for that person. This, I believe, is one of Freud's greatest discoveries. We have seen that a person's thoughts, words, activities are embedded in a web of unconscious associations which are both archaic and idiosyncratic. Just as each person, when speaking a natural language, also unconsciously speaks an idiolect, does she not also, as she participates in the culture's activities, unconsciously inhabit an idiosyncratic world? If an artifact gets its shared meaning via its location in a common web of psychological forces, it would seem that each participant, as she plays her role in the shared culture, is also at the same time performing an idiosyncratic variation on a theme. For as we watch how the unconscious uses day residues, condensation, and displacement—all the loose associations of archaic mental functioning—to disguise and express itself, we see that every public ritual, every shared artifact, is imbued with idiosyncratic meanings by each of the participants. One of the deeper consequences of Freud's discovery, I believe, is that each person, as he participates in a shared culture, is also attempting to create and inhabit an idiosyncratic polis—an *idiopolis*—the peculiar lineaments of which are largely unconscious.

There is also room within a culture for people to act out phantasies in private enactments. Imagine a middle-aged man who never married and who lives at home with his aged mother. We can imagine it emerging in analysis that he is acting out a phantasy of remaining with mother in an incestuous relation. All other women are treated as "barbarians": not to be trusted, dangerous, outside the polis. Has not this person created a micropolis with its own peculiar meanings? Of course, before analysis the meaning of his activity has remained unconscious to everyone, himself included, and thus it has been excluded from intersubjective questioning. It thus fails one of the hallmarks of social reality—though even here one must acknowledge that analysis is itself a form of intersubjective questioning by which the contours of the idiopolis come to light. And it does possess the other hallmark: the person has carved out an arena in which to live. His environment has a stable system of reference points and associations, people are endowed with idiosyncratic meanings, and the boundaries of this idiopolis are actively defended. One can say in all seriousness that this man has *given his life* to the cause of keeping the barbarians outside the gates.

Transference, as it emerges in analysis, is simply the idiosyncratic, unconscious side of the psyche's fundamental activity: to inform the world with meaning. To paraphrase the novelist L. P. Hartley: transference is a foreign country; they do things differently there. The fundamental demand of all transference is to participate in the idiopolis, and thus lend it reality. To return, for a moment, to Freud's discovery of transference in the "false connection": what is it about the connection that made it *false?* Is it not Freud's refusal of his patient's invitation to participate in a ritual, to enter a world? Just one kiss, for all we know, might have turned this *mésalliance* into an *alliance amoureuse*. It is not as though the patient was making a simple mistake; she was trying to invest the world with particular meaning. Instead of joining in, Freud pointed that out. Freud once said that the transference is a "battlefield."[22] What we see here, within the confines of a shared culture, is the battle of two microcultures, at the point where they meet. The patient wants Freud to play the role of lover; Freud insists on playing the doctor.

Freud might have "won" that battle, but it is easier to see what is going on if we imagine him "losing." Imagine, not that he kissed her, but that he misunderstood her wish. Her wish was not to be kissed, but to be rejected. It is she who wished to look on love as a *mésalliance*. She could then defensively justify her isolation as a series of rejections by others. Her problem, as she saw it, was that she was attracted to the wrong sort of person. On this interpretation, Freud unconsciously entered her idiopolis: he actively took on the significance with which she endowed him. Indeed, the discovery of transference turns out to be the gratification of her wish. The fundamental demand of all transference, underlying all the particular demands, is that the analyst, the other, should participate in a world endowed with peculiar meanings. Missing the transference meaning, as we see in this imagined instance, is tantamount to unconscious compliance with the fundamental demand.

The fundamental demand, then, is at once for intimacy and for a certain intersubjectivity. The myriad transference demands are not *simply* for love: love's required form is that the analyst should travel the hidden byways of a peculiar world. The analyst is to participate in an intimate world, and thereby lend it substance. Nietzsche admonished us to live our lives as though we were creating a work of art. The phenomenon of transference reveals, I think, that each of us is unconsciously trying to do just that. Each of us is trying to create a peculiar polis in which to live and unconsciously demanding that others recognize and participate in it. This demand, it is worth noting, is not always absurd. The artist, Freud saw, succeeds in having his imaginative expressions appreciated by others. The public recognition of artistic creation lends the creation a reality it would not otherwise possess. There is poignancy in the fact that each of us labors against the background that his or her creation could, just possibly, be recognized by others.

But while all transference demands are implicitly for participation, that is only part of intersubjectivity; and transference as it emerges in analysis typically shuns the other part. Acting out, Freud says, is a *substitute* for conscious remembering.[23] It is as though the ritualistic enactment of an idiopolis depends on the absence of conscious understanding. This, I believe, is a hallmark by which a neurotic idiopolis is distinguished. Because a neurotic conflict is repressed, it must be acted out over and over again; and this lends the neurotic idiopolis a special rigidity. There is no room for life's passing events to influence the shape of the idiopolis, for they have already been endowed with fixed meanings within it. Ironically, the sense of reality inside a neurotic idiopolis depends on its lacking one of the essential criteria of social reality: intersubjective reflection and testing. Just as the power of dream experience typically depends on there being no room within it for the thought "This is only a dream," so the power of an idiopolis depends on there being no room inside for a conscious, communal inquiry into its meaning.[24] Of course, it is no use, as Freud well knew, simply to explain to a person his intrapsychic conflicts. The problem, classically understood, is that the explanation will register only in a person's consciousness. It will be dynamically excluded from making an intrapsychic difference. This is the intrapsychic version of the barbarian defense: the consciously registered explanation cannot communicate with the relevant unconscious representations. But this intrapsychic failure reflects a prior failure of interpsychic communication. The speaker, for his part, is proceeding in ignorance of the listener's idiolect: he has no idea of the intrapsychic transferences which embed these words in a web of unconscious meanings. Thus the words he speaks drift off aimlessly, unanchored to the idiosyncratic unconscious resonances of his audience. That is why just telling a person his or her problem will not make a difference. To the ear of the unconscious, the speaker's words are little more than barbaric noise.

This barbarian defense is the interpsychic version of repression. How is it, then, that saying something could make a difference? Here it is worth returning to three Platonic insights: first, a neurotic's idiopolis is not one in which a happy life is possible, because the world itself is essentially conflicted; second, it is possible to gain a glimmer of this conflict inside the world; third, it is the task of the psychoanalyst to descend into the cave and speak the truth at the level at which it can be grasped. The question is how these insights can be applied to the analytic situation.

THE RESOLUTION OF THE TRANSFERENCE

The development of the transference in analysis is a single process with two aspects. From the analysand, there is an attempt to metabolize the analyst and the analytic situation. The analysand is performing reenactments which endow the analyst with important and familiar meanings. Freud says that the transference is "artificially constructed," and the manifest content is that it is being produced, as it were, in laboratory conditions, like a culture of bacteria. But the latent content is that it is an artifice, an artifact. The analyst is being drawn inside an idiopolis.[25] In the "true illness," as in the "artificially constructed" one, the analysand is basically engaged in the same activity. At least in the opening stages, the real difference between the true and the artificial lies not in the analysand's, but in the analyst's activity. Freud speaks of the transference as providing "new editions of the old conflicts." By that he does not mean that it is just the *latest* edition, but that it is to be a *revised* edition. As Freud says, "the new struggle around [the analyst] is lifted to its highest psychical level."[26] To understand this upward revision, we have to understand what the analyst is doing as the transference develops. At the same time as the analysand is taking the analyst into his world, the analyst is gaining a clearer understanding of what that world is like. Listening to associations and dreams, the analyst gains some understanding of the intrapsychic transferences which endow conscious thoughts with unconscious resonances. That is, the analyst achieves a working knowledge of the analysand's idiolect. Similarly, the analyst is gaining a clearer understanding of the overall structure of the analysand's intrapsychic conflicts. So, just as the analysand is getting in a position to listen, the analyst is getting in a position to speak.

Freud speaks of the transference in analysis as a "playground" in which repetitions are allowed to proliferate.[27] In this playground, unconscious intrapsychic conflicts will be acted out, and thus inadvertently put on display. The idea of the analytic situation as a playground is redolent with meaning. It is on a playground that culture has a dress rehearsal; and the regressive pull of analysis will tend to draw culture back to its infantile roots. But there is another sense in which transference, as it emerges in analysis, stands in between child's play and shared culture. On the one hand, the analysand is not just playing at creating a world, but is actually trying to create one; on the other, there is no room in the idiopolis for the kind of reflective questioning which every shared culture must allow. In order to survive, a shared culture must be able to tolerate the relevant version of "Is this subjective or is it objective?", "Is this real or only a game?", "Is this found or is it created?" These reflective questions typically dissolve transitional space, and the only way a neurotic idiopolis can cope with them is by employing the barbarian defense. If they are coming from the outside, they can be treated as so much noise.

However, condensed in the image of transference as a playground, there lurks another meaning: the analyst is now inside the game. In a maternal transference, for instance, the analysand has made the analyst into a maternal "covering," while the analyst has been learning the deeper resonances of the "mother tongue" and gaining a view of the dynamic, conflicted structure of psyche and world. The barbarian defense is no longer possible, because the analyst is no longer an outsider, making unanchored comments on an observed ritual. It is, for the analysand, as though the ritual itself is speaking. But "mother" has somehow changed her tune. In speaking the "mother tongue," the analyst tries also to reflect back to the psyche an image of itself as a conflicted whole.

No one else in the analysand's world is able to do this. All the other figures have been given limited roles and partial perspectives. The analyst is always cast in a limited role—those are the only roles there are—but he tries to use the language of each role to speak an understanding of the place of that role within the functioning of the whole. One indication of a good transference interpretation is the unique blend of comfort and discomfort it elicits. It is as though the analysand is trying to bring together an experience of recognition—Mama, it's you!—with an experience of irredeemable strangeness—Mama, what has come over you? One might call this a disturbance of memory in the idiopolis. At every stage, in every role, the analyst is trying to import self-conscious understanding into the heart of a world which must, for its survival, remain opaque to itself. However, the basic means of preserving opacity is no longer available. The analyst is no longer outside the world, making comments about it. That is why the analyst is able to give a "new transference meaning" to an analysand's symptoms, rituals, and emotions.[28] The analyst enables a characteristic emotional response to speak its own role in the dynamic functioning of the whole.

In recognizing a maternal transference, we see the analysand experiencing the analyst as a not-good-enough mother; but we tend to forget that, in the beginning, mother was the world. For whatever reason, mother was experienced as not-good-enough, disappointing the child too much, too soon, or too often. The child goes on to construct a not-good-enough world, and to experience himself as forced to live within it. It is not surprising, then, that as the fault-lines of this world emerge, we hear maternal echoes. In my analytic work, I find that I am often treated as a maternal figure around the time that the analysand has dynamic reason for experiencing disappointment. Sometimes there is an external trigger—for instance, I am about to go on vacation—but often a well-engineered disappointment is constructed to suit intrapsychic needs. Were I to play out the role of a disappointing mother, I could help damp down an emerging wish; I could also be the target for the ensuing (often unconscious) fury; and I would thus reinforce and legitimate the background assumption that the world is disappointing.

A well-placed interpretation frustrates all these functions. The drama was meant to act out a disappointment; instead the analysand is asked to reflect on why he or she needs a disappointment just now from me. The interpretation not only gives the enacted experience a name, so that it can be consciously considered *as* disappointment; it also hypothesizes the intrapsychic conflicts which give rise to a need for disappointment. It is as though the world describes not only itself but also what is going on across the border, inside the psyche, which requires the world to be the way it is experienced. The interpretation thereby frustrates the attempt to make me into a superego "covering," but it also names the associated wish which the analysand would like covered over, at just the moment when that wish is closest to conscious experience—that is, at just the moment when the wish is most closely linked with its conscious "covering." The interpretation also gives a name to the fury which inevitably follows the frustration of a wish, and describes its myriad uses: to help inhibit the wish, to punish the analysand for having it, and to punish the analyst for frustrating it. In short, in my role as "mother," I try to speak, in the mother tongue, my role within this idiosyncratic world. That is why the conflict is "lifted to its highest psychical level." "Mother," one might say, cannot ultimately survive self-understanding of what she is doing here.

Neither, ultimately, can the particular intrapsychic configuration of the analysand. The analysand's psyche stands in a dynamic relation with its world, and if key elements of that world shift, the psyche cannot remain unchanged. Human life must find its way among three sets of significant boundaries. The first are those which delineate intrapsychic structure and which collectively separate what is available to consciousness from what is repressed. The second is between what is inside a person's psyche and what lies outside. The third is between what is inside a person's world and what lies beyond the pale. Meaningful contents may travel across a boundary, but each boundary serves as a kind of buffer. Each bounded area is offered limited freedom from the pressures exerted by what lies beyond. So, for example, while it is virtually impossible for someone to hold two consciously recognized contradictory beliefs, it is easier to tolerate living with a conscious belief and an experience in the world which seems to contradict it, or to tolerate a conscious belief and a countervailing unconscious wish. These boundaries provide some respite from the holistic demand that everything fit together. Each boundary permits certain discontinuities to lie on either side.

There are, I believe, both theoretical and clinical advantages in distinguishing between a person's psyche and his idiopolis. First, this distinction helps us to do justice to the psyche's creative, artifact-making abilities. In the transference, the psyche is engaged in the same type of activity as when, in concert with others, it does its part in the maintenance of a social world. Here there is no concert: the psyche is marching to the beat of its own drum. It is, I think, a mistake to treat the idiopolis as a mere projection of the psyche. Projection is only one of a wide range of psychic tools. So, for example, a person committed to living in a disappointing world may generate disappointment in myriad ways. Genuinely disappointing events may be enhanced, ambiguous events can be given a certain spin, people may be tricked into unwittingly delivering disappointments, the person may form wishes—such as a crush on a movie star or on the analyst—whose very existence depends on the expectation that they will be disappointed. Projection may also be used: for example, a person may project her sadism onto another both to get rid of it and to experience a cruel disappointment. These are a range of distinctions which tend to get flattened when one speaks of a person's "psychological world."

Second, this artifact is experienced by the psyche as though it were a world in which the psyche is located. It is a stable structure which systematically attributes motives, emotions, and attitudes to the people in the world. The attributions purport to offer psychological explanations of all the significant actions of all the significant people in this world, the analysand and analyst included. Of course, the psyche is unaware that these purported explanations are dynamically related to intrapsychic needs. In this way, the psyche mistakes its creation for an objective world which is given to it. Although a neurotic world is essentially conflicted, nevertheless there is a certain stability, systematicity, and inclusiveness to this creation which distinguishes it from a passing illusion, phantasy, or psychological state.

Clinically, it is advantageous to be able to distinguish a person's shifting psychological states from the more or less stable world in which that person lives. A person living in a disappointing world may at various times feel angry, sullen, disappointed, resigned, comfortable, at home, reassured.

Theoretically we see that the boundary between psyche and world lends a certain resilience to the world: it can endure a person's shifting psychological states. That is why merely disappointing an analysand's wish to be disappointed would itself be of no therapeutic value. When an analysand needs a disappointment, for example, virtually anything I do, and countless things I am imagined as doing, can be woven into a tale of being let down. This stability, in turn, contributes to the experienced reality of the world. Indirectly, the world's stability ensures stability of intrapsychic structure. For while a person may go through a cascade of emotional reactions, they will tend to follow a familiar and intelligible pattern, and they will all be defined in relation to a certain type of unsatisfactory world. The only way to effect a profound shift in the psyche is via a transformation of the world in which it lives. In terms of technique, this account of transference encourages patience on the part of the analyst, and cautions against premature interpretation. If the analysand is engaged in creative activity, the analyst must exert care not to inhibit or disrupt this process. Only after the world has been woven with the analyst inside it can both the analyst and analysand together find their ways around in it.

Psychoanalysis, I believe, distinguishes itself from other forms of "talking cure" by its aim of changing the world. Although analysis may eventually help analysands establish more realistic relations with the common social world, its first task is to help analysands take apart a private world which has held them captive. That is why it is such a long and arduous task. Through repeated interpretations of the need to be disappointed, spoken by the designated disappointer in the appropriate idiolect, the psyche is fed a transference meal which it cannot metabolize in its familiar ways. The analyst is already inside the idiopolis, and he gives his interpretation in a language designed to work its way into the psyche. The interpretation makes explicit the intrapsychic transferences which have hitherto relied for their existence on remaining unconscious. The interpretation is spoken so as to awaken these unconscious resonances and thus to permeate the intrapsychic boundaries. As the intrapsychic transferences are so described, the need for them diminishes. Over time, these transference-interpretations help foster a transubstantiation of intrapsychic structure. As the multiplicity and diversity of the "disappointments" are pointed out and interpreted, the analysand comes to see that he or she is not being acted upon by a not-good-enough world, so much as creating a world in which to be disappointed.

Theorists sometimes write as though once analysands can grasp their conflicted responses, they can choose less conflicted ways to live. There is truth to this, but it tends to portray analysands as smart shoppers: now that they have been given a choice, analysands can choose better psyches than they did the last time around. It is as though the only problem with conflicts is that they are painful; and one is thus better off without them. It is Plato who saw that there are certain types of conflict which, when recognized, are not just bad, but impossible. Not all conflicts are such. The recognition of tragic conflict, for instance, can reinforce a sense of the world's reality: of its painful independence. A neurotic idiopolis is experienced as though it too were painfully independent—subjecting the person, say, to wave after wave of disappointment—and it cannot survive the pervasive recognition that it is both motivated and created. For it is of the essence of a world to present itself as given. The analysand does not choose a better world over his familiar idiopolis: the old world goes dead.[29]

By the time analysands can recognize their own activity in creating a world, that world is already on the wane. That is why making the unconscious conscious ultimately requires (and is a sign of) the transformation of the analysand's world. In this process, analysands move from experiencing themselves as passive victims to recognizing their own activity. This is what a person experiences in the deconstruction of an idiopolis. All transference, I have argued, is an attempt to create a world in which to live. But not all attempts are successful; and what analyst and analysand eventually come to recognize jointly as transference are the tryings which do not succeed. The world has gone dead, a sure sign that the transference is all but moribund. That is why, at this stage, it is so easy to think of transference as a merely psychological state. Ironically, by the time analysands can look on transference as their psychological activity, the power of this activity to inform the world has diminished. In analysis, Loewald says, "the ghosts of the unconscious are led and laid to rest as ancestors."[30] In this process a living world is transformed into a remembrance of things past.

CHAPTER 5

Restlessness, Phantasy, and the Concept of Mind

IRRATIONALITY AS A
PSYCHO-PHILOSOPHICAL PROBLEM

I have often wondered how different the history of philosophy would be if, at the last minute, Socrates had decided to cut and run. I imagine him in his cell, having just drunk the hemlock, reminiscing with satisfaction over the argument he has recently given to Crito that it is best for him to stay where he is and obey Athenian law. Suddenly his facial expression changes, and he throws up. *"Apeleuthomai euthus!"* he exclaims, which is roughly translated as "I'm out of here!" Of course, such is the stuff of a skit from Monty Python, not a dialogue from Plato; but if it were our paradigm, I wonder if the philosophical tradition would be so wedded to the idea that mind is rational.

Socrates famously argued that no one willingly commits bad acts.[1] For since everyone aims at what he or she takes to be a good outcome, the only way something bad can happen is if agents are mistaken in their beliefs about what constitutes a good outcome (or if the act somehow misfires). For

Socrates, an *akratic* (incontinent) act—the intentional performance of an act for which one believes one has less-good reasons than for another act—is not simply irrational; it is impossible. The argument purports to show that there is a presumption of rationality built into the very ideas of agency, action, and mind.[2] This is an important moment in the history of our life with the concept of mind, for ordinary psychological experience seems to demand room for the idea of an irrational act, yet Socrates' argument claims that no such space is available.

Akrasia is one type of a more general form of irrationality which I shall call *reflexive breakdown:* the inability to give a full or coherent account of what one is doing. Of course, this isn't the only form of human irrationality.[3] The terms "rational/irrational" are a contrasting pair which—like "subjective/objective," "real/unreal," "inner/outer"—can, in different circumstances, be used to delineate any one of a family of distinctions. But reflexive breakdown is an especially important form of irrationality, because humans distinguish themselves from the rest of nature by being self-interpreting animals. Pigs live within a normatively endowed environment, and we can watch them maximizing porcine utility. In this weak sense, we can see pigs "acting for reasons," and we can even see breakdowns and irrationality, as, say, when a pig starts to eat mud rather than rolling in it. But there is a stronger sense in which humans are capable of acting for reasons. Humans are able to think about what they want, to subject their desires and beliefs to self-conscious scrutiny, and to modify them in the light of criticism. Moreover, a person's actions *flow through* her understandings of what she is doing: her understandings shape and guide her action. Reflexive breakdown is important because it is a disruption of our capacity to be self-interpreting animals. And it represents a kind of irrationality, because what we are able to say or think about ourselves is contradicted by what we do.

EVER SINCE SOCRATES, philosophers have tried to make room for the idea of the irrational-mental, and though the approaches differ, they seem to agree that Socrates did succeed in showing that *some* presumption of rationality is built into the very ideas of mind and action. Roughly speaking, there are two families of solutions. The first follows Aristotle, who accounts for the *apparent* fact of akrasia while agreeing with Socrates that a pure case of akrasia is impossible. In so-called akratic acts, the knowledge of the better alternative is somehow shut down. The akratic, by this picture, is like a drunk, whose judgment momentarily shuts down. At the moment of acting, therefore, the akratic is actually operating from a kind of ignorance.

The second family divides the mind into mindlike parts. Each mindlike part is itself rational (or quasi-rational), and irrationality occurs as a by-product of conflict or interaction between the parts. So, each mindlike part satisfies the Socratic constraints, though irrationality becomes a possibility for the mind, or agent, as a whole. On this schema, the unconscious mind would be conceived of as its own locus of rationality (or quasi-rationality)—perhaps even of strategizing and intentionality—and irrationality would come about through conflict between the conscious mind and unconscious mind.[4]

I am going to argue that this is not the best way to conceptualize unconscious mental functioning or to account for irrationality, but it is important to understand the temptation of the view. We think we see people acting on the basis of desires, fears, angers of which they are unaware; and to try to make sense of this we are naturally led to the idea of an Unconscious Mind: a locus of its own rationality and intentionality. For if we take the idea, say, of unconscious fear at face value, we have to locate that fear in a rationalizing web of beliefs and expectations. As Aristotle pointed out, the emotion of fear requires that an agent believe she is some danger.[5] Fear makes an implicit claim that it is a merited response to one's circumstances. Of course, an agent may be mistaken, but without a rationalizing belief, we lose grip on the idea that what the agent suffers from is fear (rather than, say, anxiety). Thus we are led to the idea that the agent must also have an unconscious belief that she is in danger and perhaps an unconscious desire to escape. (A similar argument applies to other self-regarding emotions like shame and guilt.) We are quickly led to the idea of The Unconscious as a mindlike structure with its own rationality.

And if we inquire into the nature of the unconscious belief and desire we are led even further in this direction. The very idea of an agent's having a particular belief (or desire) depends on that belief's (desire's) being located in a web of other beliefs and desires which both rationalize it and provide the structure in relation to which the belief has the particular content it has. So, for example, if a person is afraid because she fears she is about to be attacked by a wolf, she must also believe, say, that wolves are different from dinosaurs (otherwise, why isn't it a fear of dinosaurs?), that a wolf is about to be somewhere in her vicinity (or perhaps that this is a magical wolf that can specially operate across space and time), that this wolf will have it in for her (for reasons of its own), and so on. Beliefs and desires are not things we can intelligibly assign to people one at a time. And thus to assign a belief is at the same time to assign a mindlike structure of beliefs in which that belief is located.[6]

The idea that The Unconscious is itself a mindlike structure, itself a locus of its own rationality and intentionality, seems, then, not so much an empirical discovery as a conceptual requirement. It flows from taking both seriously *and at face value* the idea that people have unconscious fears, angers, desires, and beliefs. With so much rationality seemingly built into the very idea of mind, it's a wonder we can ever take an irrational breath. Literally. The problem with such a Two-Minds account of the mind is that while it purportedly makes room for irrationality, the account makes it mysterious just how it could occur. The Two-Minds schema is like the solution to a dyadic equation. It tries to solve simultaneously for two apparently conflicting demands which are implicit in the idea of *motivated irrationality*. To secure the idea that this irrationality is motivated, that is, a genuinely psychological phenomenon, we need to secure the mentality of the motivation.[7] Doing this seems to require locating the motivation in a mindlike structure with its own rationality. But to secure the irrationality of the phenomenon, the motivation must become *from outside* the mindlike structure in which the irrational phenomenon itself occurs. On the Two-Minds schema, the mentality of the cause is secured by being placed within a rational network of propositional attitudes in one part of the mind; yet irrationality is explained by allowing that cause to have nonrational effects in another part of the mind.

But this schema leaves unanswered just how that mental cause brings its irrational effect about. It does not adequately illuminate the mentality of an irrational act. To make room for the concept of an irrational act, we must be able to account for "method in madness." We isolate something as an irrational act, as opposed to a meaningless outburst, because we see it or suspect it of having a strange logic of its own. *We want to capture the mentality of the cause not because we want to understand its rational place in this other part of the mind, but because we want to grasp the weird intelligibility it lends to the irrational phenomena it brings about.*[8] Obviously, the mental cause does not *rationalize* its irrational effect, but it does lend it a peculiar intelligibility. Method does not turn madness into sanity, but it does bequeath to madness its own intelligibility. As far as I can tell, the Two-Minds schema does not explain this *cunning of unreason.*[9]

I am tempted to say that the problem with the Two-Minds schema is that it is too conceptual a solution to a conceptual problem; but this cannot be quite right. If we follow the later Wittgenstein and Hegel in thinking that our concepts must be understood in the context of the life we live with them, then the problem with the Two-Minds solution is that it is not conceptual enough. We are not yet sufficiently at home with the concept of mind to understand the place of the irrational-mental. One sign of this, I think, is that both strategies for answering Socrates—Aristotle's and the Two-Minds schema—assume that Socrates is basically right: that the concept of mind requires rationality. By contrast, I want to argue that it is intrinsic to the very idea of mind that mind must be sometimes irrational. Rather than see irrationality as *coming from the outside* as from an Unconscious Mind which disrupts Conscious Mind, one should see irrational disruptions as themselves an inherent expression of mind. In a nutshell: mind has a tendency to disrupt its own rational functioning.

This isn't only an empirical discovery about the human mind—though it may also be that; it also comes to light when we think about what it is to be minded.[10] I can here only briefly mention two features, each of which expresses a fundamental aspect of what we take mindedness to be, and which together imply that it is part of our concept of mind that minds must be sometimes irrational. First, it is inherent to our very idea of mind that minds are restless. Minds are not mere algorithm-performing machines, and they do not merely follow out the logical consequences of an agent's beliefs and desires. Rather, it is part of the very idea of mind that a mind must be able to make leaps, to make associations, to bring things together and divide them up in all sorts of strange ways. Creativity isn't simply an empirical blessing—though it is that; it is a conceptual requirement: a mind must have at least the potentiality for creativity. This in turn requires that there be certain *forms of restlessness* embedded in mental activity. Freud's discovery of primary-process mental functioning, his discovery of certain mental tropisms like projection and introjection, and his discovery that human sexuality is not merely a biological instinct but a drive with great plasticity in its aim and object—all this can be seen as the discovery of certain forms of restlessness in the human mind. Freud took himself to have made an empirical discovery, arrived at through his attempts to interpret dreams. He was relatively unaware of the *logical* flow of his argument. So, for example, as soon as one approaches a dream as something that requires interpretation—that is, as something whose meaning is not immediately transparent, but which nevertheless has a meaning—one needs to account both for the opacity and for the meaning. How could mind be making a meaning it doesn't understand? To be making a meaning, it must be making certain associations among ideas, engaging in symbolization, however elementary; yet those associations must be opaque to conscious, rational-thinking mind. And once we recognize that mind has to be capable of making (what from the perspective of secondary process appear to be) strange leaps and associations, we see that a mind has to have something like displacement and condensation as forms of mental activity. For displacement is the bare making of associations by linking ideas; condensation is the bare making of associations by superimposing them. These activities both discover and create similarities, and together they provide forms of restlessness needed for mind to express creativity and imagination.

Second, minds must be embodied. Embodiment is here a formal requirement: it is part of the idea of mind that a mind is part of a living organism over which the mind has incomplete control and that it helps the organism to live in an environment over which the organism has incomplete control. Of course, much important philosophical work has been done, notably by Aristotle, Heidegger, and the later Wittgenstein, to illuminate the mind's necessary embodiment, but one can gain some insight by reflecting on the idea that a mind cannot be omnipotent. In our analytic work with neurotics we regularly hear echoes of omnipotent and magical thinking. In work with psychotics we see the mind in fast-forward toward flagrant forms of omnipotence. But what can be so distressing in such work is that as they approach full-blown delusions of omnipotence, we see them *lose their minds*. In omnipotence, there is no longer a distinction between mentality and reality; there is no longer anything for mind to operate on or in relation to. We cannot make coherent sense of such a mind (and neither can the poor wretches whose minds are falling apart). The authors of both the Hebrew Bible and the Christian Bible implicitly grasped this. For although it might at first seem that the idea of God is the idea of an omnipotent mind, the authors of the Hebrew Bible portray God as in a regular state of frustration, disappointment, sadness, anger, and jealousy with respect to his chosen people. For the Hebrew Bible, the Israelites are God's body. In the Christian Bible, of course, divinity is humanly incarnated in Jesus Christ, and whatever lip service might be given to God's omnipotence, there is no serious suggestion that God could have offered humans the possibility of salvation by taking some shortcut. From a Christian perspective, Jesus had to come into the world; he had to experience human resistance and sin in order to forgive it and redeem humankind. That is, it is human sin and recalcitrance which serves as the Christian God's body.

Once we can see mind as necessarily embodied and restless, there is much else about it which can come to light. For starters, we can see that the philosophical tradition's approach to irrationality has occurred, for the most part, at the wrong level. Previous attempts to make room for irrationality within the concept of mind have failed in roughly the same way that the propositional calculus fails to illuminate the concept of mathematical proof. For previous attempts have in common that they examine neither the inner structure of the contents of the propositional attitudes nor the various possible mental operations on that inner structure. Rather, they try to account for irrationality in terms of an irrational configuration of propositional attitudes, while leaving the internal structure of those attitudes unexamined. In akrasia, for example, a reason causes me to act in a certain way in spite of the fact that I supposedly have a stronger reason to act in some other way.[11] That is, akrasia is displayed as a structure of propositional attitudes leading to an action. But what this structure does not explain is the fact of irrationality itself: in this case, why the better reason did not engage.[12] That is one reason why such structures lend a static air to the irrational: even though the structure gives us the motivation for the irrational outcome, we cannot see it coming into being.

Freud's discovery of the elemental forms of mental restlessness suggests that if we are to understand the myriad phenomena of motivated irrationality, we have to understand how the mind effects transformations *on the inner contents* of propositional attitudes and other meaningful bits. Psychoanalysis is of philosophical interest not merely because it provides a fascinating picture of human motivation, but because it intimates how one might construct, as it were, *a predicate calculus of irrationality*.[13] In general, philosophical accounts of irrationality tend to fail to capture either the *immanence* or the possible *disruptiveness* of the irrational. Partitioning the mind along the fault-lines of reason, for example, fails to capture the immanence of human irrationality. Irrationality is treated as a *by-product* of the mind's being a composite of two quasi-minds. And displaying irrational outcomes, like akrasia, as organized structures of propositional attitudes makes mysterious how the mind can, on occasion, disrupt itself. I shall argue, in contrast to the philosophical tradition, that the problem with akrasia is posed not by its irrationality, but by the fact that it is *too rational* to capture the phenomena it is often used to describe.

Of course, unconscious mental functioning is not everywhere disruptive: it can infuse one's conscious, emotional life with joy and creativity. But we also need to account for the fact that it can disrupt life in untold ways. And to capture the immanence of the irrational, we should see this disruption not as coming from outside the mind, or from Another Mind (The Unconscious as a locus of its own rationality and intentionality), but as inherent in the mind's own activity. So, while Socrates may be right that the system of propositional attitudes and actions they bring about show the mind to be inherently rational, Freud is right that the disruptions of this system show the mind also to be inherently irrational. Within a single human mind there are heterogeneous forms of mental activity, not all of which are rational.

One significant form of such mental activity, from a psychoanalytic point of view, is what Freud calls the "drive" *(Trieb)*—and he again took himself to have made an empirical discovery. But if we think about what a mind must be like if it is to be embodied and restless, we can see that it must engage in something like drive-activity. An embodied mind of an organism living a directed life in an environment must be in the business of trying to represent to the organism its basic needs and direction. As Freud so neatly put it,

> By a "drive" [*Trieb*] is provisionally to be understood the *psychical representative* of an endosomatic continuously flowing source of stimulation, as contrasted with a "stimulus," which is set up by *single* excitations coming from *without*. The concept of a drive is thus one of *those lying on the frontier between the mental and the physical.*[14]

A drive, then, is one of the primordial ways in which mind represents its body to itself: namely, in its elemental forms of directedness and motivation. The idea of a drive thus lends content to the idea of a mind embodied in a nonomnipotent organism which must interact with an environment to satisfy its needs. It helps us to understand what it is to be an embodied mind. And if we also take mind's restlessness into consideration, we can see why this elemental form of motivation is *a drive* rather than what Freud called an *Instinkt.*[15] An *Instinkt,* for Freud, is a rigid, innate behavioral pattern, such as the innate pressure on and ability of a bird to build a nest. A drive, by contrast, has a certain plasticity: it can be shaped not only by experience but also by various forms of intrapsychic transformations. To put it metaphorically, a drive is what happens to an instinct when it takes up residence in a restless mind. To put it conceptually, once we recognize that mind must be restless—that we need the concept of mind precisely when we need to account for an organism which isn't just rigidly performing instinctual behavior—we can see that that restlessness must express itself in even the most elemental forms of mental activity. Otherwise we wouldn't need the concept of mind at this level; we would just have rigid, instinctual behavior. Freud's discovery that human sexuality is a drive rather than an *Instinkt* is precisely the discovery that sexuality is the primordial expression of restless, embodied mentality. Freud called it a "fact which we have been in danger of over-looking," namely, that "the sexual drive and the sexual object are merely soldered together."[16] Restlessness expresses itself at the joints.

One other feature of mind which comes to light when we consider it in its restless embodiment is that it must live with the permanent possibility of falling apart. By way of analogy, consider Plato's discussion of falling apart in the *Republic*. According to Socrates in the *Republic*, even when the human psyche is in the best of shape, even when the most basic form of political organization, the polis, is in the best of shape, each will have to struggle with internal as well as external threats to its integrity. There is always a tendency to come undone. Why should this be? Usually readers think that Plato is simply expressing what he takes to be a sad fact of human life, but that is because they read the *Republic* as a work of political philosophy and psychology. A deeper reading reveals it to be a work of logic: in the sense of revealing the logic, or logos, of a concept. The *Republic* would, I think, be more appropriately titled the *Constitution*, another acceptable translation of the Greek title, *Politeia*. For the book is an inquiry into the very idea of constitutionality. Socrates takes himself to be delineating the concept of justice—what justice is—but it soon becomes clear that what he is working out is the very idea of a differentiated unity, as that idea is instantiated in the human psyche and in the polis. The issue isn't merely that a particular instance of a differentiated unity, the human psyche, will, as a matter of empirical fact, have a hard time holding itself together, but that the very idea of differentiated unity has a hard time holding itself together. On the surface, at least, it is a paradoxical idea. How can we give the idea of differentiation its due without threatening unity? How can we give the idea of unity its due without threatening differentiation? Plato's answer is that we must understand a differentiated unity as existing in a state of tension and under conditions which perpetually threaten disintegration. The *idea* of a permanent possibility of falling apart is needed to keep the *idea* of a differentiated unity from itself falling apart. For Plato, as for Freud following him, the mind's inherent restlessness and its embodiment provide the perfect conditions for the needed threat to integrity.

From a philosophical point of view, what is exciting and significant about psychoanalysis is that it is the first working-out of a truly non-

Socratic approach to human irrationality. Rather than starting, as Socrates does, with an argument that mind must be rational, and then wondering how irrationality can be tacked on, psychoanalysis, when properly understood, begins with the idea that mind must be sometimes irrational. The possibility of disruption is built into the very idea of mind-edness. This becomes especially clear if we think of the mind as a differentiated unity *capable of growth*. For how could a differentiated unity grow other than by disrupting itself and then, as it were, healing over that disruption? All of this is obscured by the Two-Minds interpretation of psychoanalysis by which The Unconscious is Another Mind. This is the Socratic reading of Freud, and it covers over Freud's most distinctive achievement: a truly non-Socratic answer to Socrates' challenge.

THE IMMANENCE OF IRRATIONALITY

Consider, for example, this selection from Freud's description of the Rat Man's transference:

> Things soon reached a point at which, in his dreams, his waking phantasies, and his associations, he began heaping the grossest and filthiest abuse upon me and my family, though in his deliberate actions he never treated me with anything but the greatest respect. His demeanor as he repeated these insults to me was that of a man in despair. "How can a gentleman like you, sir," he used to ask, "let yourself be abused in this way by a low, good-for-nothing fellow like me? You ought to turn me out: that's all I deserve." While he talked like this, he would get up from the sofa and roam about the room,—a habit which he explained at first as being due to delicacy of feeling: he could not bring himself, he said, to utter such horrible things while he was lying there so comfortably. But soon he himself found a more cogent explanation, namely, that he was avoiding my proximity for fear of my giving him a beating. If he stayed on the sofa he behaved like someone in desperate terror trying to save himself from castigations of terrific violence; he would bury his head in his hands, cover his face with his arm, jump up suddenly and rush away, his features distorted with pain, and so on. He recalled that his father had had a passionate temper, and sometimes in his violence had not known where to stop.[7]

What is the Rat Man doing in cringing before Freud? Good question! The Rat Man himself doesn't immediately have an answer: he is momentarily in a state of *reflexive breakdown*. Momentarily, he tries out the idea that he has got up from the couch out of delicacy of feeling, but he doesn't seem to be able to live with it. Then he hits upon "a more cogent explanation" and seals over the breakdown with this self-interpretation: he is afraid that Freud is going to give him a beating. And the interpretation does have this plausibility: first, the Rat Man has just expressed hostility toward Freud and is awaiting some kind of response; second, the outbreak of cringing is affectively laden—it is, one might say, a fearful response, and the cringing is itself a primitive, bodily expression of fear; third, the Rat Man quickly associates to past fear of his father. In short, it is tempting to follow the Rat Man's own interpretation and take the cringing to be an outburst of fear of which he has hitherto been unconscious. The Rat Man himself implicitly understands that if he is to interpret himself as afraid of Freud, he must at the same time come up with a reason for his fear. Thus he suggests that he is afraid that Freud is going to give him a beating. Now the Rat Man is interpreting himself as having not only an unconscious fear of Freud, but an unconscious belief about him. And when the Rat Man asks himself why he should believe that, he himself comes up with the thought that Freud reminds him of his violent father. The Rat Man is well on his way to interpreting himself as having an Unconscious Mind with its own beliefs and intentions.

Note that in this instance, at least, the pressure to posit an Unconscious Mind comes from the Rat Man's need to rationalize his cringe. Cringing has burst forth, and the Rat Man wants to make it intelligible to himself by giving it a reason. But consciously the Rat Man understands that he doesn't really have anything to fear from Freud. He knows that his doctor is not going to beat him. So the reasons for the cringe must be Somewhere Else. And the reason for the Somewhere Else is the felt need to give reasons for the cringe. In this interpretation, the Rat Man's cringing is a case of akrasia. The Rat Man himself knows that he doesn't have a good reason to fear a beating, yet the cringing is the outburst of an unconscious fear: it is happening for reasons of which the Rat Man has hitherto been unaware and for reasons which, once they are held up to conscious scrutiny, the Rat Man himself can recognize as not particularly persuasive. But somehow the less-good reasons (to fear) have overwhelmed the better ones (not to fear), and what one sees is an akratic expression of fear.

Basically, this is the Rat Man's own interpretation—and it is important to keep in mind that the Rat Man is an obsessional. As anyone who has worked with them will know, obsessionals tend to interpret themselves as being more rational than they are. Rationalization is among the favorite forms of obsessional defense. Might this not be what is going on here? Obviously, I think the answer is yes. Let me state the thesis baldly and add nuance later: the Rat Man does not fear that Freud is going to give him a beating. And thus there is no need to posit an Unconscious Mind in which that fear is located and rationalized. In short, the Rat Man's cringing before Freud is not an expression of fear and thus not a case of akrasia. It is not a case in which a less-good reason to fear is triumphing over a better reason to remain calm. Whatever it is that the Rat Man is doing, he is not doing for a reason. It is not an expression of belief or desire: and thus it is not an action. It is what Freud called *acting out.*

In cringing, the Rat Man acts out fear. And, to put it paradoxically, acting out isn't a form of acting, it's an activity which isn't an action. It is the expression of phantasy. Why the *ph* rather than the familiar *f*-word? Psychoanalysts use the technical term "phantasy" to draw attention to unconscious aspects of our imaginative life. The ordinary English word "fantasy" is then used generically to cover a family of mental states and activities, but fantasies all have it in common that they are motivational, directed toward some kind of satisfaction, and either have some representational content, expressing a narrative, like a daydream, or express content. If there is a rationale for this distinction, it is that the power and shape of our imaginative life cannot be fully captured by attending only to the contents of our dreams and daydreams. Here I shall argue that *it is a peculiar type of mental activity,* rather than whether it is conscious or unconscious, which distinguishes phantasy. This mental activity will tend to enact a meaning or put some meaning on display, though it may also represent meaning in an imaginative scene. But phantasy will typically "show" a meaning where it does not "say"—and this is one way in which phantasy remains relatively cut off from conscious understanding. Phantasy may operate in relation to, but relatively free of, the rationalizing constraints of logos—the holistic system of an agent's beliefs and desires, fears, angers, and other propositional attitudes. Indeed, it is this relative freedom from logos which helps to explain phantasy's power. The kind of "fearful" phantasy we see expressed in the Rat Man's cringe is preserved through time precisely because it doesn't have to interact with his beliefs—in this case with his belief that Freud is not going to hurt him. In this way, countervailing beliefs cannot tame or modify the reaction. Phantasies are experienced as powerful because there is no obvious or easy way to bring them into the domain of thought. Thus, however active the mind may be in creating these phantasies, it often experiences them passively, as though it is suffering an experience over which it has little control. Because phantasies can remain relatively unintegrated, the mind may regularly have to suffer its own activity.

But what is it about the phantasy which makes it "fearful"? I am using quotation marks to signal that we do not have a ready vocabulary to talk about these mental states. The very use of language to describe these mental states and activities tends to make them look more rational than they are. Just by giving these mental states a name, we make them seem already to be within the domain of logos, while what we are in fact trying to capture is their not (yet) being there. We need to strike a convincing balance. On the one side, we need to capture the idea that this cringing is not an expression of fear. Otherwise we will also need to supply the relevant beliefs and desires which will rationalize the fear, and we will then be well on our way toward postulating an Unconscious Mind with its own logos. On the other hand, we want the "fearful" expression to stand in some intelligible relation to fear. The cringing isn't merely meaningless behavior, and it is affectively laden: in cringing the Rat Man is in a highly charged state. How can we capture the "fearfulness" of the cringe without making it into an expression of fear?

My answer to this question takes two steps, one through Aristotle's metaphysics, one through Freud's account of the development of psychic structure. The first step is the most vulnerable to misinterpretation, because most people have the unfortunate fate of having to live with a preconscious misconception of Aristotle's metaphysics. Basically, I want to argue that in the cringe what we see is *the matter* of fear—as Aristotle would put it, *that from which* fear is constituted.[18] What the cringe lacks is, in the literal sense of the term, *information*. It has not yet been fully formed, because it has not been taken up into logos and embedded in the web of beliefs, expectations, and desires which would help to constitute it as fear.

Let's get clear on what this claim is by getting clear on what it is not. The claim is not that the meaning or emotion *fear* is tacked on to what would otherwise be a meaningless cringe. Emotive texture and structure are being incorporated at every level of functioning from the most bodily to the most thoughtful. For Freud, even the most elemental psychological items, the drives—those basic impulsive forces which represent bodily needs—are incorporating information from the social environment for their very constitution.[19] Infants are capable of exhibiting fearful responses in response to fearful stimuli from the beginning of psychological life, and those responses incorporate ever more texture as a person develops. To say that the Rat Man's cringe is "fearful," but not fear, is not to deny any of this. The point is to draw attention to it. When we consider a functioning human being in a state of fear, we want to capture, on the one hand, that the fear reaches down to the most elemental bodily reactions—it expresses itself in structured forms of muscle clenching, constriction of veins, pulse, respiration—while, on the other, fear reaches out and offers a rationalizing orientation to the world. These are not *ingredients* of fear; they are two *aspects* of fear. Or, rather, they are aspects of a functioning whole: a person who is in fear.

The Rat Man's cringe is full of emotional texture and affective meaning, and yet it is only the matter of fear. How could this be? First, the distinction between matter and form is not absolute, but relative to the level of investigation.[20] Second, matter and form are not two ingredients which together make a composite whole; rather, they are two *aspects* by which we can understand the functioning of the whole. We don't tend to see them in isolation unless there has been some kind of a breakdown.

It is just such a breakdown which we see in the Rat Man's cringe. For although the cringe does have an emotional texture and structure of its own, because it is the expression of phantasy it has been kept from being integrated with the beliefs and other attitudes which would help to constitute it as fear. Many people assume that if the cringing is not an expression of fear, then it is "mere behavior"—and that formulation seems counterintuitive. But to move from "not fear" to "mere behavior" is to live in an impoverished universe of possibilities. The Rat Man's cringing is neither fear nor "mere behavior": it is affectively laden, it has texture and depth for the Rat Man, it is certainly an expression of anxiety.[21] But at the moment it appears it has not yet been taken up into the rationalizing structure of conscious and preconscious mental functioning. It is not (yet) constituted as fear, and thus it is, momentarily at least, unintelligible to the Rat Man. It is unintelligible not because the fear exists in some other part of the mind, The Unconscious, but because what is breaking through isn't fear; it is "fearful," and thus it has not yet assumed a form in which it can easily be thought.

Similarly, when we consider a full-fledged emotional reaction like fear, it is a mistake to think of it as composed of two independently existing ingredients, form and matter. Form permeates matter, and matter "embodies" form. We can mistake an aspect for an ingredient because in moments of functional breakdown it is possible to see the matter on its own—as when we see the Rat Man cringe. And if we do take the matter as an ingredient rather than as an aspect, we will tend to see the cringe as a "mere cringe," as mere bodily behavior (which of course it is not) and then look for the fear which informs it. When such a cringe is integrated into a person's expression of fear, it is as much an expression of fear as anything else. It is not as though we have a worked-out understanding of what the matter of fear is independently of observing various breakdowns and miscarriages of emotional response. The emotion of fear has its own developmental history, and breakdowns and fixation points can occur almost anywhere along the continuum. We discover the matter of fear by studying the Rat Man's cringe.

These reflections are of clinical significance. The Rat Man is himself puzzled by his behavior, and interprets it first as an expression of delicacy, then as an expression of fear: and in this way he interprets himself as more rational and mentally organized than he is. And that is so, even if the interpretation ultimately portrays the Rat Man as irrational. So, for example, the Rat Man may say that Freud reminds him of his father, and he may once have had reason to fear his father. On this interpretation, the Rat Man may be irrational—he may have better reasons not to fear Freud—but at least he is acting for a reason. The Rat Man now has a sense of what he is doing. He purports to understand himself in terms of an organized structure of propositional attitudes. *And he may even form those attitudes.* That is, in response to the anxiety aroused by not knowing what he is doing, he may actually form the belief that Freud is about to beat him. But here it is not a reason which is causing an action; it is acting out and anxiety which are causing the formation of a reason. He may then even become afraid of Freud, but *now it is not that fear is being expressed in a cringe; the cringe is bringing about the fear.* Akrasia would then be occurring *as a defensive response to irrationality,* not as an originating instance of it. It would then facilitate a defensive misunderstanding of that irrationality.

Freud finds the Rat Man's self-interpretation of fear "a more cogent explanation." But that's the problem: it is *too* cogent. Similarly with the standard philosophical account of irrationality: it collaborates with the defense. For if the Rat Man's cringing is portrayed as akrasia, it may be irrational, but at least the Rat Man is acting from reasons. But this philosophical account enters too late to capture the distinctive grade of irrationality at play. For it enters at the level of the propositional attitudes, whereas by then we are already at the level of a defensive surface. At best, the interpretation of akrasia captures only the most superficial layer of this irrational activity.

It is an ever-present danger of psychoanalytic technique that one unwittingly collaborates with a rationalizing defense. Sartre criticized psychoanalysis as a form of bad faith—and while the charge is unjustified as it stands, the charge does apply to certain misapplications of technique.[22] So, the Rat Man portrays himself as cringing before Freud because he is *already* in a state of fear; he portrays himself as suffering his own emotional states. This is a form of bad faith. And insofar as psychoanalytic interpretation corroborates such an outlook, it ends up reinforcing the resistance rather than analyzing it. If one were to interpret at this point at all, one ought, I think, to help the Rat Man recover his own sense of puzzlement at what he is doing: allow him, insofar as it is possible, to tolerate his anxiety at not already knowing the answer. If he is able to live with the experience of a "fearful" reaction while recognizing that he actually isn't afraid of Freud, he may come to a more accurate sense of how his past and his inner world are making for an irrational present. Above all, the interpretation should not help him make too much sense of what he is doing.

Note that the problem with the Rat Man's interpretation is not simply that it is positing more psychological complexity than exists. Sometimes there is occasion for an interpretation which adds complexity to an emotional response. Here is one typical example: a person may regularly keep himself in a state of unawareness and psychological disorganization as he acts in anger or with aggression. To interpret the anger is not to point out a fully formed psychological state (and the interpretation ought not to imply that it is), but the interpretation may provide the concept needed for the analysand to organize his various angry feelings and acts—and thus become conscious of his anger. In this way, a good interpretation can *inform* the analysand's behavior and emotional responses.

Of course, as every practicing analyst knows, there are people whose anger is so well organized that all which seems to be missing is the name "anger" itself. What's in a name? Well, the ability to move from a highly organized preconscious state which nevertheless remains split off from conscious life to a state in which one can recognize and consciously tolerate one's anger and begin to integrate it into the rest of one's emotional life. Here the angry responses may themselves have been well organized—thus we designate the anger as preconscious—but the interpretation nevertheless facilitates an emotional development which does not yet exist.

By contrast, the problems with the Rat Man's interpretation are: first, insofar as it posits more psychological complexity than exists, it is not aware that it is doing so, and thus it promotes self-misunderstanding; second, it promotes "bad teleology": a tendency for the Rat Man to become afraid of Freud as a way of rationalizing his own behavior. In such a case, it is not that he is coming to understand his own emotional life; it is that his understanding is laying out the tracks along which his emotional life is being directed to run. Unlike the case of unconscious anger, in which an analysand actively keeps himself from understanding his anger as a defense, and in which a proper interpretation can help analyze the defense, the Rat Man is not keeping himself from an awareness of his fear of Freud. Quite the contrary: his fear of Freud—insofar as he does become afraid—is itself the construction of a defense.

I SAID EARLIER that to understand the "fearfulness" of the Rat Man's cringe we need to take two steps, one through Aristotle's metaphysics, the other through Freud's account of the development of psychic structure. It is time for the second step. I shall only sketch a rough outline, and we must keep in mind that the interpretation is provisional: we have only a brief case history and notes to go on. But the point is not to reach absolute certainty about the Rat Man, but to get a clearer idea of how to understand a "fearful" cringe which is not an expression of fear.[23] In the end, it doesn't matter whether we are getting the Rat Man right; what matters is whether we are accurately identifying a serious occupational hazard of psychoanalytic technique.

First, the development of psychic structure, according to Freud, typically has a historical dimension. There is likely to have been an earlier time when the Rat Child did fear his father. His father may have been violent and given the child reason to fear him. He may also have seemed fearful as a result of various phantasies and conflicts. In response, the Rat Child *internalizes* the Rat Dad. Internalization is a nonrational mental activity which takes significant figures from the external world and places them inside the psyche. For Freud, psychic structure is formed around these internalizations. Once internalized, the Rat Dad is subject to phantastic distortions and primary-process associations. The Rat Child now has a punishing father figure inside him, and it acquires an intrapsychic role. Perhaps the original internalization was a defensive response: the point of the internalization was to contain and control a threatening figure in the environment. But now that the punishing father is inside, the psyche organizes itself around it.

The phantastic creation of a powerful, vindictive father may serve to inhibit public outbursts of rage. How so? Melanie Klein has argued that the earliest internalizations occur via phantasies of physical incorporation.[24] In good-enough circumstances, the comfort, reassurance, and satisfaction which the child receives at the breast is taken in with mother's milk. That is, the milk itself becomes a concrete vehicle of meaning. Goodness is the meaning of the milk. As the warm milk enters the mouth, and the child can feel herself swallow it and feel the milk fill up her tummy, it is, for her, as though mother's goodness is now physically present inside her. Similarly, the child may begin to form a superego around a prohibitive utterance: for the Rat Child, it may have been the voice of the father saying, "Don't do that!" The utterance is itself the physical movement of meaning. The father's tongue has set the air around it vibrating, and a prohibitive meaning informs that vibrating air. That meaning reaches the Rat Child's ear via its concrete vehicle and triggers a chain of neurological reactions. One outcome is that the Rat Child can hear his father; another is that he can hear the prohibitive voice over and over "inside his head." The Rat Child experiences his own rage as tremendously powerful; and one way to deal with the anxiety it arouses is, in phantasy, to move it over to invest the father's voice. This isn't a thought or a judgment; it is the nonrational, phantastic movement of content. However, though the phantasy-movement of content is not itself rational, it may acquire a dynamic, intrapsychic function. Rage gains some expression, phantastically expressed over there, in the voice of the father, and it is used intrapsychically to inhibit outbursts of rage. And so the movement of meaning in phantasy helps to shape intrapsychic structure. The Rat Child begins to live a life which is to be understood in significant part as an extended cringe before the voice of the Rat Dad.

It is important to recognize that the internal Rat Dad is not a subject of propositional attitudes for the Rat Man. Much later, after psychoanalytic treatment, the Rat Man may form certain beliefs and desires about his superego: he may come to believe that his superego is too cruel, and he may want it to give him a break, and so on.[25] But at the time of its formation, the Rat Man's superego is not the kind of thing about which he is in a position to form any beliefs or desires: it is just a bit of his psychological makeup which is coming into being. Now as a result of repeated activities of introjection and projection, the internal Rat Dad stands in complex psychological relations with the Rat Man's father, about whom the Rat Man does have beliefs, desires, hopes, loves, and hates. The Rat Man can continue to think about, fear, and love *his father,* and the internal Rat Dad is dynamically and phantastically linked to him. But the internal Rat Dad is not a character about whom the Rat Man is in a position to form even unconscious beliefs or emotions: he is, rather, a fixed point of psychic structure. This is one way in which phantasy arrogates to itself its tremendous power: because the internal Rat Dad cannot be thought about (in any obvious way), there is no obvious way in which the experience of its power can be modified by conscious thought.

The Rat Person grows up, his father dies: he no longer has reason to be afraid of his father, he no longer believes that his father might attack him, he no longer desires to avoid such an attack. Nevertheless, a structure has been laid down in phantasy which continues to have a profound effect on the way the Rat Man lives. We see a flagrant example in the transference. Anxiety is building up in the Rat Man, no doubt for all sorts of reasons, but one is that his aggression and hatred is gaining some expression in the analysis. Perhaps there is anxiety in relation to an impending attack by the internal Rat Dad. The Rat Man responds by projecting Rat Dad onto Freud. Note that the Rat Man does not *believe* that the Rat Dad is about to attack, nor does he *believe* that Freud is like his father, nor does he *believe* that Freud is about to beat him. We are not dealing with such thoughtfulness. Projection is a nonrational, though strategic, response to anxiety. The phantasy finds its target in Freud in part because the intrapsychic time is right—the Rat Man needs to find some target onto which to discharge his anxiety—in part because of some elemental, primary-process senses of similarity between father and Freud. *Indeed, the transference-projection may help to create the sense of similarity the Rat Man now experiences:* that is, it may not be because Freud reminds him of his father that he projects the Rat Dad onto him, but because he has projected the Rat Dad onto Freud that he now remembers that he used to be afraid of his father. The transference is thus not to be understood simply as a set of emotional reactions which are transferred from father to Freud. Rather there is, via internalization, a phantastic movement from father, to phantastically distorted internal Rat Dad, and then a subsequent projection of Rat Dad out onto Freud. The Rat Man does not have a reason to do this, though there may be a strategic point to each of these elemental activities. In mental expulsion, the mind phantasizes getting rid of some unpleasant bit.[26] But of course that phantasy too has a fate, and what the external observer now sees is the Rat Man cringing before Freud. But the Rat Man is not here expressing his fear of Freud; he is putting on display the structure of his mind. Intrapsychic structure ends up being displayed in the social world.

No wonder that it is precisely here that the Rat Man reflexively breaks down: he cannot coherently *say* what he *shows*. He does not understand what he is doing, and he searches for some rationalizing explanation. It is not just that as a self-interpreting animal, the Rat Man wants to understand what he is doing; he wants to understand himself as a rational animal. He wants to see himself as acting for a reason. Thus he quickly constructs his more "cogent explanation." As we have seen, reason is used as a defense to cover over unreason.

WHAT MIGHT A NONDEFENSIVE USE of reason be like? As a first step, consider Wittgenstein's description of training an infant to express her pain in language.[27] The infant expresses her pain with a "primitive," "natural" outburst. The child does not need to be taught to cry, nor need the crying occur for a reason. And the prelinguistic infant will not be able to interpret or otherwise understand her own behavior. Yet the behavior will nevertheless have meaning for her parents, who, in effect, will offer the child an interpretation. Usually the interpretation will be offered as a form of comfort: "I know it hurts now, but it will go away"; "It's only a scrape, you'll be fine"; and so on. As Wittgenstein puts it, "words are connected with the primitive, the natural, expressions of the sensation *and used in their place.*" That is, the child learns to express her pain in language. "The verbal expression of pain *replaces crying* and does not only describe it." In this way, a primitive, natural reaction of mind and body is brought within the domain of logos. The infant's outburst is not "mere behavior"; it is affectively laden, and it has meaning *for the parents,* who offer that meaning to the infant as one of many ways of inducting her into logos. The experience of pain, crying, the verbal expression of pain all come to have meaning *for her*. The child can now not only express her pain in language; she also acquires the ability to represent her pain to herself, and she likewise acquires the ability to bring other thoughts to bear on her pain. She can now *tell herself* that it is really only a scrape, and so on. In subjecting her pain to rational consideration, in the light of her other understandings, she thereby gains a certain freedom with respect to it.

Now a cringe is also a "primitive," "natural" outburst, like crying, but unlike the prelinguistic infant, the Rat Man already lives within logos. He already knows the meaning of a cringe. A child who has already learned to express her pain in language may nevertheless burst out crying—because pain overwhelms her, or because she is strategically trying to elicit the sympathy of others, or because she is trying to fool others into thinking she is in pain. In each of these cases, the crying has itself become a vehicle of meaning. It expresses a meaning *for the child*. It might be thought that the Rat Man's cringe is something like that: the primitive expression of fear by someone who has already learned to express his fear in language. But this isn't quite right. Internalization, as we have seen, effectively isolates and withdraws the Rat Dad from the system of propositional attitudes. In this way, although the Rat Dad may continue to be transformed in phantasy, and continue to be subject to primary-process elaboration and distortion, "he" also remains a piece of the archaic past. "He" cannot be effectively or consciously thought—and thus cannot be transformed by thought. So when the Rat Man projects the Rat Dad out onto Freud, he responds with a cringe—*as though* it were relatively uninformed. Of course, the cringe isn't "mere behavior"—it is affectively laden, it is something which in a more integrated response would be woven into the expression of fear—and as he turns his attention to it, the Rat Man comes to see meaning in it. But unlike the linguistic child who immediately sees meaning in her crying, for the Rat Man there is a moment of not-knowing the meaning of his doings.

The cringe is, as it were, a blast from the past. And that is why the verbal expression of fear *cannot* (as yet) replace this cringe. Because of the vicissitudes of internalization and projection, it is as though an uninformed cringe gets preserved in intrapsychic amber. The cringe is "fearful," and when taken up into logos will help to constitute fear—but in its initial expression, it is like an outburst from the archaic past. What we get to see in this outburst of irrationality, in this moment of reflexive breakdown, is the "that from which," "matter," of fear. Of course, this moment of reflexive breakdown provokes its own anxiety, the anxiety which arises from not knowing what one is doing; and the defensive use of reason rushes to the meaning of cringing and tries to give a rationalizing explanation in terms of it: "I am afraid of Freud." And once the Rat Man has this interpretation, he may form the belief that he is afraid. That is, the interpretation may become self-fulfilling.

But even so, something important has gone missing. Cringing has become a vehicle of meaning for the Rat Man, and when he interprets it, he gives the *content* of this meaning, but he thereby remains oblivious to what he is *doing* with this meaning. He takes himself to be expressing this content in his cringe—that is, to be expressing fear—and remains unconscious of the phantasy activity which expresses itself in the cringe. He is, for example, unaware that he uses the cringe to break off the elaboration of a sadistic phantasy in which he heaps abuse on the Freud/Rat Dad, he is unaware that he is projecting an internal figure onto Freud, he is unaware that in his cringe he is displaying not fear but his own phantasized crouch, the very mode of his own inhibiting activity, and so on. So far, he can understand himself only in terms of the meanings on which the phantasy activity operates, but he cannot understand the phantasy activity itself. And that is why the cringe can be preserved through cycles of internalization, projection, and reinternalization. For even in moments when the cringe is acted out in social space, as in the transference, and even when the Rat Man interprets it, his interpretation has little transformative effect. This is because the interpretation ignores the real mental activity which is being expressed in the cringe—projection, phantasy activity—and focuses on content. The Rat Man concerns himself with what the cringe *says*, and is oblivious to what it *shows*.

And this gives a clue to what a nondefensive use of reason might be like. It is the process Freud called "working-through": the enduring attempt to give a meaning to the phantasy activity itself. Rather than simply stating the meaning of a cringe, the interpretation would try to state (in understandable terms) what the Rat Man is doing with that cringe. In that way, the phantasy activity would itself come to have meaning for the Rat Man, come to be a possible object of thought, and thus gain some genuine integration into the rationality system. This is what it is for the Rat Man's cringing to acquire what Freud called a new "transference meaning."[28] In the transference, which is itself a form of phantasy activity, a figure in the Rat Man's mind has been projected onto Freud. But unlike his purely internal counterpart, Freud can offer an interpretation of his place in the Rat Man's intrapsychic structure. For the Rat Man, it is as though the punishing father can speak his own meaning, interpret his role in the phantasy activity. No other figure in the Rat Man's inner world can do this: all the other characters have relatively fixed roles, locked in certain dynamic struggles. But when the Rat Man comes to re-internalize the punishing father, he is, as it were, importing self-under-standing into a previously unreflective world.[29] In this way, phantasy begins to be transformed into, or at least brought in relationship with, preconscious and conscious imagination. The effect is that intrapsychic structure gets loosened up—and a real possibility of psychic integration emerges. It comes to be influenced by conscious thought and the propositional attitudes. Ironically, the Rat Man may have spent his life alternating between phantasized attacks on and cringes before the punishing father—but all of this preserves the Rat Dad in a relatively fixed dynamic position. The one thing the punishing father cannot survive is an adequate interpretation of his role. With this new transference meaning, the cringing loses its automatic, compulsive quality. In Wittgenstein's terms, the verbal expression of phantasy comes to replace phantasy and not merely describe it. In Freud's terms, the cringing comes to be something which can be "remembered" and not merely "repeated."

We began this section with a temptation and a challenge. The temptation was to interpret the Rat Man's cringe as an expression of unconscious fear. To take that interpretation seriously, we have to rationalize that fear with unconscious beliefs and expectations: that is, we are led to posit the Unconscious as another mind, a locus of its own rationality and strategy. In this conceptualization, an irrational outburst like the cringe is the by-product of a conflict between two mindlike entities, The Conscious and The Unconscious. The challenge was to see if we could construct an alternative picture in which irrationality is *immanent* to mind. By now it should be clear that the Rat Man's cringe is not an expression of fear and thus there is no need for an Unconscious Mind in which that fear is rationalized. Nor is there need to see the cringe as breaking through from another mind, The Unconscious. Just the opposite: *the mind is putting its own structure on display.* And thus the cringe, however irrational, is an immanent expression of mind.

A word of clinical warning: It is a mistake to use the thoughts in this essay surreptitiously to teach analysands a new theoretical vocabulary ("No, Johnny, it is not fear you are experiencing, it is 'fearful' . . ."). Rather, as clinicians, we need to make our own theoretical unconscious conscious and to do our best to continue analyzing defenses rather than unwittingly collaborate with them. I have tried to show how from such a simple and plausible step as interpreting the cringe as an expression of fear one can be led unawares to the idea that the unconscious must be Another Mind, its own center of rationality and intentionality. One can also be led to collaborate in an obsessional defense. But, having *worked through* the thoughts in this essay, it is fine by me if an analyst wants to stay close to the analysand's own vocabulary and call the cringe an expression of fear. Ironically, having come to see that it is not an expression of fear, we can say that it is! Because now we will be using the vocabulary of fear to capture the analysand's emotional life in his own vocabulary, yet we will also be trying to help the analysand tolerate the anxiety of not already knowing what he is doing, and we will also be helping the analysand to notice the defensive nature of his rush to interpretation. The point is not to create a new dogmatic vocabulary, but to make us sensitive to the ways in which the interpretation of emotions can be used to cover over psychic reality rather than reveal it. If you now want to call the cringe "fear," go for it![30]

THE DISRUPTIVENESS OF PHANTASY

But even if phantasy can supply an immanent source of irrationality, how can mind disrupt itself? This question, as we have seen, is especially pressing for the philosophical tradition, which tends to portray irrationality as organized structures of propositional attitudes. The point is not to show that unconscious mental activity is everywhere disruptive or that phantasy is necessarily disruptive. They are not. Unconscious phantasy

can enrich and enliven conscious creative life. But phantasy can also disrupt, and it is important to grasp this disruption as coming not from outside the mind or from an Unconscious Mind but as part of the mind's own
activity.

Consider, for example, this description of the Rat Man's protective
prayers.

> At the time of the revival of his piety he made up prayers for himself which
> took up more and more time and eventually lasted for an hour and a half.
> The reason for this was that he found, like an inverted Balaam, that some-
> thing always inserted itself into his pious phrases and turned them into their
> opposite. E.g., if he said "May God protect him," an evil spirit would hur-
> riedly insinuate a "not." On one such occasion the idea occurred to him of
> cursing instead, for in that case, he thought, the contrary words would be
> sure to creep in. His original intention, which had been repressed by his pray-
> ing, was forcing its way through in this last idea of his. In the end he found
> his way out of his embarrassment by giving up the prayers and replacing
> them by a short formula concocted out of the initial letters or syllables of var-
> ious prayers. He then recited this formula so quickly that nothing could slip
> into it.[31]

Again, it is tempting to see the Rat Man bursting forth with a contradictory
judgment from the one he consciously intends to utter. The utterance is
then seen as a case of akrasia: although all things considered he wants to
utter a protective prayer, an unconscious desire causes him to issue his contradictory prayer instead. But why should there be such a desire? How can
we understand it other than as part of a rationalizing network of beliefs and
desires of an Unconscious Mind? This unconscious desire makes sense if it
is located in an Unconscious Mind which also hates the Rat Man's father,
fears his revenge, and desires his own revenge. Here we again see that following out the plausible thought that this is a case of akrasia leads us to posit
Another Mind, another locus of rationality and strategy.

But to interpret this as akrasia is again to attribute more rationality to
the occurrence than is there. We are witnessing a mental activity too
primitive to be understood as the outcome of belief and desire. The Rat
Man is not uttering a contradictory judgment—and thus there is no need
to posit a desire or intention to issue such a prayer anywhere in the mind.

What the Rat Man is doing is launching a phantasized attack on his own prayer-making activity. He is not asserting a prayer contradictory to the one he consciously intended; he is, rather, primitively attacking his attempt at prayer, breaking it up by forcibly inserting a "not." He is actively disrupting his own thought.

Of course, there are many ways in which a person may disrupt his thought activity which do not involve the creation of a new meaning: by stuttering or sneezing, by repeatedly getting up to go to the bathroom, by having intrusive thoughts which break in on one's train of thought, and so on. The Rat Man has hit on an ingenious form of disruption: one which creates a new public meaning, one to which he cannot remain oblivious. On the one hand, this is not just an accident; on the other hand, it is not the utterance of a contradictory prayer. How can there be any room in between? It is phantasy which preserves the possibility of elemental forms of mental activity which are themselves meaningful but are not themselves the formation of judgments or other propositional attitudes. We have already seen how the Rat Man lives out a cringe before the internal Rat Dad; he also sporadically lives out a "hateful" rebellion. I say "hateful" because what we see here is the matter of hate: the Rat Man's hostility has not been taken up into logos and embedded in the justifying beliefs and attitudes which would inform it as hate. Precisely because the Rat Dad has been internalized in phantasy, "he" is removed from the network of propositional attitudes—and thus cannot be worked over in thought. As a result, Rat Dad remains a fairly primitive phantastic figure who elicits fairly primitive phantastic responses. Primitive expressions of hostility thus survive, unintegrated into rational thought. Let us consider how this might work.

As we know from the case history, the Rat Man was himself tortured by phantasies of a rat-torture being inflicted on his father.[32] This phantasy is elaborated from a story a cruel captain told him when he was in the army. In the torture, rats burrowed into the anus of the victim and devoured him from the inside. No doubt the conscious phantasy that this was happening to his father was itself an expression of hostility, and through it, sadistic yearnings gained some gratification. In phantasy, the Rat Man's mind is working in an aura of omnipotence: for the Rat Man, it is almost as though the torture is being carried out. This raises anxiety, and his mind leaps to a phantastic, magical gesture of undoing and reparation. There might be various such gestures, but one would be a prayer uttered under the same magical mist of omnipotence. In phantasy, the prayer has the power to protect his father—and there is a psychological truth which underlies this experience of omnipotence. Insofar as the Rat Man can concentrate on uttering a prayer, he will actually have succeeded in getting his mind to break off the elaboration of the phantasy of the rat-torture: and thus he will, at least for that moment, have brought the rat-torture to an end.

So he tries to utter a protective prayer, but at that point his hostility wells up, and he shoves a "not" into his utterance. The disruption occurs via a direct assault on a vehicle of meaning: the spoken sounds with which the Rat Man is trying to say a prayer. And the utterance is physically disrupted by the physical intrusion of another vehicle of meaning, an utterance of the word "not." That is, even as he is trying to protect his father from the rat-torture by uttering a prayer, *he reenacts the torture by shoving a "not" up the ass of his utterance.* The "not" intrudes inside the utterance and eats away at its meaning.

Such an act is a wondrous concoction of sophisticated and primitive forms of mental activity. The Rat Man is already in logos: he speaks and thinks in a natural language. (In his case it was German, but to avoid unnecessary complication, I shall simply treat him as English-speaking.) Thus he understands that "not" is a word typically used to form negations. And his phantasy activity is to some degree sensitive to the sophisticated fact that "not" has a negating meaning. But the phantasy activity itself puts this sophisticated vehicle of meaning to a primitive use. What this example shows is that the direct attack on vehicles of meaning can itself be meaningful. The Rat Man attacks his prayer-making activity, but he hears himself saying, "May God *not* protect him!" and this has a meaning for him, as for his audience. He has actively broken up his prayer, but he experiences himself as passive before the new injunction which he has ended up uttering. This is not the outcome of belief and desire. It is more like crying or cringing or bursting out: a primitive, natural expression—in this case, of aggression. But instead of crying with tears or bursting out in a scream, the Rat Man bursts out with a concrete, sophisticated vehicle of meaning. In this way, he satisfies his aggressive wishes *by being aggressive,* and in the process he creates a new hostile piece of meaning. But it is not a judgment; it is the active disruption of the mind's own judging activity.[33]

Undoubtedly the Rat Man will himself try to understand what he is doing. He will probably take himself to be issuing a contradictory judgment: and thus it will become overwhelmingly plausible to the Rat Man himself that he has another part of his mind from which the contradictory judgment issues. But all of this is *post hoc:* it is part of a rationalizing defense. And it keeps the Rat Man in ignorance of what he is actually doing. In this way, postulation of The Unconscious as another mind, a locus of its own rationality, facilitates self-misunderstanding. And it collaborates with and expresses an obsessional outlook. Of course, once the Rat Man has taken himself to have uttered a contradictory judgment, that judgment will be taken up into the system of propositional attitudes, and its influence will begin to take on a certain life of its own. But this is not the incorporation of the phantasy into the domain of logos; it is the incorporation of a defensive misreading of that phantasy. For a genuine incorporation into logos, one needs the process of working-through. Only then can the verbal expression of aggression replace its enactment.

But until these doings are properly brought within logos, as genuinely understood, the Rat Man correctly portrays himself as somewhat passive in the face of the meaning his acts end up creating. He tries uttering a curse in the hope that a similar attack on judgment will leave him uttering a prayer. Finally, he stumbles on an ingenious, if temporary, solution: to try to create a meaningful assertion from nonmeaningful bits—that is, to try to make the formation of a judgment more like the formation of a single word. He concocts a code from the first letters of various words or sentences in the prayer and tries to say them so quickly that he cannot interrupt himself. The important point is not that he can say these letters quickly, but that any attack on the performance of this ritual, though it may disturb the ritual, cannot negate it. The interruption may prevent him from creating his meaning, but it will not thereby create another meaning which he will then have to endure. Of course, such a solution can last only so long: it is only a matter of time before each of the "letters" takes on the meaning of a word, and some gesture or sound comes to mean negation.

THE POWER OF PHANTASY

One source of phantasy's power is that it can work both in and on meaning. One can see this by contrasting the efficacy of phantasy with the ways conscious imaginative activity like daydreaming works on us. (Of course, daydreams will themselves be expressions of phantasy, but I here want to concentrate on the conscious aspect.) In a typical masturbatory daydream, for example, it is a person's understanding of the unfolding sexual content which, in concert with physical masturbatory activity, will raise sexual excitement to an orgasm. Similarly, when we cry at a sad movie, our emotional reactions are following and responding to the content of the story. In contrast, phantasy can also work *directly* on the mind. It does so in part by working on the material vehicles in which the mind expresses itself. We have seen the Rat Man directly attack his attempt at prayer. He doesn't do this by operating purely at the level of sense, or meaning: he doesn't offer a contradictory judgment which negates the meaning of the original judgment. Rather, he materially attacks the concrete activity of judging—and in the process creates a new meaning.[34] It is important to see that similar acts can create the content of phantasies themselves. Consider, for example, Freud's description of the analytic session in which the Rat Man recounted the torture.

> At all the more important moments while he was telling his story his face took on a very strange, composite expression. I could only interpret it as one of *horror at pleasure of his own of which he himself was unaware.* He proceeded and with the greatest difficulty: *"At that moment the idea flashed through my mind that this was happening to a person who was very dear to me."* In answer to a direct question he said that it was not he himself who was carrying out the punishment, but that it was being carried out as it were impersonally. After a little prompting I learnt that the person to whom this "idea" of his related was the lady whom he admired.
>
> *He broke off his story in order to assure me that these thoughts were entirely foreign and repugnant to him,* and to tell me that everything which had followed in their train had passed through his mind with the most extraordinary rapidity.

Simultaneously with the idea there always appeared a "sanction," that is to say, the defensive measure which he was obliged to adopt in order to prevent the phantasy from being fulfilled. When the captain had spoken of this ghastly punishment, he went on, and these ideas had come into his head, *by employing his usual formulas (a "but" accompanied by a gesture of repudiation, and the phrase "whatever are you thinking of"?)* he had just succeeded in warding off *both* of them.

The "both" took me aback, and it has not doubt also mystified the reader. For so far we have heard only of one idea—of the rat punishment being carried out upon the lady. He was now obliged to admit that *a second idea had occurred to him simultaneously, namely, the idea of the punishment also being applied to his father.* As his father had died many years previously, this obsessive fear was much more nonsensical even than the first, and accordingly it had attempted to escape being confessed to for a little while longer.[35]

The Rat Man is recounting the story of the rat-torture when, in phantasy, a representation of his lady friend is intruded into the story. The intrusion may be visual—an image of his lady put in the place of the victim—or it may be verbal—he hears himself saying or thinking "my friend" instead of "the victim," and so on; but in every such case the intrusion is more or less physical. This is an example of what Freud meant by displacement or condensation, paradigms of primary-process mental activity. And once this intrusion has occurred, there is now a new phantasy with which the Rat Man must contend: that of the rat-torture happening to his lady friend.[36] Here we see how the holistic content of the phantasy can be altered by an atomic perturbation: for example, the momentary insertion of an image of the lady friend. The overall meaning of the phantasy shifts in response to elementary transformations on concrete vehicles of meaning. Later, he has to admit that another idea has been superimposed on that of the victim and the lady: the torture is now happening to his father as well. This activity of superimposition is what Freud called condensation. The phantasy has been operated on directly, and it creates a new meaning.

The only way he knows how to protect himself from the force of this newly formed phantasy is to attack it directly. In the transference, he breaks the story. He interrupts himself to assure Freud that all this is repugnant to him. On the surface, this looks like a conscious reassurance—

and it is certainly that. But it is also a direct attack on his phantasy. He interrupts the flow of the phantasy (which is taking hold even as he recounts it in the analysis) by breaking it off (and reassuring Freud). And in phantasy activity, he breaks up the formation of this phantasy with a sanction. The Rat Man has formed a magical symbol of negation—exclaiming "but," followed by a certain gesture, probably one which imitates the physical gesture of pushing something away or erasing it, followed by "whatever are you thinking of?!"—which when appended to a phantasy serves to negate it. Of course, one can imagine the Rat Man attacking this gesture of repudiation, and so on. But in each case there is a direct, physical attack on a vehicle of meaning which ends up creating a new meaning.

One might wonder: why does the Rat Man think that uttering a sanction will somehow undo the malign power of his phantasy? Of course, if there were a rational answer to that question, we'd be within the domain of rationality, which we are not. But I think we can see here a certain method in the madness. The Rat Man is able to invest the sanction with magical powers because the sanction actually breaks up the formation of the torture phantasy. It does actually succeed in inhibiting or undoing the phantasy; not by magic—in this way the Rat Man misunderstands himself and the power of the sanction—but through a direct attack on the phantasy.

I have focused on examples in which one can see fairly clearly the direct efficacy of some phantasy activity. But once one grasps the model, one can see much of the Rat Man's life as dominated by this nonrational form of mental activity. At the time the Rat Man is plagued with these torture phantasies, the captain, who mistakenly thinks the Rat Man owes a certain Lieutenant A. money, comes up to him and tells him that he must repay the money. The Rat Man's life is then taken up with the most contorted and complicated attempts to repay the money—when all along he knows that he doesn't actually owe Lieutenant A. anything. Why does he do this? It is even more of a strain than usual to see this as a case of akrasia, for the Rat Man does not seem to have *any* reason to pay back the lieutenant. But if one wants to go that route, one can say that he *wants* to follow the captain's orders. We are then left with the dubious challenge of trying to explain at the level of beliefs and desires why the Rat Man doesn't simply explain to the captain that no money is owed to Lieutenant A. Is it because he *fears* the captain will punish him before he gets his explanation out? But why does he *believe* that? Again, we are led to posit a whole other realm of beliefs, desires, emotions—an Unconscious—which would rationalize this one irrational act. And the basis for all of *this* structure is the irrational act we are trying to understand.

A better answer to the question "Why does he do this?" is: because it comes next. It is the temporal juxtaposition of the captain's order, coming just when the Rat Man was having torture phantasies, which allows the Rat Man to treat the order as a sanction which would negate the phantasy. It is plausible that the Rat Man also projected the internal Rat Dad out onto the captain, so that the Rat Man experiences the captain's utterance as the Rat Dad telling him what he has to do to prevent a retaliatory attack. Here we see how *the content of a phantasy can become quite sophisticated, but as the result of elementary mental activities.* There is nothing internal to the meaning of the rat-torture phantasy from which it unfolds that the Rat Man must pay back the lieutenant. The elaboration of the phantasy is not working through its meaning. Rather, the sophistication of the phantasy is parasitic on the sophistication of the captain's utterance. The utterance gains its power from the fact that the captain is the target of the Rat Man's projective phantasies and what he says comes next. In this way, meaning gets made from elementary mental operations and physical juxtapositions. One should thus view the entirety of the Rat Man's twisted attempts to pay back the money as an extended gesture of repudiation: a sanction which, appended to the torture phantasy, will magically undo it. Again, the rationality system may be wheeled in to formulate a rationalizing interpretation, and the Rat Man may even form beliefs to fall in line with his self-interpretation, but all of this is *post hoc* defensive surface.

It is important to note that rationality enters mainly as a defense. Consider this account of how the Rat Man sought help from Freud.

His determination to consult a doctor was woven into his delirium in the following ingenious manner. He thought he would get a doctor to give him a certificate to the effect that it was necessary for him, in order to recover his health, to perform some such action as he had planned in connection with

113

Lieutenant A. . . . The *chance* that one of my books happened to fall into his hands just at that moment directed his choice to me. There was no question of getting a certificate from me, however; all that he asked of me was, very reasonably, to be freed of his obsessions.[37]

It seems pretty clear that Freud is here taken in by the defense, and collaborates with the transference rather than analyzing it. From an obsessional perspective, there is no such thing as chance. A chance occurrence is in fact a physical juxtaposition of meanings. Freud's book comes to the Rat Man's attention just as he is experiencing difficulty in carrying out his sanctioning gesture. Thus it is taken by him as a sign: it points the way to how he is to continue his phantasized gesture of repudiation. Not to go into analysis would, from the Rat Man's phantasized perspective, have been tantamount to allowing the rat-torture to go ahead unimpeded by any repudiating gesture. When Freud says that there was no question of the Rat Man's getting a certificate, he is speaking from his own perspective, not the Rat Man's. And when he says that the only thing the Rat Man asked of him, "very reasonably," was to be freed of his obsessions, Freud is oblivious to the way that reason is being used to cover over unreason. From the perspective of phantasy, the Rat Man is trying to complete the gesture of repudiation. He seeks Freud's help, just as he sought to pay back Lieutenant A.: because it is the gesture which physically, and therefore meaningfully and magically, comes next. The appearance of rationality is used to disguise and rationalize essentially magical commands. Yet again, the rationalization may come to take on a life and truth of its own: the Rat Man may actually come to want and believe that Freud will help him. Even so, the rationalizing engagement remains eerily cut off from the deeper layers of phantasy which bring the Rat Man onto Freud's couch.

It is when this appearance of rationality is challenged that the Rat Man becomes positively philosophical. Why, Freud asks—and at some point the Rat Man asks himself—go through all this effort to protect your father from torture when, all along, you know he is dead? In response, the Rat Man offers a critique of the limits of human reason. What can one know about life in the afterworld? he wonders. And thus begins a phase of skeptical doubt and critique. Kant is said to have offered a critique of reason to make room for faith; the Rat Man offers his critique to make room for phantasy.

PHANTASY AS CONTENT, PHANTASY AS ACTIVITY

To understand its power, we have had to understand phantasy not merely in terms of its representational content, but as a motivated form of mental activity. So, for example, when the Rat Man hears himself utter his negative prayer, it is not merely the content of his malediction which disturbs him, but the violence of his own mental activity. Of course, some of the phantasy's power is running through its content. In phantasy, the Rat Man's mind is working in an aura of omnipotence, so that when he hears himself say "May God not protect him!" it is as though he has successfully ordered God off the scene. And this is horrifying to him. But that is only part of what is going on. It is also horrifying that he has been able to disturb directly his own mental functioning. He was able to attack his own intentional efforts to utter a prayer. Here we see that "phantasy" versus "reality" is a false dichotomy: this phantasized attack on the mind's attempt to form an intentional judgment is as real an attack as there can be.

Part of what is so shocking about this negative prayer for the Rat Man is that he experiences his mind as active, but not under his control. Phantasy is a form of mental activity—the Rat Man is shoving a "not" into his utterance—and yet this activity is not itself an intentional act. Phantasy operates around, in relation to, in the interstices of intentional action, but it is itself a form of mental activity which is not an intentional act. It might be tempting to think that either the Rat Man is (intentionally) doing something or something is happening to him: that is, that intentional acts are the only kind of activity there is, and that everything else must be a passive suffering. The phenomenon of phantasy shows that this is an impoverished universe of alternatives: phantasy is a form of mental activity which is not an action. In experiencing it as out of one's intentional control, one can feel passive with respect to it—for one's intentional system *is* then passive, as when the Rat Man's attempt at prayer is disrupted—but it is nevertheless a form of one's own mental activity, and one can experience this too: the Rat Man can experience himself as disrupting himself, and this is part of what is so disturbing to him.

If we are to understand the efficacy of phantasy, we must recognize that the full meaning of a phantasy is not given by its representational content alone. We need to understand what the person is *doing* with that content. Imagine, for example, that the Rat Man came into a session and said that the night before he had a dream: in one room there was the most beautiful woman, dressed in white, lovingly beckoning him to come in; in another room there was a horrid woman, dressed in black, whom he hated. One might be tempted to say that the Rat Man is splitting idealized and hated images of his lady friend—and he may well be doing this. But as Freud pointed out, one cannot tell this from the content of the dream alone. Freud argued that certain phantasized representations of splitting are, in fact, the mind's first attempts at *recovery:* they are the first attempt to overcome splitting by forming a representation of what has happened.[38] From the content of the dream alone we cannot tell whether the Rat Man is holding the white lady and the dark lady apart or bringing them back together. Rather, we have to understand what the Rat Man is doing with that content: we have to understand that dreaming is fundamentally a form of mental activity, and inquire whether in that activity he is holding these images apart or bringing them together. This corresponds to Freud's own understanding of the dream as essentially a form of mental activity.

And once we take seriously the idea that phantasy is a form of mental activity, a certain mystery about its force evaporates. At first, one might wonder: how can a phantasy of splitting actually split the mind? This question seems pressing when one thinks of phantasy only in terms of its representational content. For how, one may well think, can an image of, say, a motorcycle driving through one's head actually serve to split the mind? If we think only of the imagistic content of this phantasy, there is no good answer to the question. But once one frees oneself from the assumption that phantasy is fully captured by its representational content, then there is the most beautifully simple answer to the question; *the phantasy of splitting just is the activity of splitting.*

Consider, for example, the Rat Man's stroll along a road on which he expects his lady friend's carriage soon to travel. He sees a boulder in the road and clears it out of the way; a bit later he turns around, goes back to that spot, and replaces the boulder. How are we to understand this? By now it should be clear that if we try to interpret all this in terms of the Rat Man's beliefs and desires we will land in a familiar interpretive impasse. What the Rat Man is doing here is *acting out:* he is actively holding loved and hated representations of the lady friend apart, while in dynamic relation. He thereby holds apart, and expresses, affectionate and hostile responses in himself. This activity of holding apart *is* the phantasy. One doesn't then have to wonder how phantasy can be efficacious; phantasy just is a form of mental efficacy.

It follows that when we talk about the *content* of a phantasy, there is an important ambiguity. This is because phantasies are doings which themselves may have representational content which may be expressed in a material vehicle. So, first, the content of a phantasy may be its representational content: as when we have a conscious sexual daydream which itself provides some sexual excitement and gratification. Second, the content may be the appropriate interpretation of phantasy activity: as when we correctly *say* what the Rat Man is *showing* in his cringe. Here the interpretation allows the activity to be thought, and thus to be "remembered" rather than merely "repeated." Third, one may wish to refer to the particular material vehicle in which meaning is embedded: for example, the Rat Man's particular, concrete utterance of "May God . . ." For when one sees content concretely embedded in a material utterance one can see how phantasy activity can directly affect content—for example, by concretely shoving in a "not." One needs to keep these three distinct meanings of meaning clear if one is to understand how phantasy works.

FORMS OF RESTLESSNESS

I said at the beginning of this essay that it is part of our very idea of mind that mind is restless—and it is one of Freud's distinctive achievements to show us the basic forms of restlessness. It is this restlessness of mind which the philosophical tradition has by and large ignored. In brief, the psychoanalytic tradition has isolated three forms of restlessness: first, there are *mental tropisms,* of which projection and introjection are paradigms; second, there are *drives,* of which sexuality is a paradigm; third, there is *primary-process mental activity*—displacement and condensation—which expresses a pure form of mental restlessness. I shall conclude by saying something about each.

ONE CAN THINK of the Rat Man's own turn to philosophy as wishful: in becoming skeptical of our knowledge of the other world, he comes to believe that his father may be alive there. But how does this wishful formation of belief occur? The philosophical tradition has had little more to say than: it just does. And as Socrates has shown, if we stay at the level of propositional attitudes there is very little more one *can* say. One might then view the formation of this wishful belief as the outcome of a simple, nonrational movement of thought: the Rat Man just moves from anxiety that his father might not be all right to wishful belief that he is. A *mental tropism* is a subintentional, nonrational mental activity which has a strategic point: namely, relieving the mind of anxiety.[39] On this view, a conviction that *P* is the mind's response to its anxiety that, perhaps, *not-P*. But *how?* The very idea of a tropism might tempt one to think that if there is a causal bridge from anxiety to anxiety-reducing belief, that is all one needs to know: *the mind just does it,* subintentionally, nonrationally, and for a strategic purpose.[40] But it is an important fact about the human mind that for a wide range of cases, the mind doesn't just do it. And when one inquires what the mind does do, one sees that tropisms are at work below the level of propositional attitudes.

Consider, for example, the Rat Man's response to anxiety that his father is in trouble in the next world. He does not simply move from anxiety that his father is in trouble to wishful belief that he is fine. Rather, the psychic situation is more like this: in response to phantasies of the rat-torture being applied to his father, the Rat Man becomes anxious. His father may be in trouble in "the other world." Because he misunderstands his phantasy life, he mistakes a danger to the Rat Dad in his inner world for a danger to his deceased father in "the next world." In any case, he responds to this anxiety in a strategic way: he projects Rat Dad out of his inner world and onto the captain. This subpropositional activity, projection, is the tropism: the point of projection is to relieve the anxiety around the Rat Dad. But one of Freud's great insights is that even a simple mental tropism like projection can have a fate. Now that the captain has taken on a paternal role, when he speaks it is as though the Rat Dad is telling him what he should do.

The Rat Man *may* thereby move from anxiety that his father is not okay, to wishful belief that if he pays back Lieutenant A. he will be okay. But this formation of wishful belief is not the fundamental mode of anxiety reduction. Paying back Lieutenant A. has now become a magical undoing of his previous hostile phantasy, which sent rats up his father's ass. So if the Rat Man *were* to form a wishful belief that paying back Lieutenant A. will help his father in the next world, it would be as a rationalizing defense of his acting out. It would not be that he was performing this act because he wishfully believed that it would help his father; rather, he would be forming the wishful belief in order to help himself understand what he is doing. The anxiety is no longer directly about his father, but about being in a state of reflexive breakdown.

This is what Freud called a "propositional reflection" of phantasy—and it serves to cover over the more elemental forms of tropistic activity.[41] One can see this if one reflects on the fact that the activity of trying to pay back the lieutenant generates as much anxiety as the original phantasy it is supposed to undo. This would be very odd if the tropism were working at the level of the propositional attitudes. But it makes perfect sense if the anxiety reduction is operating at the level of projecting the Rat Dad—to get him out—but with the accidental fate that the target then gives him an impossible task to perform.

THOUGH HIS THEORY CHANGED, Freud always characterized the mind as operating under the influence of two contradictory principles. In his last theory, the mind operated under the sway of eros, a drive directed toward forming differentiated unities, and the death drive, an entropic force directed toward decomposition and undoing. His aim was to portray the mind as inevitably conflicted. But he also succeeded in portraying the mind as inherently restless. Restlessness is not itself a teleological goal of mind; it is the inevitable outcome of mind's operating under the influence of conflicting teleological principles. At its best this restlessness expresses itself in creative associations, poetry, delightful wanderings of mind; at its worst, in mental discontent, irritability of mind, intrusive and dominating thoughts, traumatic associations. But this restlessness isn't a goal of mind; it's an expression of it.

It is in reflecting on such restlessness that Freud came to think that the most fundamental form of mental activity is what he called a drive *(Triebe)* rather than an instinct *(Instinkt)*—a rigid, innate pattern of behavior. One can think of psychoanalysis as beginning with Freud's recognition that human sexuality is not an instinct in this sense. And that is why a drive cannot be understood as a tropism. A mental tropism is "a characteristic pattern of causation between types of mental states, a pattern whose existence within the mind is no more surprising, given what it does for us, than a plant's turning toward the sun."[42] But the problem with understanding the vagaries of human sexuality, Freud came to realize, is not just that the *position* of the sun keeps changing, but *that what it is to be* the sun keeps changing. Indeed, *what it is* to move in a certain direction also keeps changing, so much so that the sexual drive may come to turn away from its sun. A drive, unlike an instinct, may change in all sorts of strange ways in its goal, object, aim, and characteristic form of activity.

To take a familiar example, sexual desire for another person can undergo a transformation of object and thus be replaced by desire for knowledge. As a result of what Freud called the overvaluation of the sexual object, a person may then form the wishful belief that knowledge is of overwhelming value—so much so, that it may cause anxiety and thus lead to the formation of a defense against acquiring it. Plato distinguishes the philosopher, the one who desires knowledge, from the sophist, the one who thinks he already has it. The philosopher thus gains his or her identity from the idea of pursuit—pursuit of an object which is portrayed as being as desirable as it is distant. But, as Freud pointed out, insistence on pursuit may become a reassurance that the supposedly desirable object will *never* be attained. Pursuit, ironically, becomes a means of keeping the object of pursuit at bay. At the grotesque limit, we have the figure of Casaubon, infinitely preparing to begin his great work unlocking the key to all mysteries. In all these transformations, is there a reduction of anxiety or an expression of it?

The sexual drive and its object are, as Freud put it, merely soldered together. And once the sexual object is repressed it undergoes all sorts of primary-process transformations. It slips along a skein of associations which altogether expresses an archaic sense of similarity. Unlike a tropism or a drive, both of which are motivated forms of mental activity—one aimed at reduction of anxiety, the other at gratification—condensation and displacement are pure expressions of restlessness. And yet they perform an invaluable service, allowing the mind to function under conditions of repression. For conscious mind to function, certain ideas need to be repressed. But these are wishful ideas and phantasies—forms of motivation which seek satisfaction. Under conditions of repression, they undergo a series of primary-process transformations until they are sufficiently unlike the intolerable idea so as to escape repression, but sufficiently linked with it so as to provide some gratification.

And precisely because we have these forms of restlessness, there is no need to conceive of an Unconscious Mind strategizing to get itself expressed in Conscious Mind. To see this, consider, by way of analogy, the change of outlook which Darwin's theory of natural selection occasioned. For thousands of years it was tempting to view the natural world as the product of Another Mind, God's, located outside it and making plans for it. It was Darwin who showed that the appearance of design can be mimicked by a crude form of censorship—death—along with certain forms of restlessness by which different genetic combinations are "tried out." One can think of a DNA molecule as an unconscious idea, a unit of genetic information which is struggling to get itself expressed. At the level of the molecule these ideas are transformed by a primary process—mutation, arbitrary syntactic transformations, and so on—until they finally find a form which evades censorship. That is, in sexual reproduction, two "unconscious ideas" are brought together to form a "conscious judgment"—a living member of the species who may or may not live to pass on his "ideas" to the next generation. Sexual reproduction would then form a kind of "secondary-process" transformation of genetic material. Similarly, though the emergence of unconscious material in conscious life can often look stunningly apt—and thus display a kind of "reason in madness"—there is no need for an Unconscious Mind as the locus of that reason. All that is needed is censorship and unconscious forms of restless mental activity.

In this way, the forms of restlessness lend content to the drive. Freud took himself to have made an empirical discovery of the drives. But I think we can see the idea of something like drives as flowing from the idea of a restless mind. From Socrates and the ensuing philosophical tradition we have learned that a mind capable of propositional attitudes, such as belief, desire, hope, and fear, must be sensitive to the content of those attitudes in such ways as to maintain rational relations among them. This requires sensitivity to the inner structure of the contents of those attitudes, so that transformations of subject and predicate can be made which preserve the overall rationality of the system of propositional attitudes. But if the mind is to be restless, in the sense I want to capture, there must be systematic ways of disrupting that system, systematic ways of moving on. Some of those ways, like projection and introjection, are tropisms. Others, like sexuality, are drives. But others, like displacement and condensation, seem simply to be principles of mental activity. In their wake, meaning is created, and the associations may be put to various uses, but, strictly speaking, they have no purpose: they are just forms of restlessness. In the Rat Man's psyche, paying Lieutenant A. comes to express an idiosyncratic meaning; but it acquires this meaning, really, for no better reason than that it comes next. It is this restlessness which guarantees the immanence and disruptiveness of irrationality in our lives.

CHAPTER 6

The Introduction of Eros: Reflections on the Work of Hans Loewald

THE TASK

Freud's essay "On Narcissism: An Introduction" would have been more aptly called "On the Introduction of Narcissism," not merely because it is a more accurate translation of the German, but because the aim of the essay is not so much to introduce the reader to narcissism as to introduce narcissism into psychoanalytic theory. In hindsight, it seems that Freud should also have written an essay titled "On the Introduction of Eros." For from 1920 on, he seems increasingly aware that he had, incredibly enough, left eros out of psychoanalytic thinking.

When we talk of a legacy our speech is often tinged with an ambiguity which suggests ambivalence. There is, of course, the straightforward sense of a bequest—as with Freud's passing on to us the idea of the repressed unconscious. But there is also a sense of legacy as that which a person did *not* hand down (but should have). Here the legacy is a task: it is the unfinished business which the child needs to complete in order to manifest love, atone for ambivalence, and succeed the parent.[1]

This is Freud's legacy-as-task: to develop a psychoanalytic account of the erotic. Although he places eros at the center of psychoanalytic theory, he says remarkably little about it. Of course, he speculates grandly: he introduces eros as one of two cosmic principles which, together, make the world go round. In the realm of the human psyche, eros and the death drive are the basic drives which, in complex particular forms, account for all neurotic conflict. Eros itself is ultimately responsible for human development. But grand speculation masks an inner emptiness. We lack an understanding of what eros is. Eros has, as it were, been introduced into psychoanalysis without an introduction.

The temptation is to treat eros as a minor emendation. After all, Freud has been talking about the sex drive, about libido, from the beginning. It is all too easy to see eros as a philosophical flourish, resting on the foundation of human sexuality. From this perspective, it is the introduction of the death drive which seems novel, ominous, and questionable. It takes a profound mind to see that the situation is precisely the reverse.

> . . . the proposition of a duality of Eros and Thanatos, the life drive and the death drive . . . for the first time establishes . . . an independent psychic force that does not follow the constancy or Nirvana principle. The metapsychological . . . meaning of pleasure, in the old pleasure principle, was the abolition or diminution of unpleasure or "stimulus tension" in pursuit of the return to a state of absolute rest or "death." This tendency in psychic processes is now called the death drive. In this sense the death drive is nothing new, but merely a new conceptualization of the constancy principle. What is new in Freud's last drive theory is the life drive as a force or tendency sui generis, not reducible to the old pleasure-unpleasure principle.[2]

> It remained an insoluble problem for Freud to fit his life drive [or eros] into his new definition of drive . . . The inertia or constancy or unpleasure or Nirvana principle . . . fits in perfectly with the death drive, insofar as the latter is "the expression of the inertia inherent in organic life." In this sense, the death drive is really nothing new, not a conception that should have taken psychoanalysts by surprise . . . What is new, and this does not seem to fit with the inertia principle . . . is the concept of Eros, the life or love drive.[3]

By making it clear that eros is new, unfamiliar, and needed, Loewald is, in effect, offering an interpretation—an interpretation by which psycho-analysis may come better to understand itself.

But a good interpretation, according to Loewald, does more than make the unconscious conscious. It offers the opportunity to integrate this newly found understanding into one's overall organizational structure. Loewald's work constitutes an interpretation of Freudian psychoanalysis in this sense: it makes manifest how eros comes to be a conceptual requirement; then it shows how the idea of eros might be developed and integrated into psycho-analytic thinking and practice. It is a corollary of the oedipus complex that creativity requires that one come to grips with the legacies of one's intellec-tual parents. Within the broad domains of psychology and psychiatry, there have been embarrassingly many attempts to kill off Freud; but even within psychoanalysis, the proliferation of schools and schisms has often, if not al-ways, hidden a wish to murder the father. Loewald's work is remarkable for its unique blend of creativity and faithfulness. On the one hand, the essays present themselves as vibrant explications of Freud. There is no room for the reader of these essays to decide to become a "Loewaldian," whatever that might be: in being gripped by these essays, the reader is led to believe that he is learning what it is to become a Freudian. From this perspective, these essays appear as a work of profound humility. But the humility is "profound" in the sense that it contains not a drop of slavish devotion or castrated submission. For, on the other hand, this "interpretation of Freud" is of remarkable originality. Certain Freudian themes are enhanced: their consequences are pursued beyond anything Freud imagined. Every good interpretation is as much a critique as an explication. And although Loe-wald treats eros as what is genuinely new in Freudian theory—and thus as Freud's contribution—the point is that Freud himself was not sufficiently aware of the significance of this concept for psychoanalysis. To say that it re-mained an "insoluble problem" for Freud to integrate eros into his theory of drives is to say not only that Freud came to eros relatively late in his think-ing, almost as an afterthought, but that he never really figured out what to do with it. In turning to this unfinished business, Loewald displays real filial piety in the very creative acts by which he goes beyond anything Freud thought.

What Is It to Abandon the Seduction Theory?

It is ironic that such heavy weather has been made in recent years about Freud's so-called abandonment of the seduction theory, since there is a deep sense in which he was never really able to give it up. It is well known that in his early work on hysteria, Freud thought that neurosis in adults was a causal outcome of abuse or seduction in childhood. By 1897 he realized that not all purported memories of seduction were veridical, but that some had been shaped by phantasy. He never abandoned the idea that childhood sexual abuse occurred, more often than generally acknowledged; nor did he ever abandon the belief that childhood seduction was an important cause of psychological harm. What he abandoned was the belief that all cases of hysteria and obsessional neurosis could be traced to an actual seduction.

The lure of the seduction theory is that it purports to offer an explanation of symptoms which, on the surface, appear incomprehensible. So, for example, a young woman's fear of entering shops unaccompanied appears bizarre on its own but becomes intelligible when it is linked to previous abuse which the woman unconsciously fears will be repeated.[4] This is meant to be a *psychological* explanation; and the point of such explanation is to restore a particular type of intelligibility. In seeing her current fear as a response to a now-forgotten past event, Freud is trying to bring the explanation within the web of personal motivation. Of course, Freud is inviting us to broaden our conception of what we might recognize as motivation; but within this expanded domain, we now see that the person's behavior is motivated: she fears that she will be molested again. Ultimately there may be no good reason to link the past with the present—that may be the source of irrationality—but, given the linkage, we can see that the current symptom has a certain intelligibility to it. There is "method in her madness."

Only thus can psychoanalysis be a talking cure. Unless we can see the symptom as a causal outcome of a person's motives—however broadly construed and however hidden from the person—there would be nothing of therapeutic significance to say. Symptoms present themselves as apparently unintelligible. The point of talking is to make the implicit rationality of the symptom explicit and conscious, and thus amenable to revision in the light of one's other motivations. Freud was aware of this, and he thus insisted on a *fundamental assumption* of psychoanalytic practice: "psychoanalysis must keep itself free from any hypothesis which is alien to it, whether of an anatomical, chemical or physiological kind, and must operate entirely with purely psychological . . . ideas."[5]

However, he did not see that the seduction theory covertly violates this fundamental assumption. For in appealing to a real event—an actual seduction—one is trying to get outside a person's "purely psychological ideas." Indeed, one is trying to explain those ideas by appeal to an objective reality which plays a causal role in bringing those ideas about. The real-life seduction is not itself part of the person's psychological world: it is a part of objective space-time which has helped to shape the psychological world. The search for a past seduction is thus for the external Archimedean point from which the analysand's psychological world has already been moved. Freud did not see the conflict between the seduction theory and his fundamental assumption, because he took reality for granted. He assumed that reality came with its own inherent meaning. If there was an actual seduction, that fact existed independently of how it was interpreted by the participants—indeed, it was this independent reality which caused the participants to interpret it as a seduction. It was thus that the seduction supposedly entered the realm of a person's "psychological ideas."

The seduction theory, in its broad significance, is thus not about seduction per se: it is about the role "reality" is to play in psychological explanation. To abandon the seduction theory, on this understanding, is not to say that actual seduction is not important or that there are no important differences between actual and phantasized seductions (of course there are). Abandoning the seduction theory is, fundamentally, abandoning the idea that citing any actual event could be the end of one's psychological-explanatory activity. One needs to know how that event (or nonevent) is taken up into a person's imaginative life; how it is metabolized in phantasy. Whether the seduction is actual or phantasized or both, the important point is that in each case one must go on to understand what psychological significance attaches to these events. To discover an actual seduction does not absolve one of the task of analyzing what meaning this event has for the analysand—in particular, how the memory of that event gets woven into the analysand's phantasy life.

In abandoning the seduction theory, Freud opened the door to seeing the psyche as imaginative and active in structuring its experience.[6] But Freud was not able to pursue the significance of this insight, because he could not wean himself from dependence on an unquestioned conception of reality.[7] He simply assumed, for example, that science, as he understood it, would reveal reality as it is in itself. In the generation after Freud, a number of notable psychoanalysts, for example Winnicott and Bion, took seriously the idea that the individual psyche emerges from a less differentiated field of psychic forces. But it is Loewald who worked through the *theoretical* significance of the thought that reality is always reality for a subject, that its meaning is never simply given, nor can it ever be simply invoked. It is Loewald who brings to our conscious awareness what is deeply involved in abandoning the seduction hypothesis.[8]

In his first essay, "Ego and Reality," Loewald argues that psychoanalysis has tended to look at the ego and its relation to reality *from sideways on.* That is, it is as though analyst, analysand, and reality form three points of a triangle, and the analyst is looking on at the analysand trying to establish some rapport with reality. On this view, even the ego is taken to be, as it were, outside of reality attempting to establish some relation with it. It is in making the transition from the pleasure principle to the reality principle that the ego bridges the gap and reaches out to this independent reality. From this sideways-on perspective, the ego and reality are both taken as given, and the question becomes how the one relates to the other. This, of course, is an illusion of a scientific perspective—one which flows from three sources. First, there is the image of the objective scientist as detached from the reality he is observing. Second, there is Freud's model of the psyche as an apparatus designed to reduce stimulation. On this model, reality is conceived as an external source of unpleasant stimulation. Third, the clinical basis of this picture is the report of neurotic patients about their difficulties in adjusting to their life situations. From a neurotic perspective, reality does seem hostile and impinging. "Psychoanalytic theory," Loewald argues, "has unwittingly taken over much of the obsessive neurotic's experience and conception of reality and has taken it for granted as 'the objective reality.'"[9]

One of Loewald's gifts is his ability to bring out the complexity of Freud's thought. While the picture of the ego as a pathetic "frontier creature," trying to fend off intrusions of the external world, is a dominant image in Freud's writing, Loewald reminds us that it is not the only image to be found there. Loewald will typically find a variant strain in Freud's thought, enhance it, and thus give back to us a Freud who is unfamiliar and original, yet genuinely Freud. We come to see that the Freud we had assumed is a caricature—an image which even Freud might have had of himself—but one which does not do justice to the full range of his thought.

There is, Loewald points out, another perspective in Freud's writing on the ego's relation to reality. In *Civilization and Its Discontents,* Freud takes up the perspective of the emerging ego of the newborn child. The newborn, Freud argues, does not yet distinguish an ego from an external world. There is, as it were, a field of experience in which the emerging ego eventually differentiates a breast which is not always available to it.

> In this way for the first time something like an "object" becomes constituted, an outside against an inside, and therewith a border between the two . . . This state of affairs can be expressed either by saying that "the ego detaches itself from the external world," or, more correctly: the ego detaches from itself an outer world. Originally the ego contains everything. Our adult ego feeling, Freud says, is only a shrunken vestige of an all-embracing feeling of intimate connection, or we might say, unity with the environment.
>
> In other words, the psychological constitution of the ego and outer world go hand in hand. Nothing can be an object, something that stands against something else, as long as everything is contained in the unitary feeling of the primary, unlimited narcissism of the newborn, where mouth and mother's breast are still one and the same. On the other hand, we cannot, in the strict sense, speak of an ego, a mediator between id and an external world, where there is as yet nothing to mediate.[10]

This is the perspective *from the inside,* from the ego.[11] The external world is no longer taken for granted, and so the question now becomes: what is required for the ego to be able to experience the world as objective? This is, of course, a psychological achievement. In particular, for the ego to be able to experience a world of objects, it must experience itself as a subject set amongst these objects. But to experience itself as a subject is part of the process of the emerging ego constituting itself as a subject. Thus the world of objects is simply the experiential correlate of the psychological constitution of the ego.[12]

For the young child, this development of subject and object typically takes a particular form. The infantile ego emerges from an experiential field, a mother-and-child dyad.

> The less mother and child are one, the more they become separate entities, the more will there be a dynamic interplay of forces between these two "systems." As the mother becomes outside, and hand in hand with this, the child an inside, there arises a tension system between the two. Expressed in different terms, libidinal forces arise between infant and mother. As infant (mouth) and mother (breast) are not identical, or better, not one whole, any longer, a libidinal flow between infant and mother originates, in *an urge towards re-establishing the original unity.*[13]

From this perspective, libido is the force by which the ego tries to remain connected to reality, even as it differentiates reality from itself. By changing perspective, from outside to inside, we begin to see the ego in a new light. It is the essence of the ego to maintain, on ever more complex levels of differentiation, the original unity of subject and object. Thus:

> *What the ego defends itself, or the psychic apparatus, against is not reality but the loss of reality,* that is, the loss of an integration with the world such as it exists in the libidinal relation with the mother.[14]

Libido is the force, emerging from the ego, by which the ego strives to keep itself connected with the world from which it is differentiating itself. It attempts to reinstate the "original unity," but at a more complex level of organization and integration. Loewald reminds us that from a properly psychoanalytic perspective, reality must always be understood as reality as it exists for an ego. The ego's developmental task is not merely to develop itself, but to develop its relations with what, for it, is an ever more complex world. To grasp that these are not two different tasks, but two aspects of a single process, is what it is to abandon the seduction theory.

ARISTOPHANES' CHALLENGE

But why should the ego have any developmental task at all? On Loewald's view, the ego has an inner potential to develop; and development consists in becoming more complex as it establishes more complicated relations to reality. How so? The answer, for Loewald's Freud, is eros, a drive which is posited precisely to account for this trajectory. For Loewald, this development should be understood as the reestablishment, at a higher level of organization, of the lost unity of the mother-child dyad. This image of human development as aimed at reunification is reminiscent of Aristophanes' famous myth in Plato's *Symposium.*

Originally, Plato's Aristophanes tells us, human nature was different than it is today. Humans were originally round creatures with two heads, four arms, four legs: some had both male and female genitals. Aristophanes tells a tale of rivalry and retribution: the original humans tried to ascend to heaven to attack the gods and were split in half as punishment. Eros, according to Aristophanes, is the force innate in every human which "calls back the halves of our original nature together; it tries to make one out of two and heal the wound of human nature." "'Eros' is the name for our pursuit of wholeness, for our desire to be complete."[15]

It does not seem stretched to see Loewald as giving a psychoanalytic interpretation of Aristophanes' myth. However, there is one important difference between Aristophanes and Loewald which needs to be addressed. Although Aristophanes' myth is told in rivalrous terms, the point is that the original humans are trying to ascend to a divine level of existence. The gods see this as a threat: and the point of splitting them in half is not merely to punish them, but to distract them. If humans are now impelled to spend their lives searching for their other halves, they are drawn into the political-social realm in search of human completion. That is, this absorption in the purely human realm serves as a distraction from the transcendent. In this myth, *eros functions as a resistance to ascent.*

There is much in the psychoanalytic thinking which supports Aristophanes' view. Certainly, Aristophanes' eros is compatible with those libidinal forces Freud called transference. For, as Loewald has argued, transference is human love life as it manifests itself in the social realm.[16] Psychoanalysis as a mode of therapy was, Freud thought, crafted specifically for the so-called transference neuroses; for it is these neuroses which demand that others conform to set roles. Transference is of its essence a form of political engagement: it is an attempt to shape society, or at least the immediate social environment, according to a certain image. That is, transference is an attempt to make the world over—in phantasy and actings out—according to an image of what would gratify basic wishes, under certain conditions of conflict. Though an expression of erotic longing, transference is the erotic attempt to end that longing by "finding" what one is missing. Thus the image might broadly be construed as of the person's "other half."

Psychoanalysis can be efficacious only because the analysand's transference will tend to make the analyst over into various images of the analysand's "other half." It is this erotic engagement of the analysand for the analyst which can be put to therapeutic use. This is remarkable, because transference manifests itself regularly as a *resistance to analysis*. Transference is an archaic and insistent demand that one's immediate world satisfy one's longings. There is no room within that demand for reflection upon itself; nor is there tolerance for anything which will undermine its power. Transference itself, the human-erotic engagement in the social world, stands as a constant obstacle to its own analysis.

Analysis of the transference is the mode of analytic therapy, but on this conception of transference it is a mistake to think of eros as itself a developmental force. Eros is here functioning as an obstacle to development: it is a demand that the world remain forever fixed according to a certain image of one's other half. Ironically, analytic therapy requires an obstacle to be overcome. Eros as transference is necessary, not as a developmental force, but as providing the gradient against which development can occur. Transference in this sense is like Plato's cave: that it can be turned from a prison to the wall against which we can scale must constitute one of the great reversals in the history of the human psyche's attempt to treat itself. As Freud put it, "Transference which seems ordained to become the greatest obstacle to psychoanalysis becomes its most powerful ally."[17]

On my reading of the *Symposium*, Aristophanes is challenging the Socratic idea of eros as a developmental force. That same challenge can now be put to Loewald. Why should we think of eros as a force *for* development, rather than *against*? Why not, with Aristophanes, think of eros as a distraction and resistance? There are clearly Aristophanic as well as Socratic strains in Freud's thought (just as there were in Plato's): why opt for the Socratic? Here the aim is not to prove that Loewald's account is correct (or incorrect). It is, rather, to illuminate his work by considering what his answer to this challenge might be.

DRIVES

The basic phenomenon which needs to be explained is the therapeutic action of psychoanalysis. How is it that psychoanalysis can be a talking cure? Psychoanalysis is an organized flow of words—a *field of logos*—in which analysand speaks to analyst, purportedly, anything and everything which comes to conscious awareness, and the analyst eventually speaks back. Why should this particular form of speech be of help? What sort of help is it? For Loewald, the psychoanalytic field is constituted by a differential in psychological organization: the analyst is more highly organized than the analysand. The psychoanalytic process facilitates a transmission of organization across this field. What is it about the human condition and the psychoanalytic process which allows this transmission to occur?

In response to Aristophanes, Socrates tells a story which he says he once heard from a priestess who taught him "the art of love." Diotima, the priestess, questions Socrates, and from their dialogue it emerges that eros can be neither an immortal god nor a mere mortal. Rather, eros lives in an "intermediate region," between the divine and human realms, and shuttles back and forth as a messenger. This, says Diotima, is what it is to be a *spiritual being:* to interpret each realm to the other. Spiritual beings carry prayers and sacrifices from humans to gods and bring back commands and gifts from gods to humans. On this interpretation, eros bridges the gap between the transcendent and immanent realms. Eros would thus create a "transitional space" whereby mundane life is invested with deep value and meaning.

For Loewald, the analytic relationship is a recreation, at a higher level of organization, of the mother-infant field.[18] For the emerging infantile perspective, parents occupy a realm of ultimate meaning. Eros, for Loewald, constitutes the field through which meanings flow. Mother, one might say, plays the roles both of divine and of messenger. On the one hand, she occupies her place in a transcendent realm, infinitely remote from infantile concerns and meanings; on the other, she is able to communicate adult meanings to the child in the appropriate infantile language.[19]

Now if one truly abandons the seduction theory, one can no longer take the individual as given.[20] The individual begins to emerge from the infant-mother dyad largely in response to the communications flowing though that field. To use the Platonic metaphor, it is as though eros-as-messenger brings the recipient of the message to life. But if the individual is coming into being, we cannot take for granted an inside or an outside (for that person). And if we cannot take an "inside" for granted, then there is a need to rethink the theory of the drives: for drives are a paradigm of items inside the person which play a prominent role in psychological life. Eros, of course, is treated by Freud as a drive—and it is Loewald who sees that we cannot understand the role of eros until we reconceptualize the theory of drives so as to free it from any dependence on the seduction theory.

It has become fashionable simply to throw out Freud's drive theory, either as reductionistic scientism or as wild speculation. By contrast, Loewald argues that it is a mistake to give up on drives altogether. The point of a theory of drives is to give us an account of the elements of mental life. We want to understand *that from which* mature mental life emerges. The point is not to capture how the mental develops from the nonmental, but how it develops from the protomental. This is especially important for psychoanalytic theory, which hopes to understand how psychic organization, in particular the healthy developed personality, develops from less organized states.

Admittedly, Freud's conceptualization of drives is confusing. On the one hand, a drive is depicted as a stimulus applied to the mind—as though it were impinging on it from outside. On the other hand, a drive is also depicted as a *"psychical representative"* of a stimulus—as a force *within the mind.* It is, on this construal, a constituent of mental life, not a biological force operating upon it. The way is thus open to depict the mind's activity in terms of representing stimuli rather than in terms of getting rid of them. This is not a path which Freud ever pursues wholeheartedly. For Freud, it is a basic theoretical postulate that stimulation is unpleasant. The psyche's task is to rid itself of this excitation, and thus its fundamental activity is governed by the avoidance or diminution of unpleasure (= stimulation) and by the production of pleasure (= discharge, and return to unstimulated state).[21]

Freud tended to group drives and forms of mental functioning into pairs of opposites—for example, the sexual versus the self-preservative drives, pleasure principle versus reality principle. But until his mature theory of the drives, both sides of the opposition aimed at the discharge of tension. The mind working according to the reality principle may take a more circuitous route—taking reality into account, and thus postponing discharge—but the aim is still the reduction of stimulation (given the constraints of reality). It is only with the last theory—where eros is pitched against the death drive—that one side of the opposition does not have reduction of tension as its goal. The aim of eros is "to form living substance into ever higher unities, so that life may be prolonged and brought to higher development."[22]

Ironically, just as Freud formulates this truly fundamental opposition, he defines a drive as "an urge inherent in organic life to restore an earlier stage of things."[23] This definition, as Loewald points out, harks back to the constancy principle.[24] But by this definition, eros does not even count as a drive! Only the death drive, a tendency in every living organism toward decomposition, would strictly speaking be a drive. So, although Freud thinks of the death drive as going "beyond the pleasure principle," Loewald sees that it is really eros which represents something new in psychoanalytic thinking.

One of the innovations in this mature theory is that the drives are no longer simply assumed to be inside a given psyche. Rather they are posited as forces which permeate animate nature. Even if we disregard Freud's penchant for cosmic speculation, these drives are well suited to a psychoanalytic theory truly purged of the seduction theory—one which hopes to chart how the individual emerges from less-organized psychological states. If we take neither the individual nor the world of objects (which the individual inhabits) for granted, but see them both as differentiating out of a mother-infant field, then it is theoretically helpful to have a force which can be conceptualized as flowing through that field. It is the mother's ministrations, her loving attention and attuned attachment, which communicate an ordered and loving world to the infant:

> objects are not givens. On the contrary, a highly complex course of psychic development is required for environmental and body-surface stimuli to become organized and experienced as external, in contrast to internal . . . In other words, what is naively called objects plays an essential part in the constitution of the subject, including the organization of instincts as psychic phenomena and of the subject's developing "object relations"; and what is naively called subject plays an essential part in the organization of objects (not merely object representations) . . . *drives, understood as psychic, motivational, forces, become organized as such through interactions within a psychic field consisting originally of the mother-child (psychic) unit.*[25]

Thus drives as *internal* sources of motivation are constituted from a field from which an individual and an erotically related world of objects emerge. But this field is a *field of logos:* the mother-infant dyad is essentially a field of communication. For Loewald, the infant emerges as essentially in communication with the world from which he differentiates himself. And the drives, now internalized, are the elements of all communication. Though they now represent intrapsychic and *even bodily demands,* the form of these demands has taken shape through communication with the mother. The drives are *essentially communicative* not merely because they are born *from* a communicative field, but because they are communicative *in* that field.[26] And though, from the perspective of mature, adult life, drives may appear stubbornly insistent, they are in fact ready to be influenced by certain forms of communication from the outside world. Therein lies the possibility of the therapeutic action of psychoanalysis.

TRAGEDY OR COMEDY?

At the end of the *Symposium,* almost all the original participants have left or have fallen asleep. Only Socrates, Aristophanes, and Agathon remain awake and in active conversation. Even Aristodemus, who supposedly provided the original account of the evening, had fallen asleep for a while. He thus could not remember exactly what they had been saying, "but the main point was that Socrates was trying to prove to them that authors should be able to write both comedy and tragedy: the skillful tragic dramatist should also be a comic poet."[27]

Why should it be important that a poet be able to write both tragedy and comedy? If the question is taken to mean "Why should it matter that the same person be able to write, say, *Oedipus Tyrannus* and *The Clouds?*" the answer must be that it couldn't matter at all. Of course, it might be pleasing to the author to be able to write both plays, but given that we have both plays, it couldn't really matter to us whether they were written by one person or two. That is, it couldn't *really* matter. It would seem that the reason it is important for a poet to be able to write both comedy and tragedy is that there is something important about the human condition that can be conveyed only in a drama which can be read both as a tragedy and as a comedy. The point, then, is that the author create a single drama which allows comic and tragic interpretations.

This, I believe, embodies Loewald's understanding of the therapeutic potential of psychoanalysis. On the psychoanalytic understanding of human development, each of us is author of a drama in which we ourselves play central roles.[28] In a typical development, a child faces a tragic moment, summed up as the oedipal crisis, which the child may negotiate more or less well. "Less well," and tragedy embeds itself in memory, in the unconscious, in phantasy—in our character. The child has, as it were, received an oracle, a communication from "the gods," and his psyche now sings a tragic song of life. The oracle may of course be elaborated in phantasy, its shape being influenced by inner forces of which the child is unaware: but has there ever been an unelaborated oracle? What we, as analytic observers, tend to see as neurotic repetition is, in effect, the enduring refrain of the chorus of drives.[29] The child has received a devastating message from on high, and the psyche proceeds through life singing songs of defeat and resignation. But however repetitive, however impervious these neurotic refrains may appear, it is important to see this chorus as essentially engaged in communication. And yet the message is

137

opaque—above all to the person whose song it is. It is the analyst who can hear this song and interpret it back in a language which is both understandable to the singer and emotionally real. The analyst serves as a *spiritual being,* at least in Plato's sense: bringing a message from the depths of a person's soul to conscious awareness. In that sense, the analyst functions as a manifestation of eros.

In neurotic enactments there is, as Freud showed, a need to repeat painful emotional experiences, sometimes to confirm them, sometimes with a wish to undo them. But there is also, as Loewald points out, *"a wish for re-doing the past*—not exclusively a wish to do away with what happened to the patient by dint of unfeeling parents or evil fates, but also a wish to experience, to deal with whatever happened in a different way."* This wish is often defeated, and what then ensues is another neurotic repetition. But there is, for Loewald, the permanent possibility of a restorative recreation. It is this possibility which, Loewald thinks, is revived in the process of working through:

> Working through seems to be the work of the ego to repeat "actively" what was experienced "passively," to repeat on a higher level—a level of more dimensions and further differentiated and integrated experience and functioning. Working through has decidedly to do with redoing, not with undoing, the past. The repetition involved here is not duplication or reiteration, but recreation, to be distinguished from reproduction.[30]

Thus Loewald makes what, for him, is the fundamental distinction between repetition and recreation. The psyche is out to repeat its tragic drama but is led to recreation and comic restoration instead.

The field of this dramatic recreation is the transference neurosis, as it occurs in the analytic situation. "The transference neurosis," says Loewald, "is the patient's love life . . . as it is re-lived in relation to a potentially new love-object, the analyst."[31] Precisely because instincts are essentially communicative, a person will thrust meanings onto significant people in the very act of libidinally engaging with them. That is why Freud was able to use the concept of transference in two related ways: first, as the transfer of libido from the ego onto objects; second, as the transfer of infantile relations from the past onto the current situation with the analyst in the analytic setting.[32] Since libido is informed with meaning—since eros is logos—the transfer of libido will necessarily be the transfer of meaningful relations.

Loewald also identifies a third use which Freud makes of transference: a repressed idea will tend to transfer its libidinal energy onto a preconscious or conscious idea, and thus get itself "covered" by it. Of course, this is not just a transfer of energy. The conscious idea now serves as a "covering": it symbolically represents the "covered" idea.[33] Thus there is a chain of transfers—from repressed to conscious idea, from ego to social world—by which daily carryings on get imbued with deep psychic meaning. Meaning is flowing from the depths of the soul out into the social environment. It is the analyst who is able to recognize this as a communication and who is able to communicate back: from the social world to the depths of the soul.

The transference neurosis, says Loewald, is an "operational concept," an "ideal construct."[34] That is, it is not so much a psychological configuration to be found in the analysand in a clinical setting, as it is the clinical setting itself—as that setting has been given meaning by the analysand. The analysand is about to weave the analyst into a repetitive drama of ancient, automatic, unconscious meanings. What is novel about the analytic situation is that the drama speaks its own meaning back to the analysand. Herein lies the crucial difference, for Loewald, between transference and transference neurosis. Transference is just the ubiquitous, automatic attempt to repeat unconscious meanings. It marks the opening phase of analytic work, as it marks all significant social interactions. What is special about the analytic situation is the possibility for endowing an ancient drama with "a new transference meaning":

> We may regard [the transference neurosis] as denoting the retransformation of a psychic illness which originated in pathogenic interactions with the important persons in the child's environment, into an interactional process with a new person, the analyst, in which the pathological infantile interactions and their intrapsychic consequences may become transparent and accessible to change by virtue of the analyst's objectivity and the emergence of novel interaction possibilities. The illness, which had become an autonomous process and an automatic response regardless of environmental changes and

reactions and even attracting and provoking pathogenic reactions similar to the original ones, becomes alive again and clarified as originating in pathogenic interactions with the environment . . .

Understood in this light, the transference neurosis is indeed a creature of the analytic situation and not simply a repeat performance or continuation of the old illness . . . The difference between transference manifestations and transference neurosis . . . then, would be that the former are essentially automatic responses, signs and symptoms of the old illness; whereas the transference neurosis is a creation of the analytic work done by analyst and patient, in which the old illness loses it autonomous and automatic character and becomes reactivated and comprehensible as a live responsive process and, as such, changing and changeable . . . As promoted by the analyst, the transference neurosis is curative; as taking place in the patient, it is a healing process.[35]

This is the essence of Loewald's response to Aristophanes' challenge. From a psychoanalytic perspective, the ultimate reason we have for thinking of eros as a developmental force is that a person's disparate transference manifestations can, in an analytic setting, develop into a transference neurosis. What had been experienced passively as fixed, rigid, and tragic comes to take on new meanings. The analysand comes to see that he is a dramatist: creator of meanings, rather than passive victim of a tragic world. The possibility thus arises to take up these meanings and go on in new ways.

This transformation occurs, in part, "by virtue of the analyst's objectivity." But because he has abandoned the seduction theory, Loewald must have a conception of objectivity which differs profoundly from Freud's. For Freud, an objective observer is detached from the reality he is describing: he views that reality *from sideways on,* his descriptions are not part of that reality, nor do they interfere with that reality. For Loewald, by contrast, an analyst is objective insofar as he presents himself to the analysand *as an object.* First, the analyst renounces libidinal-aggressive involvement with the analysand so as to ensure a certain type of emotional neutrality.[36] This does not mean that the analyst has no feelings toward the analysand, but that he does not intrude them into the erotic-communicative field which is being established. This field can then become "a *tabula rasa* for the patient's transferences." That is, it becomes a field in which the analysand can come to see his own activity shaping the field according to preestablished patterns. Second, the analyst focuses on interpreting the analysand's myriad transference distortions. In so doing, he detaches himself from the patient's phantasy and presents himself as part of a world which need not be distorted in order to be lived in.

> This objectivity cannot mean the avoidance of being available to the patient as an object. The objectivity of the analyst has reference to the patient's transference distortions. Increasingly, through the objective analysis of them, the analyst becomes not only potentially but actually available as a new object, by eliminating step by step impediments, represented by these transferences, to a new object relationship . . . The analyst in actuality does not only reflect transference distortions. In his interpretations he implies aspects of undistorted reality which the patient begins to grasp step by step as the transferences are interpreted. This undistorted reality is mediated to the patient by the analyst, mostly by the process of chiselling away the transference distortions, or, as Freud has beautifully put it, using an expression of Leonardo da Vinci, *per via di levare* as in sculpturing, not *per via di porre* as in painting. In sculpturing, the figure to be created comes into being by taking away from the material; in painting, by adding something to the canvas. In analysis, we bring out the true form by taking away the neurotic distortions.[37]

So the objectivity of the analyst cannot imply his detachment from the field: his communications with the analysand help to constitute the field of study. Nor is the analysand to remain unaffected by the analyst's observations: the whole point of the "observations" is a therapeutic intervention. Indeed, the analysand is invited to become an objective observer himself. The point of analysis is not simply to observe the field of study, but to change it.[38]

Reality, says Loewald, is "mediated to the patient by the analyst." This mediation is a form of communication which Socrates defined as erotic. The real world—that is, the world as it is undistorted by powerful phantasies—had become for the analysand a transcendent realm. The world had become inaccessible because it was hidden behind a veil of phantastic distortions. Thus genuine communication with the world had become impossible, for the analysand was, in effect, "communicating" with himself. That is, what he took to be communication with others was in fact an interaction with his own phantasies, projected onto the external world. Through repeated interpretations of transference distortions, through proper handling of the transference neurosis, the analyst is able to communicate an objective world—a world of objects rather than phantastic facsimiles—to the analysand. The analysand becomes ever more able to live in a world which is not dominated by phantasy and repetition. What has hitherto been a transcendent realm becomes immanent and inhabitable.

Through his interpretations, the analyst conveys a more highly organized understanding of self and world. In response, the analysand becomes better organized, and Loewald conceives of this as the transmission of psychological organization across a field constituted by analyst and analysand. Precisely because Loewald does not take the individual for granted, but regards individuation as a psychological achievement, it is useful to conceptualize eros as constituting a field across which psychological contents and organization may flow. And because the analyst's communications tend to facilitate psychological growth in the analysand, there is reason to conceive of eros as developmental. But, for Loewald, there is a deeper reason to conceive of this field as erotic: it is a manifestation of love.

> It also needs to be said that the love of truth is no less a passion because it desires truth rather than some less elevated end. In our field the love of truth cannot be isolated from the passion for truth to ourselves and truth in human relationships. In other fields, too, the scientist is filled with love for his object precisely in his most creative and "dispassionate" moments. Scientific detachment in its genuine form, far from excluding love, is based on it. In our work it can be truly said that in our best moments of dispassionate and objective analyzing we love our object, the patient, more than at any other time and are compassionate with his whole being.[39]

The analytic relation is itself a recreation—a recreation of the mother-infant relation—and it opens up the possibility of further recreations of both past and future. Tragic fates can be undone; comic restoration becomes a permanent possibility, an object of practical faith.

BEYOND EROS?

In conclusion, I think it fitting to outline what I take to be Loewald's legacy-as-task. His work understandably concentrates on the erotic, for he correctly saw that this was the genuine innovation in Freud's later theorizing, and thought it would provide the deepest explanation of the therapeutic potential of psychoanalysis. The death drive, insofar as it represented the latest formulation of the constancy principle, was "really nothing new." True, but it is also important to recognize that Freud invoked the death drive to explain three very different types of phenomena—aggression, unanalyzable behavior, and psychological entropy. And if we begin to question whether these three types should be lumped together, that gives us reason at least to question the basic formulation of eros versus the death drive.

There would be no reason to conceptualize the death drive as a drive if it were posited merely to account for a certain entropic tendency. If psychological organization tended simply to come undone, there would be no need for an active agent of disintegration. Rather, following Plato, organization would be like form imposed on matter. Matter itself would have no organizational or actively disruptive principle: it would just have an inherent tendency to lose form eventually. The only active principle would be eros. However, Freud also wants to account for behavior which appears *driven*. In particular, he wants to account for human destructiveness and for certain kinds of repetition compulsion. It was easy for Freud to bring these two phenomena together, for the repetitions he was concerned with tended to be violent, at least in phantasy. There were the repetitions involved in the so-called traumatic neuroses and war neuroses. Patients would live and relive with the most violent intensity the horrific experiences of war and trauma. Freud came to think that these compulsive repetitions could not be understood as disguised and conflicted attempts at gratification, so he concluded that their explanation must lie "beyond the pleasure principle." But, more importantly, these repetitions seemed recalcitrant to a talking cure. The death drive is invoked not merely to account for human destructiveness but also to mark the limits of psychoanalysis as a form of therapy. It is as though there is a force in the human psyche which is beyond words, beyond logos. As Freud so memorably put it, the death drive "works in silence."[40]

So it came to be that, in Freud's thinking, human destructiveness was linked, on the one hand, with falling apart—for destructiveness breaks down psychological structure—and, on the other hand, with the limits of analysis. But on reflection it seems odd that these phenomena should be linked by a single overarching principle. Why should destructiveness be linked with entropy? Why should either destructiveness or entropy be linked with the limits of logos? To take the most obvious point: certain forms of destructiveness are analyzable, and certain forms may even promote psychic development. To take a less obvious point: the difference between aggression and destructiveness does not seem to mark a difference in psychological state. Rather, "destructiveness" seems to suggest that a person's aggression has been successful in destroying things in the world. That is, "aggression" seems to focus on the psychological state of the actor, whereas "destructiveness" seems to focus on *the worldly outcome* of the aggression.

If so, then any theorist of the death drive faces the following dilemma. On the one hand, aggression may well promote psychological growth and development; and there is no reason to think that aggression is *in itself* unanalyzable. There would then seem to be no need to invoke something like the death drive to account for human aggression per se. On the other hand, certain forms of destruction may seem beyond the bounds of the human ability to understand or analyze, and the destruction may bring down organization all around. But it seems odd that destruction should be invoked in a psychological theory, since "destructiveness" does not seem to mark a different psychological state of the actor from "aggressiveness," but merely suggests that the "aggressiveness" has a devastating worldly effect. Should a basic category of a psychological theory depend, not on a psychological state, but on certain worldly effects of that state?

Loewald offers a remarkable answer to this problem in his account of the negative therapeutic reaction.[41] There are certain patients who notoriously get worse rather than better in response to a talking cure. The moral masochist, for example, will often get worse in analysis, at least for a while, because, as Loewald puts it, "improvement to him is a sign of a lessening of that self-punishment that he requires."[42] This masochism may well be analyzable as, say, an unconscious sense of guilt; and the initial deterioration of the analysand's condition may ultimately be understood in terms of a libidinal fixation to a neurotic organization of experience. In such cases, the analysand may eventually come to understand his self-destructiveness as an expression of a guilt which can be worked through, and eventually abandoned. But, says Loewald, in some cases there may be an "irreducible residue" of self-destructiveness which remains. That which resists all attempts at analysis is *a fortiori* unanalyzable. It is this surd negativity for which, Loewald thinks, the death drive needs to be invoked.

Loewald suggests we can understand this unanalyzable negativity as the outcome of severe, early disturbance of psychological development. If the child has a bad-enough parent, disturbing development early enough, often enough, and severely enough, he will never get to the psychological stage where aggressive forces can be organized—for example, as an unconscious sense of guilt. Only then can analysis yield understanding and insight. But without that initial organization, "the patient cannot be persuaded he feels guilty—*he feels sick.*"[43] That is, he lacks the psychological organization to move from having a stomachache to feeling guilty: feeling pain in his stomach is, for him, the psychological end of the line.

One fascinating consequence of Loewald's account is that "destructiveness" does, after all, become a psychological category. The bad-enough parent's aggression is a form of destructiveness because it has a certain destructive effect in the world. But the part of the world in which that effect occurs is *inside the psyche* of her child. And the effect has been so fundamentally devastating that the child's psyche is not merely disorganiz*ed*, but disorganiz*ing*. It cannot grow in response to normal nurturing, for in its disorganized state, it tends to dis-organize its own experience. This psychological state is destructive: it tears asunder what would normally be organizing worldly experiences, while remaining actively disorganized itself. "One might say in epigrammatic form the patient does not say no to the therapist or to any other person, but to himself."[44] In this way, Loewald rescues "destructiveness" as a topic for psychology and plausibly links it to the limits of analysis.

Yet there remains a question why these phenomena need to be linked by a fundamental principle like the death drive. To be sure, the child's disorganizing psyche is now both destructive (of psychological structure) and unanalyzable. But why couldn't this just be the unfortunate and contingent outcome of forces—say, the mother's aggression and other deprivations—which are themselves analyzable? From the mere fact that bad parenting can produce a disorganizing psyche, it does not follow that there needs to be a fundamental disorganizing principle.

Furthermore, there is the ironic possibility that positing a *fundamental* force for disorganization might have a disorganizing effect on psychoanalytic theory. Any attempt at theorizing will be an effort to carve up psychological reality at the joints. The death drive brings together destructiveness and the limits of analysis into a basic unity. Might we thereby be blinding ourselves to more natural unities? So, for example, suppose we simply took the *limits of analysis* as a category, and made no presumption as to whether what lay beyond the bounds was destructive or constructive. Then we would include in that category not only the unanalyzable destructiveness of the negative therapeutic reaction but also the creative genius which Freud acknowledged lay beyond the bounds of psychoanalytic understanding. In that case, the fundamental category might be *the sublime.* The sublime, one might say, is sublimely indifferent as to whether its manifestations are, from a human perspective, constructive or destructive. And in place of the opposition of eros versus the death drive, we might have instead the opposition of *the sublime versus the mundane.* The limits of analysis would then, plausibly enough, coincide with the limits of human understanding.

This is not the place to pursue these thoughts. But it is worth noting, in closing, that even on this reconceptualization, eros would retain a fundamental role. For Socrates, eros links the sublime and mundane realms, and thereby invests human life with meaning and value. In the absence of eros, we have tragedy: the sublime and mundane realms may intersect, sometimes with horrible consequences, but the meaning of that intersection remains humanly incomprehensible.[45] In the presence of eros, we have the permanent possibility of comic restoration. Hans Loewald dedicated his life to exploring redemption as an erotic possibility. The death drive was "nothing new." But perhaps we now need something new which will serve as a genuine complement to eros. This, I believe, is one legacy of Hans Loewald's work.

CHAPTER 7

Eros and Unknowing:
The Psychoanalytic Significance
of Plato's *Symposium*

The *Symposium* is the only attempt ever made to plumb the philosophical significance of party-crashing. Not that it was much of a party: Alcibiades' drunken entrance puts an end to a series of sober, sometimes ponderous, speeches on the nature of love. It is only with Alcibiades' disruption that the fun really begins. But what, precisely, is being disrupted? At one level, the answer is obvious: the symposium. Not only does Alcibiades disrupt the party-game, substituting a speech about Socrates for the conventional praise of the god Eros; he engages in a jealous and comic struggle with Socrates, ostensibly over Agathon, making further speeches impossible. A group of drunks then wanders in: "there was noise everywhere, and everyone was made to start drinking in no particular order" (223b).[1] At that point, many of the original guests leave. The *Symposium* is thus as much concerned with the symposium's undoing as it is with rendering an account of the symposium itself. Why should that be?

I do not think one can answer this question satisfactorily so long as one assumes that Alcibiades' speech humorously and indirectly confirms the Socratic account of the erotic. On one familiar reading, Alcibiades' speech reveals Socrates as impervious to Alcibiades' sexual advances, and thus as further up the "ladder of love" than Alcibiades, who is stuck on a lower rung. It then becomes difficult to view the disruption as more than incidental farce. And yet Alcibiades' entrance and the subsequent undoing of the symposium is the most dramatic event of the evening. The suspicion arises that what is being dramatized is not merely the undoing of the symposium, but the undoing of the *Symposium*'s account of love. The drama of the *Symposium* would, on this interpretation, stand in an uneasy relation to the speeches: indeed, Alcibiades would be seen as *acting out* a refutation of Socrates' theory of love. Of course, Alcibiades makes a speech too, like all the other symposiasts. But the importance of the speech lies not in what he *says* in it, but in what he *does* with it. Alcibiades is using his erotic attachment to Socrates to stay just where he is; and Socrates is unwilling or unable to do anything about it. It is, I think, too easy to account for Alcibiades' failure to ascend to higher forms of erotic engagement as due to a flaw in his character or, perhaps, to a lack of empathy on Socrates' part. That may be true; but the point is not to illustrate the failures of two particular individuals, but to call into question the very idea of eros as a developmental force.

ONE PLACE TO BEGIN is with the *Symposium*'s hazy ending. Aristodemus, the supposed eyewitness who provided the original account of the evening, had fallen asleep for a long time. When he woke, Socrates was talking to the only two people who had not left and were still awake, Aristophanes and Agathon (223d): "Aristodemus couldn't remember exactly what they were saying—he'd missed the first part of their discussion and he was half-asleep anyway—but the main point was that Socrates was trying to prove to them that authors should be able to write both comedy and tragedy: the skillful tragic dramatist should also be a comic poet."

For as long as there is anything we can recognize as Western philosophy, interpreters will be puzzling over this tantalizing morsel. Enough is said to suggest that Socrates is making (what Plato takes to be) an important point; but there is no explanation. Why should it be important that a poet be able to write both tragedy and comedy? The answer cannot ultimately be about the author—that he or she should be so versatile as to write two different types of drama—but must be about the dramatic work itself. Socrates' point, I believe, is that a tragic poet ought to be able to write a single drama which can be read both as a tragedy and as a comedy. Perhaps the *Symposium* is just such a drama. After all, why should Plato be offering advice to the poets and not be trying to follow it himself? The end of the *Symposium* would then provide a clue as to how it itself is to be read.

The comic dimensions of the *Symposium* are fairly straightforward. There are, most notably, Alcibiades' drunken entrance and his bitchy squabble with Socrates over who is the victim in their love affair—and there is, of course, their hilarious rivalry for Agathon. Alcibiades enters blind drunk: he literally cannot see what he is doing. He is full of passion for Agathon, but has to be helped by friends to a seat next to him. As he is led to his seat, "he kept trying to take his ribbons off so that he could crown Agathon with them, but all he succeeded in doing was to push them further down his head until they finally slipped over his eyes. What with the ivy and all, he didn't see Socrates, who had made room for him on the couch" (213a).

In true comic fashion, it is in sitting next to the intended object of his desire, Agathon, that Alcibiades also unintentionally sits next to his old love, Socrates. He is unwittingly starting an affair in the presence of an old boyfriend, whom he has not got over, and with whom he will soon enter into an absurd rivalry (213b–c):

> "We can all three fit on my couch," Agathon said.
> "What a good idea!" Alcibiades replied. "But wait a moment! Who's the third?" As he said this, he turned around, and it was only then that he saw Socrates. No sooner had he seen him than he leaped up and cried: "Good lord, what's going on here? It's Socrates! You've trapped me again! You always do this to me—all of a sudden you'll turn up out of nowhere where I least expect you!"

Socrates, for his part, takes on a comic role of such proportion as to be unique in the Platonic corpus (213c–d):

"I beg you, Agathon," Socrates said, "protect me from this man! You can't imagine what it's like to be in love with him: from the very first moment he realized how I felt about him, he hasn't allowed me to say two words to anybody else—what am I saying, I can't so much as look at an attractive man but he flies into a fit of jealous rage. He yells; he threatens; he can hardly keep from slapping me around! Please, try to keep him under control. Could you perhaps make him forgive me? And if you can't, if he gets violent, will you defend me? The fierceness of his passion terrifies me."

The image of a cringing Socrates, hiding behind Agathon, is truly ridiculous.

BUT WHERE IS THE TRAGEDY? The answer must be "nowhere" if Diotima's ascent is taken at face value. What could be tragic about the erotic if, when pursued, it takes us ever upward toward true beauty? In fact, I think there is a tragedy in the *Symposium;* and it consists in the very same meeting of Socrates and Alcibiades.

As Diotima questions Socrates, it emerges that Eros can neither be divine and immortal, nor can it be merely mortal. Rather, Eros lives in an "intermediate region" and shuttles back and forth as a messenger. This is what it is to be a *spiritual being:* to interpret each realm to the other. Spiritual beings carry prayers and sacrifices from humans to gods and bring back commands and gifts from gods to humans (202e). On this interpretation, Eros bridges the gap between the transcendent and immanent realms. Eros thus creates a "transitional space" whereby mundane life is invested with infinite value and transcendent meaning. Eros would then provide the profoundest of legitimations for the greatest of truly human concerns.

We have a tragedy when there is a recognition that neither Eros nor any other being can perform the tasks which Diotima assigns to it. Though the divine and human realms intersect, with profound and often painful consequences for human life, there remains an unbridgeable gap in the sense that the deepest meaning of that intersection will remain humanly incomprehensible. In that sense, tragic consciousness arises when there is a recognition that there can be no truly spiritual beings. As Jean-Pierre Vernant puts it, "The particular domain of tragedy lies in this border zone where human actions hinge on divine powers and where their true meaning, unsuspected by even those who initiated them and take responsibility for them, is only revealed when it becomes a part of an order that is beyond man and escapes him."[2] In the meeting of Socrates and Alcibiades, divine and human manifestations of the erotic intersect; and it is their failure to communicate which casts doubt on the idea that anything like Diotima's path of ascent from the mundane to the transcendent could be possible. Though intrigued, fascinated, and captivated by Socrates, Alcibiades can neither learn from him nor grow in response to him. As any contemporary reader of the *Symposium* would have known, Alcibiades will go on to betray his polis with tragic consequences for Athenian civilization.

IT IS ARISTOPHANES who raises the possibility that love is a distraction from, indeed a retribution for, trying to ascend to a higher level of existence. Of course, the myth is told in rivalrous terms—the original humans tried to ascend to heaven to attack the gods and were split in half as punishment (190c–d); but the point is that they were attempting to approach a divine level of existence. Eros is the force innate in every human which "calls back the halves of our original nature together; it tries to make one out of two and heal the wound of human nature" (191d). But if humans are now impelled to spend their lives searching for their other halves, they are drawn into the political-social realm in search of human completion. That is, this absorption in the purely human realm serves as a distraction from any tendency to strive for the transcendent. "'Eros' is the name for our pursuit of wholeness, for our desire to be complete" (192e). In this myth, eros functions as a *resistance* to ascent.

It is, I believe, this formulation of the erotic which Freud called "transference." For transference just is human love life as it manifests itself in the social realm.[3] Psychoanalysis as a mode of therapy was, Freud thought, crafted specifically for the so-called transference neuroses:[4] for it is these neuroses which demand that others conform to set roles. Transference is of its essence a form of political engagement: it is an attempt to shape society, or at least the immediate social environment, according to a certain image. That image might broadly be construed as an image of the person's "other half." That is, transference is an attempt to make the world over according to an image of what would gratify one's most basic wishes. Though an expression of erotic longing, transference is the erotic attempt to end that longing by "finding" what one is missing. Psycho-analysis can be efficacious only because the analysand's transference will tend to make the analyst over into various images of the analysand's missing half. It is this erotic engagement of the analysand for the analyst which can be put to therapeutic use.

It is remarkable that transference should have any therapeutic value, since, as Freud noted, transference regularly manifests itself as a *resistance* to analysis. Transference is an archaic and insistent demand that one's immediate world satisfy one's longings. There is almost no room within that demand for reflection upon itself; nor is there tolerance for anything which will undermine its power. Transference itself, the human-erotic engagement in the social world, stands as a constant obstacle to its own analysis.

So, for example, in the immediate aftermath of an interpretation, it is common for the analysand to take up a transferential attitude with re-spect to it. She might say, "I can't believe I didn't think of that myself! Here I've been in analysis for years, and you still have to make that point for me: I seem incapable of getting it for myself. You must think I'm hopeless—you're rolling your eyeballs, thinking, 'God, won't she ever get it?'! I bet you can't wait to get rid of me." Here the analysand is casting herself in the role of helpless little girl, and the analyst as benign but exas-perated parent. Of course, it is precisely her "helplessness" which is de-signed to keep the analyst bound to her forever: eternally fixed as the be-nign and exasperated parent who will put up with her infinite inability to grow up.[5] The point of this ordinary example is to show that forming an attitude to the interpretation serves as a way of ignoring its content. What was actually said by the analyst has hardly been heard, and its signifi-cance is clouded over in a storm of emotional reactions. The only way for-ward is to analyze this too.

Analysis of the transference is the mode of analytic therapy, but on this conception of transference it is a mistake to think of eros as itself a developmental force. Eros is here functioning as an obstacle to development: it is a demand that the world remain forever fixed according to a certain image of one's other half. Ironically, analytic therapy requires an obstacle to be overcome. Eros as transference is necessary, not as a developmental force, but as providing the gradient against which development can occur. As Freud put it, "Transference which seems ordained to become the greatest obstacle to psychoanalysis becomes its most powerful ally."[6]

Now Socrates and Diotima are themselves masters of reversals. Socrates, through a variety of frustrations and seductions, is able to convert Alcibiades from the loved one *(eromenos)* into the lover *(erastes)* (compare, for example, 219e and 217a). Diotima, for her part, reverses the preferred erotic position from *eromenos* to *erastes*.

First, she undermines the traditional praise of eros, diagnosing it as based on a confusion of loving and being loved (204c; compare 201e). The *loved one* may have beautiful properties, but the lover himself must be lacking: he is filled with longing for that which he does not have (200a–b, d; 201b–c; 202d; 206a). But, having undermined the traditional praise, Diotima undermines the idea that this revised conception of eros diminishes it. For although the lover is filled with desire, this desire is ultimately the desire to give birth (206c–e). What love wants is not beauty, but to give birth in beauty (206e). Beauty provides the environment in which the lover can give birth to his greatest creations. And in reproduction and creation humans approach immortality. Should one create something truly fine, one will convert even the gods from loved ones to lovers: "The love of the gods belongs to anyone who has given birth to true virtue and nourished it, and if any human being could become immortal it would be he" (212a–b).

But for all their reversals, neither Socrates nor Diotima seems to understand that eros itself stands in need of a reversal; at least, if it is going to function in a developmental process. Diotima correctly sees that endurance and stability in the human realm depends on constant acts of creativity (207d–208b):

"mortal nature seeks so far as possible to live forever and be immortal. And this is possible in one way only: by reproduction, because it always leaves behind a new young one in place of the old . . . And it's not just in his body but in his soul too, for none of his manners, customs, opinions, desires, pleasures, pains or fears ever remains the same, but some are coming to be in him, while others are passing away . . . And in that way everything mortal is preserved, not, like the divine, by always being the same in every way, but because what is departing and aging leaves behind something new, something such as it had been. By this device, Socrates," she said, "what is mortal shares in immortality."

That one needs constant creation in order to keep one's manners and customs—one's culture—in place is precisely the insight that transference is the erotic insistence that the world be a certain way. One needs to be forever creating the world according to a certain image in order for that world to endure. Freud saw transference as a repetition, but that is because he took the world for granted. Whether one sees an action as a repetition or as a continuation of the enduring structure depends on how one is counting. If one assumes a given intersubjective world, one will see a person as repeatedly treating people in his environment on the model of, say, his mother. However, if one does not assume a given world, but treats a person's transference as his attempt to create a meaningful world in which to live, then it appears not so much that he is treating a succession of people as mother so much as he is trying to keep "mother" alive. From this perspective, mother is not repeated; she endures.[7]

Diotima sees that we must continually create our customs, manners, and opinions in order for them to remain the same. And she sees eros as the motive force for this creation. Why, then, does she not see eros as a form of fixation, forever tying us to a stultifying way of life? Isn't neurosis an attempt at immortality: an attempt to create a rigid structure, a world, impervious to alteration? No experience can change this world, because all experience is already interpreted to fit. Neurosis is a constant effort "to give birth in beauty": it's just that the neurotic creates his loved one as beautiful. That is, in the positive transference the analysand makes the analyst into a loved one and, in the presence of this created beauty, proceeds to create her world. The problem is that were there no analysis of transference as a resistance, there would be no reason to think that the analysand would grow at all. Diotima seems to think that people are going to develop by the force of logic alone. At the first stage, for example, the lover is a lover of one body:

> then *he should realize* that the beauty of any one body is brother to the beauty of any other and that *if he is to pursue beauty of form,* he'd be very foolish not to think that the beauty of all bodies is one and the same. *When he grasps this he must become a lover of all beautiful bodies,* and he must think that this wild gaping after just one body is a small thing and despise it. (210a–b; emphasis added)

But Diotima has given us no reason to believe that the erotically engaged lover is pursuing beauty of form, nor that even the lover of form will not become so erotically hooked on a single beautiful instance that he is incapable of looking anywhere else. "After this *he must think* that the beauty of people's souls is more valuable than the beauty of their bodies" (210c). Why *must* he think *that?*[8] The assumptions seem to be, first, that it is true that a beautiful soul is more beautiful than a beautiful body; and, second, that a lover's heart will track the truth. These are powerful assumptions. And if the question at issue is "Why think that eros is a developmental force, rather than a force which retards development?" it becomes difficult not to conclude that Diotima's account begs the question.

IT IS AT THE END of Socrates' speech that Alcibiades makes his boisterous entrance. And his performance is, I think, a demonstration of what is missing in Diotima's conception of eros. Alcibiades is going to manifest his refusal or inability to develop according to Diotima's path of ascent. Since he is the incarnation of the human-erotic, his drama must cast doubt on the very idea of eros as a force for ascent. Freud recognized an inverse relation between the ability consciously to entertain wishes, phantasies, and memories and the impulsion to act them out in dramas whose full significance escapes the actor.[9] But if there is this inverse relation, then acting out must serve as a test of any therapeutic method designed to promote conscious awareness. If acting out does not abate, there must be something going wrong in the therapy. And one must face the possibility that the problem lies in the therapeutic method itself. It is even possible that a fundamental concept on which the therapeutic method is based—in this case, eros—is itself impugned.

Alcibiades enters drunk, and it is instantly clear that he is locked in a cycle of repetition, not on a path of ascent. He has come to seduce Agathon, as he has seduced countless times in the past. Nothing is to change; the same drama of seduction is to endure forever. It is Socrates who, by his mere physical presence on the couch, is going to get in the way of this being just another seduction. And yet there is even here a hint of repetition: "It's Socrates! You've trapped me *again! You always do this to me*" (213c). On Diotima's account, Alcibiades' speech ought to be his creation in the presence of beauty. Officially, though, the encomium is delivered in the spirit of revenge. "I shall never forgive you!" he tells Socrates. "I promise you, you'll pay for this!" (213d–e). And he asks his audience: "Should I unleash myself upon him? Should I give him his punishment in front of all of you?" (214e). No doubt this "punishment" is meant to be sadomasochistically exciting; it is one more attempt at seduction (whether of Socrates, Agathon, or both). But that is hardly a form of growth in the presence of Socrates. Rather, it is a massive resistance to any potential for growth which the example of Socrates might offer.

The portrait Alcibiades paints is of an erotic Socrates containing a divine principle within. On the outside he looks like a satyr, possessed of powerful sexual appetites and the power to arouse others; but on the inside, like a Silenus statue, he is full of tiny statues of the gods (215a–d) Alcibiades sees this as blasphemy. He compares Socrates to the satyr Marsyas, whose music was divine but who dared rival the gods and was flayed alive in punishment. Indeed, from Alcibiades' perspective, Socrates is even more impudent than Marsyas: "The only difference between you and Marsyas is that you need no instruments; you do exactly what he does, but with words alone . . . let anyone—man, woman or child—listen to you or even to a poor account of what you say—and we are all transported, completely possessed" (215c–d).

It is as though Socrates is the original human of Aristophanes' myth: complete unto himself, already possessing his "other half," and thus with no distraction from becoming as divine as possible. This, from Alcibiades' vantage, is a very dangerous position to be in. It invites divine retribution.

One would expect Alcibiades, the incarnation of eros-as-distraction, the one who is forever locked in the search for his other half, to avoid Socrates' fate at all costs. And so he does. Alcibiades portrays Socrates' influence as a kind of rape. His words completely possess any listener; and thus the listener is absolved of responsibility. Alcibiades seems to be saying, "Please, gods, do not punish me for having any association with this blasphemer; his influence is totally out of my control, and completely his fault." This is transference as resistance: Alcibiades as embodiment of human eros will do anything to resist following Socrates' example toward the divine.

On the one hand, Alcibiades insists that Socrates is absolutely unique in his experience (215e, 216b, 219c, 221c). On the other hand, Alcibiades is determined not to learn anything from him. Alcibiades says that Socrates is the only person who has made him feel ashamed; but he is unaware that shame itself is a distraction. He can go on forever beating his breast that he is not worthy; and all that will take up time which would have better been spent inquiring seriously into how he should live. Apollodorus goes around beating his breast too (173d)—Socrates seems to have that effect on young men; but all that is a repetition, sound and fury signifying distraction from the important task at hand. Alcibiades is perfectly aware that this is so (216b–c):

> "I know perfectly well I can't prove he's wrong when he tells me what I should do; yet, *the moment I leave his side, I go back to my old ways:* I cave in to my desire to please the crowd. *My whole life has become one constant effort to escape from him and keep away,* but *when I see him, I feel deeply ashamed, because I'm doing nothing about my way of life,* though I have already agreed with him that I should." (Emphases added)

Alcibiades recognizes that his relation with Socrates is having no developmental effect on him. He is locked in a transferential repetition: they do their familiar dance together, Alcibiades reverts to his same old ways, then feels ashamed; and so it goes, round and round again. Alcibiades is absolutely correct that his life has been given over to escaping from Socrates—*that* is his erotic response. What he does not understand is that shame is just one more way of keeping away from Socrates' influence.

Alcibiades gives this account of the basis of Socrates' influence over him: "I once caught him when he was open like Silenus' statues, and I had a glimpse of the figures he keeps hidden within: they were so godlike—so bright and beautiful, so utterly amazing—that I no longer had a choice—I just had to do whatever he told me" (216e–217a). This account is suspicious for various reasons, most notably because Alcibiades has just told us that he has *never* been able to do what Socrates has told him. Alcibiades says that he no longer had any choice: again there is the pretense that nothing he does around Socrates is up to him. And the account of why he has lost control is unconvincing. He has come up against something which awes him, but he is doing everything in his power to avoid understanding what it is.

Now Alcibiades does go through the motions of wanting to learn from Socrates. "Nothing is more important to me," he tells Socrates, "than becoming the best man I can be, and no one can help me more than you to reach that aim" (218d). But it soon becomes clear that this is just an attempted seduction. After a brief exchange, Socrates makes the following proposition: "Let's consider things together. We'll always do what seems the best to the two of us" (219b). Instead of following the proposed method, Alcibiades exults that his seduction has finally worked: "His words made me think my own had finally hit their mark, that he was smitten by his arrows" (219b). His response is to get in bed with Socrates. The purported effort at self-improvement is nothing more than an erotic distraction from any such real effort.

Socrates, as is well known, spends the night between the sheets with Alcibiades, sexually unmoved. Instead of reflecting on why that might be, Alcibiades prefers the melodrama of insult, outrage, and humiliation (219c–d):

> this hopelessly arrogant, this unbelievably insolent man—he turned me down! He spurned my beauty, of which I was so proud, members of the jury—for this is what you are: you're here to sit in judgement of Socrates' amazing arrogance and pride . . .
>
> How do you think I felt after that? Of course, I was deeply humiliated, but also I couldn't help admiring his natural character, his moderation, his fortitude.

The outrage, like the shame, is one more way of avoiding any lesson the example of Socrates might have to offer. To be sure, Alcibiades also admires him. But in this context, the admiration leads to nothing: Alcibiades cannot learn from Socrates, nor can he let go of him and move on. He is fixed in a meaningless repetition in which no growth is possible.

Even the absurd rivalry with Socrates over Agathon is a distraction. He cannot let go of the idea that his interaction with Socrates is in the field of seduction and betrayal: if he is not going to seduce Socrates, he will spend his time worrying that Socrates will seduce someone else, perhaps even the person he, Alcibiades, would like to seduce after his failure with Socrates. If he can't succeed at seducing Socrates, at least he can waste his time being jealous. Suffering a jealous rivalry with Socrates is preferable to learning anything from him.

❖ ❖ ❖

FOR HIS PART, Socrates is at times indifferent to the human-erotic; at times he takes advantage of it. At the end of Alcibiades' speech, Socrates offers what Lacan has called an interpretation (222c–d):[10]

> You're perfectly sober after all, Alcibiades. Otherwise you could never have concealed your motive so gracefully . . . As if the real point of all this has not been simply to make trouble between Agathon and me! You think that I should be in love with you and no one else, while you, and no one else should be in love with Agathon—well, we were not deceived; we've seen through your little satyr play. Agathon, my friend, don't let him get away with it: let no one come between us!

If this is an interpretation, it is a poor one. Alcibiades is obviously putting the make on Agathon, and his jealous rivalry with Socrates is flagrant. What is concealed is that Agathon has no importance other than as a pawn in Alcibiades' erotic game with Socrates. Instead of pointing that out, Socrates plays along. He does not say, as an analyst might, that all of Alcibiades' goings-on about Agathon are an attempt at distraction: an attempt to distract himself from the fact that the real issue for him is his relation with Socrates; and an attempt to distract Socrates into a rivalrous triangle. In short, Socrates avoids the transference-meaning of Alcibiades' actings out, and thus he collaborates with Alcibiades' evasion. Indeed, Socrates seems to want to show that if the game is jealous rivalry, he can win. Socrates has only to point out that should Agathon stay next to Alcibiades, then he, Socrates, will not be able to praise Agathon. It is, Socrates says, a speech he would very much like to give. The old seducer! "Alcibiades, nothing can make me stay next to you now," Agathon says. "I'm moving no matter what. I simply *must* hear what Socrates has to say about me" (223a). If Socrates' performance is to be evaluated along the lines of analytic technique, he must be either dismissed as incompetent or condemned as a lecherous sadist, taking advantage of transference, rather than analyzing it.

At times Socrates seems divinely remote from human eros; at other times he seems like a camp queen. Here he is willing to let Alcibiades spend the night next to him with an erection, with only his own frustration to go on as a source of education. Many males who have spent such a night might look back on it as a "learning experience," but few will think of it as a path of ascent. In a sense, Socrates is only making himself available to those few. Only those who *already* have a divine-erotic principle within them will be able to learn from Socrates' example, but they are the ones who don't really need him. Socrates may provide an occasion for their growth, but they, like Socrates, will find their occasions. The others Socrates leaves to their own devices. He seems unwilling to engage with the resistance of human eros.

But Socrates' indifference is not uniform. When Alcibiades discovers his presence next to Agathon, Socrates vamps: "I beg you, Agathon, protect me from this man! You cannot imagine what it's like to be in love with him" (213c–d). What could such a performance do, other than inflame Alcibiades? Both his desire for revenge and his erotic engagement: "I shall never forgive you! I promise you, you'll pay for this!" How many lovers have had this exchange just before engaging in sexual activity in which love and revenge are hopelessly mixed? Instead of helping Alcibiades understand this, Socrates eggs him on. If eros be the music of resistance, Socrates seems to be saying, play on!

❖ ❖ ❖

SOCRATES IS OFTEN TREATED as a proto-psychoanalyst. And there certainly are resonances between Socratic and psychoanalytic technique. First, his method of cross-examination is designed to elicit contradictory beliefs which had remained hidden inside the interlocutor. In that sense, Socrates, like an analyst, is engaged in an effort to make the unconscious conscious. Second, Socrates had a fundamental question—"How shall I live?"—which, I believe, is also the fundamental question of psychoanalysis. Humans are the unique animals who can pose that question to themselves and take steps to shape their lives as an answer. Indeed, for Socrates, humans constitute themselves as distinctively human by their efforts to ask and answer this question: that is why, for him, the unexamined life is not worth living. The point of Socratic inquiry is to ask and answer that question well. Similarly, people enter analysis because they suspect they are not answering the question well. Analysis is itself a manifestation of the analysand's fundamental question; it is also an inquiry into the ways the attempt to answer the question have been distorted, as well as a therapeutic attempt to undo those distortions. Third, Socrates has a fundamental rule—state only what you believe—which bears a family resemblance to the fundamental rule of psychoanalysis. Although the fundamental rule of analysis enjoins the analysand to state whatever comes into his mind without censorship, the rationale for this rule is that free association reveals one's psychic commitments. That is the point of the Socratic rule: the interlocutor must be committed to what he says. It is precisely because he is committed that if he becomes aware that he is in a contradictory position, he will be changed by that awareness. The real difference between the Socratic and psychoanalytic versions of the fundamental rule is that psychoanalysis has a broader conception of what constitutes a psychic commitment. It is not concerned merely with the commitment of belief, but also with the commitments of wish and phantasy. Finally, for both Socratic and psychoanalytic practice, the fundamental task is the improvement of one's psyche. For Socrates, it was the only truly important task; it is a regulative principle of psychoanalysis. Should anything be shown not to contribute to psychic improvement, it must thereby be excluded from psychoanalytic technique.

But there the resemblance ends. The most significant dissimilarity lies in the conception of what constitutes psychological improvement. In Diotima's tale of ascent, a person leaves his particularity behind. He moves from a love of one beautiful body to a love of all beautiful bodies, from a love of bodies to a love of souls, from that to a love of laws, and then on to a love of wisdom. Having moved along this path, he is ready to grasp "the goal of loving," the beautiful itself (211a–d):

> The beautiful will not appear to him in the guise of a face or hands or anything else that belongs to the body. It will not appear to him as one idea or one kind of knowledge. It is not anywhere in another thing, as in an animal, or in earth, or in heaven, or in anything else, but itself by itself with itself, it is always one in form . . . This is what it is to go aright, or be led by another, into the mystery of love: one goes always upwards for the sake of this beauty, starting out from beautiful things and using them like rising stairs . . . so that in the end he comes to know just what it is to be beautiful.

From the point of view of these "rites of love," beautiful individuals have only instrumental value: they are to be used, stepped on, like rungs on a ladder which leads away from any concern *for them*. And after one has climbed the ladder, the best thing would be to kick it away. Diotima says (211d–212a):

> But how would it be, in our view, if someone got to see the Beautiful itself, absolute, pure, unmixed, not polluted by human flesh or colors or any other great nonsense of mortality, but if he could see the divine beauty itself in its one form? . . . in that life alone, when he looks at beauty in the only way that beauty can be seen—only then will it become possible for him to give birth, not to images of virtue (because he's in touch with no images), but to true virtue (because he's in touch with true beauty).

By falling in love with beauty itself, one comes to see human flesh and colors as a pollution, a "great nonsense of mortality." From a divine perspective, beauty is not immanent: "it is not *in* another thing, as in an animal, or in earth" (211a–b).

This conception of the divine is the source of the tragedy of the *Symposium*. The "rites of love" proceed via a series of identifications. The lover becomes ever more like the object of his love: as the object of his loving changes, so does he. That is why loving ever better objects is psychologi-cally beneficial. So "the goal of all loving" is not simply to love something without particularity, but to leave any particularity in oneself behind. It is clear that in loving the divine one becomes like the divine: "The love of the gods belongs to anyone who has given birth to true virtue and nour-ished it, and if any human being could become immortal, it would be he" (212a–b).

One must, then, become disdainful of one's own mortal nature, treat-ing it as not part of one's true self. This accounts for Socrates' indifference to Alcibiades' struggles. Socrates has made the journey, he has become as divine as humanly possible, and though he remains in the human realm, he is no longer part of it. He looks on the humanity of the human world with the indifference of the gods. Alcibiades is, of course, as human as they come. He is trapped in the human-erotic, and the only help which Socrates offers is as an exemplar in the human realm of divine beauty: that is to say, he offers Alcibiades no help at all.

It misses the point to say that Socrates did not understand that human eros functions as a resistance. Nor does it seem accurate to say that he did not understand how to analyze resistance. Socrates had no interest in an-alyzing resistance. Why should a god care if the human realm resists the divine? It is only humans who care about that, and, in becoming divinely inspired, Socrates has left his humanity behind. Socrates is interested in Alcibiades only insofar as he has the potential to develop a divine princi-ple within himself. To that end, Socrates need only stand as the exemplar that he is. But insofar as Alcibiades is trapped in the human-erotic, he can, from Socrates' perspective, go fuck himself. It does not matter to Socrates what the consequences are. From the vantage of Athenian cul-ture, this encounter between Alcibiades and Socrates must be judged a failure of inestimable cost. Nothing less is at stake than the future of one of world's great civilizations. And yet, from a divine point of view, human politics is by and large a distraction.[11] It just does not matter which partic-ular form the distraction takes.

This is the tragedy of the *Symposium*. For 2,500-odd years Western civi-lization has been trying to comprehend the demise of classical Greece. Plato seems to suggests that there is something in this undoing which must remain incomprehensible. Indeed, the *Symposium* is a dramatization in miniature of this disintegration. The party falls apart, as does Greece, because there is an intersection of the divine and human realms, the full meaning of which is incomprehensible in purely human terms. In human terms, it looks as though the tragedy is divine punishment for humans' being erotic animals. At least, that is what I imagine the chorus singing.

On the interpretation I have suggested so far, one would read the *Symposium* first as a comedy, then as a tragedy. The tragedy would give the deeper meaning. But I doubt this can be Plato's intention. The question would thus be: how can one now go on to read the *Symposium* again as a comedy? I think one would have to ascend to a divine perspective, like that of Zeus after he has split humans in half. Watching humans spending all their time groping for their other halves must be a ridiculous sight indeed. Perhaps Socrates occupied something like that perspective. If so, then the reason an author needs to be able to write both comedy and tragedy is that he needs to be able to portray an event like the meeting of Socrates and Alcibiades from both a human and a divine perspective. Tragedy purports to give an account of the intersection of divine and human realms, but it does so from a purely human perspective. Comedy represents the best human attempt to give an account of that same intersection from a divine perspective.

BY NOW IT SHOULD BE CLEAR that the psychoanalytic approach to the human-erotic differs fundamentally from the Socratic. First, psychoanalytic "ascent" is toward individuation rather than away from it. Instead of a process by which one sheds one's particularity, one's particularity is enhanced by an increasing sense of one's own subjectivity. Phantasy is an activity which becomes idiosyncratic through and through. The very idea of a day residue suggests that in crafting a dream or a phantasy, we tend to take up chance experiences of the day, often insignificant in themselves, and invest them with peculiar meanings. So not only is there an idiosyncratic route we each take through the world; there is an idiosyncratic choice of experiences to invest with phantastic meaning. Moreover, though archaic thinking tends to be concrete, imagistic, and fluid, there

165

are idiosyncratic ways in which that concreteness and fluidity are expressed.[12]

It is our idiosyncratic phantasy lives which, from a psychoanalytic perspective, lie at the heart of our creativity. Of course phantasy life does tend, as Plato might put it, to be "polluted by human flesh" and "the great nonsense of mortality." Phantasy takes up the body and the bodily to express itself, and may enliven the body in so doing. The aim, then, is not to leave the human realm behind, but to get deeper into it—its smells, feels, textures, and the imaginary meanings we give to them. Whatever "higher" or "deeper" meanings there may be, they do not transcend human life, but lie immanent in it. The body, its drives, and the bodily expression of mind all lend vitality to "higher" mental functions and to social life. It is this particular subjectivity with which we are pregnant: and it is from this that we give birth in beauty.

The psychoanalytic situation provides the beautiful environment in which to give birth. Of course, this requires that the analysand create the analyst as beautiful. In short, the analysand has already given birth before the official labor begins. Paradoxically, though, the beautiful environment serves as a resistance to the birthing process. In making the analyst beautiful, one also makes her into someone from whom one wants love, not analysis. The myriad demands for love thus function as a resistance to the process of analysis. The repressed then tends to be acted out in these demands, and, indirectly, they become the subject matter for analysis. It is because the erotic is repressed that giving birth in beauty is always a difficult labor—a labor of love. This is what Diotima's ascent lacks: the resistance which needs to be overcome. And herein lies the biggest difference between the Socratic and psychoanalytic approach to the human-erotic. For Socrates, eros may function as a divine source of ascent, but for those in whom it functions as a source of social distraction, there is nothing to be done. From a psychoanalytic perspective, by contrast, this erotic distraction needs to be worked with and worked through if human life is to be afforded a comic restoration. This, I believe, is a possibility Plato saw; and he saw that it was a possibility which Socrates ignored. It is Socrates' failure to grasp this possibility which is dramatized in the *Symposium*. And it is this possibility which Freud takes up when he thanks the "divine Plato" for inspiration.[13]

CHAPTER 8

Testing the Limits:
The Place of Tragedy
in Aristotle's Ethics

Can mind comprehend its limits? Since Kant this has become a familiar question for theoretical reason, but for Aristotle it was crucial for practical reason. It is, after all, a primary task of practical reason to create, shape, or sustain the polis; and, for him, the boundaries of the polis ought to capture the domain of robust human logos. That is, citizenship ought to be granted to all and only those capable of the practical reason involved in ruling and being ruled.[1] Legislators are to use their practical reason to determine who else is capable of the practical reason necessary for citizenship. So, in determining the shape and extent of the polis, practical reason should set its own boundaries. The polis becomes the field of human logos, at least in the sense that it is the arena in which practical reason achieves its full and proper expression.[2] Moreover, when legislators exercise their practical reason well, they craft a polis which both encourages and makes room for the exercise of theoretical reason on the part of those who are capable of it. The polis, then, is the place where both practical and theoretical reason reach fruition.

But there is also a deeper sense in which, for Aristotle, the polis is the field of logos. The polis is neither a brute element of the universe, nor is it the outcome of rigidly instinctual behavior, as is, say, a beehive.[3] The structure of the polis ought to be the outcome of a certain kind of debate *inside the polis* as to what the polis ought to be like. Obviously, this is nothing like a modern liberal debate, in which radically different conceptions of the good can fight it out or make room for each other, as the case may be. That, for Aristotle, would not be an exercise of practical reason. Only virtuous people are capable of practical reason—indeed, the virtues constitute practical reason—so the debate will be carried out by people who have already been educated into a broadly shared outlook. This Aristotle took to be the outlook of a truly excellent human being. These fine human beings are already living good lives, and it is their task, as legislators, philosophers, and citizens, to discuss among themselves what this good life consists in and how it can best be facilitated within political space. Legislators will enact this practical wisdom into law. In short, the shape of the polis is to be decided by a few good men.

Let us for a moment set aside concerns we might have about the restricted social world which Aristotle thought capable of the full exercise of reason. Then I think we can see Aristotle as committed to the autonomy of human reason in this sense: through debate in the polis, human reason is setting its own standards of what constitutes a good life. This point is easy to miss if one is reading Aristotle in the shadow of Kant. For in Kant's anatomy of the psyche, reason has a "pure" form distinct from, and often set over against, human desires and passions. Aristotle does think that the debate on the good life must take into account basic biological facts of human existence, the nature of human desire, the emotions, and so on. These conditions of human existence are ones to which any adequate debate must be responsive. The debate within the polis, then, is obviously not one Kant would recognize as an exercise of pure practical reason.

However, rather than viewing these conditions as exercising a heteronomous constraint, it is, I think, more illuminating to see Aristotle as trying to work out an embodied conception of human reason. First, the "nonrational" part of the psyche is by nature responsive to the dictates of reason. And when a person is well brought up, that is, brought up to virtue, the "nonrational" and rational parts of the psyche together constitute practical reason: "they" function together as a harmonious and seamless whole.[4] So when the debate about the good life takes certain conditions of human existence into account, this, for Aristotle, is part of the process by which human logos determines its own shape. The debate is constrained, to be sure, but not by something which is ultimately to be understood as external.

Second, the citizens of the polis, those who exercise practical reason, are themselves the final arbiters of what constitutes adequate responsiveness to these conditions of human existence. Being adequately responsive to the "facts of human nature" is equivalent to being taken to be adequately responsive by those who have practical reason. In that sense, there is no tribunal outside of reason to determine whether a given exercise of reason is or is not the exercise of correct reason *(orthos logos)*.

Third, Aristotle's claim that humans are by nature political animals implies that human nature is not an external constraint on the debate. For it is logos which, in Aristotle's opinion, distinguishes human nature. Humans differ even from other social animals in that they alone have logos or reason; and it is clear that this reason is normative and ethical.[5] The deepest reason that humans are by nature political is not, then, that a given nature forces them to huddle together, like sheep in a storm, but that human nature is realized in the political debate and enactment of what constitutes a good life. The debate is itself one of the higher expressions of human nature.

The human task, then, is to create an environment in which humans can become most fully themselves. The polis, for Aristotle, emerged naturally out of earlier forms of association—the household and village—which were themselves the outcome of natural instincts and drives, notably for sexual union and protection.[6] Nature, working so to speak from below, facilitates forms of social organization which are ever-less-direct expressions of instinct. The polis culminates the development of human forms of life: it is the minimal (and maximal) self-sufficient unit which can successfully achieve its aim of securing the good life for humans.[7] And self-sufficiency here implies not merely that it is capable of catering to the material needs of the inhabitants, but that it is self-sufficient for determining through debate what the good life for humans is. A polis in good shape will be able to establish its own standards of the good life, enact them into law, and transmit them to future generations through ethical education. And the claim that the polis is the minimal unit of human self-sufficiency implies that human autonomy is paradigmatically political. By actively participating in a healthy polis, virtuous people will themselves endorse and enact the lives which the polis, through its own internal debate, has determined to be good lives.

For Aristotle, the polis existed by nature, but he notoriously kept this realm of nature a restricted preserve. In the best polis, women are excluded, as are metics, slaves, and anyone else without education or virtue, such as manual laborers and merchants—though they are all needed to support polis life. Only "the best" men, Aristotle thinks, should be granted citizenship; for only they are capable of ruling and being ruled. So, in shaping the ideal polis, Aristotle went well beyond the restrictive practices of his day. Were this merely an argument about citizenship, one might be tempted simply to dismiss it. But the political argument is grounded in a claim about the scope of human reason: all those creatures capable of exercising reason should be allowed inside. Of course, Aristotle interprets this constraint stringently. Although he admits that women, slaves, and so on have various inferior capacities to respond to reason, he restricts citizenship to those who are able to have reason in the strong sense of having practical wisdom. A high standard perhaps; but for Aristotle it is only at this level that humans reach their telos, and thus fully realize their nature. If relatively few members of the biological species are granted citizenship, that is because only they are capable of becoming fully human.

This is an astonishing conclusion, but Aristotle seems willing to accept it. Humans are, for him, the only creatures who almost never realize their nature. Of course, he attempts various palliatives: that it is the nature of a slave to be such as he his, the nature of a woman to be such as she is, and so on. But this is tantamount to saying that for a vast range of biological human beings, it is their "nature" never fully to realize human nature. That is, most of humanity in the biological sense isn't fully human in Aristotle's sense. Throughout the rest of nature, the members of a species tend to become what it is their distinctive nature to be. Indeed, for Aristotle, this is virtually a methodological principle, albeit one confirmed by experience. For the rest of nature, Aristotle observes what he takes to be typical members in the characteristic activities and environment of maturity, and concludes that these activities manifest the nature of the species. When it comes to humans, though, Aristotle shifts his ground: he resorts to philosophical reflection on the good life for humans. The effect of this shift is dramatic, though perhaps not obvious because nature everywhere is normative. For any creature to fulfill its nature is what it is for that creature to live a good life. This is as true for humans as it is for chickens. But the shift in method has the following consequence: while almost all other animals are living good lives—for their lives conform to the pattern of a typical member of the species—almost no humans live good human lives—for they fail to achieve the standards set by philosophical reflection. The upshot is that though the polis should contain everyone capable of realizing their human nature, virtually no one gets to belong.

There are two types of criticism of Aristotle's strategy. The first is a social criticism which points out the anti-egalitarian, antidemocratic base on which Aristotle's ethics rests. Though it is true that much modern discussion of Aristotelian approaches to ethics has ignored the elitist strain in Aristotle's thought, I find the social critique unsatisfying. For it remains unclear how crucial Aristotle's elitism is to his ethical-political outlook. Is it possible for a modern democrat to treat the elitism as a contingent bias of Aristotle's historical time and class, which can be eliminated from an acceptable, modern Aristotelianism? This question has not been adequately answered. Moreover, the social critique results in a standoff. It assumes a democratic, inclusive standpoint and invites us to condemn Aristotle's elitism. That may be fine, if the social critique deliberately assumes an audience broadly committed to a democratic outlook; but that is certainly not an outlook Aristotle and his audience would share. From a democratic perspective, Aristotle's politics will of course appear objectionably elitist; while from Aristotle's perspective, the democratic outlook will appear incapable of grasping the truth about ethical life. This truth, as Aristotle eloquently argues, can be grasped only from within the perspective Aristotle himself holds. Of course, a modern democrat might not feel obliged to muster an argument which would persuade Aristotle. But from a philosophical perspective, one wonders whether there might not be something going wrong *within* Aristotle's philosophy. Might there not be strains inherent in Aristotle's outlook? If so, one could formulate an objection which was more than a bare dismissal of the outlook. Indeed, it would be one which even Aristotle would have to take seriously.

Here I should like to explore a second possible objection, one which is internal to Aristotle's strategy. Has Aristotle begged the question of what constitutes human nature by simply excluding any possible counterexample? On this objection, Aristotle's conception of logos or reason trivially emerges as the distinguishing characteristic of human nature, because only those who can robustly exercise it are counted as fully human. From this perspective, Aristotle's ideal polis looks like an attempt to avoid disquieting thoughts about human nature. For his method begins to look as though it were designed to yield a noble conception of human nature: all those whose existence might challenge this alleged nobility are dismissed from consideration.

For Aristotle, the ultimate vindication of his ethical outlook was the judgment of the practically wise. Of course, practical wisdom is characterized by Aristotle as the exercise of correct reason; and for reason to be correct it must adequately capture the truth about the situation it is judging. *Orthos logos* is by definition accurately in touch with reality. One would expect the practically wise to study human nature, history, other forms of social organization, just as Aristotle did; but all of this study is seen from the distinctive perspective of the practically wise. Ultimately, it is the practically wise who are themselves determining what being adequately in touch with the truth consists in. There is thus the danger that those who take themselves to be "practically wise" are setting standards which confer an illusory vindication.

The significance of this issue transcends any qualms one might have with the specific limitations of Aristotle's social vision. Indeed, it confronts any ethical system which values autonomy. For there is, I think, an incipient tension between valuing autonomy and valuing that to which autonomy might lead. How much does any ethical theory which values autonomy have to restrict what it counts as "us," so that what "we" end up legislating turns out to be recognizably ethical? Kant restricts "us" to purely rational wills as he purports to offer a proof that such beings will autonomously will the categorical imperative. Aristotle, for his part, restricts "us" to virtuous people. In an ideal polis, such citizens are, for Aristotle, in an "ideal speech situation": the outcome of their debate is *a fortiori* legislation of the good. But has the speech situation been made so "ideal" that genuine debate is short-circuited? Aristotle's virtuous man may be uniquely able to grasp the value of virtuous activity; but might he also be peculiarly unable to grasp the logos in women and slaves? It is therefore important that any attempt to draw the bounds of logos also supply certain tests that its delimitation is legitimate. This, I think, is the most general philosophical question raised by Aristotle's social exclusivity: how can any ethical system which offers an "internal" validation provide sufficiently strong internal tests that its claims to validity are more than self-serving ideology?

Aristotle himself tested the limits he had drawn in three ways. First, in the *Nicomachean Ethics* he offers an internal vindication of the virtuous person's outlook as manifesting logos. Second, in the *Politics* he surveys existing *poleis* and tries to show that they are attempts to instantiate a field for logos which fail for comprehensible reasons. So, for example, an oligarchical polis fails because its judgment is distorted by too much appetite. The *Ethics* and *Politics* together thus constitute an attempted empirical vindication of Aristotle's boundaries.

But Aristotle also turned to the imagination. He wanted, I think, to test the boundaries with something stronger than any actual example could provide; and he thus turned to tragedy. The classic tragedies, for him, represent attacks upon the primordial bonds which hold the polis together. And he encourages plots of family destruction: "Whenever the tragic deed is done among friends—when murder or the like is done or meditated by brother on brother, by son on father, by mother on son, or son on mother—*these* are the situations the poet should seek after."[8] These are "unnatural acts," to be sure, but within the context of Aristotle's political philosophy, tragedy is also a mimesis of a destructive attack on the elementary structures of reason. The polis is meant to provide protection from the ravages of uncivilized nature; yet there seems need for a representation of the unnatural inside nature, the *alogon* inside logos. Why should the polis, the field of human logos, seek to contain within itself representations of attacks upon logos? Aristotle's answer, I believe, is that these representations help test the adequacy of logos or reason to account for human nature. That is why he insists that these destructive acts be perpetrated (or intended) by basically good people.[9] Tragedy, for Aristotle, represents the extremes of destructiveness to which a basically good person can fall. Such a person is good-enough to be a citizen and thus good-enough to be a representation of human nature, as Aristotle understands it. The philosophical significance of tragedy, for Aristotle, is that it shows that reason can give an account of even the most apparently "unnatural," *alogon*, irrational acts which truly *human* beings commit. The *Poetics,* then, is an attempted vindication of his ethical and political realism: it aims to show that the polis is adequate to capture all of *human* nature.

Here I would like to investigate Aristotle's use of tragedy as a constituent in the internal validation of his ethics. First, I shall discuss the Platonic legacy. Plato is important not merely because he sets the context for Aristotle's discussion, but also because he has a darker view of the limitations of human reason. For Plato, the ultimate opacity of human destructiveness plays a crucial role in his decision to banish tragedy from the polis. From Plato, I turn briefly to Freud. Plato's darker view of the human condition sheds light on Freud's postulation of a death drive. But, more importantly, Freud's argument provides a model of how logos might recognize that something beyond it is part of human nature. Finally, I shall turn to Aristotle's account of tragedy, examining his use of tragedy as a test of his conception of human nature, and thus as a legitimation of his ethics.

The Platonic Legacy

What lie beyond logos for Plato are certain forms of violence and undoing. Plato banished tragedy from the polis because he thought it encouraged a strain of destructiveness which logos could not contain. It does this by perverting the process of psychosocial development. The human psyche, for Plato, stands in a dynamic relation to the social world it inhabits.

Primarily in youth, but throughout life, a person internalizes cultural influences; and these influences, once internalized, become motives. They are organized with other motives into an "inner polis," the psyche. In maturity, a person externalizes these metabolized influences in activities which help to shape, sustain, or undo the social world. Tragic poetry, Plato thinks, turns this dynamic process into a vicious downward spiral.[10]

This deleterious trajectory is due in part to a type of desire in the human psyche which Plato calls *paranomos*. *Paranomos* is usually translated as "lawless," which suggests that these desires resist being informed, or even controlled, by law *(nomos)* and thus by logos. "They are probably present in everyone," Plato says, "but they are held in check by the laws and by the better desires with the help of logos. In a few men they have been eliminated or a small number are left in a weakened state, while in others they are stronger and more numerous."[11] They are incapable of lawful citizenship within the psyche, and the best case, in Plato's view, seems to be benign repression.[12] Even "the very best of us," Plato thinks, may have *paranomoi* desires, albeit in a weakened condition.[13] His reason for thinking this seems to be the dreams which even the best of us may have. These dreams, for Plato, represent *paranomoi* desires existing in the psyche, though repressed in daily life:

> They are aroused during sleep, whenever the rest of the soul, the reasonable, gentle and ruling part, is slumbering; whereas the wild and animal part, full of food and drink, skips about, casts off sleep and seeks to find a way to its gratification. You know that there is nothing it will not dare to do at that time, free of any control by shame or prudence. It does not hesitate, as it thinks, to attempt intercourse with a mother or anyone else—man, god or beast; it will commit any foul murder and does not refrain from any kind of food. In a word, it will not fall short of any folly or shameless deed.[14]

But, should the focus of attention shift from the activities these desires motivate inside the psyche to the activities they motivate in the polis, they come to appear *paranomoi* in a stronger sense. They are now "against the law" in the sense of being destructive of law. It is these desires, expressed dramatically in dreams and in tragedy, which motivate attacks upon the elementary structures of human social relations.

Herein lies a basic tension in Plato's conception of human nature. Humans are by nature polis animals; but they seem to achieve fullest expression only by repressing an ineliminable part of themselves. Human nature, in Plato's vision, contains within itself motivation for attacks on the very structures in which it can be realized.[15] This dark thread running through Plato's account of human nature is occasionally masked by Socrates' enthusiastic hymns to the possibility of harmony in the psyche and in the polis.[16] But even in these hopeful trills there are intimations of darkness: this harmony is, after all, virtually impossible to achieve in actual life; and should it ever be achieved, it would eventually decay.[17]

Plato makes an equivocal attempt to offer a logos of this destructive tendency. He conceives the *paranomos* in human nature as a type of desire. It is as though there are omnivorous appetites which, in themselves, know no limit. Unless there is some constraint—whether political or intrapsychic (like shame)—these desires will motivate unbounded consumption. Human destructiveness, on this view, is a by-product of appetite or desire lurching out of control. But as desire starts gobbling up everything, we begin to lose our grip on the idea that this force is a form of desire.[18] What can a truly unlimited and unchecked desire be a desire for? The answer cannot even be "everything": for should the *paranomos* ever have complete sway, it would succeed not in acquiring "everything," but in destroying everything. We see this in Plato's portrait of the tyrant. He does not acquire the polis but destroys it—as he is himself undone in the process.[19] The tyrannical psyche falls apart into a teeming mass of *paranomoi* "desires": there is no longer any organizational principle holding the psyche together. In full bloom, the *paranomos* cannot motivate the human subject to acquire anything, let alone everything; for the subject has already decomposed. The attempt to explain human destructiveness in terms of unlimited desire seems itself to fall apart under the weight of what it is trying to explain.

It seems, then, that in Plato's conception of human nature, there is a force for decomposition, the *paranomos*, which itself resists further explanation or understanding. The *paranomos* is *paralogos*—incomprehensible. The polis can, then, be a field of logos only by forcibly suppressing an ultimately ineliminable part of human nature.

Tragedy, for Plato, is the return of the repressed. It not only loosens the important bonds of repression; it helps the *paranomos* to flow out of the psyche into polis life. Mimesis sets up homeopathic resonances in the psyches of the audience: even "the best of us" are susceptible.[20] It stirs up the emotional and appetitive parts—the *alogistikon*—and thus encourages the audience to act out on the political stage the destructive impulses acted out in the theater. Because mimesis sets us at no significant distance from the attacks on logos it represents, tragedy provides the bridge by which the worst products of the human imagination are made real. Tragic mimesis is thus a repetition which encourages repetition. It also plays a crucial role in legitimating tyranny.[21] The tyrant comes to feel justified in acting out the destructive attacks on his parents' estate, on his friends, family, and fellow citizens.[22] And in establishing his tyranny, he must expel from the polis the brave and the wise, and surround himself with the cowardly and base.[23] "A fine catharsis!" Plato says.[24] Tyranny thus emerges, for Plato, as the true meaning of tragedy. By encouraging the *paranomoi,* always just below the surface of human nature, tragedy facilitates attacks upon the elementary structures of human logos. The only way to deal with tragedy is to do away with it. By banishing tragedy, Plato is trying to get rid of the *paranomoi* in psychic and political life. Of course, he realizes that there is no final solution: even in the best case there will be *paranomoi* desires in the psyche which are either weakened or repressed.

More importantly, Plato recognizes another source which is "against the law" in a deeper, if less violent, sense than the *paranomoi* desires. Even the best-organized polis, Plato thinks, must eventually fall apart as a result of an inner tendency toward decomposition.[25] The finest guardians will eventually make a mistake about the proper time for mating; for their judgment must combine logos with perception. An inferior generation is born, and the polis is on a path of dissolution. What undoes human logos is matter: the stuff which is perceived but not ultimately understood; the stuff which may be informed for a while, but which eventually looses itself from form. Matter is a principle in opposition to logos. In the human realm, this is manifest both in the fact that it is ultimately responsible for the undoing of humanity's finest instantiation of logos and in the fact that it resists being understood. The ideal polis is undone for no reason at all. Matter, for Plato, is the basic *paranomos*.

FREUD ON THE DEATH DRIVE

Plato, then, thinks there is a strain in human nature which lies beyond the bounds of logos. In its most violent manifestation this strain becomes an attack on logos. But how can one conclude that this destruction is genuinely *alogon*, as opposed to having a logos which has thus far remained hidden? Aristotle holds, in opposition to Plato, that tragic destruction does have a logos, though one which may remain opaque to the participants. It may at first appear that Aristotle thereby accepts the reality of human destructiveness and gives it a proper place in polis life. But on further reflection, there is a question whether precisely by giving it a place, Aristotle evades the reality of human destruction by assigning to it an ersatz logos. Here a comparison with a modern example may be of help.

At the beginning of his career, Freud thought that logos was adequate to give an account of human nature. That is, even the most bizarre neurotic symptoms could, he thought, be made intelligible through psychoanalysis. He treated the psyche almost like an inner polis, and, like Aristotle, the only things he recognized as "citizens" had logos, at least in the minimal sense of being intelligibly directed toward a goal. Neurotic symptoms were the surface manifestation of civil strife. They were the outcome of conflicting lines of motivation, each line of which was intelligible. Freud's early work with neurotics convinced him that the human mind was basically pleasure-seeking. A person could be inhibited by societal prohibitions, and conflicted by internalization of those norms; but the mind's basic task was to find pleasure under the constraints of reality. What on the surface appeared to be irruptions of irrationality were revealed to be intelligible, if nonoptimal, attempts to perform this basic function. The early Freud thought he was justified in treating logos as adequate to capture human nature: after all, he could take purportedly extreme counterexamples and show that even there logos was at work.

However, Freud gradually shifted from this Aristotelian position to a more Platonic outlook in which some part of human nature must be recognized as beyond logos—indeed, as set over against logos. What changed his mind was a certain type of mimesis. In a classic discussion of repetition, Freud described how he became the audience of a tragic mimesis acted out on a small stage within the micropolis of a family.[26] A little boy would throw away a wooden spool attached to a string and cry out an infantile version of "fort" ("gone"), and then pull the spool back with a joyful "da!" ("there"). Freud interpreted this as an enactment of the disappearance and return of the boy's mother. Significantly, the question of whether the drama is a tragedy or a comedy, at least in the modern senses of those terms, is up to the child. If the drama ends in "fort," it is a tragedy; if it ends in "da," the mother has returned, and there has been a comic restoration. The child exerts imaginative control not merely over the ending of the drama but also over its form.

Freud was puzzled that the "fort-da" game should regularly end at "fort." There is no doubt some truth in the thought that the child is trying to gain imaginative mastery over a painful situation which, in real life, he passively suffered. But this thought does not explain why, if the game is really up to him, it should so regularly end as a tragedy rather than as a comedy. We seem to need a deeper understanding of what it is for the ending to be "up to him." Freud linked this drama with the repetitive enactments of people suffering from the so-called war neuroses and traumatic neuroses. It was not the destructiveness of the First World War which changed Freud's mind about the place of logos in human nature, but one psychological consequence of that destruction. Freud saw people repeat, in nightmares, daymares, and compulsive rituals, the horrifying experiences they had suffered. The brute passivity of these enacted scenes, their compulsive durability, and the fierce anxiety they provoked convinced him that they could not be understood as restorative or pleasurable in any way. Though he was a master in finding pleasures disguised in painful symptoms, when Freud finally looked hard at the horrific dramas of war neurosis, he abandoned the hypothesis that the archaic mind always seeks pleasure. There must be a force which lies, as he put it, beyond the pleasure principle.[27]

In trying to account for these dramas, Freud imported a new force into the domain of psychoanalytic theory. The theory of the drives is refashioned so that, following Plato, one is eros, a force which holds psyche and polis together. Sexuality is a manifestation of eros, as is logos. But there is another entropic force, tending toward decomposition. Freud called it the death drive; and it has long been puzzling how he could have thought of it as providing an explanation. For, unlike eros, the death drive is conceptualized as a purely biological force, having no psychological representation.[28] Freud thus abandons his regulative principle of providing psychological explanations for psychological phenomena.[29] So while the death drive is imported into psychoanalytic theory, it remains, as it were, a resident alien. And because it is a biological force, from a psychological perspective one can infer it only from its results: as Freud put it, the death drive "works in silence."[30]

It is tempting to dismiss this conceptualization of the death drive as a manifestation of Freud's scientistic commitment to biological reduction.[31] But perhaps there is deeper motivation for his choice. We are motivated to discover an explanation of eruptions of human destruction. In Aristotle's terms, we want a logos of attacks on the elementary structures of logos. In postulating a purely biological force, Freud is in effect admitting that there is a limit on any such attempt. In fact Freud's thinking seems to vacillate among shades of darkness, almost like a shopper in front of a rack of dark suits hesitating as to which goes best. When he stresses the biological basis of the death drive, there is a disguised Aristotelian optimism underlying his surface Platonic pessimism. For as a brutely biological force, the death drive will lack a logos from the perspective of psychoanalysis—that is, it will be unalterable by any talking cure—but presumably it will have a biological account. There would still be the hope of understanding it from a biological point of view, and perhaps of altering it via biological intervention.

However, in his mature theory, eros and the death drive take on the aspect of basic metaphysical principles. The death drive becomes a brute entropic force, running through the universe: a fundamental and inexplicable tendency toward decomposition. Certain forms of human violence are manifestations of this tendency; and thus they are utterly inexplicable. This is the deepest reason why the death drive must "work in silence": we will forever be taken by surprise, because such destruction has no logos. We can never see it coming: that is why it will always appear to us as an eruption. From this perspective, there could be no such book as, say, *Strife and Its Place in Nature*. The point of postulating a biological death drive rather than a minded Strife is that, from the point of view of psychological motivation, there is nothing to be said about it. To understand it would be to bring it within the domain of logos, and it is of the essence of the death drive to attack any attempted assimilation. On this view, it remains a permanent possibility for human destructiveness to catch us by surprise; for there must be an element in human violence which remains inevitably surd. These are the moments when we suspect that all this carnage has happened for no reason at all.

These thoughts represent a challenge to psychoanalysis. For it is a regulative principle of psychoanalytic practice that it is possible, though perhaps only in the long run, to give a logos to the apparently disparate flotsam and jetsam which emerge from attempts to free associate. Interpretation is, by its nature, an organizing and unifying activity. On Freud's mature theory of the drives, it makes sense that psychoanalysis should be especially successful in interpreting sexual motivation. For sexuality, on the mature theory, is a manifestation of eros, a unifying and organizing force, which has, as other important manifestations, interpretation, understanding, logos. Sexuality may be repressed, it may be confusing, and it may fuel the intrapsychic civil wars we call "neurosis," but it is comprehensible. As psychoanalysis has moved ever more toward the analysis of aggression, violence, and destructiveness, however, it becomes less clear that what it is analyzing is analyzable. There are certainly intimations in Freud's later writings that, in attempting to analyze human destructiveness, analysis is bumping up against its own limits.

ARISTOTLE'S TEST

As Plato is packing tragedy's bags, he allows Socrates to issue his famous caveat: "if poetry that aims at pleasure and mimesis has any argument to bring forward to prove that it must have a place in a well-governed polis, we should be glad to welcome it."[32] In this context, the *Poetics* takes the shape of a political argument: a plea to the State Department to revoke a deportation order. Aristotle accepts Plato's constraint on how a justification is to be given. It must be via logos: an argument that tragedy earns its

181

place in a well-ordered polis.[33] But why should the polis permit representations of attacks on its elementary bonds? Aristotle's answer, I believe, is that tragedy plays a significant role in the self-validation of logos. The point of tragedy, for Aristotle, is to reveal logos manifest even in attacks upon logos, and thus to establish the adequacy of logos to account for even the most destructive aspects of human nature.

In myriad ways, Aristotle insists on the inherent rationality of a tragic plot. First, the events must occur plausibly or necessarily,[34] they must occur on account of one another rather than in mere succession,[35] and the protagonist must make a certain mistake *(hamartia)* which rationalizes his downfall.[36] Second, tragedy must exemplify the ethical structure of logos: it cannot portray a virtuous person falling to bad fortune or the rise of a bad person to good fortune.[37] The protagonist must have just the right amount of goodness: good-enough to inspire our pity and fear, but not so virtuous that he cannot plausibly make a mistake which will intelligibly lead to his downfall.[38] Third, the reversal and discovery, though a surprise to the protagonist, must follow intelligibly from preceding events and thus make sense to the audience. In this way too, the audience can distance itself from, and thus domesticate, the eruption of horrifying surprise. The upshot of these constraints is that the unnatural acts of tragedy take on a peculiar logos of their own—a logos concealed within the drama, but available to the audience. In the light of the overall argument, it would seem that, for Aristotle, tragedy achieves its catharsis by offering a logos for the terrible events (the objective *pathē*) which provoke the tragic emotions (the subjective *pathēmata*). There are relief and reassurance in the thought that the portrayed destruction does not, in the end, represent a totally incomprehensible attack upon logos, but an attack which can be understood within the domain of logos. Aristotle thus reiterates "a fine catharsis!" but without Plato's irony.

Anyone who loves Greek tragedy will, I suspect, come away from the *Poetics* with a sense that, at some level, Aristotle "just didn't get it." But it is difficult to give a precise diagnosis of what is going wrong. It is tempting to think that Aristotle smothered tragedy with logos: that by insisting on logos inherent in tragedy, Aristotle abets the elimination of what he was purportedly trying to save. And yet Aristotle's constraints are there in *Oedipus Tyrannus*. Indeed, Sophocles has Oedipus work through an argument of Euclidean rigor. Thus, even if, as I believe, Aristotle's account of tragedy is ultimately a failure, we must ask whether our sense of disappointment in his account flows from that failure or whether, ironically, it flows from his success in describing certain aspects of tragedy. Jean-Pierre Vernant has brilliantly described how tragedy exists in a "border zone" "where human actions are hinged together with divine powers where, unknown to the agent, they derive their true meaning by becoming an integral part of an order that is beyond man and eludes him."[39] Strictly speaking, it is not a border zone, but an illusion of such a zone. Through a brilliant use of language and dramatic structure, Sophocles invites his audience into an imaginary world: a world in which they can share Oedipus' ignorance, pretend to be confronting the unfathomable, play with horrific surprise. Aristotle, in effect, is pointing out that this is just play. There is, of course, no room inside the play for such recognition.[40] The question, then, is whether our sense of disappointment in Aristotle's account is actually a symptom of its accuracy: whether by pointing out the dramatic structure of an illusion, he disillusions us.

Aristotle does seem more interested than Sophocles in rationalizing Oedipus' downfall. Thus the focus on Oedipus' mistake. Such a mistake pulls the downfall into (or at least toward) the realm of the human explicable; whereas for Sophocles, the origin of that downfall transcends the human realm as well as the human ability to understand. Yet Aristotle insists that the mistake is necessary for the play to be truly tragic. What entitles him to assume that only the plays meeting his constraints are tragic? Aristotle gives a psychological justification: only plays meeting these constraints can elicit pity and fear from the audience and thus effect the requisite catharsis. His guide to judging tragedy is thus not its accuracy in portraying human nature, but its success in eliciting a certain psychological response in the audience.[41] The plot must be persuasive to the audience; and this persuasiveness, Aristotle thinks, rests on the plot manifesting logos. It is not he, Aristotle can say, but the audience who is insisting on logos: only then can tragedy evoke the tragic emotions.[42]

Again, it is tempting to object that Aristotle should be concerned with the truth of human destructiveness, not a mere psychological reaction in the audience. After all, tragedy is meant to be a mimesis of a serious action, and there should be a question whether the mimesis is an accurate representation. What is to prevent tragedy from being a "noble" falsehood: an illusion which sustains a misleading image of human nature and political order? Aristotle's conception of human nature is meant to block this skeptical possibility. By insisting that humans are by nature polis animals, Aristotle is claiming that there are no deeper facts about human nature than those which could be revealed in polis life. Of course, polis life does give room for reflection on destructiveness; and tragedy, in Aristotle's opinion, is a particularly significant example. If tragedy is found persuasive inside the polis, there is no tribunal outside—human nature as such—with which one could compare tragedy's account and find it wanting. For Aristotle, there can be no further truth about the nature of human destructiveness: the emotional truth of mature citizens is all the truth tragedy could possibly have. So the fact that tragedy is experienced as psychologically convincing, far from opening the door to skepticism, is treated by Aristotle as evidence for its truth.

At this point it is difficult to avoid the sinking feeling that this is all too easy. Aristotle is using tragedy to test the boundaries of logos manifest in the polis; but he is using the polis to legitimate tragedy. Of course, for Aristotle any legitimation of logos must be internal. But here the circle seems too tight for comfort—or, rather, too comfortable to be uncomfortable. Our feeling of dissatisfaction has its source, I believe, in Aristotle's decision to cite pity as a tragic emotion. The point of pity, for Aristotle, is to secure a particular emotional relationship between the audience and the dramatized events. We feel pity *for others*—thus we must be at a certain distance from the dreadful events—but for others who are *like us*—and this allows a certain imaginative proximity to those same events.

> We pity those who are like us in age, character, disposition, social standing or birth; for in all these cases it appears more likely that the same misfortune may befall us also.[43]

In the imaginative setting of the theater, pity makes fear possible. Because the characters are enough "like us" that we can pity them, we can also imaginatively identify with them and feel fear. And even if we do not identify with them, in pitying them we experience ourselves as sufficiently close to their condition to be threatened by it. For fear is elicited by the thought that a terrible event threatens one: "we shall not fear things that we believe cannot happen to us."[44] And yet pity also ensures that there is not too much fear. If events become too terrible, dread drives out pity.[45] Aristotle cites the tale of Amasis, who did not weep when his son was taken away to his death, but did weep when he saw a friend begging. Pity, as Aristotle's own example shows, sets us at a luxurious distance from the portrayed events: it's safe enough to indulge one's fears while generously extending pity to the other.

In that sense, pity serves as a defense against terror: the very condition which makes fear possible insures us against terror. Pity thus domesticates fear, ensuring that it will not get out of hand. And once pity is installed as a necessary constraint, the tragic plot must also manifest logos. The reversal and recognition—the surprise!—must follow intelligibly from the preceding actions: if not, pity would be driven out by terror.[46] If terrible deeds can befall us, out of the blue and for no reason, then, for Aristotle, there is no room for pity. Moreover, pity's requirement that the characters be "like us" is in fact a requirement that they be *taken by us to be like us.* That is, we, the audience, will feel no emotional tug toward pity if we do not feel the characters are like us, whether or not they are such. Pity thus provides ample room for idealized self-images to go unchallenged, and for darker strains of our own nature to be disavowed. In particular, we can take ourselves to be fundamentally creatures having logos, and thus fail to feel pity for creatures we do not take to be such. This ensures, as Aristotle clearly saw, that the protagonists of tragedy be "good-enough."

The inclusion of pity as a tragic emotion also enables the audience to play its own "fort-da" game with terror. As the child enacts a tragedy by throwing a spool, so the ancient audience can imaginatively throw itself into the drama, but always with the tacit knowledge that it could at any moment pull itself back. This tacit knowledge is guaranteed by pity. The audience needs to feel not only like the characters on stage, but assured that in their imaginative identifications they will not be overwhelmed by dread. The device of the chorus plays an important role in making pity a possible response. The chorus is meant to express the audience's fears, but the chorus also renders the audience twice removed from the portrayed disaster. The chorus of *Oedipus Tyrannus* is, after all, bound up in the miasma, as the audience is not. As the audience watches a dramatically involved audience, it can both identify with it and step back from it. In its forward position, the audience experiences terror; in its return, there is pity alongside relief that the audience lives centuries later in a polis structured so as to insulate them from these "unnatural" happenings.[47] In every tragedy, there is thus a hidden comedy, at least in the modern sense of that term.

Pity thus makes tragedy "safe for human consumption"—especially in Aristotle's conception of the human. For pity to be a possible emotional response to a drama, even the most horrific reversals must have an inherent logos. Of course, Oedipus is going to be taken by surprise, but, from Aristotle's perspective, the audience is reassured that the reversal is the outcome of a particular blindness on his part, not a surd eruption of meaningless devastation. In this way, he attempts to domesticate surprise. For consider what sorts of experiences might lead us to conclude that human destructiveness lies beyond the bounds of logos. It would seem to be that despite our best efforts to understand, human destructiveness repeatedly takes us by surprise. After each outburst we may retrospectively try to offer an account, but we find that this does nothing to insure us against future surprise. This, it would seem, is the phenomenology we should expect if human logos is inadequate. Precisely because logos cannot grasp human destructiveness, it will forever be surprised by it. Of course, there can never be a definitive proof that destructiveness lies beyond logos' pale: there may forever be the hope that an account lies just around the next corner. But the enduring repetition of surprise may eventually suggest that there is something about human destructiveness which lies beyond logos. This lends added poignancy to the spectacle of Oedipus working out his own surprise. On the one hand, we can imaginatively enact our own susceptibility to surprise; on the other, we defend against it by seeing Oedipus use logos to arrive at his surprise and by taking up the position of an omniscient audience which knows all along what is going to happen.

It is, I think, by including pity as a tragic emotion that Aristotle fails to provide a sufficiently robust test of his conception of human nature. For if tragedy is meant to test the limits of human destructiveness, all destruction which lacks logos is thereby eliminated from the realm of the human. All human attacks on logos must themselves manifest logos—otherwise, they will not be counted as human. Tragedy thus "legitimates" logos' ability to account for human destruction because it ignores any destruction which doesn't fit. Of course, I do not think one can *prove* that Aristotle begged the question: one person's "begging the question" is another person's "internal legitimation." From Aristotle's perspective, the point of tragedy is to test logos *from the inside:* to move around within the domain of logos, explore its outer reaches, and see how far destruction can go while still remaining intelligible. Aristotle obviously does not think he begs the question by citing pity as a tragic emotion. Pity is there precisely because Aristotle wants to secure the autonomy of human nature. Humans are the unique animals whose task it is to determine their own nature, through debate, legislation, education, and other cultural activities, for instance tragedy. These activities all occur within the polis, which is itself a creation and manifestation of human logos. In feeling pity, an audience of citizens sets its own outer bounds on what counts as human. Aristotle thus legitimates the ability of logos to account for human destruction—at the cost of excluding unintelligible, horrific destruction from the domain of the human. By contrast, Plato and Freud are less interested in human autonomy and more interested in pursuing the darker threads of human behavior, even if doing so points beyond the bounds of intelligibility. They thus have a more inclusive conception of human nature; and they are willing to countenance the thought that certain forms of human destruction are brute attacks upon logos which themselves have no logos at all.[48]

Those of us who find Aristotle's account of tragedy flat-footed, and would like an account which allowed tragedy to explore this darker conception of human nature, might try eliminating pity as a tragic emotion. But we need to recognize pity's central theatrical value: it keeps the audience emotionally connected to the dramatized events. Too closely connected, perhaps; but Aristotle is certainly right that some balance needs to be struck between an audience's sense of dread and its sympathetic emotional involvement. The possibility of tragedy obviously relies on a delicate balance of conflicting emotional currents; but it remains unobvious what that balance is. It is beyond the scope of this essay to lay down an alternate set of abstract conditions; and that is just as well, since I do not know what I would propose. But in any case, I think the strategy for anyone who wants to probe the possibility of pitiless tragedy is to investigate those extant tragedies for which pity seems inappropriate. Aristotle focused on Oedipus, and Freud has brought to our attention deep reasons why we might take Oedipus to be "like us"; but need we feel pity for Medea or Antigone? Might not our awe, our wrenching upset, and our terror come from a profound recognition that they are not "like us"?

Aristotle's reluctance to countenance the opacity of *human* destruction is, I believe, the central failure in his account of tragedy. In reflecting on this failure, I think we may gain insight into certain strengths and weaknesses of his ethical realism. Aristotle's ethics is an attempt to work out the idea of autonomy, subject to the constraints of outlook of a brilliant philosopher of mid-fourth-century Athens. His hope is for meaningful and rich human existence inside the polis, a social structure which is at once a manifestation of reason and transparent to reason's inquiry. Precisely because humans are to work out their own nature by reasoned debate inside, Aristotle has to exercise care about who is allowed to participate. The ethics represents Aristotle's attempt both to contribute to and to anticipate the outcome of that debate. His account of tragedy is an attempt to reclaim the opacity of human destructiveness: to lend it intelligibility and thereby confer upon it some political value.

If one feels disappointed by Aristotle's lack of breadth, that is likely to be for one of two reasons. Either: like Plato and Freud, one places less significance on autonomy and greater significance on exploring the darker realms of human existence. One is, as it were, willing to accept that humans are not rational animals; and insofar as they lack rationality, it is not obvious that they should be autonomous. Or: one does value autonomy but is disappointed with the severe social restrictions placed on those who were allowed to exercise it. This, I think, would be the most widespread source of disappointment today. It is, after all, difficult to read Aristotle's discussions of slaves and women without discomfort.

These may be reasons for disappointment. But we use them at our peril simply to dismiss Aristotle. By the standards of his social world, Aristotle was not a bigot or a crank. He did not think that Athens was a perfectly ordered polis, but it provided the framework within which he made the adjustments he thought necessary to craft a just society. That is, the world in which he lived provided a framework for and constraint upon his philosophical imagination. Is that not true of us all? The point is not to forgive Aristotle for living twenty-odd centuries before the Enlightenment, but to recognize that his is a creditable attempt to articulate and legitimate an idea of autonomy, subject to the constraints of his social world. So described, could we hope to do more? This question is particularly pressing for anyone who wishes to formulate an ethics in which autonomy or virtue plays a significant role. The virtues, notoriously, are legitimated internally: a coward, for instance, cannot see the value or the pleasure inherent in brave acts. But how, if we have acquired a purported virtue and are enjoying the distinctive outlook which virtue permits, can we avoid complacent smugness? How, that is, can we avoid dismissing any challenge to our virtue as a brave person dismisses a coward's demurrals? From within the perspective of the alleged virtue, it is not at all clear how we might come to recognize that our perspective was distorted by illusion. This problem has not yet been sufficiently addressed by those who wish to revive a broadly Aristotelian approach to ethics.

As for autonomy, any ethical system which values it will place restrictions on who is allowed to exercise it. There will always be a question whether those restrictions are legitimate. Certainly, one does not automatically purchase sufficient inclusiveness by saying that autonomy should be exercised by any rational being. Aristotle, as we have seen, thought that any fully rational being should be a citizen, but that did not prevent him from having a restricted view of who counted as capable of sufficient rationality. There will always, then, be a question of social inclusiveness. Similarly, there will also be a question of psychic inclusiveness: are the parts of our psyche which make the decisions sufficiently inclusive that the decisions are genuinely an expression of ourselves? Or do we beg the question by simply refusing to countenance the excluded bits as parts of ourselves? These are serious questions, and it is difficult to know how to answer them. The reflections here suggest that any attempt to offer an internal legitimation of an ethical system which values autonomy will be in danger of ignoring the very challenges it should take seriously. This is an occupational hazard of internal legitimations, to be sure. But we overlook that hazard at the risk of being overtaken by horrific surprise: the very surprise it was the aim of tragedy to depict.

CHAPTER 9

Catharsis

Tragedy, says Aristotle, is a mimesis of a serious and complete action, having magnitude, which through pity and fear brings about a catharsis of such emotions.[1] But what Aristotle meant by what he said—in particular, what he meant in claiming that tragedy produces a catharsis—is a question which has dominated Western philosophy and literary criticism since the Renaissance.[2] In the last hundred years it has been widely accepted that by catharsis Aristotle meant a purgation of the emotions.[3] Now, there is a sense in which the interpretation of catharsis as purgation is unexceptionable: having aroused the emotions of pity and fear, tragedy does leave us with a feeling of relief; and it is natural for humans to conceive of this emotional process in corporeal terms: as having got rid of or expelled the emotions.[4] But at this level of generality, the interpretation is as unhelpful as it is unexceptionable. For what we wish to know is how Aristotle conceived of the process of catharsis as it occurs in the performance of a tragedy. Even if we accept that Aristotle drew on the metaphor of purgation in naming this emotional process "catharsis," what we want to know is: did he really think that this process was an emotional purgation or did he merely use the metaphor to name a process which he understood in some different way? At the level of metaphor there seems little reason to choose between the medical metaphor of purgation and its traditional religious competitor, purification, not to mention more general meanings of "cleansing," "separation," and so on.[5] In fact, Aristotle's preponderant use of the word is as a term for menstrual discharge.[6] As far as I know, no one in the extended debate about tragic catharsis has suggested the model of menstruation. But why not? Is it not more compelling to think of a natural process of discharge of the emotions than of their purging?

It is only when we shift from the question of what metaphors Aristotle might have been drawing on to the question of what he took the process of catharsis in tragedy to be that there is any point in choosing among the various models. Of course, the task of figuring out what Aristotle meant by catharsis is made all the more alluring, as well as frustrating, by a passing remark which he makes in the *Politics* while discussing the catharsis which music produces: "the word 'catharsis' we use at present without explanation, but when later we speak of poetry we will treat the subject with more precision."[7] We seem to be missing the section of the *Poetics* in which Aristotle explicitly set out what he meant.[8]

Here I will first isolate a series of constraints which any adequate interpretation of catharsis must satisfy. These constraints will be derived from a consideration of Aristotle's extended discussion of the emotions, of the effect of tragedy, and of how tragedy produces this effect. The constraints may not be tight enough to delimit a single acceptable interpretation, but I shall argue that they are strong enough to eliminate all the traditional interpretations. Second, I will offer an interpretation of tragic catharsis which satisfies all the constraints.

LET US BEGIN with the suggestion that a catharsis is a purgation of the emotions. To take this suggestion seriously one must think that, for Aristotle, catharsis is a cure for an emotionally pathological condition: tragedy helps one to expel or get rid of unhealthily pent-up emotions or noxious emotional elements.[9] The only significant evidence for this interpretation comes from Aristotle's discussion in the *Politics* of the catharsis which music produces:[10]

> We accept the division of melodies proposed by certain philosophers into ethical melodies, melodies of action, and passionate or inspiring melodies, each having, as they say, a mode corresponding to it. But we maintain further that music should be studied, not for the sake of one, but of many benefits, that is to say, with a view to education, to catharsis (the word catharsis we use at present without explanation, but when hereafter we speak of poetry we will treat the subject with more precision)—music may also serve for intellectual enjoyment, for relaxation and for recreation after exertion. It is clear, therefore, that all the modes must be employed by us, but not all of them in the same manner. In education the most ethical modes are to be preferred, but in listening to the performances of others we may admit the modes of action and passion also. For emotions such as pity and fear, or again enthusiasm, exist very strongly in some souls, and have more or less influence over all. Some persons fall into a religious frenzy, whom we see as a result of the sacred melodies—when they have used the melodies that excite the soul to mystic frenzy—restored as though they had found healing and catharsis. Those who are influenced by pity or fear, and every emotional nature, must have a like experience, and others in so far as each is susceptible to such emotions, and all receive a sort of catharsis and are relieved with pleasure. The cathartic melodies likewise give an innocent pleasure to men. Such are the modes and melodies in which those who perform music at the theater should be invited to compete.[11]

It does seem that Aristotle distinguishes cathartic melodies from those "ethical melodies" which help to train and reinforce character—and thus that the point of catharsis cannot in any straightforward way be ethical education.[12] But the only reason for thinking that catharsis is a cure for a pathological condition is that Aristotle's primary example of catharsis is as a cure for religious ecstasy.[13] However, even if we accept that religious ecstasy is a pathological condition, the idea that catharsis is meant to apply to a pathological condition can be sustained only by ignoring an important claim which Aristotle makes in the quoted text. Having begun his discussion of catharsis with the example of those who are particularly susceptible to religious frenzy, Aristotle goes on to say that the same thing

193

holds for anyone who is influenced by pity and fear and, more generally, anyone who is emotionally influenced by events.[14] In case there should be any doubt that Aristotle means to include us all under that category, he continues: "and a certain catharsis and lightening with pleasure occurs for everyone."[15] But "everyone" includes virtuous people, and it is absurd to suppose that, for Aristotle, virtuous people were in any kind of pathological condition.

Nor does the idea of a purgation seem a plausible analogue for tragic catharsis. In a medical purge, as the Aristotelian author of the *Problems* says, "drugs are not concocted—they make their way out carrying with them anything which gets in their way: this is called purging."[16] The idea of a purgation seems to be that of the introduction of a foreign substance, a drug, which later gets expelled from the body untransformed along with the noxious substances. But the idea of a purgation as it is suggested by the commentators is of a homeopathic cure: we introduce pity and fear in order to purge the soul of these emotions.[17] The problem is that though the idea of a homeopathic cure was available in Aristotle's time, there is no evidence that he was aware of it and lots of evidence that he thought that medical cure was effected by introducing contraries.[18] But once we abandon the idea that for Aristotle a medical purgation was a homeopathic cure, there seems to be little to recommend the medical analogy. What foreign substance is introduced to expel what contrary noxious substance in the soul? Why should one think that the virtuous man has any noxious elements in his soul which need purging?

Indeed, if we look to Aristotle's account of the emotions, they do not seem to be the sort of things which are readily conceived as purgeable. Fear, for example, is defined as a pain or disturbance due to imagining some destructive or painful evil in the future.[19] That is, the emotion of fear is not exhausted by the feeling one has when one feels fear. In addition to the feeling, the emotion of fear also requires the belief that one is in danger and a state of mind which treats the danger as worthy of fear. All three conditions are required to constitute the emotion of fear.[20] If, for example, one believes one is in danger but one's state of mind is confidence in being able to overcome it, one will not feel fear.[21] An emotion, then, is not merely a feeling; it is an orientation to the world. But if an emotion requires not merely a feeling, but also a belief about the world one is in and an attitude toward it, then it is hard to know what could be meant by purging an emotion. An emotion is too complex and world-directed an item for the purgation model to be of significant value.

I DO NOT WISH to spend time on the idea that tragic catharsis effects a purification of the emotions, for though this view has had proponents since the Renaissance, it is not seriously held today.[22] The major problems with the idea of purification are, first, that virtuous people will experience a certain catharsis in the theater, but their emotional responses are not impure; second, it is not clear what is meant by purifying the emotions. One possibility was suggested by Eduard Muller: "Who can any longer doubt that the purification of pity, fear, and other passions consists in, or at least is very closely connected with, the transformation of the pain that engendered them into pleasure?"[23] The fact that we do derive a certain pleasure from the pitiable and fearful events which are portrayed in tragedy is, I think, of the greatest importance in coming to understand tragic catharsis. However, it is a mistake to think that, in tragedy, pain is transformed into pleasure. Pity and fear are not abolished by the tragedy; it is just that in addition to the pity and fear one feels in response to the tragic events, one is also capable of experiencing a certain pleasure. More-over, even if there were a transformation, to conceive of it as a purifica-tion is to assume that the original emotional response of pity and fear is somehow polluted or unclean. But this isn't so. Aristotle makes it abun-dantly clear that pity and fear are the appropriate responses to a good tragic plot.[24] The pain of pity and fear is not an impurity which needs to be removed; it is the emotional response which a virtuous man will and ought to feel.

PERHAPS THE MOST SOPHISTICATED view of catharsis, which has been argued for in recent years, is the idea that catharsis provides an education of the emotions.[25] The central task of an ethical education is to train youths to experience pleasure and pain in the right sort of ways: to feel pleasure in acting nobly and pain at the prospect of acting ignobly.[26] This is accomplished by a process of habituation: by repeatedly encouraging youths to perform noble acts they come to take pleasure in so acting. Virtue, for Aristotle, partially consists in having the right emotional response to any given set of circumstances.[27]

Tragedy, it is argued, provides us with the appropriate objects toward which to feel pity and fear. Tragedy, one might say, trains us or habituates us in feeling pity and fear in response to events which are worthy of those emotions. Since our emotions are being evoked in the proper circumstances, they are also being educated, refined, or clarified. By being given repeated opportunities to feel pity and fear in the right sort of circumstances, we are less likely to experience such emotions inappropriately: namely, in response to circumstances which do not merit pity and fear. Since virtue partially consists in having the appropriate emotional responses to circumstances, tragedy can be considered part of an ethical education.

There are two overwhelming advantages to this interpretation, which, I think, any adequate account of catharsis ought to preserve. First, this interpretation relies on a sophisticated, and genuinely Aristotelian, conception of the emotions. Tragedy provides (a mimesis of) certain objects toward which it is appropriate to form certain beliefs and evaluative attitudes as well as to feel certain pains. Second, this interpretation offers an account of the peculiar pleasure we derive from a performance of tragedy.[28] Aristotle, as is well known, believes in an innate desire to understand, and a special pleasure attends the satisfaction of that desire.[29] If tragedy helps to provide an ethical education, then in experiencing it we come better to understand the world, as fit object of our emotional responses, and better to understand ourselves, in particular, the emotional responses of which we are capable and which the events portrayed require. It is because we gain a deeper insight into the human condition that we derive a special cognitive pleasure from tragedy.

This interpretation does have a genuinely Aristotelian ring to it: it is a position which is consonant with much that Aristotle believed, and it is a position he might have adopted. But I don't think he did. First, as we have seen, a virtuous person will experience a certain catharsis when he sees or hears a tragedy performed; but he is in no need of education.[30] Second, the *Politics'* discussion of music clearly distinguishes music which is educative of the emotions and should be employed in ethical training from music which produces catharsis.[31] The best attempt I have seen to meet this problem is an argument that the type of catharsis which Aristotle is contrasting with ethical education is only an extreme form derived from orgiastic music:

> Once attention is shifted to types of katharsis connected with more common emotions and with those who do not experience them to a morbidly abnormal degree (and both these conditions are true of the tragic variety), it is possible to discern that katharsis may after all be in some cases compatible with the process which Aristotle characterizes in *Politics* 8 as a matter of habituation in feeling the emotions in the right way and towards the right objects (1340a16–18) . . . Simply to identify tragic katharsis with a process of ethical exercise and habituation for the emotions through art would be speculative and more than the evidence justifies. But to suggest that these two things ought to stand in an intelligible relation to one another (as the phrase "for education and katharsis" at *Pol.* 1341b38 encourages to see them) is only to argue that tragic katharsis should be capable of integration into Aristotle's general philosophy of the emotions, and of their cognitive and moral importance, as well as into the framework of his theory of tragedy as a whole.[32]

Of course, tragic catharsis and ethical education might stand in an "intelligible" relation to each other even if they served completely different purposes; but when one sees the phrase "for education and catharsis" quoted out of context, it is tempting to suppose that education and catharsis are part of a single project. Unfortunately, the text will not support this supposition. Aristotle explicitly says that although one should use all the different types of melodies, one should not use them for the same function.[33] And when he says that music may be used "for the sake of education and of catharsis,"[34] he is unambiguously listing different benefits which may be derived from music.[35] Nor is it true that in this passage Aristotle is only contrasting education with an extreme, orgiastic form of catharsis. For although, as we have seen, he begins by talking about the catharsis of religious frenzy, he very quickly goes on to mention a certain catharsis had by everyone, and the fact that two lines before he explicitly mentions those who are susceptible to pity and fear suggests that he had tragic catharsis in mind.[36] Thus the contrast which Aristotle draws between ethical education and catharsis cannot easily be brushed aside.

Moreover, Aristotle continues by saying that vulgar audiences will have vulgar tastes and that professional musicians ought to cater to those tastes, since even vulgar people need relaxation.[37] But if even some melodies are ethically educative, why doesn't Aristotle insist that the vulgar be confined to such uplifting tunes? The answer, I think, is that it's too late. Aristotle contrasts two types of audience: the vulgar crowd composed of artisans and laborers on the one hand, and those who are free and have already been educated on the other.[38] In each case the characters of the audience have been formed, and ethical education would be either futile or superfluous.

Aristotle clearly thinks that tragedy is among the highest of art forms. Aside from the fact that tragedy is the culmination of a teleological development of art forms which began with dithyrambs and phallic songs,[39] and aside from the fact that Aristotle explicitly holds it in higher regard than epic, notwithstanding his enormous respect for Homer, Aristotle criticizes certain forms of inferior plots as due to the demands of a vulgar audience. For example, Aristotle criticizes those allegedly tragic plots which end with the good being rewarded and the bad being punished: "It is ranked first only through the weakness of the audiences; the poets merely follow their public, writing as its wishes dictate. But the pleasure here is not that of tragedy."[40] The implication seems to be that a proper tragic plot would be appreciated and enjoyed above all by a cultivated person. It is hard to escape the conclusion that, for Aristotle, education is for youths, and tragic catharsis is for educated, cultivated adults.

The third reason why the education interpretation of catharsis ought to be rejected is that there is a fundamental sense in which tragedy is not evoking the proper responses to events portrayed. Should we be spectators to tragic events which occur not in the theater but in real life to those who are close to us, or to those who are like us, the proper emotional response would be (the right amount of) pity and fear. To take any kind of pleasure from these events would be a thoroughly inappropriate response. Thus there is a sense in which tragedy provides a poor training for the emotional responses of real life: first, we should not be trained to seek out tragedy in real life, as we do seek it in the theater; second, we should not be trained to find any pleasure in real-life tragic events, as we do find pleasure in the tragic portrayals of the poets. Although a mimesis of pitiable and fearful events must to a certain extent be like the real-life events which they represent, the mimesis must, for Aristotle, also be in an important respect unlike those same events. For it is precisely because the mimesis is a mimesis that a certain type of pleasure is an appropriate response to it. Were it not for the fact that Aristotle recognized a salient difference between mimesis and the real-life events it portrays, Aristotle would have had to agree with Plato that poetry should be banned from the ideal state. Aristotle disagrees with Plato not over whether tragedy can be used as part of an ethical education in the appropriate emotional responses, but over whether a mimesis is easily confused with the real thing. Aristotle's point is that although the proper emotional response to a mimesis would be inappropriate to the real event, a mimesis is sufficiently unlike the real event that there is no danger of its having an improper educational effect on the audience. From the point of view of ethical education alone, poetry is allowed into the republic not because it has any positive educational value, but because it can be shown to lack any detrimental effects. If poetry has positive value, it must lie outside the realm of ethical education.

"There is not the same kind of correctness in poetry," Aristotle says, "as in politics, or indeed any other art."[41] The constraints on the poet differ considerably from the constraints on the politician. The politician is constrained to legislate an education in which youths will be trained to react appropriately to real-life events; in particular, to feel the right amount of pity and fear in response to genuinely pitiable and fearful events. The tragedian is constrained to evoke pity and fear through a mimesis of such events, but he is also constrained to provide a catharsis of those very emotions. It is in the catharsis of those emotions that the emotional response appropriate to poetry goes beyond that which is appropriate to the corresponding real-life events. Thus in coming to understand what

199

catharsis is, we will be approaching an understanding of the special contribution poetry makes to life.

The final reason why the education interpretation of catharsis ought to be rejected is that in the end it does not explain the peculiar pleasure of tragedy.[42] Of course, a proper appreciation of tragedy does require a finely tuned cognitive appreciation of the structure of the plot, and there is no doubt that the exercise of one's cognitive faculties in the appreciation of tragedy does afford a certain pleasure. But the pleasure we derive from tragedy is not primarily that which comes from satisfying the desire to understand.

In fact there is little textual support in the *Poetics* for the hypothesis that the peculiar pleasure of tragedy is a cognitive pleasure. The main support comes from *Poetics* 4, where Aristotle explains the origins of poetry:

> It is clear that the general origin of poetry was due to two causes, each of them part of human nature. Imitation [*mimesis*] is natural to man from childhood, one of his advantages over the lower animals being this, that he is the most imitative creature in the world, and learns at first by imitation. And it is also natural for all to delight in works of imitation. The truth of this second point is shown by experience; though the objects themselves may be painful to see, we delight to view the most realistic representations of them in art, the forms for example of the lowest animals and of dead bodies. The explanation is to be found in a further fact: to be learning something is the greatest of pleasures not only to the philosopher, but also to the rest of mankind, however small their capacity for it; the reason of the delight in seeing the picture is that one is at the same time learning and reasoning what each thing is, e.g., that this is that; for if one has not seen the thing before, one's pleasure will not be in the picture as an imitation of it, but will be due to the execution or coloring or some similar cause.[43]

Aristotle is here concerned with the origins of a process which culminates in the development of tragedy. Children begin learning by their early imitations of the adults around them, and in learning they derive a rudimentary form of cognitive pleasure; but this is only an explanation of how elementary forms of imitation naturally arise among humans. It is not an explanation of the peculiar pleasure of tragedy.

One must also be cautious in interpreting Aristotle's claim about the pleasure in learning. Aristotle is trying to explain why we take pleasure in viewing imitations of objects which are themselves painful to look at. Now, it is tempting to assimilate this passage with Aristotle's admonition in *Parts of Animals* that one should not shy away "with childish aversion" from studying blood and guts and even the humblest of animals: for the study of even the lowest of animals yields a pleasure which derives from discovering the intelligible causes of its functioning and the absence of chance.[44] For Aristotle there contrasts the cognitive pleasure derived from coming to understand causes from the pleasure derived from an imitation:

> For even if some [animals] are not pleasing to the sense of sight, nevertheless, creating nature provides extraordinary pleasures for those who are capable of understanding causes and who are by nature philosophical. Indeed, it would be unreasonable and strange if mimetic representations of them were attractive, because they disclose the mimetic skill of the painter or sculptor, and the original realities themselves were not more interesting, to all at any rate who have eyes to discern the reasons that determined their formation.[45]

Aristotle is saying that there are two distinct pleasures to be derived from animals which are in themselves unpleasant to look at: a cognitive pleasure in understanding their causes, and a "mimetic pleasure" in appreciating an artist's skill in accurately portraying these ugly creatures. It is this distinctively "mimetic pleasure" which Aristotle is concentrating on in *Poetics* 4. The reason he focuses on the artistic representation of an ugly animal is that he wants to be sure he is isolating the pleasure derived from the mimesis, rather than the pleasure one might derive from the beauty of the animal itself. In explaining this "mimetic pleasure," Aristotle does allude to the pleasure derived from learning. But that Aristotle has only the most rudimentary form of "learning" in mind is made clear by his claim that this pleasure in learning is available not only to the philosophically minded, but to all of mankind, however small their capacity for it. What one is "learning" is that this is that: that this (picture of a dead mouse) is (an accurate representation of) that ([a] dead mouse). The "reasoning" one is doing is confined to realizing that one thing (an artistic representation) is an instance of another. The pleasure, Aristotle says, is precisely that which would be unavailable to someone incapable of formulating this elementary realization: that is, to someone who had never seen a mouse or someone who, for whatever reason, was not able to recognize representation as a representation.[46] Thus it is a mistake to interpret this passage as suggesting that the reasoning is a reasoning about causes. *Poetics* 4, then, is about the most elementary pleasures which can be derived from the most elementary forms of mimesis. Although this is a first step toward an understanding of tragic pleasure, it does not lend support to the thesis that tragic pleasure is a species of cognitive pleasure.

Now, Aristotle does repeatedly insist that a good tragedy must have an intelligible plot structure. There must be a reason why the tragedy occurs: thus Aristotle says that the events must occur plausibly or necessarily,[47] that the events must occur on account of one another rather than in mere temporal succession,[48] and that the protagonist must make a certain mistake or error *(hamartia)* which is responsible for and explains his downfall.[49] And I think there is no doubt that the proper effect of tragedy on an audience is brought about via the audience's cognitive appreciation of the intelligible plot structure. The question, then, is not whether an audience must exercise its cognitive faculties, nor whether it may find pleasure in so doing; the question is whether this cognitive exercise and its attendant pleasure is the proper effect of tragedy. Is this cognitive pleasure the pleasure appropriate and peculiar to tragedy? To see that the answer is no, consider one of Aristotle's classic statements of the demand for intelligibility: "Tragedy is a mimesis not only of a complete action, but also of fearful and pitiable events. But such events occur in the strongest form when they occur unexpectedly but in consequence of one another. For the events are more marvelous [*thaumaston*] when they occur thus than if they occur by chance."[50] Aristotle's point is that a plot structure in which the events do not merely succeed each other in time, but stand in the relation of intelligible cause to intelligible effect, albeit a relation in which the intelligibility comes to light only with a reversal and recognition, is the best plot structure for portraying truly pitiable and fearful events. What it is to be a pitiable and fearful event is to be an event capable of inducing pity and fear in the audience. But pity and fear is clearly not the proper effect of tragedy: it is merely a necessary step along the route toward the proper effect. For Aristotle says that it is from pity and fear that tragedy produces a catharsis of these emotions.[51] Therefore, the audience's cognitive appreciation of the plot's intelligible structure and attendant pleasure is important, but they are causal antecedents of the proper effect and proper pleasure of tragedy.

Aristotle does say that events are more marvelous when they occur unexpectedly but in an intelligible relation to each other. And this fact is invoked by those who wish to argue that tragic pleasure is a cognitive pleasure. For in the *Metaphysics* and *Rhetoric,* Aristotle links the wondrous or marvelous with our desire to understand.[52] It is owing to wonder, Aristotle says, that man first began to philosophize: the rising and setting of the sun, for example, provokes man's wonder, and this wonder sets him on a journey to explain why this phenomenon occurs.[53] Thus it is suggested that the wonder that is produced in a tragedy provokes the audience to try to understand the events portrayed, and the pleasure which attends coming to understand is tragic pleasure.[54]

If there were already a strong case for thinking that tragic pleasure was cognitive pleasure, then the link between the marvelous and tragedy, on the one hand, and the desire to understand, on the other, would be suggestive. However, in the absence of a strong case, there are three reasons why Aristotle's remarks on the marvelous cannot be used to lend any significant support to the idea that tragic pleasure is cognitive. First, in the *Poetics* passage just quoted Aristotle seems to be suggesting that the relation between wonder and understanding is precisely the opposite of that suggested by the *Metaphysics:* it is by cognitively grasping that the events, though unexpected, are intelligibly linked to one another that wonder is produced in us. So whereas in the *Metaphysics* wonder provokes us to understand, in the *Poetics* understanding provokes us to experience wonder. Second, although in the quoted passage Aristotle associates intelligibility with wonder, toward the end of the *Poetics* Aristotle also associates wonder with irrationality.[55] One advantage of epic over tragedy, he says there, is that it is better suited to portraying irrational events *(to alogon).* For since the audience of an epic narrative does not actually have to see the irrationality acted out onstage, it is less likely to notice it as irrational.

However, Aristotle says, it is the irrational which chiefly produces wonder. And he says that the experience of wonder itself is pleasant.[56] So in this case it cannot be that wonder provokes understanding which is pleasant—for irrationality ultimately resists understanding. And at the end of the *Poetics* Aristotle suggests that the pleasure proper to epic and the pleasure proper to tragedy are of the same type,[57] even though tragedy is a higher form of art. Yet if the pleasure proper to epic can be derived from a plot containing irrationalities, it hardly seems that this pleasure can be cognitive. Finally, even granting a link between wonder and cognitive pleasure in itself does nothing to support the thesis that tragic pleasure is cognitive. For an anticognitivist like myself does not believe that there is no role for cognition and its attendant pleasure in the appreciation of a tragedy; he only denies that cognitive pleasure is to be identified with tragic pleasure. For the anticognitivist, cognitive pleasure is a step which occurs en route to the production of the proper pleasure of tragedy.

The final text cited in support of the cognitivist thesis is Aristotle's claim that poetry is "more philosophical" than history:

> Poetry is more philosophical and more serious than history: for poetry speaks more about universals, while history speaks of particulars. By universal is meant what sort of thing such a sort of person would plausibly or necessarily say or do—which is the aim of poetry though it affixes proper names to characters; by a particular, what Alcibiades did or had done to him.[58]

Of course, philosophy is an exercise of man's cognitive faculties, and, as is well known, Aristotle repeatedly insists that it is universals which man understands.[59] However, even if we interpret this passage just as cognitivists would like us to—as suggesting an intimate link between the appreciation of tragedy and the exercise of our cognitive abilities—nothing in this passage would help us decide between the cognitivist and the anticognitivist theses. For, as we have seen, the anticognitivist does not deny that a cognitive understanding of the plot is essential to the proper appreciation of a tragedy; he only denies that tragic pleasure can be identified with the pleasure which attends understanding.

But, more importantly, I don't think we should interpret this passage as the cognitivists would like us to. There is a certain plasticity in the idea of a universal which facilitates the transition from poetry to cognition. The true objects of knowledge, for Aristotle, are essences, and these essences are "universal" in the sense that two healthy human beings will instantiate the same essence: human soul. But the reason that essences are linked with knowledge is that in coming to understand a thing's essence we come to understand what that thing is really like. In coming to understand human essence, we come to understand what it is to be a human being. Now, when Aristotle says that poetry is "more philosophical" than history because it deals with universals, it is tempting to read him as saying that poetry provides us with deeper insights into the human condition. This is a temptation which ought to be resisted.[60] If we look to what Aristotle means by "universal" in the passage under discussion, it is clear that he does not mean "universal which expresses the essence of the human condition," but something much less grandiose: that poetry should refrain from describing the particular events of particular people and instead portray the sorts of things a given type of person might say or do. Aristotle later gives an example of what he means by the universal element in poetry:

> The following will show how the universal element in *Iphigenia*, for instance, may be viewed: a certain maiden having been offered in sacrifice, and spirited away from her sacrificers into another land, where the custom was to sacrifice all strangers to the Goddess, she was made there the priestess of his rite. Long after that the brother of the priestess happened to come: the fact, however, of the oracle having bidden him go there, and his object in going, are outside the plot of the play. On his coming he was arrested, and about to be sacrificed, when he revealed who he was—either as Euripides puts it or (as suggested by Polyidus) by the not improbable exclamation, "so I too am doomed to be sacrificed as my sister was"; and the disclosure led to his salvation. This done, the next thing, after the proper names have been fixed as a basis for the story, is to turn to the episodes.[61]

Aristotle's point is simply that poetry deals with types of actions and type of persons, even though the poet, after having constructed the "universal" plot, later assigns names to the characters.[62] Aristotle does say that such a universal plot is "more philosophical" than history, but by this he did not mean that poetry gives us ultimate understanding of humanity.

Rather, he meant that it has emerged from the mire of particularity in which history is trapped and thus has taken a step along the way toward philosophy. Whether fairly or unfairly, Aristotle had a very low opinion of history (he seemed to hold history in the same regard as we hold newspapers), and thus something doesn't have to be very philosophical to be more philosophical than history.[63]

What then is the point of Aristotle's requirement that poetry deal with universals, if it is not to insist upon poetry's ultimate cognitive value? If we read *Poetics* 9 through to the end it becomes clear that Aristotle's overall concern is with the formation of a plot which effectively produces pity and fear in the audience.[64] But in order to feel pity and fear the audience must believe that there is a certain similarity between themselves and the character in the tragedy: and the reason they must believe in this similarity is that they must believe that the events portrayed in the tragedy might happen to them. For a person to feel pity and fear, he must believe that he himself is vulnerable to the events he is witnessing. That is why Aristotle says that the poet's function is to portray not events which have happened, but events which might happen—and that these possible occurrences must seem plausible or even necessary.[65] The point of portraying events which might plausibly happen is that the audience will naturally come to believe that these events might happen to them. And this is a crucial step in the production of pity and fear in their souls. Poetry uses universals for the same purpose. Because poetry is not mired in particularity, but concerns itself with types of events which occur to certain sorts of people, it is possible for the audience to appreciate that they are the sort of people to whom this sort of event could, just possibly, occur. The universality Aristotle has in mind when he talks about the universality of poetry is not as such aiming at the depth of the human condition; it is aiming at the universality of the human condition.[66]

THE EDUCATION INTERPRETATION, however attractive it is, must be rejected as an account of what Aristotle meant by tragic catharsis. But having already rejected the purgation and purification interpretations, we have abandoned all the important traditional accounts. What then did Aristotle mean by tragic catharsis? It is to this question that I now turn.

Although the work so far has been largely critical, I think something of positive value has emerged. For in seeing how previous interpretations fall short, we have isolated a series of constraints which any acceptable interpretation of catharsis must satisfy. These constraints may not be so narrow as to isolate a single, definitive interpretation, but they at least set out a field in which the truth must lie. In this section I would like to state the constraints on any acceptable interpretation of catharsis and to offer an interpretation which fits those constraints.

One of the major constraints on any interpretation is:

1. There is reason for a virtuous person to experience the performance of a tragedy: he too will experience a catharsis of pity and fear.[67]

Precisely because of (1), it follows that

2. Tragic catharsis cannot be a process which is essentially and crucially corrective: that is, it cannot be a purgation, insofar as purgation is of something pathological or noxious; it cannot be a purification of some pollution; it cannot be an education of the emotions.

This is not to deny that a cathartic experience may be corrective. Aristotle, as we have already seen, thought that cathartic melodies can help to restore those who are particularly susceptible to religious frenzy; and one might similarly suppose that a tragic catharsis could restore those who are particularly susceptible to the tragic emotions of pity and fear. Nor do I mean to deny that a virtuous person may experience relief in a cathartic experience—a relief which it is natural to conceive of in terms of the release of pent-up emotions. However, the virtuous person is not in a pathological condition, nor is he polluted with some impure element which needs to be removed. Nor is he in need of any further training of the emotions: indeed, it is because he is already disposed to respond appropriately to the situations of life, in judgment, in action, and in emotion, that he is virtuous. The idea that catharsis provides an education of the emotions suffers further from the fact that

3. What one feels at the performance of a tragedy is not what one would or should feel in the real-life counterpart.

For although tragedy provokes pity and fear in the audience, it also elicits an appropriate pleasure. This pleasure would be thoroughly inappropriate to real-life tragic situations. But the fact that a good person (at least) feels pleasure in the performance of a tragedy, but would not do so in real life, suggests that

4. A proper audience does not lose sight of the fact that it is enjoying the performance of a tragedy.

Although the audience may identify emotionally with the characters in the tragedy, this identification must remain partial. Throughout its emotional involvement, the audience keeps track of the fact that it is an audience. For in a real-life tragedy a person would feel fear and, if he stood in the right relation to the tragic event, pity, but he would derive no pleasure from the tragic event. This implies that

5. The mere expression or release of emotions is not in itself pleasurable.

For Aristotle, pity and fear are unadulterated pains.[68] The mere opportunity to feel these painful emotions does not in itself provide relief: everything depends on the conditions in which these painful emotions are to be felt. Those who have assumed that a catharsis, for Aristotle, was a release or discharge of pent-up or unexpressed emotions have also assumed that the mere experience of emotions, even painful ones, has a pleasurable aspect to it. There is pleasure to be had in a good cry. Such an idea may have a certain plausibility to it, but it is foreign to Aristotle. For him, it depends on what one is crying about. If one is crying in the theater, a certain pleasure may ensue, but there is, for Aristotle, no pleasure to be had in crying over real-life tragic events. This is the problem with taking catharsis to be the mere release of emotion. For Aristotle there is nothing pleasurable per se about experiencing pity and fear.

These conditions under which we can derive pleasure from pity and fear and the conditions under which a catharsis of pity and fear occurs are intimately linked, for

6. Catharsis provides a relief: it is either itself pleasurable or it helps to explain the proper pleasure which is derived from tragedy.[69]

Constraints (3)–(6) together suggest that if we are to understand tragic catharsis, we should look to the special ways in which tragedy produces its emotional effects.

Aristotle, as we have seen, defines tragedy in part by the effect it has on its audience: it is a mimesis of an action which by arousing pity and fear produces a catharsis of those emotions.[70] It might seem odd to a modern reader to see Aristotle define tragedy in terms of its effect, for in a modern climate we tend to think that a work of art should be definable in its own terms, independently of whatever effect it might have on its audience. But it would be anachronistic to insist that Aristotle could not have been defining tragedy in terms of its effect on the audience. Poetry, for Aristotle, is a type of making, and the activity of any making occurs in the person or thing toward which the making is directed.[71] For example, the activity of the teacher teaching is occurring, not in the teacher, but in the students who are learning; the activity of the builder building is occurring, not in the builder, but in the house being built. It stands to reason that, for Aristotle, the activity of the poet creating his tragedy occurs ultimately in an audience actively appreciating a performance of the play.[72]

Not only does Aristotle define tragedy in terms of its effect; he thinks that various tragic plots can be evaluated in terms of their effects on an audience.

We assume that, for the finest form of tragedy, the plot must be not simple but complex; and further, that it must imitate actions arousing fear and pity, since that is the distinctive function of this kind of imitation. It follows, therefore, that there are three forms of plot to be avoided. A good man must not be seen passing from good fortune to bad, or a bad man from bad fortune to good. The first situation is not fear-inspiring or piteous, but simply disgusting. The second is the most untragic that can be: it has no one of the requisites of tragedy; it does not appeal either to the human feeling in us, or to our pity, or to our fears. Nor, on the other hand, should an extremely bad man be seen falling from good fortune into bad. Such a story may arouse the human feeling in us, but it will not move us to either pity or fear; pity is occasioned by undeserved misfortune, and fear by that of one like ourselves; so that there will be nothing either piteous or fear-inspiring in the situation.[73]

The important point to note about this passage is that Aristotle is evaluating plots not on the basis of feelings, but on the basis of the emotions. The reason we do not feel pity and fear in witnessing the fall of a bad man from good to bad fortune is that pity requires the belief that the misfortune is undeserved, and fear requires the belief that the man who has suffered the misfortune is like ourselves.[74] (Presumably Aristotle assumed that the proper audience of tragedy would not believe themselves to be sufficiently like a bad person to believe that the things which befall him—most likely as a consequence of his badness—might befall them.)

Similarly with the disgust we feel when watching a good man fall from good to bad fortune: such disgust isn't a pure feeling which can be identified on the basis of its phenomenological properties alone. Disgust requires the belief that there is no reason at all for this good man's fall. It is sometimes thought that Aristotle contradicts himself, for he elsewhere seems to suggest that tragedy is paradigmatically about admirable men falling to bad fortune.[75] But if we take the rest of chapter 13 as explicating what Aristotle means when he denies that the fall of a good man can be the basis of a properly tragic plot, I think we can see a consistent point emerging. In tragedy, Aristotle insists, the central character must make some mistake or error which leads to his fall.[76] The *hamartia* is a mistake which rationalizes the fall. So what Aristotle is excluding when he prohibits the fall of a good man is a totally irrational fall: one which occurs through no fault of the good man at all. Aristotle certainly does allow the fall of a good man to be the subject matter of tragedy, but not of a man who is so good that he has made no mistakes which would rationalize his fall. This distinction illuminates what is meant by disgust: disgust is an emotion which is partially constituted by the belief that there is no reason at all for the misfortune. Disgust is something we feel in response to what we take to be a total absence of rationality.

Aristotle thinks that the mere fact that tragedy must arouse pity and fear in the audience justifies him in severely restricting the range of tragic plots.

It is not necessary to search for every pleasure from tragedy, but only the appropriate pleasure. But since it is necessary for the poet to produce the pleasure from pity and fear through a mimesis, it is evident that he must do this in the events in the plot. We should investigate, then, what sorts of events appear to be horrible or pitiable. In respect to such actions, it is necessary that the people involved be either friends with each other or enemies or neither of these. But if enemy acts on enemy, there is nothing pitiable about this—neither in the doing of the deed, nor in intending to do it—except in relation to the terrible event itself [*kat' auto to pathos*]. The same is true when the people stand in neither relation. But whenever the terrible events occur among loved ones [friends, kin], for example if a brother should kill or intend to kill or do some other such thing to a brother, or a son to a father, or a mother to a son, or a son to a mother: we should search for these things.[77]

Aristotle is clear that the peculiar pleasure of tragedy is produced by evoking pity and fear in the audience and that this is accomplished by constructing a mimesis of a special type of terrible event *(pathos)*. Aristotle uses the same word, *pathos,* both to signify a terrible event, catastrophe, or serious misfortune and to signify emotion. When, for example, Aristotle cites *pathos* as one of the three ingredients needed in a plot, along with reversal and recognition, in order to produce pity and fear, he is not requiring a certain emotion to be portrayed onstage; he is requiring that there be a destructive act.[78] So one might say that, for Aristotle, there is an objective *pathos* and a subjective *pathos;* and the two are related. For what Aristotle is trying to do in this passage is delimit the precise type of objective *pathos* which is adequate to bring about a particular type of subjective *pathos*—pity and fear—in response.[79]

The objective *pathos* required to produce the tragic emotions is a terrible deed done between kin or loved ones. That is why the great tragedians have correctly focused on just a few families which have been ripped apart by terrible deeds.[80] But what is it about the portrayal of a terrible deed done among kin which makes it particularly well suited to evoking pity and fear?

Perhaps a start may be made in answering this question by recognizing that at least a necessary condition for the audience to feel pity and fear in response to such terrible deeds is that they believe that such events could happen to them. For fear, this is obvious. Aristotle, as we have seen, defines fear as a pain due to imagining some painful or destructive event befalling one. And he further requires that the fearful event be both imminent and capable of causing great pain.[81] For we do not fear distant pains, for example death, nor do we fear imminent but minor pains: "From the definition it will follow that fear is caused by whatever we feel has great power of destroying us, or of harming us in ways that tend to cause us great pain."[82] Aristotle is explicit that we feel fear only when we believe that we are ourselves vulnerable to an imminent and grave danger: "we shall not fear things that we believe cannot happen to us."[83] A further condition on fear is that we must believe that there is at least a faint possibility of escape from the danger.[84]

At first sight, it appears that pity is the paradigm of an other-regarding emotion. We feel pity for others when they suffer what we believe to be undeserved pain.[85] However, Aristotle makes it clear that in order to feel pity for others we must also believe that the terrible event which has befallen them might befall us or our loved ones and, moreover, might befall us soon. Thus in order for us to feel pity for others, we must believe that the others' situation is significantly similar to our own. One might at first think that pity can be felt for those who are in some relevant respect like us—in either social standing, or character, or age—even though we do not believe we could end up in their situation; but Aristotle denies this. We do feel pity for those who are like us, but the reason we do, Aristotle thinks, is that in such cases we think it more likely that the misfortune which has befallen them can befall us.[86] This likelihood explains Aristotle's otherwise puzzling remark in the *Poetics* that we fear for someone who is similar to us.[87] Why not simply pity him? Aristotle's point is that fear is an appropriate emotion to feel in response to a similar person's misfortune: for through his similarity we recognize that we stand in the same danger he did.

Likewise with pity. Aristotle's only caveat is that the perceived danger cannot be too immediate, for in that case fear (for oneself) will drive out pity (for others).[88] Pity will also be driven out of the souls of those who, already ruined, believe that no ill can further harm them, and of those who believe themselves omnipotent and impervious to harm.[89]

Those who think they may suffer are those who have already suffered and have safely escaped from it: elderly men, owing to their good sense and their experience; weak men, especially men inclined to cowardice; and also educated people, for they are able to reason well.[90]

Aristotle clearly recognizes pity as a reasonable emotion for an educated and thoughtful person: and since good tragedy is ideally for an educated audience, it follows that, for Aristotle, the pity which good tragedy evokes is a reasonable emotional response to the events portrayed.

IT FOLLOWS that a normal, educated audience, going to a performance of a good tragedy, believes that the terrible events portrayed—infanticide, parricide, matricide, the tearing apart of the most primordial bonds of family and society—could happen to them. If they lacked that belief they would, in Aristotle's eyes, be incapable of experiencing the tragic emotions. This shared belief allows us to impose a further constraint, at least upon the emotions from which a tragic catharsis is produced:

7. The events which in a tragedy properly provoke the pity and fear from which a tragic catharsis occurs must be such that the audience believes that such events could happen to them.

First I would like to dispose of two objections which might be raised against this conclusion. The most serious objection is that the audience need not believe that the terrible events could happen to them: they are able to experience the tragic emotions because they are able to identify imaginatively with the central character and thus empathically feel what he feels. Within Aristotle's world, it is clear that the objection has the situation the wrong way around: for Aristotle, it is only because we think ourselves to be sufficiently like another that we can identify with him.[91] On Aristotle's view, we cannot identify with the very bad or with the gods: it is precisely because we are so distant from such beings that our emotions must retain a similar distance from theirs. That is why, for Aristotle, there is no important distinction to be made between our feeling our fear and our feeling Oedipus' fear. The very possibility of our imagi-natively feeling Oedipus' fear is grounded in the recognition that we are like him: that is, it is grounded in the possibility of our fearing for our-selves.[92] Moreover, this objection does not take seriously the emotion of pity. We cannot feel pity in imaginatively identifying with Oedipus: part of what makes Oedipus such a remarkable and admirable figure is his lack of self-pity. But if our pity isn't an imaginative reenactment of Oedipus' self-pity, then it must, as we have seen, be grounded in the belief that his fate could be ours.[93]

The less serious objection is that the audience doesn't come to the per-formance believing that the terrible events portrayed in the tragedy could happen to them: they are persuaded that this is so by the performance it-self. The shortest answer to this objection is also the best: tragedy is not rhetoric; it is poetry. Because fear sets us thinking about how to escape from the perceived danger, an orator may wish to persuade his audience that they are in danger;[94] but a tragedy doesn't try to persuade its audi-ence of anything. The only effect on the audience which a tragedy aims to produce is a certain emotional response (the content of which we are try-ing to uncover). Of course, if tragedy is to succeed in this, it must portray events which are convincing, plausible, events which plausibly could occur.[95] But Aristotle's point in insisting that the poet construct plausible, convincing plots is not so that the poet may persuade the audience of anything but so that he may portray an event which the audience can recognize as one which could, just possibly, happen to them.

Now, if a normal, educated audience attending the performance of a good tragedy believes that the terrible events to be portrayed could, just possibly, happen to them, there seems to be a striking fact which is true of them both before they enter and after they leave the theater: they seem to have the beliefs which would justify the experience of pity and fear, but they are not experiencing those emotions.[96]

A misleading way of putting an important truth is this: that when a normal, educated person experiences a performance of a good tragedy, he is able to unify certain beliefs he has with feelings which are appropriate to those beliefs. He came to the theater believing that he could commit or suffer terrible deeds. In the theater he is able to feel those beliefs. But before we jump to the conclusion that catharsis is a unification of belief and feeling, a unification of the tragic emotions, let us stop to consider why this mode of expression is misleading. It is misleading because it suggests that what we feel in the theater is what we ought to feel in real life: that in real life the appropriate feelings are somehow kept at bay from the beliefs which would rationalize them.

But this cannot be right. For constraint (1) requires that the virtuous person experience a catharsis in the performance of a tragedy, but his emotional reactions are already appropriate to the real-life situations in which he lives; and constraint (3) requires that our emotional response to tragedy is not what we would or should feel in response to real-life counterparts. Tragic pleasure depends crucially on the belief that one is emotionally responding to a mimesis of tragic events. Without this belief, tragic pleasure is impossible. Therefore, constraint (7)—that the audience believe that tragic events could happen to them—must be interpreted in a way which does not suggest that the virtuous person, in not feeling pity and fear in ordinary life, is somehow cut off from a proper emotional response to his situation. It is completely un-Aristotelian to suppose that what we feel in the theater is what we ought to feel in real life, but for some reason do not. In real life the virtuous man feels just what he ought to feel. But then, how could he believe that terrible, tragic deeds could, just possibly, befall him and not feel fear and dread?

Everything depends on the strength of the modal operator. The virtuous man believes that terrible, tragic events could happen to him, true, but the possibility that those things will happen is, in his opinion, too remote for the actual feeling of fear to be warranted.[97] Although a tragic breakdown of the primordial ties of human life is possible, the virtuous man also recognizes that this is less likely to happen to him than almost anything else. That is why it is misleading to say that tragedy restores the appropriate feelings to our already existing beliefs. Our belief that tragic events could, just possibly, befall us already has the appropriate feeling attached to it outside the theater. No unification is needed, for, at least in the case of the virtuous person, there is no split which needs to be overcome.

And yet the belief that tragic events could, just possibly, happen to us does exert some pressure on our souls—even on the souls of us virtuous people. This is precisely the pressure which takes us to the theater. For in the theater we can imaginatively bring what we take to be a remote possibility closer to home. As Aristotle himself said: "those who heighten the effect of their words with suitable gestures, tones, appearance, and dramatic action generally are especially successful in exciting pity: they thus put the disasters before our eyes, and make them seem close to us, just coming or just past."[98]

The tragic poet, for Aristotle, plays a role in the world of emotions somewhat similar to the role of the skeptic in the world of beliefs. The skeptic awakens us to the fact that we ourselves believe in certain epistemic possibilities which in ordinary life we ignore: for example, that we could be asleep, dreaming, or perhaps deceived by an evil demon. On the one hand, these possibilities are extremely remote, so we are justified in ignoring them in ordinary life; on the other hand, they lend content to the idea that in ordinary life we are living "inside the plain": and they fuel our desire to get outside the plain of everyday life and see how things really are, absolutely.[99]

The tragic poet awakens us to the fact that there are certain emotional possibilities which we ignore in ordinary life. On the one hand, these possibilities are remote, so it is not completely unreasonable to ignore them in ordinary life; on the other hand, they lend content to the idea that in ordinary life we are living "inside the plain": and they fuel our desire imaginatively to experience life outside the plain. Even if tragedy does not befall us, it goes to the root of the human condition that it is a possibility we must live with. And even if remote, the possibility of tragedy is not only much more imminent than the skeptical possibilities; it is much more threatening. For while skeptical possibilities are so designed that they make no difference to the experience of our lives, in tragedy our lives are ripped asunder.

But there is a genuine problem about how to experience tragic possibility. On the one hand, the possibility of tragedy in ordinary life is too remote to justify real fear; on the other hand, it is too important and too close to ignore. Tragic poetry provides an arena in which one can imaginatively experience the tragic emotions: the performance of a play "captures our souls."[100] However, it is crucial to the pleasure we derive from tragedy, that we never lose sight of the fact that we are an audience, enjoying a work of art. Otherwise the pleasurable catharsis of pity and fear would collapse into the merely painful experience of those emotions. Aristotle is keenly aware of the important difference between a mimesis of a serious action and the serious action of which it is a mimesis. The emotional response which is appropriate to a mimesis—tragic pleasure and catharsis—would be thoroughly inappropriate to the real event.

It is this experience of the tragic emotions in an appropriately inappropriate environment which, I think, helps to explain our experience of relief in the theater. We imaginatively live life to the full, but we risk nothing. The relief is thus not that of "releasing pent-up emotions" per se; it is the relief of "releasing" these emotions in a safe environment. But to say that it is this experience of relief to which Aristotle gave the name "catharsis" is not to characterize it fully: one needs also to know the content of our relief, what our relief is about.

Here I will only mention briefly certain consolations which are integral to Aristotle's conception of tragedy. The world of tragic events must, Aristotle repeatedly insists, be rational. The subject of tragedy may be a good man, but he must make a mistake which rationalizes his fall.[101] The mere fall of a good man from good fortune to bad fortune for no reason at all isn't tragic, but disgusting. The events in a tragedy must be necessary or plausible, and they must occur on account of one another. Insofar as we do fear that tragic events could occur in our lives, what we fear is chaos: the breakdown of the primordial bonds which link person to person. For Aristotle, a good tragedy offers us this consolation: that even when the breakdown of the primordial bonds occurs, it does not occur in a world which is in itself ultimately chaotic and meaningless.

It is significant that, for Aristotle, *Oedipus Tyrannus* is the paradigm tragedy rather than, say, *Antigone*.[102] For the point of tragedy, in Aristotle's eyes, is not to portray a world in which a person through no fault of her own may be subject to fundamentally irreconcilable and destructive demands. In Aristotle's conception of tragedy, the individual actor takes on the burden of badness, and the world as a whole is absolved.[103] And there is further consolation is recognizing that even when they are responsible for their misfortunes, humans remain capable of conducting themselves with dignity and nobility.[104] Even in his humiliation and shame, Oedipus inspires our awe and admiration.

In the *Rhetoric* Aristotle says that those who have already experienced great disasters no longer feel fear, for they feel they have already experienced every kind of horror.[105] In tragedy, we are able to put ourselves imaginatively in a position in which there is nothing further to fear. There is consolation in realizing that one has experienced the worst, there is nothing further to fear, and yet the world remains a rational, meaningful place in which a person can conduct himself with dignity. For Aristotle, even in tragedy the fundamental goodness of man and world is reaffirmed.[106]

CHAPTER 10

Inside and outside
the *Republic*

An engaged reader of the *Republic* must at some point wonder how—or if—it all fits together. There seem to be jumbled within that text a challenge to conventional justice, a political theory, a psychology, a metaphysics, a theory of education, and a critique of art, music and poetry. A brilliant work; but is it an integrated whole? A just republic, for Plato, turns out to be a harmonious, though differentiated, unity; and so the question can be rephrased: is the *Republic* a just *Republic?* Most of the illuminating discussions of the *Republic* can be seen as attempts to answer this question. I would like to suggest that this problem of unity arises in a particularly acute form for modern readers, because we are disposed to see the *Republic* as existing in bits. For we tend to conceive of psychology as the psychology of the individual. Since Plato, in the *Republic,* is concerned with the constitution of the individual psyche, it is easy for us to assume that his psychology is revealed in that account. But this omits what, I believe, is the most distinctive aspect of Plato's psychology: a dynamic account of the psychological transactions between inside and outside a person's psyche, between a person's inner life and his cultural environment, between *intra*psychic and *inter*psychic relations.[1] If we ignore these dynamic transactions, we cannot understand even individual psychology. We miss what, for Plato, holds a person together—and also what holds Plato together. For if one assumes that psychology is individual psychology, the *Republic* will then look as though it is composed of various bits—among them, a psychology and a political theory—and there will inevitably be a question of how they fit together. In Plato's psychology, as I understand it, this question should not arise. For *psyche*-analysis and *polis*-analysis are, for Plato, two aspects of a single discipline, psychology, which has at its core the relation between inside and outside. What holds the *Republic* together is Plato's understanding of what holds people and polis together.

Here I shall concentrate on two topics which lie at the heart of the *Republic*. First, there is the analogy between polis and psyche. Plato thought that there were important structural isomorphisms between polis and psyche, and thus that he could use discoveries about one to prove results about the other. It is now widely accepted that Plato uses this analogy to fudge his arguments. Plato, so the charge goes, uses a vague analogy fallaciously, and he is thereby able to hide a fundamental tension which underlies his ideal polis. That is, he disguises the repressive relation between the ruling class and the ruled by an illegitimate comparison with the structure of the psyche. I shall argue that these criticisms look valid because Plato's psychology is not well understood.

Second, Plato's critique of the poets has inspired a wealth of deep and imaginative discussion,[2] but all of it has tended to concentrate on two questions: what is the effect of poetry on us? and what is the moral value of art? Plato's argument is intriguing because, roughly speaking, we tend to think that art is good for us, while Plato argues that it is bad. Modern psychoanalysts and psychologists often think that art offers a kind of psychic salvation; while Plato treats acquaintance with Homer and the great Greek tragedians as a psychological catastrophe. And so we are led, like bees to nectar, to find a flaw in Plato's argument or, less often, to reevaluate our own aesthetics. Perhaps it is this fascination which has blinded us to the fact that we have been living on a restricted diet of questions. There are other questions, central to Plato's psychology, which as far as I know have not been asked, let alone answered. For example: who, psychologically speaking, are the poets? What, from a psychological point of view, are the poets doing in making poetry? And what is Plato doing, psychologically speaking, in banishing the poets? These are questions which, I think, tend to be obscured by assuming psychology to be the study of the individual psyche, but they come to the fore when psychology is taken to span the boundary of an individual's psyche. For we will then see poetry as coming from some psyches and entering others, and the question naturally arises: what, from a psychological perspective, is going on?

My hope is that the discussions of the polis-psyche relation and of poetry will illuminate the approach to Plato's psychology which I am advocating, and help to confirm it. As a by-product, I hope we shall also see the *Republic* as more unified than it is often taken to be.

INTERNALIZATION

At the beginning of book 2 Socrates takes up the challenge, which will occupy the rest of the *Republic*, to describe justice and injustice as an "inherent condition inside the psyche."[3] Although he proposes to look first at justice writ large in the polis,[4] in fact Socrates turns almost immediately to the psyche. For he begins his construction of the ideal polis with a discussion of the education of young children. And he justifies this strategy by saying that "the beginning of any project is most important, especially for anything young and tender. For it is then that it takes shape and any mold one may want can be impressed upon it" (2.377a–b). If we carelessly allow children to hear any old stories, he says, they may "take into their psyches" beliefs which are contrary to those they should hold as adults (377b). Nursemaids and mothers must be allowed to tell only certain stories to their children and so "shape their psyches." Children should not be allowed to hear the classic tales of warring gods, because the young cannot distinguish what is allegorical from what is not, and the opinions they form at that age tend to be unalterable.[5] For Plato, humans enter the world with a capacity to absorb cultural influences. The young human psyche is like a resin, able to receive the impress of cultural influences before it sets into a definite shape. And it is clear that, for Plato, the stakes

221

are high. The goal of achieving a well-governed polis depends on there being no one in the polis either asserting or hearing any tales which suggest that God is the cause of anything bad (380b–c). Plato believes these tales will shape the character of the future citizens.[6] Mothers must not be allowed to terrify their children with bad tales about gods sneaking about in disguise, "for at the same time as they blaspheme the gods, they make their children cowardly" (381e).

If, for example, one is an honor-loving person, one should be brought up on stories of brave men doing brave deeds so as to fear slavery more than death (387); be allowed to play at and later imitate only the deeds appropriate to a guardian, "lest from imitation they take in the reality" (3.395c); be brought up in a rigorous program of music and gymnastics that reinforce the honor-loving part of one's psyche;[7] and be taken out even as a youth to observe battles (5.466e–467a); so that when one is grown, it is through the activities of guardianship that one achieves happiness.[8] If this program of education and culture is successful, the qualities appropriate to guardianship should "settle into one's character and into one's nature" (3.395d). Plato seems to be saying that through proper imitations from youth, one actually constitutes oneself as a certain type of person. Whether one develops into a noble and brave person, at one extreme, or a base coward, at the other, depends significantly on the myths one has heard from youth, the education one has received, the models one has been given to imitate. Leaving divine inspiration aside, Plato thinks that were it not for this training, one would not develop the character or nature of a guardian.[9]

The *Republic* is a study in the health and pathologies of polis and psyche. And the conditions of polis and psyche are interdependent. The variety of pathologies of the psyche, for example, depends on the person's taking in pathological structures from the culture. Culture penetrates so deeply that a fractured polis will produce a fractured psyche. For Plato, it is only the ideal polis that can properly be called a polis or a city (4.422e). Other actual cities or *poleis* are only apparently such. In fact, each lacks sufficient internal unity to count as *a* polis: each is, in truth, many *poleis* or, more properly, polis-parts (422e–423d). But, Plato argues, for every pathological polis there is a corresponding pathology of the psyche (books

8–9). The conclusion of the syllogism is that a pathological psyche is not, in fact, *a* psyche, but various psychic parts. So, for example, just as an oligarchy is not *a* polis, but two parts, a rich part and a poor part (8.551d), so an "oligarchical psyche" is in fact two psychic parts: a ruling part and a ruled (553c–554e). For Plato, there is not sufficient integration in the functioning of the parts for them to count as a genuine unity, a psyche. Indeed, even among the oligarchical person's appetites there will be division and faction.[10] Being thrifty and acquisitive, the oligarchical person will satisfy only his necessary appetites and "enslave" his other appetites (554a). Because of his "lack of culture," his unruly and unnecessary appetites spring up in him, but they are "forcibly restrained" by the better part.[11] The oligarchical person is, says Plato, someone double (554d). For Plato, being double is a way of not being an integrated person: it is a divided and conflicted existence.[12] In fact, the pathologies of psyche Plato examines turn out, strictly speaking, to be studies in the failures to become a psyche.[13]

BY NOW IT SHOULD BE CLEAR THAT, for Plato, satisfying the human need for culture is a process of taking cultural influences into the psyche. Let us call this process, whatever it is precisely, *internalization*. Although Plato did not have an articulated theory, he did think that imitation *(mimesis)* was a paradigmatic means of internalization. It is youthful imitations which settle the shape of one's character and nature (3.395c–d). That is why musical education is preeminent: "because rhythm and harmony permeate the inner part of the psyche, bring graciousness to it, and make the strongest impression, making a man gracious if he has the right kind of upbringing; if not, the opposite is true" (401d–e). And it is clear that Plato thought that internalization was a largely unconscious process. Guardians should not be brought up among images of evil lest they "little by little collect all unawares a great evil in their own psyche."[14] One cannot change the modes of music, Plato says, without upsetting fundamental constitutional laws (4.424c); and it is clear that the causal route of this destabilization proceeds via internalization. For lawlessness, Plato says, easily creeps into music without our noticing, and, "having little by little settled in there it flows into the characters and pursuits" of people (424d). And so, in our education and rule of children, one should not let them be free until "a constitution is set up inside them just as in the polis" (9.590e).

For Plato, we are culture-vultures: we "feed" our psyches by internalizing cultural influences. That is the psychological point of culture; and it is why education and upbringing, on the one hand, and the shaping of culture, on the other, play such a predominant role in the *Republic*. It would seem, then, that internalization is a fundamental psychological activity.[15] The fact that we are so dependent on internalization for our psychological constitution makes us susceptible to cultural luck. Our ultimate dependency is manifest in the fact that we internalize these influences before we can understand their significance. We are dependent on culture for the constitution of our psyches, but on what does culture depend? How is culture itself shaped and formed?

EXTERNALIZATION

Plato suggests that culture is formed by an inverse process of psychological activity, moving outward from psyche to polis. For example, Plato says, "there must be as many types of character among men as there are forms of government. Or do you suppose that constitutions spring from the proverbial oak or rock and not from the characters of the citizens, which as it were, by their momentum and weight in the scales draw other things after them?" (8.544d–e). And character, Plato says elsewhere, is inherent in the psyche.[16] The same forms, he says, will be found in the polis and in the individual psyche (4.435c), and the shape of the polis has to be understood as deriving from the shape of the psyche:

> we are surely compelled to agree that the same forms and character-types are in each of us just as in the polis. They could not get there from any other source. It would be ridiculous if someone supposed that spiritedness has not come to be in the polis from individuals who are reputed to have this quality . . . or that the same is not true of the love of learning . . . or the love of money.[17]

It would seem, then, that for a significant range of psychopolitical predicates F,

224

If a polis is F, there must be some citizens whose psyches are F who (with others) have helped to shape the polis.

This is easiest to see in the case of the just polis. It will be shaped by the philosopher-king, whose thoughts are directed toward realities (6.500b–c). And though he will try to shape the city according to a divine paradigm (500e), he does so by first imitating these eternal realities, fashioning himself as far as possible in their likeness.[18] It is by associating with the divine order that the philosopher himself becomes ordered and divine, insofar as that is possible for humans (500c–d). The philosopher, Plato suggests, has a paradigm of the internal realities inside his psyche.[19] Although there is no existing ideal polis on earth—and thus no ideal cultural template to internalize—there is a paradigm of it in heaven, and a person studying it can constitute himself its citizen (9.592b). Only after the philosopher has shaped his own psyche by internalizing divine order is he able to shape the polis according to what has now become the order in his psyche.[20]

Let us call *externalization* the process, whatever it is, by which Plato thought a person fashions something in the external world according to a likeness in his psyche. Then, for Plato, the polis is formed by a process of externalization of structures within the psyches of those who shape it. And, more generally, externalization is a basic psychological activity. For Plato suggests that cultural products in general are externalizations. Good rhythm, harmony, and diction, for example, should follow and fit good speech; and speech, in turn, follows and fits the character of the psyche (3.400d–e). In painting and all artistic works, weaving, embroidery, architecture, the making of furniture, harmony and grace are closely related to and an imitation of good character (400e–401a). And character, as we have seen, is inherent in psyche.

Notoriously, Plato believes that education must begin by telling young children false tales (2.376e–377a). These myths are distinguished from unacceptable myths and legitimated, first, because there is truth in them (377a), but, second, because that truth is a reflection of a truth in the poet's psyche. A falsehood which is merely a falsehood in words "is an imitation of something in the psyche, a later reflection," which is therefore not completely untrue (382b–c). It is because this merely verbal falsehood is an externalization of something true within the poet's psyche that it can be used, with caution, as a medicine (382c–d). By contrast, falsehood in the psyche, falsehood taken as truth, is what people hate most of all (382b). This is ignorance in the psyche. Though Plato does not say so explicitly here, the implication is that unacceptable myths and poems are externalizations of this real falsehood.

AND SO IT SEEMS that in the ideal polis, after we internalize our cultural roles by a process of education, we externalize them in our social roles. It is by a process of internalization and externalization that we are able to conform to the rule of each performing his own task. Incoherence is avoided because Plato's is a developmental psychology. Internalization is going on primarily in unformed youths; externalization is going on primarily in adults who have already formed themselves through prior cultural internalizations. Psyche and polis are mutually constituted by a series of internalizations and externalizations, with transformations occurring on both sides of the border. We tend to think of the economic model in psychology as concerned with the distribution of a fixed quantity of energy—and, indeed Plato lends support to this model, since he believes that when a person's desires incline strongly toward something, they are correspondingly weakened for other things.[21] However, if we consider Plato's psychology as a whole, it would seem that a more promising economic model would be of trade across a border. Plato's psychology is basically one of interpsychic and intrapsychic trade. What is being traded across a boundary is not unformed energy, but psychological products. They are crafted both outside and inside an individual's psyche and are traded back and forth across the boundary of the psyche. Once inside, they become citizens of a more or less federated republic and are subject to the vicissitudes of intrapsychic conflict, before being externalized again across the border.

Plato decides first to look for justice writ large in the polis because, he says, he will then be able to read the small print of the individual psyche (2.368d–369a). By now it should be clear that he is not relying on a mere analogy of polis and psyche, but on an isomorphism which must hold because of the way we function psychologically. Psyche and polis, inner world and outer world, are jointly constituted by reciprocal internalizations and externalizations; and the analogy is a by-product of this psychological dynamic.

THE ANALOGY OF PSYCHE AND POLIS

One way to see the virtue of an interpretation is to see how the *Republic* looks without it. In his classic essay "The Analogy of City and Soul in Plato's *Republic*," Bernard Williams offers the most penetrating critique we have of Plato's analogy.[22] According to Williams, Plato's argument is incoherent, and the analogy disguises a fundamental tension in his account of psyche and polis. If Williams is right, the *Republic* is a brilliant mess. Here I would like to try to rescue the analogy from Williams' critique by attending to the psychological principles which underlie it.

The analogy, for Williams, is founded on two principles. First, there is *the whole-part rule*:[23]

> a. A city is F if and only if its men are F.

Second, there is the *analogy of meaning* (derived from 435a–b):

> b. The explanation of a city's being F is the same as that of a man's being F (the same *eidos* of F-ness applies to both).

Although it appears that these two principles support each other, Williams argues that is not so: the whole-part rule in fact "defeats" the analogy of meaning:

> For if we say that "F" is applied to the city just because it is applied to the men, we have already explained how the term can be applied to both cities and men, and to go on from there to look for a similar explanation of how "F" applies to men is at least pointless, since the phenomenon which set off the search for the analogy in the first place, viz. the fact that "F" applies to both cities and men has already been explained. If, moreover, the rule applying "F" to cities is taken as itself the common *logos* that we were looking for, then we have not just pointlessness but absurdity, since the common *logos* will have to be something like "x is F if and only if x has constituent parts which are F," which leads to a regress.[24]

However, Plato does not in fact think that F is applied to a polis "just because" it is applied to its citizens. Even if he were committed to principle (a) (or some variant), the principle cannot fully capture Plato's intentions. For the principle describes a formal relation between polis and citizens, whereas Plato believes the formal relation holds in virtue of causal-psychological transactions. Plato's point at 435e is that a spirited polis, say, is spirited not simply in virtue of having spirited citizens, but in virtue of having spirited citizens who are successful in shaping the polis in their image. And so one has not "already explained" how spiritedness can be applied to both polis and psyche. Plato has not yet given us the explanation; he is showing us where to look for one. He is saying that there is an externalizing psychological relation from citizen to polis. The explanation of what it is that makes either polis or man spirited lies in the future. So far Plato has given us only the methodology of a research project, one based on his psychology. If this is a general point which holds for significant psychopolitical predicates, it is not pointless to move from an explanation of, say, justice in the polis to an explanation of justice in the psyche. If a just polis is an externalization of just citizens who shape it, it would be reasonable to work one's way backward down this externalization to learn about the psyches of these citizens. This reasoning can occur before one has any idea what the structure of justice is.

To be sure, Socrates does say that a just person and a just polis will be alike in respect of the form of justice; and he defends this claim by appeal to a semantic principle: "things called by the same name are alike in respect to which the name applies" (435a–b). This is the basis for Williams' principle (b). Yet even if Socrates accepts this semantic principle, there remain questions about it: for example, why should such a semantic principle hold? Why does it hold in the realm of psychopolitical predicates? Given that it does hold, how could it be legitimate to call a certain sort of person and a certain sort of polis just? Again, the semantic principle is the beginning, not the end, of a research project. Only a few sentences after he introduces it, Socrates explains that a wide range of political characterizations of the polis are to be understood as externalizations of the same qualities from within the psyches of the historically significant citizens (435e). I read this not simply as making a psychological-causal point about the relation of the polis to its citizens, but also as providing a psychological grounding of the semantic principle, at least within the range of psychopolitical predicates. The semantic principle is introduced in the course of a dialectical inquiry, and it therefore remains open to further explication and defense. It also remains vulnerable to future emendation and revision. It should not be treated as an obvious axiom beyond criticism or inquiry. The psychological principles of internalization and externalization help us to understand why the semantic principle might hold in spite of the fact that there is a range of predicates which apply both to polis and to psyche.

Principles (a) and (b) do not, therefore, give us Plato's reason for thinking there is an isomorphism between polis and psyche. The isomorphism depends on psychological relations Plato believed to hold between inside and outside. If justice, for example, can be found outside (in the polis), it must have come from inside (that is, it must be a causal outcome of just men's shaping the polis according to their conception of justice). Given the psychologically dynamic relations between inside and outside, a weak version of a whole-part rule will follow as a corollary.[25] And so there is neither regress nor absurdity in Plato's argument, for there is no reason to think that he has thus far given us the common logos. It is often thought that Plato uses his analogy to derive his psychology: that by simply claiming the analogy and looking at the structure of the polis, he derives his psychology. But once we see that psychology is not just individual psychology, we can see that the situation is pretty much the reverse: his psychology is used to legitimate belief in isomorphism.

Williams thinks that there is a "contradiction . . . powerfully at work under the surface of the *Republic*."[26] The contradiction lies in the fact that if we apply principle (a) to the case of a just polis we get:

a'. A polis is just if and only if its men are.

But a just polis will have a majority of appetitive persons who, by the analysis of justice, ought to be doing their proper jobs. An appetitive person, however, is not a just one; and that must contradict (a'). By now it should be clear that Williams is not entitled to attribute (a) to Plato, but:

a". If a polis is F, then some of its men are F.[27]

And so he is entitled to derive not (a') but:

a'''. If a polis is just, then some of its men are just.

This generates no contradiction.[28]

But it is clear that Williams thinks there is a contradiction here which goes beyond the validity or invalidity of this formal argument. For, he reasons, the appetitive class must exercise some reason of its own, even if it is only in the service of obeying its rulers, sticking to its tasks, and so on.

> But now if the epithymetic [appetitive] class has in this way to exercise some *logistikon* [reason], and this helps it stick to its tasks, recognize the rulers and so forth, and if we read this result back through the analogy to the individual soul, we shall reach the absurd result that the *epithymetikon* [appetitive part] in a just soul harkens to the *logistikon* in that soul through itself having an extra little *logistikon* of its own. Recoiling from this absurdity, we recognize that in the individual soul, the *epithymetikon* cannot really harken; rather, through training, the desires are weakened and kept in their place by *logistikon*, if not through the agency, at least with the co-operation of *thymoeides* [the spirited part]. If with this fact in our hand we come back once more across the bridge of the analogy to the city, we shall find not a *dikaios* [just] and logistically co-operative working class, but rather a totally logistic ruling class holding down with the help of a totally thymoeidic military class, a weakened and repressed epithymetic class; a less attractive picture. The use of the analogy, it begins to seem, is to help Plato to have it both ways.[29]

Plato's commitment to the analogy, according to Williams, forces him into absurdities within the realms of both politics and psychology. That is the way it will look if one takes the analogy to be merely an analogy. If, by contrast, we view the isomorphism as a manifestation of internalization and externalization, it seems we can use the "analogy" to form a clearer idea of how Plato understood psychological structure.

Plato identifies the distinct parts of the psyche via each part's ability to enter into fundamental conflictual relations with the other parts. Psychological structure is delineated most obviously in intrapsychic conflict. The question then is: how are we to understand psychological structure in the absence of conflict? Instead of assuming we know what psychic parts are and using the analogy to derive absurdities, let us use Plato's principles of

230

internalization and externalization to try to find out more about what it is to be a psychic part. In the just polis, the appetitive class does have to exercise some reason of its own, to stick to its tasks, recognize its rulers, and so forth. What intrapsychic condition (of a member of the appetitive class) might have this socially harmonious behavior as an externalization?[30]

Plato believes this requires a certain type of intrapsychic harmony appropriate to an appetitive person. This requires that the appetitive part of his psyche harken to reason in that psyche. The question is how one might avoid the absurdity of the appetitive part's needing to have a little extra *logistikon* of its own. Not surprisingly, we need to understand the psychic part as having been formed by previous internalizations. Plato, as is well known, divides appetites into the necessary and the unnecessary (8.558d–559c). The necessary appetites are either unavoidable (for example, for basic nourishment) or for things which do us some good. Unnecessary appetites, by contrast, both are avoidable by proper training from youth and lead to no good (or even to bad). In an ideal polis, then, an appetitive person will be brought up so as not to have unnecessary appetites. That is why, in contrast to his pathological cousin, the oligarchic man, he does not need to hold them down by force (554b–e). As a result of his education, there is nothing in him which requires forcible restraint. Such a person will have appetites only for the bare necessities of life and for things which genuinely do him good. In the well-ordered polis, Plato says, each class will enjoy the happiness which suits its nature (4.421c). Assuming that the things which do a person good are the things which give him the happiness that suits his nature, in Plato's vision the appetitive person in a well-ordered polis should have just those appetites which the polis gives him the opportunity to satisfy (9.576c–d).

The appetitive part has thus been shaped to be responsive to reason in the psyche. The idea that appetite needs extra reason of its own derives from the thought that appetite "cannot really harken"; and this thought in turn flows from taking the conditions in which the psychic parts are isolated to be the essential conditions in which they must operate. We identify the appetitive part by seeing it functioning in opposition to reason. If this is the way it must operate, then of course appetite cannot harken to reason. And one can be tempted to make this inference by the thought that this is the way appetites must be.[31] On this view all domination by reason would ultimately have to be repression, and Plato's alleged distinction between the oligarchic person and the appetitive person in the just polis will look like propaganda.

Moreover, if a psychic part must be the way it is when it is originally isolated, it is natural to identify appetitive persons with the appetitive parts of their psyches. For since, on this assumption, the appetitive part can have no real commerce with the other psychic parts, there seems to be no other option for appetitive persons than to be driven by their appetites. This apparent lack of options conflicts with the claim Plato makes about the difference between the oligarchical psyche and that of the appetitive person in the just polis; but again this will look as if it is Plato's problem. However, once we recognize internalization and externalization as basic psychological activities, we can see that the psychic parts can be shaped, and thus that the conditions under which we first identify them need not be the conditions under which they operate. We can then see that an appetitive person need not simply be someone driven by the appetitive part. And once we see that psychic parts need not always be functioning in the conflictual ways in which they are first identified, we can then grant culture a greater role in psychic formation than would otherwise be thought possible.

Consider, for example, the money lover, a paradigmatic character-formation of an appetitive person. How did his appetites ever come to love *money?* Money is the paradigm cultural artifact: it has no existence *hors de culture.* So if the appetites can be directed onto money, it would seem that culture can permeate and inform the lower elements of the psyche.[32] The appetitive personality will organize his personality around his appetites; and a paradigm, for Plato, is the money lover who devotes himself to the pursuit of wealth. For such a person, reason will be directed instrumentally toward figuring out ways of satisfying this desire, he will feel honor in achieving wealth-related goals, and there is a peculiar pleasure in achieving them.[33] The pursuit of wealth, then, is setting the overall agenda for this person's projects, and honor and reason are disciplined to serve this outlook. But within this schema there is room for the oligarchic personality, the democrat, the tyrant, and (as I shall argue) the poet, all of whom are appetitive types. "Appetitive" is thus a genus of personality organization, and the variety of species results from the fact that internalization can inform the appetitive part of the psyche.[34]

It might at first seem paradoxical that, on the one hand, the appetitive part is the ruling principle of an appetitive person (9.581), while, on the other, the appetitive person should believe along with everyone else that reason should rule (4.431d–e). Plato is trying to have it both ways; but within the framework of his psychology, he can get away with it. The appetitive person thinks that the peculiar pleasures available to his way of life are the best, and since the appetitive part rules in his psyche, his reason will be directed toward figuring out ways to secure those pleasures. But given that this appetitive person has been brought up to have just the appetites which the well-ordered polis can satisfy, his reason ought to be telling him that the best way to satisfy his appetites is to harken to the reason manifest in the laws of the philosopher-king.

In the temperate polis, Plato says, the same belief about who should rule will be inside both the rulers and the ruled (4.431d–e, 433c–d). This belief helps to constitute the reason of the appetitive person in the just polis. Ironically, it is because the reason in his psyche is subservient to the appetitive part that the appetitive person submits himself to the rule of reason in the polis. Just as the appetitive person will abjure junk food for healthy bread and relishes, so he will abjure junk bonds for municipal bonds. And all the while he will be telling himself, correctly, that this is the really good investment for himself and his family. This is how the appetitive person's role in a well-ordered polis looks from an appetitive perspective. On the one hand, his reason is focused on securing gain; on the other, he concludes that the best way to do this is to follow the rule of reason in the polis. This would not have been possible if he had not been brought up in such a way as to internalize appropriate cultural influences and get rid of unnecessary appetites. Yet for all that, he remains basically an appetitive type, organizing his life, values, and thoughts around production and acquisition. For him, justice is basically a matter of doing and getting one's own.[35] Temperance in the polis is like "a certain harmony" which "spreads throughout the whole" (4.431e–432a). But if temperance spreads throughout the whole, there would not be genuine harmony in the polis if the psyche of an appetitive citizen were at war with itself. Plato does not believe the appetitive person has the virtue of temperance, but in a well-ordered polis, as a result of well-crafted internalizations, such a person will be well disposed to temperance, both inside and outside himself.

So too for the honor-loving members of society: each will commend the distinctive pleasures of the honor-achieving life as the best (9.581c–d) and will try to organize his life and character around this pursuit. In a just polis, honor lovers will be educated to hold fast to the laws and to fear only those things which the lawgivers think are fearful (4.429b–430a). These people will be brought up to be soldiers: they will be educated so as to be free of unnecessary appetites and to have their other appetites disciplined to the pursuit of honor. Their reason too will be directed toward honor, but they will have been educated so as to understand that the way to achieve true honor is to defend and safeguard the law (laid down by the philosopher-rulers) (429c). Therefore, although honor is the fundamental principle of this person's life, on that very account he will, when brought up in a just polis, believe that reason should rule. Whatever one thinks about Plato's prescription for attaining health, one must, I think, acknowledge that his conception of a healthy, harmonious psyche is not just a dodge to cover up an irresolvable tension, but a natural consequence of his psychology.

The analogy between polis and psyche is a manifestation of the fact that there are important structural similarities between interpsychic relations and intrapsychic relations. But for Plato these structural similarities are themselves a manifestation of important psychological transactions, back and forth, between interpsychic and intrapsychic. This is true in sickness as in health. If we examine Plato's tale of political decline, we see that the degeneration occurs through a dialectic of internalization of pathological cultural influences in individuals which provokes a degeneration in character structure (as compared to the previous generation), which is in turn imposed on the polis, which thus acquires and provokes deeper pathology.[36] Plato does not merely want to show that the same neurotic structure can exist in both psyche and polis, but that the pathology in each helps to bring about pathology in the other. This has not been easy to see, I suspect, because Plato's conception of pathology is not well understood.

It is, for example, easy to read his accounts of the rise of the democratic polis and the emergence of democratic man as two parallel accounts which have only a structural analogy in common. In fact Plato traces a sophisticated interaction between polis and psyche which helps to account for both. Consider, for example, Plato's account of the rise of democratic man (8.558–562). He emerges from an oligarchic family, the values and goals of that family being set by the father, who is himself a manifestation of an oligarchic personality. The oligarchic father is thrifty and frugal; he has organized himself around the pursuit of wealth and tries to instill this same structure in his family (554b–555b). He has been able to keep his unnecessary appetites in check, but because he has not had a proper upbringing, because he has not experienced or internalized true culture, these appetites must be held in place by the only means available to him: brute force. This is a man whose personality is held together by forcibly holding down an inner world of unruly appetites. He presents a good face to the world but in fact exists in two bits (554d). The emergence of the democratic man is, roughly speaking, the return of the repressed in the next generation. The oligarchic father creates in his family and immediate social environment a microculture, a template for internalization, which embodies contradictory demands. On the one hand, there is the demand inside his family for frugality so as to accumulate wealth. There is some suggestion that this demand on its own is self-contradictory. For to pursue wealth is to organize the family around the appetites; and Plato does say there is a tendency to spoil the children (556b–c). Yet to insist on frugality is to hold those appetites in check. The appetites are thus simultaneously encouraged and forcibly restrained. The only way the father knows how to instill frugality is by force. Since he has failed to internalize a more harmonious psychic structure, forcible restraint is the only means at his disposal, and he imposes it on his family as well as on himself. Thus the child is brought up in a miserly fashion without real education (559d). On the other hand, the oligarchical father encourages prodigality *outside* his family (555c–e). By lending others money and encouraging wasteful-

235

ness, he hopes eventually to acquire their property. These people, made poor, will eventually revolt and usher in democracy (557a).

Here we see how the oligarchic father, by pursuing his own ends, recreates on the interpsychic stage of his family and immediate social environment a model of his own intrapsychic relations. His son, having his appetites both encouraged and held down, becomes an interpsychic correlate of the appetites within the father. However, as a member of the outer world, the son is open to other polis influences. The oligarchical father encouraged prodigality outside the family, but Plato's point is that this prodigality cannot, finally, be kept outside. The prodigal youth, encouraged by the oligarch, is an externalization and interpsychic correlate to the unnecessary appetites within the oligarch's psyche. Because the son's appetites have been both encouraged and held back, he is susceptible to appetitive influences around him. "Just as the polis changed when one faction received help from like-minded people outside, so the young man changes when help comes from the same type of appetites outside to one of the factions within himself" (559e). But these appetites outside are also offspring of the father. It is these appetites—whose pedigree goes back to the father—which are re-internalized in the intrapsychic battle within the son. For a while, a struggle rages both inside and outside his psyche. The father lends his influence to aid the internalized repressing forces; the young thugs on the block egg the appetites on.[37] But this is a struggle which the appetites have to win, because this youth never had the opportunity to internalize good cultural structures. When the appetites come knocking on the door of his psyche, they find no one home (8.560b–c). The psyche is easily reshaped, and a "democratic man" is born.

There is a problem, though, about the relation of the democratic polis and the democratic man. The democratic polis is one which contains every sort of character, like a garment of many colors.[38] However, as Williams points out, the democratic man is described as always shifting, following the appetite of the moment, without any expertise (561d). And here Williams tightens the noose:

A democracy is a state in which the many rule, and if it gets its character from that of its rulers, then the majority must have a "democratic" character.

This, on the face of it, sorts none too well with the claim that the democratic state will particularly tend to contain all sorts of character—the "democratic" character seems in fact to be a special sort of character. Moving between the social and the individual level once more, Plato seems disposed to confound two very different things: a state in which there are various characters among the people, and a state in which most of the people have a various character, that is to say, a very shifting and unsteady character.[39]

Surely a society of many colors does not require that each of its members be a patchwork quilt. Have we finally reached the true absurdity of Plato's analogy? I don't think so. That a polis allows and even prides itself on the fact that it has various sorts of characters (8.557b–558a) is, for Plato, a manifestation of the fact that it does not have a firmly established sense of better and worse. There can be no agreed or enforced set of values, beyond tolerance: thus the political possibility of various types. It is as though citizens are allowed to decide for themselves what will constitute their own goods. However, for Plato, this is not a serious psychological possibility: humans need a socially grounded culture to internalize.[40] A person may decide, say, to be a politician, but such a decision is superficial and eminently shakable by external events. By historical luck the person may succeed at the appearance of statecraft, but Plato's point is that this is thin stuff. And so, even in democracy's finest hour, when it appears a many-colored fabric, full of different individuals each performing their own tasks, Plato's point is that this cannot be more than appearance. For although at that moment the citizens will not all be shifting their characters, they will all have characters which are shift*able*. Thus their characters are unsteady, however firm they may appear.

Williams concludes:

> There have been those who thought that the working classes were naturally of powerful and disorderly desires, and had to be kept in their place. There have been those who thought that they were goodhearted and loyal fellows of no great gifts who could recognize their natural superiors and, unless stirred up, keep themselves in their place. There can have been few who have thought both; Plato in the *Republic* comes close to being such a one.[41]

This thought is amusing, but not absurd. Indeed, if one takes the role of internalization seriously, it would seem to follow that in one political environment the working class will be a disorderly mob which has to be kept in its place, while in another it will consist in good-hearted fellows who recognize their superiors. Again and again, what presents itself as an absurdity dissolves once one takes seriously the idea that humans are dependent on internalization for acquiring psychological structure.

The initial appearance of absurdity depends once more on assuming that psychic parts are invulnerable to cultural influence. If the appetitive part must be in the conflictual relation with reason in which it is originally identified, then the working class will have to be a direct manifestation of contentious appetite. If intrapsychic conflict is unavoidable, then, given the analogy, so is political conflict. It will then look, just as it does to Williams, that when the mask is pulled away we will see that Plato's just polis has the same repressive structure which Plato himself diagnoses in oligarchy. And, I think, it is tempting to go along with Williams' argument in part because Plato's ideal polis does look to us as though it has repressive features.[42] But the point of the present argument is not to rescue Plato's polis; it is to understand the psychological basis of the isomorphism. Once one sees that the isomorphism is not a mere analogy, but is grounded in internalization and externalization, one sees that there is room to influence the shape and content of the psychic parts, and this allows room to influence the specific type of say, appetitive person, which in turn allows room to influence the specific type of appetitive class in the polis. This is hard to see in part because Plato concentrates so much on pathology, and pathological structures are inherently conflictual. Plato's psychology, like Freud's, is "wisdom won from illness."[43] Plato finds himself in a pathological social situation,[44] and, given his psychological principles, he deduces that this pathology is both cause and manifestation of pathology within the psyche. And it is his task to work his way back from the conceptualization of this pathology toward a conception of health.[45] His strategy was to assume a dynamic psychological relation between psyche and polis, and to construct an idealized genealogy of illness.[46]

For Plato, the hallmark of pathology is a lack of harmonious relations between inside and outside. That is one reason why the principles of internalization and externalization have been difficult to recognize. For it is a sign of oligarchy's being a pathological structure that it cannot simply be internal-

238

ized and externalized without further ado. The oligarchical father does externalize the structure of his psyche. And it is such externalizations which shape the oligarchical polis: by encouraging one class to accumulate wealth, the other class to forfeit it. The son, for his part, does internalize the polis influences. But because oligarchy is a pathological configuration, the internalization cannot stably reproduce the psychic structure of the previous generation. The instability is manifest in the inability of inside and outside to maintain a mirroring relation—and in the ensuing failure of the son to grow up in the image of the father. All this in spite of the fact that internalization and externalization are basic psychological activities.[47]

The point of Plato's argument is to show that there is only one relatively stable equilibrium position between inside and outside.[48] Only the just polis and its citizens are so structured that the various internalizations and externalizations will maintain harmony in each; and harmony between them. Justice, for Plato, is a certain harmony within the psyche; it is also a certain harmony within the polis.[49] But now we can see that each of these harmonies is possible only if there is a larger harmony—between inside and outside—which encompasses and explains them.[50] Justice when properly understood is each part, inside and outside, doing its own task. That is why it is ultimately misleading to think of there being merely an analogy between polis and psyche.[51] That is how it might look at the beginning of inquiry, but not how it should look at the end. When it is first introduced, the isomorphism may appear to be little more than an argumentative device. But then we, at that stage, are deep in the cave, confronted by what appear to be contradictory arguments about whether justice is good or bad.[52] The remainder of the *Republic* works through these contradictions, and what we come to see is that, roughly speaking, psyche is internalized polis and polis is externalized psyche. What initially appeared as two things which stood in a merely analogous relation come to appear as the internal and external workings of a psychological universe which may exist in various states of harmony or disharmony.

Poetic Justice

Internalization and externalization also explain why, for Plato, poetry corrupts our psyches. Given our psychology, there are two features of poetry which make it an especially potent drug. First, the music and rhythms with which poetry is expressed pour directly into our psyches.[53] Second, poetry tends to be expressed in imitative style: the characters speak as though from their own first-personal perspectives (3.393b–d). In this way, poetry can preserve the first-personal perspective throughout its transmissions.[54] Whether we are poet, performer, or audience, we imaginatively take up the perspective of the characters: even the best of us abandon ourselves and imaginatively take up their feelings (10.605). It is as though imitation blurs the boundary between inside and outside. Through imitation we get outside ourselves imaginatively, but psychologically we take the outside in. By pretending to be these characters, we unconsciously shape our characters around them.[55] The mimetic poet, says Plato, sets up a bad constitution in the psyche of each person (605b–c).

Poetry feeds our psychological hunger to take things in, but it feeds us a diet of illusion.[56] Its ability to draw us into such a world indicates that it is appealing to a primitive level of mental functioning: Plato calls it a vulgar part of the psyche (10.603a). For Plato, poetry has a hotline to the appetites.[57] It is able to bypass reason, the faculty which corrects for false appearance (601b, 602d–603b), and go straight to the psychic gut. So while reason may tell us to be moderate in our grief, poetry encourages lamentation, excess, and loss of control (604–605). Poetry thus sets us up for intrapsychic conflict.[58] For poetry encourages the irrational part of us to hold on to illusion in spite of reason's corrections. It establishes a split-off part of the psyche to which reason is not accessible. And that is why poetry cannot, for Plato, be just a stage in the developmental cave we work our way through. Other images may generate conflicts which lead us toward reality (7.523), but poetic imitations keep us imprisoned at that level. So, on the one hand, poetry promotes intrapsychic conflict; on the other, it keeps us unconscious of that conflict, for the irrational part of our psyche cannot hear reason's corrections. That is why poetry, with its throbbing rhythms and beating of breasts, appeals equally to the nondescript mob in the theater and to the best among us (10.604e–605d).

But if poetry goes straight to the lower part of the psyche, that is where it must come from. First, imitation by its very nature encourages poet, actor, and audience to go through the same motions. Although imitation is only play (10.602b), it is in this play that we unconsciously shape our psyches (606b). If poetic imitation sets our appetites in motion, it is reasonable to infer similar motions within the poet. Second, when a part of our psyche is strengthened from outside, it tends to be by an interpsychic manifestation of that very same part of the psyche. So, for example, the budding democrat's appetites are reinforced by the appetitive thugs on the block.[59] The fact that poetry deals in illusion and the throbbing lamentations of the irrational part of the psyche testifies to its lineage. Third, when Plato in his thought experiment wants to move from a minimal polis to a fevered one, he adds imitators: poets, actors, rhapsodes, chorus dancers, theatrical managers (2.373b). He takes himself to be introducing a pathogen into a healthy organism. And the disease the polis contracts is *pleonexia:* the polis gives itself over to the unlimited acquisition of wealth (373d–e). Only after the polis is rid of poets who tell tales of gods eating, fighting, and deceiving each other does Plato conclude that he has purged the fevered polis.[60] Introduce the poets, and the polis becomes pleonectic; banish them, and you cure it. Finally, as we have seen, logos follows and fits the character of the psyche (3.400d–e). If poetry is an appetitive falsehood, it must come from an appetitive source in the psyche. And so it seems that just as law in a good society is an externalization of reason (of the philosopher-king, who has already internalized the eternal realities), so poetry seems to be an externalization of the irrational part (of the poet, who may already have internalized appetitive-poetic elements of culture) (10.604d, 605b, 605e–606b).

We can see these appetites in the gods. The gods of the poets spend their time castrating and devouring each other; they are constantly at war, and tend to engage in single-minded pursuit of satisfaction (2.377e–378d). In short, these gods behave like lawless, unnecessary appetites (9.571b–d); and, given Plato's psychology, it seems reasonable to hypothesize that this is just what they are: appetites externalized and projected onto Olympus. A moment's reflection will show that there is nowhere else for them to go. Plato calls the lawless appetites "something wild and terrible" within us (572b). He speaks of eros as a "tyrant within" the psyche.[61] Undisciplined appetites are all-powerful within, so when they are externalized it makes sense that they be represented as tremendously powerful. They need a virtually transcendent arena in which to struggle.[62] And so externalization from inside the poet's psyche turns out also to be an inversion: from bottom of the psyche to top of the world. These poetic myths provide a cultural template for youths to internalize, thus inverting their own psyches and, inevitably, the societies in which they live. Children, says Plato, will come to think there is nothing wrong in punishing their father to the limit, in fighting with their family and fellow citizens, if they think they are only following in the gods' footsteps (2.378b–c). And it is precisely by those acts, Plato thinks, that the tyrant is born (9.565d–566b). According to legend, a person who eats human entrails is turned into a wolf; just so, the person who sheds the blood of the tribe by unjust accusations against fellow citizens, who banishes and slays them, has "tasted kindred blood," and is transformed into a tyrant. The tyrant is formed by transgressing the basic norms of human relations. In fact the tyrant is behaving toward other humans as the Homeric gods behave toward each other. Plato criticizes Euripides for praising tyranny as "godlike"; but he is objecting not so much to the description as to the fact that it is being used as a form of praise (8.568a–b). Tyranny *is* an imitation of the Homeric divine; but there is nothing praiseworthy about that.

This brings us to the most serious charge against the poets: they provide not only an externalization of the appetites, but also a legitimation of them. That is why the poetic myths are the "greatest lie about the greatest things," "an ugly falsehood" (2.377e). The poets externalize their appetites, but their poetry sends them upward as well as outward. The appetitive gods are re-internalized with a normative tinge.[63] Since the young are not able to distinguish myth from reality (378d–e), the tales they hear at their mother's knee provide the means by which the appetites can travel up and infect the norms and values of the developing person. In youth, we begin taking in psychological content and structure, before we know how to distinguish truth from falsity. At a later stage of development, we attempt to take in true beliefs and expel falsehoods (382; 3.412e–413b). However, if we already have a falsehood inside our psyches, even in mythic form, we will end up taking in more and more falsehood (as though it were true) and getting rid of more and more truth (as though it were false). Introduce this initial virus, and our intake-expulsion machine will start pumping in the wrong direction. That is why having falsehood inside the psyche is what humans loathe most of all (382a–b). And that, for Plato, is what mimetic poetry introduces: a falsehood taken as truth.[64]

Plato is charting the interpsychic and intrapsychic vicissitudes of the appetites. He is following the fate of the poetic trajectory; and what he finds is that the externalized appetites will tend to return, strengthened and legitimated. Poetry thus provides both a legitimation of the appetites and a cultural template for tyranny. One can see this in Plato's account of the rise of the tyrant. The tyrant is a child of democracy: the son of democratic man (9.572c–573c). The democratic father is himself a compromise formation, shaped by a thrifty, oligarchical father who encouraged only the acquisitive appetites and by a "sophisticated" element which encouraged the unnecessary appetites. The pathology of this solution is again revealed by the instability between inside and outside. The son is brought up in the ways of the father, but is thereby susceptible to lawless influence from outside. It is the "dread magicians" who both whet his lawless appetites and encourage him to expel from his psyche any remnants of shame which would keep the appetites in check. That the intake-expulsion machine is pumping in the wrong direction is testimony to there being a falsehood taken as truth within. And just as, *intra*psychically, the lawless appetites overtook the original, better ones in his psyche, so, *inter*psychically, the tyrant comes to feel justified in taking over his parent's estate, and then going on to rob, punish, and enslave family, friends, and fellow citizens (9.574a–c; 8.569b). In fact the tyrant reenacts on the interpsychic stage of the polis the situation which exists inside his psyche: he must expel or get rid of the brave, wise, and wealthy, treating them as his enemy (8.567b–c). "A fine purgation," Plato says, "and just the opposite of what a physician does with our bodies: for while they remove the worst and leave the best, the tyrant does the opposite" (567c). He recreates the polis in the image of his psyche.

And the poet gives him the cultural vehicle by which he can, at least to his own satisfaction, legitimize his acts. Hearing tales about the warring gods, Plato says, children will be encouraged to think this type of behavior appropriate (2.378b–c). The gods of the poets are the lawless appetites externalized in Olympus; the tyrant brings this lawlessness back to the

243

polis—sometimes literally. The tyrant is often someone who, because of previous attacks on society, has been banished from the polis (8.566a–b). There he remains poised for a triumphant return in the name of democracy; which for Plato is nothing more than a lawless society of appetites. Plato's point is that if you really want to get rid of the tyrant, you also have to get rid of the cultural vehicles which make him look attractive: you must also banish his poetical counterpart. For it is the poets who "draw the constitutions towards tyrannies and democracies" (568b).

One might say that the tyrant acts out what the poet only dreams; but, for Plato, both the poet and the tyrant are dreamers, though in slightly different ways. To understand the tyrant, Plato says, we must not settle for his outward appearance, the external pomp and circumstance; we must even strip him of the garb in which tragedy clothes him (8.557b) and must, in thought, enter into his character (9.577a). What we find inside is a tyranny of lawless desires (575a, 577c–e). These are the desires we encounter in our dreams, when the rational part of our psyche sleeps, and the wild and animal part wakes up. "There is nothing it will not dare to do at that time, free of any control by shame or prudence. It does not hesitate to attempt sexual intercourse with a mother or anyone else—man, god, or beast; it will commit any foul murder and does not refrain from any kind of food. In a word it will not fall short of any folly or shameless deed" (571c). These, of course, are the very deeds with which the gods of the poets occupy themselves. Indeed, the tyrant is a parricide (8.569b); and Zeus's parricide is the founding act of Homeric heaven. It is this dreamworld which the poets have externalized in Olympus, and which the tyrant has re-internalized. The dreams of the poets enable the tyrant to turn his waking life into a bad dream: a daymare.

Poet and tyrant are essentially dreaming the same dream; indeed, they are bedfellows. From Plato's perspective, poet and tyrant are the same type of person: a Dr. Jekyll and Mr. Hyde of the appetites. Both have organized themselves around their appetites, though they have different strategies for dealing with them. The tyrant keeps his appetites inside: because of them he outwardly enslaves the polis and inwardly is enslaved by them. The poet externalizes his appetites; but there they form a cultural template which, when re-internalized, enslaves us all. Poet and tyrant ultimately enslave us, but while the tyrant enforces external compliance, poetic enslavement reaches inside the psyche and reorganizes it so that we remain unconscious of our slavery.

That is why the poets must be banished from the polis. One might say that Plato is recapitulating the poet's activity, only at a philosophical level. The poets, after all, have externalized their appetites, setting them up outside the polis in a heavenly beyond. What Plato sees is that the "poetic solution" to the problem of the appetites in fact provokes a psychosocial disaster. The Platonic solution is inspired by his psychological principles. Plato knows that every externalization is fodder for internalization; and his "final solution" is designed to put an end to this cycle. The important thing for Plato is not to get the poets out of the polis, so much as to get the appetites out of culture. This, he thinks, can be accomplished only by banishing the poets.[65]

Of course, there is plenty of room to doubt whether Plato's solution is called for or whether it would be successful. Does poetry not serve a healthy function? Is poetry not more (or other) than mimesis? Would the banished not find another way to return, if not from poetic heaven, then from beyond the philosophical pale? Is Plato's prescription so removed from anything we have ever experienced that we have no idea what is being prescribed? Rather than try to answer these questions, I shall close by explaining why we have only recently become ready to evaluate Plato's argument from a psychological perspective. Most recent discussions of the psychological value of art rely on an early psychoanalytic conception of the mind. The mind, on this conception, is divided along the lines of repression. The point of therapy was to loosen repression so that the unconscious could express itself, if only in words. In this context the creation and enjoyment of art appeared as another socially acceptable way of expressing unconscious forces. Thus artistic creation and appreciation came to be seen as therapeutic. As psychoanalytic theory developed, it became less concerned with the unconscious per se, and more concerned with the structure of the psyche. The psychoanalytic valuation of art has not kept pace with the development of theory.[66] In fact, Plato's remains one of the few discussions of the psychological value of art in the context of a structural theory of the psyche. Plato's point is that it is not enough to assume that the release of the repressed is a good thing. If one wants to justify art from a psychological perspective, one must understand its role in the context of a structured psyche. And that may require an account of the psychological transactions inside and outside the psyche. This is a challenge which, it seems to me, we are only now ready to take up once again.

CHAPTER 11

Transcendental Anthropology

Even a sympathetic reader of Wittgenstein's later philosophy must, I think, conclude that it represents an unfinished work. The *Philosophical Investigations,* as Wittgenstein himself says, "is really only an album": discrete paragraphs are juxtaposed, and the reader is left to extract an argument or a point of view. This was not the result of a deliberate attempt at aphorism—to be a latter-day Heraclitus—but of what Wittgenstein called a failure "to weld my results together" into a continuous whole.[1] Biographically speaking, there may be many reasons for this failure. But from a philosophical point of view, the interesting question is whether this failure had to occur because Wittgenstein was pursuing disparate strands of thought which cannot be coherently reconciled. The two strands in greatest conflict are what I shall call his *anthropological* and his *transcendental* approaches to philosophy.

Language, for Wittgenstein, is one of the many activities in which humans engage; and if it is to be understood, it must be seen as embedded in the context of humans living their lives. A "language-game" is not merely a language, but a "whole, consisting of the language and the actions into which it is woven."[2] And "the term 'language-game' is meant to bring into prominence the fact that the speaking of a language is part of an activity, or of a form of life."[3] This would suggest that the proper study of language requires that one take an anthropological stance: one views a language in the context of the customs, institutions, practices of a community. It is one of the myriad ways in which a group of people interact with each other, with their environment, with themselves.

The anthropological stance would seem to encourage a naturalistic outlook: "What we are supplying," says Wittgenstein at one point, "are really remarks on the natural history of human beings; we are not contributing curiosities, however, but observations which no one has doubted, but which have escaped remark only because they are always before our eyes."[4] Moreover, the anthropological stance is all-embracing. Even philosophical problems are formulated in language, and thus their meaning depends on the customs and practices in which language is used.

> if the words "language," "experience," "world" have a use, it must be as humble a one as that of the words "table," "lamp," "door" . . .
>
> When philosophers use a word—"knowledge," "being," "object," "I," "proposition," "name"—and try to grasp the essence of the thing, one must always ask oneself: is the word ever actually used in this way in the language-game which is its original home? What we do is bring words back from their metaphysical to their everyday use . . .
>
> When I talk about language (words, sentences etc.) I must speak the language of every day . . .
>
> One might think: if philosophy speaks of the use of "philosophy" there must be a second-order philosophy. But it is not so: it is, rather, like the case of orthography, which deals with the word "orthography" among others without then being second-order.[5]

Philosophy, as it has traditionally been practiced, has been an attempt to step outside our customs and practices in the hope of gaining a nonlocal perspective on how things really are. Wittgenstein's critique of traditional philosophy is not confined to pointing out the futility of this hope. Our striving for the philosophical perspective is itself subjected to the anthropologist's gaze. Going after the absolute truth is one of the things we think we do, and the true meaning of the activity can be understood only by coming to see the illusions which are embedded in and expressed by our traditional philosophical practices. Everything we do, according to Wittgenstein, is only more material for the anthropological stance.

Of course, the anthropological stance is not itself supposed to support an illusion of detachment. We cannot step outside our form of life and discuss it like some *objet trouvé*. Any attempt to *say* what our form of life is like will itself be part of the form of life; it can have no more than the meaning it gets in the context of its use. This insight has often been thought to imply a kind of relativism; in fact, I think it points in the opposite direction. For Wittgenstein is not here talking about one culture among others. To see this, let us begin by considering an elementary example from arithmetic and logic. (I shall deal with issues of cultural variation later.) Let us say that a person is *minded* in a certain way if he has the perceptions of salience, routes of interest, feelings of naturalness in following a rule, and so on which constitute being part of a certain form of life. And consider, for example, the alternative answers to the following questions:

What does 7 + 5 equal?
   (a) 12.
   (b) Anything at all, just as long as everyone is so minded.
What follows from *P* and *If P, then Q?*
   (a) Q.
   (b) Anything at all, just as long as everyone is so minded.

To each of these questions, (a) gives the correct answer: 7 + 5 equals 12, and anyone who tries to offer a different integer as an answer is in error. *Q* does follow by *modus ponens* from *P* and *If P, then Q,* and—though many other sentences also follow—anyone who, say, claimed to derive *not-Q* would be in error.

After reading the later Wittgenstein, one might be tempted to say that (b) also expresses some sort of truth. But it is important to realize that (b) does not actually succeed in *saying* anything. For if (b) were true, then the following counterfactuals ought to express genuine possibilities:

7 + 5 would equal something other than 12, if everyone had been other-minded.

Q would not follow from P and If P, then Q, if everyone had been other-minded.

But these counterfactuals cannot for us express real possibilities; for, in this broad context, there is no coherent notion of people being "other-minded." The possibility of there being persons who are minded in any way at all is the possibility of their being minded as we are.

Our problem is that being minded as we are is not one possibility we can explore among others. We explore what it is to be minded as we are by moving around self-consciously and determining what makes more and less sense. There is no getting a glimpse of what it might be like to be "other-minded," for as we move toward the outer bounds of our minded-ness we verge on incoherence and nonsense.

Here we encounter a modal form of the duck-rabbit: the fact of our being minded as we are flashes before us now as contingent, now as necessary. In one *gestalt*, one becomes aware that there is nothing to guarantee one's continued correct use of language beyond the fact that one happens to share with one's fellow human beings routes of interest, perceptions of salience, feelings of naturalness, and so on. From this perspective, one's continued hold on the world can appear the merest contingency.[6] (Does anything help me keep my grasp on the world? What holds me back from the abyss?) As the *gestalt* shifts, one comes to see that there is no genuine possibility of having radically different routes of interest and perceptions of salience, for that is the spurious possibility of becoming other-minded. The illusion of possibility is engendered by considering our form of life as one among others.

> If someone says "If our language had not this grammar, it could not express these facts"—it should be asked what "could" means here.[7]

Imagine, for example, a tribe whose chief cannot be brought to see how Q follows from P and If P, then Q.[8] It seems that there is nothing to say to the chief, for we have already presented him with whatever arguments we could muster. There is, according to Wittgenstein, only the nonexplanatory "This is how *we* go on." But this Wittgensteinian standoff is a far cry from the relativist's claim that there is no "fact of the matter" as to who is right, that the truth can be decided only by criteria internal to each theory. This becomes evident if one asks who the chief is. The answer is that he's nobody, and that he could not be anybody. We cannot begin to make sense of the possibility of someone whose beliefs are totally unresponsive to *modus ponens:* we cannot get any hold on what his thoughts or actions would be like. The chief is a mere posit, a heuristic device to help us in our exploration of our mindedness. Wittgenstein occasionally postulates a tribe whose interests and activities differ from ours. Their function is to help us see how our activities are dependent upon the interests we have. But it is a mistake to think of these tribes as providing concrete examples of other-mindedness. Insofar as we can make sense of their activities and interests, that is, insofar as we can fill out the picture, they do not turn out to be other-minded. We are discovering more about what our form of life is like, not what another form of life would be like.[9] Insofar as we cannot fill out the picture, as in the case of our chief, we have not reached a case of other-mindedness; we have simply passed beyond the outer bounds of our mindedness into incoherence.

The appearance of exhaustiveness in the above dilemma can be misleading. For there is no sharp line which divides an example of our mindedness from incoherence. And in some of Wittgenstein's examples of other tribes' interests and practices, it is not clear whether we can fill out the picture or not. For certain systems of, say, magical beliefs, it may be unclear whether or not we can understand them. One task of philosophy is to explore this twilight of what does and does not make sense. Further, one need not, with Kant or the early Wittgenstein, assume that one is investigating a fixed, ahistorical framework of thought.

> The mythology may change back into a state of flux, the river-bed of thoughts may shift. But I distinguish between the movement of waters on the river-bed and shift of the bed itself; though there is not a sharp division of the one from the other.[10]

Perhaps as we explore the riverbed, shifts will occur: certain things will begin to make more sense, other things less. There is no reason to treat this as the discovery of a sense (or nonsense) which already existed before the exploration.

But the appeal (or threat) of relativism stems not from such reflections, nor from the serious empirical study of cultural differences, but from an extrapolation. We are encouraged to consider our entourage of beliefs, customs, and practices as forming a "world view" and to entertain the possibility of other world views "incommensurable" with ours. That is, relativism's appeal (threat) stems from taking the claim:

* Only because we are minded as we are do we see the world the way we do.

to express an empirical truth: as delimiting one possibility among others. Thus the relativist must make sense of the counterfactual:

If we were other-minded, we would see the world differently.

From a Wittgensteinian point of view, this counterfactual must be non-sense. One outcome of Wittgensteinian reflection is that we come to accept the claim (*) while denying that it delimits one possibility among others. But then the anthropological stance is not in any obvious sense yielding empirical insight.

A TRANSCENDENTAL INQUIRY, according to Kant, was an a priori investigation into how concepts apply to objects.[11] And an object *(Objekt)*, for Kant, was anything of which a concept could be predicated in a judgment. Wittgenstein's investigation is obviously not a priori, but it nevertheless bears a certain family resemblance to a transcendental inquiry. First, a concept for Kant has no life outside the judgments in which it is used. And the function of a concept is to unify disparate representations under it. A rule for Wittgenstein has no life outside the actual contexts in which it is used. And we may think of the actual instances of following a rule as the "particulars" which are unified under the "universal" rule. A rule is a "one over many." And a judgment in which a concept is applied to an object is a special case of rule-following. Second, although we are to consider our rule-following procedures in the context of our customs and practices, the result of the investigation is not meant to be an empirical explanation of our ability to follow rules, nor does it give us any new empirical facts about who we are or what we do. Rather, it provides some other form of insight into and appreciation of how we go on.[12]

It is commonly thought that Wittgenstein's later philosophy could not be seen as a transcendental inquiry, not merely because he insists upon the anthropological stance, but because there is no room for the Kantian distinction between the world of appearance and the world as it is in itself. For one cannot filter out the mind's contribution to experience and consider it independently. There is thus no room for the concept of the world as it is independently of that contribution. In contemporary discussion, the term "transcendental investigation" is often used to describe an inquiry into the necessary structure of the mind, of the world, or of both. This is not how Kant defined the term; though it is a plausible extension of his usage, since, for him, an a priori inquiry into the application of concepts to objects would ultimately yield necessary truths about the formal structure imposed by mind. But I am suggesting an alternative. I suggest that we go back to Kant's definition *and loosen it,* so that a nonempirical inquiry into rule-following may count as a transcendental investigation. Wittgenstein's later philosophy can then be seen as something like a transcendental inquiry even though it displays no interest in necessary structures.

The most interesting question about Wittgenstein's later philosophy is, I think, how one can adopt the anthropological stance and the transcendental stance simultaneously. On the face of it, the anthropological stance would seem to pull one in the direction of an empirical explanation of how we go on. Succumbing to this pull, however, would violate the stricture that philosophy should have no such concern. And it would threaten Wittgenstein's repeated demand that philosophical reflection should leave our practices and customs intact.[13] For if philosophy were to bequeath us an empirical explanation of how we go on, it would seem to be open to us to decide that certain practices of ours were unsatisfactory and ought to be changed. Even if the explanation itself explained why we couldn't alter our condition—like for instance an anthropology which explained why it is psychologically impossible for us not to believe in God—this feature alone could not be sufficient to transform anthropology into philosophy. What we are looking for is a philosophical understanding of why philosophy should be nonrevisionary, not a psychological one.

Here a comparison with Kant might be helpful. When Kant argued that even basic laws of logic or arithmetic could ultimately not be understood independently of the activities of a judging mind, that insight was not supposed to undermine the laws. Rather, a transcendental consideration which revealed these laws to depend on a subjective contribution of mind was intended to provide insight into why, from an empirical perspective, these laws were genuinely objective and necessary. Kant attempted a remarkable juggling act: to preserve a full-blooded sense of objectivity, but to give a philosophical account which revealed it as dependent upon mind. Whether or not Kant was successful, there is at least a serious attempt at a radical philosophical analysis which reflectively reinforces rather than undermines the beliefs we had before we engaged in philosophical inquiry. Is there any effort in Wittgenstein to show why his investigations should not be reflectively destabilizing? Why should we not come to view the law of noncontradiction as merely one of the deeply held tribal beliefs of our tribe? If, however, the anthropological stance would seem to pull us toward empirical explanations and relativism, the requirements of a transcendental investigation would seem to pull us away from any kind of anthropological insight.

The interest in the relation between a transcendental and an empirical inquiry spreads beyond a problem internal to Wittgenstein's philosophy. Ever since Hegel's critique of critical philosophy, it has seemed that Kant's attempt at a purely formal philosophy did not succeed.[14] The a priori and the a posteriori, the transcendental and the empirical, the formal and the material cannot be kept as distinct as Kant thought they could. Yet in the wake of this realization it remains unclear what to do about it. The danger, on one side, is that philosophy will collapse into the purely empirical: concern itself solely with methodological problems in the empirical sciences. On the other side, the danger is that philosophy will become vacuous by remaining a purely a priori inquiry. Studying the relation between the transcendental and anthropological strains in Wittgenstein's later philosophy provides a way of focusing on a central problem in the history of post-Kantian philosophy.

In Wittgenstein's mature thought the transcendental and the anthropological appear to be intended to form a coherent whole. Indeed, as we have begun to see, the anthropological seems to be invoked in the service of the transcendental. If we are to gain reflective, nonempirical insight into how concepts apply to objects, we must become aware of how we go on. Clearly, Wittgenstein is trying to gain deeper insight into the application of concepts to objects than is afforded by such conditions as "x satisfies 'is one meter long' if and only if x is one meter long." Nor would it help to give a more informative condition, for example, "if and only if x is the same length as the standard meter rod in Paris." He believes a deeper insight is available than could be given by any empirical account of the correct application conditions for a concept to an object. And this insight becomes available to us by reflectively considering how we use the concept: how the concept is "woven into" our customs, practices, and institutions. Transcendental insight seems to require the anthropological stance. Yet if we have to consider our interests, projects, and desires before we can fully appreciate the basis for the application of a concept to an object, is not Wittgenstein just offering a very different sort of empirical account? If so, then isn't he vulnerable to this objection: "If the moon has a circumference of n meters, then the circumference would have been such whether or not human life had ever existed; and whether or not human beings had ever devised the metric system of measurement"? One would like to be able to treat this objection analogously to the response Kant would make to the claim that there would have been physical objects even if there had been no observers. As an empirical claim the "objection" may be true, but it is not then an objection. For Kant is not making a rival claim; he is investigating the transcendental content of all such claims. There would have been physical objects even if there had been no observers: but what it is to be an object can be fully understood only by reference to the synthetic activities of a discursive intelligence.[15] The question is whether an analogous response is open to Wittgenstein.

One leaves the arena of empirical explanations on a *via negativa*: by a process of elimination one discovers that the obvious forms of empirical explanation could not possibly answer the question which is being asked. A purely physical account cannot explain language mastery. If we treat the person as a complex physical machine—say, a computer which is programmed in the course of language training—we leave out of account what it is about his behavior that makes it the speaking of a language. Language-speaking is permeated with norms: there are ways one ought and ought not to behave if one is to speak a language. And these oughts, Wittgenstein believes, cannot be derived from the is of a physically based disposition to respond.[16] That I am disposed to call this object "red" may be physically explicable, but my physical programming (if there be such) could explain neither why my calling it "red" is correct nor why my utterance is an actual predication and not a meaningless vocalization.

Nor will a mental explanation give us what we thought we wanted. We discover, first, that our actions are ultimately unconditioned in the sense that whatever reasons we might have invoked as explaining our actions give out. Ultimately we just act.

> But how does he know where and how to look up the word "red" and what he is to do with the word "five"?—Well, I assume he acts as I have described. Explanations come to an end somewhere . . .
>
> . . . if a person has not yet got the concepts, I shall teach him to use the words by means of examples and by practice.—And when I do this I do not communicate to him less than I know myself . . .
>
> How can he know how he is to continue the pattern by himself?—whatever instruction you give him?—Well, how do I know?—If that means, "Have I reasons?" the answer is: "my reasons will soon give out. And then I shall act without reasons" . . .
>
> "How am I to obey a rule?"—If this is not a question about causes, then it is about the justification for my following the rule in the way I do. If I have exhausted the justifications I have reached bedrock, and my spade is turned. Then I am inclined to say: "This is simply what I do" . . .
>
> When I obey a rule, I do not choose. I obey the rule blindly.[17]

Second, we discover that within the realm of the mental, at least on a certain familiar conception of that realm, our actions are completely unconditioned, in the sense that nothing available to an individual's consciousness (as it is portrayed within this conception) could direct or explain language mastery. No "mental" item, such as an image, idea, formula, rule, can dictate how it itself is to be used, nor can it guide the use of its correlated linguistic expression.[18] But it is the use we make of an expression which seems to give it its life, its meaning. If the mental item floats free of the use we make of the expression, then it floats free of the meaning as well. (Of course, Wittgenstein's critique is not confined to pointing out the inefficacy of such items: the very idea of the mind as an individual's container of these special items, and correspondingly the idea of his consciousness as his special access to the contents of such a container, are under attack.)

There is thus no image, and more generally no "mental" item of that kind, which guides language use, and this activity cannot be explained by appeal to any such item. This does not imply that there is no substance to the grasping of a concept or the following of a rule; but whatever substance there is must be understood in terms of how a person acts and the context into which his actions are woven. "There is," as Wittgenstein famously said, "a way of grasping a rule which is not an interpretation, but which is exhibited in what we call 'obeying the rule' and 'going against it' in actual cases."[19] One can say that someone has grasped a rule, and even that his linguistic activity is faithful to it: but the rule he has grasped does not explain his activity; his activity gives substance to the claim that he has grasped the rule.

Precisely because mental items, on the conception under attack, cannot explain use, one must look to the use itself. And this use is communal. In this way the lack of mental explanation seems to force us to adopt the anthropological stance. "Language" as a term can easily suggest something fixed and frozen, something objectlike. But, for Wittgenstein, language is not a thing we possess, in virtue of which we are able to engage in the activities of speaking a language: the myriad activities are the language. And it is in virtue of participating in these activities that we say that someone "understands the language."

The form of life in which a language is embedded is, for Wittgenstein, an activity. Consider, for example, measuring. It is obviously a contingent matter that we measure as we do: not merely that we use feet and meters, but that we go in for exact measurement. The interesting point, for Wittgenstein, is not that we measure as we do, but that what measuring is is to some extent determined by the ways we measure. These ways of measuring are expressive of our interests and purposes. To become reflectively aware of this, we may imaginatively present ourselves with people whose practices are expressive of other interests: for example, people who use flexible measuring rods to deal with each other flexibly, or a tribe who "piled lumber in arbitrary, varying height and then sold it at a price proportionate to the area covered by the piles."[20] To make it even prima facie plausible that these activities are alternative forms of measuring, we must surround the practices with a set of interests and concerns which give life to them. The point is not merely that it is contingent that we go in for exact measurements. For what it is for something to be an exact measurement is itself partially constituted by our practices.

There are several important aspects of this thought experiment which it is easy to overlook. First, this entire imaginative and reflective exercise is being conducted from our perspective. We are deciding what to countenance as an alternative form of measurement. Even when we try to come to grips with a form of "other-mindedness," it is we who have posed it and we who are trying to come to grips with it. The only reason the tribe counts as going in for an alternative type of measuring is that we see a family resemblance in their practices to what we take measuring to be. Second, the result of the thought experiment is not that this other tribe's measuring activities can be assessed only by standards internal to that tribe. The tribal practices do bear a "family resemblance" to measuring practices, and thus we can imaginatively envisage them as "an alternative form of measuring." But the point of Wittgenstein's thought experiment is not to establish the existence of alternative forms of measurement, still less to prove that relativism is true with respect to incommensurable measurement systems. The point is to help us reflectively grasp the fact that our own form of measuring—that is, measuring—is itself expressive of and partially constituted by our interests and practices. We find it easier to realize this about ourselves after we have imaginatively "observed" a tribe whose practices are expressive of other interests. So it is a mistake to conclude from the thought experiment that there is no fact of the matter as to who is measuring correctly, we or they. Since what it is to measure correctly is partially constituted by our practices, in failing to conform to those practices they fail to measure correctly. They may be doing other things well—like facilitating diplomatic relations by engaging in a flexible trade policy—and those who are good at it may in an extended sense be said to be "measuring correctly"—that is, according to the interests and point of the practice. But ultimately and strictly, we must conclude that their practices do not constitute correct measurement.

So, if we wish to interpret the man who says: "If the moon has a circumference of n meters, the circumference would have been such whether or not human life had ever existed" as speaking truly, we must interpret him as presupposing our current practices. That is, we must interpret him as saying that the moon's circumference is not dependent on human decision (in the way that the circumference of the Berlin Wall was), and (given the practices of measuring we actually do employ) that circumference is n meters. So (a) given the truth of the antecedent, the conditional as a whole is true. But if we take the conditional as asking us to abstract completely from current measuring practices, then, for Wittgenstein, the conditional loses content. For (b) if we do not presuppose our present mindedness, we cannot assign a determinate truth value to the conditional. It would not be false (as it would be if, in those conditions, the moon were of circumference m—less than n—meters). The reason for (b) is: (c) if we do not presuppose our mindedness, we cannot assign determinate content to the antecedent. So the conditional fails not because it is impossible to determine the truth of the consequent, given the truth of the antecedent, but because the antecedent ceases to express a condition.

Although, as we have seen, there is a naturalistic strain in Wittgenstein's thought, he is pretty clear that the anthropological stance is not intended to yield a natural history. We imagine various tribal practices not to study them seriously but to cure our (natural) tendency toward conceptual platonism:

> we are not doing natural science; nor yet natural history—since we can also invent fictitious natural history for our purposes.
>
> I am not saying: if such-and-such facts of nature were different people would have different concepts (in the sense of a hypothesis). But: if anyone believes that certain concepts are absolutely the correct ones, and that having different ones would mean not realizing something that we realize—then let him imagine certain very general facts of nature to be different from the ones

we are used to, and the formation of concepts different from the usual ones will become intelligible to him.[21]

But even if we are ultimately concerned with ourselves and not with other tribes, why isn't Wittgenstein's account of measuring a piece of empirical anthropology? Why can we not explain measuring as the outcome of the interests we have? And why would this explanation not serve to explain the shifts in interests and concerns which might lead us to adopt other practices—to become other-minded?[22] Is there any room for a distinctively philosophical account of our practice?

ONE WAY OF DEALING WITH THIS PUZZLE, which I shall call the *split-level interpretation*, would be to maintain that there are two levels of discourse, the empirical level, where one can offer a genuine explanation of our activities; and the philosophical level, which provides a reflective account of what such an explanation consists in. Thus the empirical anthropologist's explanation of our practice of measuring—that we act in these ways for these reasons—need not be in conflict with the philosopher's claim that we obey rules blindly. The philosophical claim that we obey rules blindly is intended only to make clear what it is to act with reasons: for example, that it is not a matter of having reasons present to consciousness (in the philosophically loaded sense).

On this interpretation, the empirical and transcendental anthropologists are not making rival claims; the latter is giving a reflective analysis of the former's explanation. For example, when I assume the role of empirical anthropologist—put on my pith helmet, hide behind a chair, and watch me cooking dinner—I see my behavior as rule-governed. I am engaged in various actions, among them occasionally measuring out ingredients; and these actions have explanations in terms of intentions, reasons, and desires. Now, after a certain amount of philosophical reflection, I am also supposed to see myself as acting blindly. The empirical anthropologist in me has seen me as acting for reasons; the philosopher in me asks, "What is it for me to be doing such?" In philosophical reflection I discover that there need be nothing "in my mind" which guides my behavior. I can be said to be following a rule if I have been initiated into the custom or practice, if I am relatively alert, and if my behavior conforms to the rule. Thus if I pour out the required amount of flour, I am genuinely following a recipe, even if my thoughts are absorbed in this essay. And this rule-following behavior is to be distinguished from the behavior of a man who has never before encountered cooking or recipes but happens to pour out the same amount of flour. The latter man's behavior, as Kant would say, has mere legality: it is in accordance with the rules, but it doesn't follow them. There is, on the split-level interpretation, no disagreement between philosopher and empirical anthropologist at the reflective level of explaining actions in terms of reasons, beliefs, and desires. If there is to be a disagreement, it would have to be at the metareflective level: over what it is to give such an explanation. The philosophical claim that we obey rules blindly would be a rival only to an equally metareflective claim: for example, that acting for reasons can consist only in consciously experienced reasons causing the actions. On the split-level interpretation, Wittgenstein is not challenging the empirical anthropologist; he is challenging an alternative philosophical account of what it is for the empirical anthropologist to give an explanation.

The main problem with the split-level interpretation concerns the plausibility of there being two levels of discourse, one empirical, one philosophical, which are relatively unimpugned by each other's claims. Kant was able to introduce the distinction between an empirical and a transcendental consideration of a subject matter because, for him, our ability to think far outstrips the conditions of our sensible experience. Thus, Kant thought, we can consider an object both as it appears to a human knower and as it is in itself, independent of the conditions of human knowledge. Our knowledge of the object is of course confined to objects only insofar as they satisfy the conditions of knowledge. Thus, for Kant, it is possible to say of an object both that it is real and that it is merely appearance without thereby making rival claims.

But how, for Wittgenstein, could there be any distinctively philosophical consideration of a subject matter which would leave an empirical consideration of that subject matter unaffected? The idea of a separate philosophical level of discourse would have been anathema to him; thus it is fairly clear that he, at least, would have been hostile to the split-level interpretation. Wittgenstein insisted that philosophers must "speak the language of every day," for an expression could have no more meaning than the use which was made of it. But the important point for a Wittgensteinian should be that meaning remains *responsible* to use, not that meaning cannot outstrip everyday use. Wittgenstein was of course concerned to deny the possibility that words gain their meaning from superhuman source—platonic ideas, for example. And he was equally concerned to deny the possibility of a transcendent perspective from which one could, as it were, see how well we were doing. But one can grant this and still insist that an expression may acquire meaning in philosophy which outstrips everyday use. (Consider, for example, Wittgenstein's own use of "language-game.") A Wittgensteinian ought to be able to show how his claims are grounded in legitimate philosophical activity—to show that he is not simply trying to speak from God's perspective. He should not have to "speak the language of every day."

The problem with the split-level interpretation, then, is not that philosophical activity may not stretch everyday use. It is rather that there is no way to keep the distinction between the empirical and the philosophical stable. If there were a distinctive activity, philosophy, which bore no relation to the rest of our lives, then words might get special meanings within that activity which differed from the meanings they had in our ordinary lives. The uses would occur, and continue to occur, independently of each other. But philosophy is not so divorced from the rest of our lives. This may be unobvious if we restrict our attention to Wittgensteinian tribes, who are all *unreflectively* engaging in their activities. But remember: (a) the divide between the philosophical and the empirical is supposed to have the philosopher on one side and the empirical anthropologist on the other; (b) much of the everyday lives of the readers of this essay will include a fair amount of reflection. It is thus a mistake to assume that the difference between the empirical and philosophical can be assimilated to a difference in the level of reflective awareness involved. Kant could make such an assimilation because he believed that the empirical coincided with the phenomenal world from which one could step outside, if only in thought. But if we abandon the distinction between world of appearance and world as it is in itself, the distinction between empirical and transcendental becomes less easy to draw. At first, it does look like a distinction between levels of reflection. For in Wittgenstein's own philosophy the transcendental coincides with a reflective consideration of unreflective activities. However, the reason that reflective consideration can plausibly be called "transcendental" is not simply that it is reflective, but that it purports to provide nonempirical insight. Prima facie, there is room for an alternative study which is equally reflective, but which offers empirical explanation instead. It is therefore too early to assume that empirical anthropology must be a less reflective discipline than transcendental anthropology. Empirical anthropology may incorporate a tremendous amount of self-reflection and self-understanding. To remain empirical, it need only continue to offer explanations of the tribe it studies: explanations which may cover the anthropologists in the tribe who are doing the explaining.

There can, therefore, be no isolated and immune level of philosophical discourse; though not for the reasons usually advanced. Words may acquire a special meaning in philosophical activity. However, since our lives form a (perhaps webbed) whole, this use tends to work its way into "ordinary use." Further, philosophical activity is not the only reflective activity there is. Insofar as the special use is the outcome of reflection, it may engage with the claims of other reflective enterprises, such as empirical anthropology.

IN GENERAL, Wittgenstein's philosophy is limited by its lack of consideration of reflective activity. If we take the simple cases of tribal behavior Wittgenstein actually considered—for example, selling piles of lumber—both the empirical and the transcendental anthropologist seem to be on the outside looking in. (None of the people piling lumber is wondering how this activity could best be understood.) But now suppose the form of life encompasses us as well. Then Wittgenstein must be seen as trying to get some members of "the tribe" to revise their practices: "We must do away with all explanation."

To whom is this injunction addressed? Who are the "we" who must do away with all explanation: we philosophers? we anthropologists? On the split-level interpretation, the injunction would be restricted to philosophers, and it might be understood in the following way. Within a practice there may be certain types of explanations which would justify various aspects of the practice in the sense of providing the reasons why the agents in the practice act as they do. For example, my flour-measuring activity may be explained by my interests in cooking, eating, and feeding others. These interests permeate the community; indeed, I have been taught the standard practices which manifest them. No doubt I would measure out flour differently if I belonged to a community which ate only raw food, had no cooking practices, but did on occasion pour out flour in order to predict the weather. Thus my reasons do provide an explanation of my flour-measuring activity, but both my flour-measuring activity and my reasons for it are "internal" to the cooking practices. On the split-level interpretation, these "internal" explanations are all right. And so are the causal explanations which try to isolate the empirical causes of a community's evolution. The injunction is directed only at the philosopher who wants to continue the justificatory process: to justify the justifications, to provide a justification of the form of life as a whole. It is the philosopher who must recognize that reasons soon give out, that justifications are soon exhausted, that "what has to be accepted, the given, is—so one could say—forms of life."[23] What has to be accepted, one might say, is living.

There are two apparent virtues of this interpretation. First, we are not forced to interpret Wittgenstein as implausibly denying the commonsense belief that we can explain my flour-measuring activities in terms of my reasons and interests. Second, an otherwise mysterious (and potentially threatening) injunction is explained in terms of other aspects of Wittgenstein's philosophy with which we are by now familiar. For Wittgenstein, explanations by reasons do eventually give out, there are no justifications of forms of life; and it is reassuring to read Wittgenstein's injunction as no more than a reiteration of those points.

However, the danger of interpreting the unfamiliar in terms of the familiar is that we may forfeit insight into the genuinely unfamiliar. Wittgenstein, as we have seen, was himself aware that the *Investigations* was an unfinished work. And a problem which is crying out for attention (perhaps it is left crying because Wittgenstein was skeptical that one could give it adequate attention) is how we are to understand reflective philosophical activity when it goes on within a form of life. Nevertheless, it is clear that, for Wittgenstein, there is no reason to suppose that there is any distinctive and isolated realm of philosophical reflection.

If the split-level interpretation is to be rejected, if philosophy is not a self-contained activity providing insight into our other activities which are themselves unaffected by philosophical reflection, then the injunction that we must do away with all explanation begins to look more puzzling. Even if we do come to this injunction via philosophical reflection, and even if the reflection is (as the split-level interpretation says) that ultimately we act without reasons or justifications, one would expect that insight to ripple through various aspects of our (reflective) lives. This would suggest a *dialectical interpretation* of Wittgenstein's injunction: after a certain process of philosophical reflection—for example, working through the *Philosophical Investigations*—we come to adopt a different attitude to the practice of explanation by reasons. This is not a specifically "philosophical" attitude, nor is it confined solely to "philosophical" explanations.

Let me give a perhaps fanciful example of how this might work. Suppose we come to realize not merely that reasons must ultimately peter out, but that the practice of reason-giving presupposes that this is not so. For example, suppose that the implicit telos of any reason-giving is ultimately a structure which terminates in self-justifying reasons. Then if we come to realize that reasons must simply give out, we ought also to realize that even in our most primitive reason-giving explanations, we were engaging in an activity which could not ultimately be legitimated. At least, the activity could not be legitimated according to a certain illusion of what a legitimation must be. What we work through is a myth of legitimation: an illusion that giving reasons will provide an ultimate ground of our activity. Having worked through the illusion, the philosopher in the kitchen may well still give reasons for his particular cooking activities—in this sense philosophy leaves everything as it is—but he no longer suffers a self-inflicted misunderstanding of what his explanation might do for him.

LET US ASSUME that the dialectical interpretation is correct: that as we work our way through the *Investigations*, the insights gained will not be specifically philosophical, but will permeate our various reflective activities. How then might the anthropological and transcendental strains in Wittgenstein's thought form a coherent whole? Remember, first, that the distinction between the empirical and the transcendental is not a distinction of subject matter, but a distinction in the way that subject matter is considered.[24] A transcendental consideration of what we are like is considering the very same people as an empirical inquiry into human nature, but it purports to yield some form of nonempirical insight. Second, it is important to realize that Wittgenstein does not confine us to reflecting solely on what can be gleaned from the anthropological stance. Wittgenstein himself regularly makes use of the first-person access we have to our lives ("perspective" is the wrong word) to draw us to his philosophical outlook. For example,

> *while* I am being guided everything is quite simple, I notice nothing *special;* but afterwards, when I ask myself what it was that happened, it seems to have been something indescribable. *Afterwards* no description satisfies me. It's as if I couldn't believe that I merely looked, made such-and-such a face, and drew a line.—But don't I *remember* anything else? No; and yet I feel as if there must have been something else; in particular when I say *"guidance," "influence,"* and other such words to myself . . . "For surely," I tell myself, "I was being *guided."*—Only then does the idea of that ethereal, intangible influence arise.
>
> When I look back on the experience I have the feeling that what is essential about it is an "experience of being influenced," of a connexion—as opposed to any mere simultaneity of phenomena: but at the same time I should not be willing to call any experienced phenomenon the "experience of being influenced." (This contains the germ of the idea that the will is not a *phenomenon.*) I should like to say that I had experienced the *"because,"* and yet I do not want to call any phenomenon the "experience of the because."
>
> I should like to say: " 'I experience the because." Not because I remember such an experience, but because when I reflect on what I experience in such a case I look at it through the medium of the concept "because" (or "influence" or "cause" or "connexion").[25]

It is only because we can reflect on our own inner experience that we can come to a proper understanding of what really happens when we want to say we "experience the because." The nonobservational access we have to our lives necessarily escapes the anthropologist's gaze. And it is only because we have such an access to our lives that Wittgenstein's observations about acting blindly or acting ultimately without reasons begin to seem plausible.

The outcome of Wittgenstein's investigation is, of course, not meant to be the empirical discovery that, as it happens, there is no mental item, present to consciousness (in that philosophically loaded sense), which determines my rule-following behavior. The outcome is supposed to be the philosophical realization that no such mental item could possibly explain or legitimate rule-following activity. But how can we get such a strong conclusion from consulting the quality of our inner life? Certainly the appeal to our inner life cannot be a step in a purely a priori argument. Where does the argumentative force of Wittgenstein's reflections come from? And what must we be like to be able to work our way through these philosophical reflections?

Although our consultation of inner experience is not a priori, it is a priori that we can make such a consultation. Kant, as is well known, argued that it must be possible for the "I think" to accompany all my representations. This, Kant argued, was a transcendental condition of self-consciousness: indeed it was an analytic principle, defining what it is for something to be a representation of mine. It is important not to conflate pure apperception with an "I think." Immediately after introducing the analytic principle of apperception, Kant says: "I call it pure apperception, because it is that self-consciousness which, while generating the representation 'I think' . . . cannot itself be accompanied by any further representation."[26] There must be an I which is distinct from any "I think" that I actually think. (And not for the reason that it is an "I think" which someone else thinks.) Each "I think" that I actually think is itself a representation, and thus is subject to the possibility of having an "I think" attached to it. This permanent possibility of reflective consciousness is original apperception: that which generates the representation "I think." Original apperception is a form of consciousness. It is not the "I think" which is predicated of a given representation. Nor, since it is a permanent possibility, is it even an "I think" which is predicable of a representation in the sense that it could actually be predicated. When I actually predicate an "I think" of a representation *R*, I judge that the representation is mine. The judgment "I think *R*" may represent a form of self-conscious awareness, but one must recognize that this judgment is no more than a judgment which is occurring within the conscious life of a self-conscious being: it is one more representation. Of course, I can now step back from the reflective judgment and consider it—I can actually predicate the "I think" of "I think *R*"—but now I am treating the judgment "I think *R*" as an object of predication. The activity of judging or predicating cannot be fully captured by any judgment.

However, there is a form of awareness of the predicating, which is distinct from the predication itself. It is an awareness which is required for the representation "I think *R*" to be itself part of a larger single self-consciousness, which is distinct from all its representations. It is a consciousness which can simply accompany the activity of predicating. The "I think" which I actually predicate thus serves mainly as a dialectical tool which leads me to recognize a form of self-awareness distinct from it. But then Kant should have given it a different name, if only to distinguish it from the genuinely predicable "I think." Let us call the original synthetic unity of apperception an "I:." (I use a colon to symbolize the idea that this is the consciousness which must be able to accompany each of my representations.) Kant should then be amended so as to claim that the "I:" must be able to accompany all my representations, whereas the "I think" must be predicable of all of them. Once I have recognized the distinct forms of apperception, I can kick away the "I think": any predicating or judging I do—any activity of applying a concept to an object—may be accompanied by this awareness.

That I must be able to accompany my rule-following activity with consciousness is a transcendental condition of subjectivity. (By contrast, the realization that what it is like to be a bat is inaccessible to human consciousness is empirical, discovered by reflection on the differing lives and neurophysiological constitutions of bats and humans.)[27] So the point is not merely that Wittgenstein makes appeal to a nonobservational access we have to our lives; it is a transcendental condition of our subjectivity that we have this access. This condition has a dual in the first person plural. If the form of life is constituted by our rule-following activities,

268

then the nonobservational consciousness with which each of us can accompany our rule-following activities ought, a fortiori, also to provide a nonobservational consciousness of the form of life itself. That we (that is, each of us) must be able to accompany our rule-following activities with consciousness is a transcendental condition of our subjectivity.

If we are able to work through the *Investigations,* we must also be beings who can reflect on what our nonobservational consciousness can accompany. And reflecting on what this nonobservational consciousness does accompany, we realize that nothing in it could explain or legitimate rule-following: nothing in it could be that extra something which turns my behavior into rule-following or guarantees that my rule-following is correct. Yet this consciousness accompanies activity which is partially constitutive of the form of life. For Wittgenstein, as we have seen, the activity of following a rule need not occur in the mind of an individual thinker: there is a way of grasping a rule which is exhibited in our customs, practices, in actual instances of obeying and disobeying it. Yet each of us can simply accompany our rule-following activities with consciousness, and reflection on what the "I:" can accompany may alter the judgments we wish to make about them. I discover that I act blindly. And I have an access to my blind actions which is denied to the empirical anthropologist watching me (even when I am the anthropologist). I can go along with them. My actions may be accompanied by consciousness, and that should be a consciousness of unconditioned activity. That is a form of awareness of my actions which does not consist in looking down on them. It is not a form of reflective consciousness, but its presence does give more material for reflective consciousness. For, tempted as I am to say that I "experienced the because," I know at first hand that I didn't.

A concept for the later Wittgenstein is merely the ontological shadow of a predicate. And the life of a predicate consists in the use we are so minded to make of it. Thus if I am a competent speaker of a language, the "I:" which can accompany my use of a predicate ought to provide a consciousness of the unfolding of a concept. Ironically, though, what is so remarkable about the quality of this consciousness is that there is nothing remarkable about it. We are not in direct contact with the concept, still less with the Absolute Idea. The fact that my consciousness is of the unfolding of the concept is ultimately a fact not about my consciousness but about the location of my activity in a larger context of customs and practices. When I use an expression, I exercise my practical ability to participate in the practice, but I may have little reflective understanding of how the expression is used.[28] Therefore, Kant's analytic principle of apperception needs to be qualified. While making an assertion R, I may self-consciously think "I think R," but the full content of that to which the "I think" attaches may not be within my grasp. For Kant, the mind was completely aware of at least the representational content of its representations. But for Wittgenstein the content of the thought "I think R" will depend on a context of use in which I can participate, to which I can practically commit myself, but of which I may lack reflective understanding.

Therefore, to work through Wittgenstein's philosophical dialectic, we must also be able to take up the anthropological stance: it is by considering our activities as embedded in the context of customs and practices that we come to see how they could be genuine cases of rule-following. Yet, even leaving aside for the moment the question of its coherence with transcendental inquiry, it is hard to see that the anthropological stance is even possible. When I take on the anthropological stance with respect to my cooking activities, I cannot genuinely be in the role of observer. The "sideways-on perspective" is not a perspective; it is an imaginative fiction. Now, of course, there is an obvious sense in which I can observe myself: as when I keep a careful record of what I eat or of what sorts of event make me anxious. But it is illusion to imagine that I thereby step outside myself and gain a genuine sideways-on perspective. Similarly for the first person plural. Though we may be able to make various studied judgments about the state of our culture, there is a deep sense in which we cannot stand as observers to ourselves.

The anthropological stance would thus appear to be both necessary and impossible. In trying to grasp the content of an expression, we cast ourselves as anthropologists observing the context in which an expression is used. But on further reflection we discover that we could never be such anthropologists, nor could we genuinely take up such an observational stance. Does this imply that meaning is ineffable? Is it only God—who can look down from a completely detached vantage point and see the entire context of use—who is able to grasp the meaning of our meaningful activities? The answer to these questions is no; but it is important to recognize the tacit presuppositions about meaning which might tempt us to answer affirmatively. If we think of ourselves along the lines of a Wittgensteinian tribe, we will implicitly assume that meaning is constituted by our nonselfconscious activities. As tribesmen, we grasp the meaning "in a flash"—we require practical competence with an expression, but we have little or no reflective understanding of the context in which our rule-following activities are set. It is only the observer, standing outside the practices, who will be able to survey the context and reflectively grasp the meaning of our activities. On this picture, there is a determinate meaning constituted by nonselfconscious activities and unaffected by self-conscious reflection, which is fully available only to a being who can fully survey the activities. Meaning is not like that. And neither are we. We are self-conscious, reflective beings, and the meaning of our activities does not determinately exist, waiting to be grasped by self-conscious reflection on the context of use: self-conscious reflection is partially constitutive of the context and thus of meaning. The context of an expression's use includes agents who are taking the anthropological stance with respect to that context, and the content of the expression is partially constituted by the self-conscious judgments of the self-appointed anthropologists as to what the expression means. Meaning is by its nature an unfinished business: it continues to be constituted by those self-conscious interpreters who seek to comprehend it by "observing" the context in which it is used.

This would suggest that the anthropological stance is not what it pretends to be. It is not genuinely an observational stance; it is rather an artifact of philosophical inquiry: one in which we discover that nothing in an individual's consciousness could legitimate his rule-following activity and that one must "look" to the community practices in which the activity is embedded. We take up the anthropological stance not when we actually go out and observe various tribes, but when, in philosophical reflection, we construct various tribal practices and imaginatively locate rule-following activity within them. In psychoanalytic terms, the anthropological stance is in fact a projective identification which we do not recognize

271

as such. We project some part of our imaginative activity out into anthropological space, and take ourselves to be investigating a tribe. To understand how the transcendental and anthropological stances fit together, we have to recover the projective identification and come to see it as part of our own philosophical-imaginative activity. Therefore, the answer to the question "How is the anthropological stance possible?" also answers the question "How do the anthropological and transcendental strains in Wittgenstein's thought cohere?" For when we penetrate its deceptive self-presentation, we discover that the anthropological stance is not at war with transcendental inquiry; it is of a piece with it.

Wittgenstein made an analogy between philosophy and therapy: each is used to free us from the grip of various illusions about who we are, how we go on, what we mean. I believe this analogy can be extended. In psychotherapy, a person may (in the presence of another) create a representation of herself: of her beliefs, desires, wishes, anxieties, and character, all set in a social context of parents, friends, and loved ones' personalities, the environment of childhood, the institutions in which she now operates. The ultimate value of the therapeutic process, though, is not the creation of this artifact. Although the agent will become a better "observer" of herself, the point of the therapy is not the observation of an accurately represented person, but nonobservational insight into the person creating the representation.[29] It is insight into the forms of active creativity. As the forms of mental activity too become conscious, they too can be represented—and thus thought about and modified. In this way, insight into activity—not into any particular mental representations, memories, facts, and so on—can lead to a change in the form of living. In this way, the creation of the artifact can be partially constitutive of a change in the creator. Philosophers have sometimes complained that psychoanalysis is not an empirical discipline, that it is not a "science." This seems to me a reason for hope, not disdain: for perhaps reflection on the therapeutic model will shed light on how to proceed philosophically in a way which is neither a methodology of the sciences nor a purely transcendental investigation.

If the analogy between psychotherapy and philosophy is to hold, then the anthropological stance must be seen as only a step along a philosophical dialectic: "observing" the context in which rule-following activity is embedded will not yield the full meaning of that activity, nor is the anthropologist the philosopher's final role. Perhaps, though, Wittgenstein should have distinguished between the "We" and a *form of life* in much the same way that Kant should have distinguished the "I:" from the "I think." "Form of life" is a predicate which may be predicated of various objects. We may use the term narrowly and label disparate social groups alternative "forms of life"; or we may use the term widely to mark the form of life which we all constitute. The problem is thus not that self-reference is impossible. We can refer to ourselves, though such self-reference is only one more act within the form of life. The problem is, rather, that what we are trying to gain insight into is not, strictly speaking, a form of life. The relation in which we stand to ourselves is similar to the relation in which I stand to myself. Just as when I try to become reflectively self-aware I end up with an "I think" rather than an "I:," it is characteristic of our position that when we try to become reflectively self-aware, we end up with a form of life. We should eventually come to appreciate that when we talk philosophically about "our form of life" what we are trying to describe is not an object—and thus not a possible object of judgment. (This, I believe, is the germination of the idea that the will is not a phenomenon.) We are trying to gain nonobservational insight into that which from a "sideways-on" perspective is a form of life. The activity is manifested in all our rule-following activities, including all our judgments, but is not the object of any of them.

The anthropological and transcendental strains in Wittgenstein's thought are, then, coherent, but they do not form a coherent whole. The problem with Wittgenstein's later philosophy is not inconsistency but incompleteness. One unfinished task, I have argued, is to provide a critique of the anthropological stance: to expose its pretense of pure observer, to recognize that it is an artifact of philosophical inquiry, and to weave it into a richer conception of philosophical consciousness.

Let us speculatively consider one way to begin. The very idea of an explanation by reasons is intimately linked with the anthropological stance: such an explanation is that which the anthropological stance produces. Insofar as the anthropological stance is unproblematically assumed, the notion of an explanation by reasons will seem inevitable and invulnerable: conversely, it is difficult to imagine how the anthropological stance could suffer a critique while the notion of explanation by reasons remained untouched. It has been plausibly argued that when we take the anthropological stance with respect to others, and try to construct an explanation of their actions on the basis of their beliefs and desires, we must, to a significant degree, assimilate them to ourselves.[30] That is, we attribute to them beliefs and desires we have, or, perhaps, beliefs and desires we think we would have if we were in their circumstances. Although our observation of others appears prima facie to be the purest case of observation, it turns out that the very possibility of making this observation depends on the possession of a vast amount of information which is not itself derived from the observation.

How is this information derived? How do we come to know what our own beliefs and desires are? I cannot now answer these questions in any detail, but it suffices for my present purposes to recognize that the answers are not straightforward. Our own beliefs and desires are not immediately transparent to consciousness, nor can we take a purely observational stance with respect to ourselves. It seems that we must construct a representation of ourselves as agents acting on beliefs and desires. In part this is done by reflecting on beliefs and desires which are relatively obvious to us, in part by imaginatively taking the anthropological stance with respect to ourselves. For example, when we construct an explanation by reasons of our measuring activities, it seems that we subject ourselves to our anthropological gaze. We see ourselves in our various measuring activities, and construct a teleological explanation of those activities in terms of our desires and beliefs.

This teleological conception is the self as it appears to itself: a representation we construct when we try to explain to ourselves who we are and what we are like. The self as it is in itself would be that which the representation is trying to represent: the human agent who embodies the beliefs and desires which the representation ascribes. Thus the self as it is in itself is not a Kantian noumenal agent, located outside space and time; it is an ordinary human being engaged in living his life. One of his projects may be the acquisition of self-understanding, and this will be pursued by the formulation of a conception of himself as an agent acting on beliefs and desires. Some people are more sensitive than others, and some self-conceptions will be more accurate than others. However, one outcome of the present inquiry is that every representation of the self, no matter how accurate, must fail to capture fully the self as it is in itself. That consciousness which must be able to accompany each of my representations cannot itself be adequately represented by any of them.

Switching to the first person plural, *form of life* is a reflective concept, used by philosophers and anthropologists when they try to construct a representation of us. It is "We" as "We" appear to ourselves. We take the anthropological stance and construct a conception of ourselves as acting in similar (ritualized) ways on the basis of shared interests, beliefs, and desires. But again some aspect of our subjectivity must be left out of this representation. Even if we represent ourselves as reflective thinkers trying to understand who we are, by the very nature of the anthropological stance we will end up with a form of life, not with what I have gestured at calling "We." What we are confronted with is not the limit of the world, but the limit of the anthropological stance.

Now if it is "We" into whom we wish to gain insight, it would seem that we must do away with explanation. Perhaps, though, the injunction is too strong. We must do away with explanation in the sense that nothing which could be explained could possibly count as that into which we are trying to gain insight.

THE CENTRAL PROBLEM for post-Kantian philosophy has been to steer a course between the empirical and the transcendental. I am not in a position to state a general solution to the problem, but I would like to conclude this essay by giving one example which might show a middle course. In Wittgenstein's later philosophy the tension between the transcendental and the empirical manifests itself in the following dilemma: Who are we?[31] If, on the one hand, we are one group among others, then Wittgenstein's remarks about forms of life lacking justification would seem to encourage a slide toward relativism. If, on the other hand, the "We" encompasses us all, encompasses any being who might in the

275

widest of senses count as one of us, then doesn't the first person plural lose its force? Are we not left with a bare Metaphysical Subject, that for which these truths are true? This is one instance of the more general dilemma: either contentful and (too) empirical (and probably false) or transcendental and vacuous. In this instance at least, I believe there is a middle course.

There are certain truths about us which, though they must be expressed anthropologically, are not confined to any particular form of life. Nor are they merely universal in the sense of occurring in all forms of life. Rather they try to express the conditions of being minded in any way at all. For example, the reflective philosophical claim that what correct measurement is is itself dependent on our interests, desires, practices is not supposed to be a local claim about what constitutes correct measurement around here. Nor is it a universal sociological claim about human groups. It is a philosophical claim about the constitutive conditions of a form of life.

Thus the motivation for radical relativism derives from evidence which, in fact, tilts in the opposite direction. The argument for relativism proceeds, roughly, as follows. First, through philosophical reflection one comes to see that the practice of measuring correctly is partially constituted by our interests, practices, customs, which are themselves contingent. That is, we move reflectively from:

This is correct measurement.

to:

We are so minded as to believe: this is correct measurement.

Such insight does not undermine our measuring practices, precisely because they are genuinely expressive of our interests, and these are not changed by reflection. Second, one infers that:

Were there an other-minded tribe, there would be no fact of the matter as to who was measuring correctly, we or they.

Third, one infers that this situation holds for all our beliefs and practices:

Were there an other-minded tribe—a group which did not share our beliefs practices, interests—there would be no fact of the matter as to whether their beliefs or ours were true. All our true beliefs are really only true for us.

The relativist argues that we ought to infer, whenever we believe that *P*, that:

Were there an other-minded tribe, it might be that *not-P* (for them).

That we cannot imagine what it would be like for it to be the case that *not-P*, the relativist contends, is no argument against the inference. It only shows that the belief that *P* is one of the beliefs to which we are very attached. To argue that there simply could not be a form of life, or a world, in which *not-P*, the relativist continues, is simply to assume a form of verificationism. We simply assume that for something to be a form of life, like-minded or other-minded, we must be able to recognize it as such, and anything we could recognize as a form of life would have to involve believing that *P*.

This argument for "general relativity" is invalid, for both inferences are septic. As we have seen, we cannot conclude from the thought experiments that these other practices would be another form of correct measurement. So the first inference, to the relativity of incommensurable systems, is invalid. And the second inference, to general relativity, is also invalid. For although we can posit a tribe with practices which fill a roughly analogous role to our practices of measuring, this is because we have conceptual space for a tribe which manages with rough measurements. There is no space for tribes with radical alternatives to all our beliefs and practices.

One way to see this is to apply the relativist's argument to a reflective, philosophical belief. For example, the relativist wants to affirm that:

Were there an other-minded tribe, it might be that some other practice would be correct measurement (for them).

Since we are convinced of that, we may add the prefix "We are so minded as to believe":

We are so minded as to believe: were there an other-minded tribe, it might
be that some other practice would be correct measurement (for them).

Of course, this sentence is of the form "We are so minded as to believe:
P." So if the relativist's argument were valid, one ought to be able to infer
the relevant instance of "Were there an other-minded tribe, then it might
be that *not-P* (for them)":

Were there an other-minded tribe, it might not be the case (for them) that:
were there an other-minded tribe, it might be that some other practice would
be correct measurement (for them).

But the relativist cannot afford to allow this conclusion in any sense in
which it would undermine the following:

Were there an other-minded tribe, it would (even so) be the case that: were
there an other-minded tribe, it might be that some other practice would be
correct measurement (for them).

(Here what follows the colon says how in the envisaged circumstances, at
least according to the relativist, things would be for us, minded as we now
are.) Variations of this argument are about as old as philosophy itself. If
relativism is not to be self-refuting, the philosophical belief that our beliefs are relative must itself stand outside its own compass.

That the relativist's argument fails might at first suggest that the "We"
shrinks to a bare formal subject. Eventually we reach truths which express basic conditions of being minded, and the "We" is just the subject
for whom these truths are true. To show that this suggestion ought to be
resisted, let us consider the most challenging case: basic logical laws.

That there must be agreement in judgments, says Wittgenstein, "seems
to abolish logic, but does not do so."[32] Logic seems to be abolished because
various pictures we have of logic do get abolished. First, there is the picture of logical laws guiding or determining the behavior of a person making logical inferences: we see that person "operating a calculus according
to definite rules."[33] But if rule-following is unconditioned, this picture is
transcendental illusion. The situation is in fact almost the reverse: the
meaning of any abstract formulation of the law of noncontradiction—say,
"Not: *P* and *not-P*"—depends in part on the fact that in actual cases we

278

generally regard sufficient evidence that *not-P* to be grounds for withdrawing our assertion that *P*. Second, there is the picture of logic as providing the metaphysical structure of the world.[34] Man's desire to know the basis of everything empirical is, Kant argued, what leads him to metaphysics. And it is this very desire, according to Wittgenstein, which lends significance to logic: which inclines us to regard it as sublime.[35] The laws of logic do not delineate the metaphysical structure of the world; they tell one how one ought to behave in arguing, in setting out deductions, in asserting.[36]

Logic, however, is not abolished. Logic itself is the outcome of reflection on our practices of arguing rigorously, of asserting and denying. Philosophy's task, as Wittgenstein sees it, is to remind us of that. Logic does not point to a transcendent truth beyond the practices; it is a normative codification we have made of the normative practices themselves. That insight, however, does not disturb the reflective equilibrium of the codification itself. "One might say: the axis of reference of our examination must be rotated, but about the fixed point of our real need."[37]

Our real need is, I believe, the need to say something: to act within a shared form of life. We are beings partially constituted by this need: without it we cease to be who we are to such an extent that it seems fair to say simply that we cease to be. The correct conclusion to draw then is not:

If we were other-minded, we would not have this need.

but

Having this need is a condition of our being minded at all.

The basic laws of logic are abstract formulations of how one should act to meet this need. There is nothing local about this need: logic provides an abstract formulation of rules which must generally be obeyed in actual cases if our activity is to be an expression of mindedness. We can continue to say "our mindedness" if we want, but we ought to understand that we are not thereby restricting the claim. This is not verificationism, for no claim is being made that we (humans) must in principle be able to recognize every form of life. Perhaps there are Martians who speak a language which because of some kinks in our hardwiring we will never be able to recognize as such. The point is that if they are speaking a language, living a form of life, they too will be generally obeying the law of noncontradiction. We (humans) may not be able to recognize all of us, but in this broad context being minded in any way at all makes you one of us. So when, in philosophical reflection, we prefix "We are so minded as to believe:" to the law of noncontradiction, that cannot legitimately be the first stage of an argument which restricts its validity to one tribe among others.

Has the "We" collapsed to a bare formal condition of thought? The outline of a Wittgensteinian answer should now be clear. The question looks as though it requires a positive answer if we conceive of logic as presenting the "laws of thought." The "We" then collapses into the mere subject which obeys those laws. But this conception itself collapses when we recognize that the "laws of thought" themselves have no content in abstraction from the myriad activities in which we engage. A rule depends for its content on what counts as obeying it and going against it in actual cases. Far from the "We" disappearing, it is only by keeping the "We" vivid that we can ensure any content for the laws of thought.

One should not, therefore, even for logic, adopt a redundancy theory of the "We are so minded as to believe:." Studying logic, we come to assert the law of noncontradiction. In philosophical reflection, we prefix "We are so minded as to believe:." Yet even though we recognize that in this context there is no possibility of being other-minded, such an exercise does not simply lead us back to where we started. First, as we have seen, certain pictures of logic to which we are naturally inclined are dismissed as illusion. Second, a transcendental consideration of our subjectivity need not be totally removed from empirical experience: it may enhance what we can learn from it. There are, as I have said, two distinct forms of reflection on our ordinary rule-following activities. We may reflect on the consciousness which may accompany our activities—and thus discover what is really happening when we want to say we "experience the because"; or we may take the anthropological stance. Both of these reflective stances are informed by the insight that the law of noncontradiction is true. The first person, either singular or plural, which can accompany our activities is not a bare Metaphysical Subject, a limit of the world.[38] It is we in our ordinary lives who can accompany our activities with consciousness. It is only in these activities that the law of noncontradiction has any life, so, reflecting on the consciousness which can accompany them, we gain insight into what the law of noncontradiction asserts. However, the law of noncontradiction is also a statement, one more move in the language-game. And since it makes a general claim about our statement-making activities, we must also take up the anthropological stance both with respect to these activities and with respect to the law itself, if we are to have a reflective understanding of its content. Here, it seems to me, there is room for a transcendental anthropology: a reflection on our ordinary activities which yields nonempirical insight into them.

CHAPTER 12

The Disappearing "We"

There is a model of transcendental arguments with which we are all familiar, which I shall call antiskeptical. A transcendental argument for a conclusion x, on the antiskeptical model, proceeds by arguing that for a condition y to be possible, x must be the case. Since the value of a transcendental argument is thought to consist in its ability to combat skepticism, y should be a condition the skeptic must accept and x a condition he calls into doubt. Some transcendental arguments let y be the condition of speaking a language and then argue that the skeptic's very ability to state his doubts about x show that x must be the case. The strongest form of transcendental argument is thought to let y be self-conscious experience. For no interesting skeptic can deny that we have such a mental life; so if the transcendental argument is valid, it is thought, the skeptic is genuinely undermined. The paradigm of a transcendental argument is thought to be Kant's Transcendental Deduction of the categories. However, had Kant thought that the Transcendental Deduction merely showed that for experience to be possible it must conform to the cate-gories, he would have considered his argument a failure.[1]

Indeed, before he even mentions the need for a Transcendental Deduc-tion, Kant has already argued that all our thinking must conform to the categories. Kant argues, in the "Analytic of Concepts," that every act of the understanding is a judgment and every judgment must employ its as-sociated category. So if self-conscious experience involves any thinking, it will have to employ the categories. The Transcendental Deduction, by contrast, aims to show that we are entitled to employ the concepts which Kant has already argued we must employ in any thinking. It is, of course, possible to see that the Transcendental Deduction is concerned with the legitimation of the categories, even if one construes Kant's argument along the lines of the antiskeptical model, but one will naturally miscon-strue what the legitimation is. One will think the categories to be legiti-mated—and the skeptic answered—by showing that they are necessary for thought or experience.[2] But these words mean something different coming out of our mouths than they meant for Kant. First, Kant is not in-terested merely to show that the categories are necessary conditions of thought or experience. For Kant, the categories are also necessary in the sense that they are partially constitutive of both thought and experience; and, as necessary, they represent our contribution to experience. Second, Kant's notion of "experience" is much richer than ours. In contemporary discussions of transcendental arguments, "experience" is used, as I began to use it, in a minimal sense, to refer to the type of mental life which even a skeptic cannot interestingly deny we have. Kant, by contrast, defines "experience" as empirical knowledge.[3] Experience, for Kant, is a type of knowing.

It has often been thought that in the Transcendental Deduction Kant begins with the premise that we have experience in the minimal sense of self-consciousness and tries to work his way to the conclusion that we must therefore have experience in the rich sense of empirical knowledge. I cannot find evidence that this was Kant's strategy. He does seem to allow for two varieties of experience, but both are types of empirical knowledge. The paradigm of empirical knowledge is an explicit judgment in which an object given in intuition is brought under a concept.[4] However, there is also a type of empirical knowledge which is not explicitly judgmental. If my intuition is genuinely of an object, it is empirical knowledge, even though it precedes all explicit thinking of the object.[5] Let us call such knowledge intuitive experience. As far as I can determine, Kant never suspends the belief that we have intuitive experience, though he does investigate the transcendental content of such experience.

The question of right arises over whether the concepts with which we must think, which are not themselves derived from experience, legitimately apply to objects given in intuition. To settle this question would be to establish that our explicit judgments could count as empirical knowledge. Kant thinks he can do this by showing "how subjective conditions of thought can have objective validity, that is, can furnish conditions of the possibility of all knowledge of objects."[6] In part, this is established by arguing that the categories "serve as antecedent conditions under which alone anything can be . . . thought as an object in general."[7] The categories would be shown to be not merely an artifact of our subjective constitutions, but the formal conditions for thought of an object. But if intuitive experience is a type of knowing, and if objective validity can be secured by showing that the categories furnish conditions of the possibility of all knowledge of objects, then the categories must already be at work in the constitution of our intuitive experience.

Self-consciousness plays a crucial role in the Transcendental Deduction but, perhaps surprisingly from a contemporary perspective, not as the ultimate *tu quoque* against the skeptic. It is cited in an explanation of what underlies experience of an object. The analytic unity of apperception—that it must be possible for the "I think" to accompany all my representations—implies a certain synthetic unity: I must be able to unite my various representations in one consciousness. Since in the bare "I think" "nothing manifold is given," the only way I can represent myself as a single consciousness is via a synthetic unity among the representations. From a transcendental perspective, the knowledge manifested in a given intuition "consists in the determinate relation of given representations to an object; and an object is that in the concept of which the manifold of a given intuition is united"; and thus "it is the unity of consciousness that alone constitutes the relation of representations to an object, and therefore their objective validity and the fact that they are modes of knowledge."[8] So not only are the categories constitutive of the concept of an object; the synthetic unity of apperception constitutes our intuitive experience as experience of objects. Thought and intuitive experience must thus be harmonious. But this harmony is not preestablished; it is constituted.[9] That our representations are of an object is, as it were, a precipitate of the unity of consciousness, its objective correlate.[10] The point is not adequately made by saying that I must think in terms of objects—though that is so—nor by saying that I must experience a world of objects—though that is also true: for an object simply is that in which the manifold of our representations is united.[11]

Here we have carried out within the realm of pure reason the first stage of a "master-slave" dialectic. For although it is the synthetic unity of apperception which ultimately constitutes the relation of representations to an object, I am nevertheless dependent on my representations' being so united to be able to represent myself as a single consciousness. The unity of the act by which a determinate combination of a manifold is imposed "is at the same time the unity of consciousness."[12] I must constitute the objects of experience in order to "constitute" myself. Of course, the validity of this result is restricted to discursive intelligences, but it is only in relation to such intelligences that there could be such a thing as an object, and so one might say that the entire field of objective validity lies within this "restricted range."[13]

I do not intend to probe the details of Kant's argument here, only to suggest that if we go back to Kant we will find an alternative model for transcendental arguments to the antiskeptical model with which we are familiar. In homage to Kant, I shall simply call it *transcendental*. A transcendental argument for X is concerned with establishing the legitimacy of X, and this may of course have antiskeptical consequences, as indeed Kant's Transcendental Deduction did. But it will secure this legitimacy not by forcing the skeptic into some form of self-contradiction, but by revealing in its broadest and deepest context what it is to be X. It will answer the question "How is X possible?" when that question is asked with a straight face rather than a skeptical sneer.[14] This is a potentially liberating shift of emphasis, for we are no longer constrained to begin our inquiry with premises the skeptic must accept. Ironically, once we abandon the overarching concern for "refuting the skeptic," we may at last be free to conduct a sufficiently broad inquiry that one outcome will be that skepticism no longer seems threatening. Ancient skeptics, at least, would have relished such a situation.

It has been suggested by Saul Kripke that one might read Wittgenstein's *Philosophical Investigations* as providing a skeptical solution to a skeptical paradox.[15] The skeptic argues that there is no fact about me which shows that I mean one thing rather than another by my utterances. A skeptical puzzle thus arises as to how any language is possible. Wittgenstein's solution is said to be broadly Humean in structure: it is conceded that the individual (event) considered in isolation cannot legitimately be said to mean (cause) anything, but it is argued that we can nevertheless say that he means (it causes) something by virtue of his (its) relation to the larger context of a community of regularities—a form of life (causation)—of which he (it) is part.

Though any interesting analogy runs the risk of obscuring important differences, I would nevertheless like to cast Wittgenstein as a post-Kantian rather than as a neo-Humean.[16] The *Investigations* as a whole forms an extended study of the multifarious relations between subjective and objective perspectives. One example of this is the relation between my inner experience of comprehension and my objective ability to use the word correctly. Wittgenstein's question is not the skeptical version of "How is language possible?" but its transcendental counterpart.

It is now common to approach the study of meaning from a purely third person perspective: we observe a group of "natives" speaking an unknown language and consider the requirements for interpreting their utterances.[17] Wittgenstein does occasionally confront us with a tribe, but this is not his primary approach: if there is a "problem about language" which haunts him throughout the *Investigations*, it is the indissoluble, necessary tension which exists between first and third person perspectives. On the one hand, the *Investigations* leads us to believe that the meaning of a word consists in the use we make of it. "But," on the other hand, "we understand the meaning of a word when we hear or say it; we grasp it in a flash, and what we grasp in this way is surely something different from the 'use' which is extended in time!"[18] "Meaning is use" is a slogan used to sum up Wittgenstein's thoughts about language, but the problem Wittgenstein seems to be facing is that meaning isn't just use.

> When someone says the word "cube" to me, for example, I know what it means. But can the whole use of the word come before my mind, when I understand it in this way?
>
> Well but on the other hand isn't the meaning determined by this use? And can these ways of determining meaning conflict? Can what we grasp in a flash accord with a use, fit or fail to fit? And how can what is present to us in an instant, what comes before our minds in an instant, fit a use?[19]

For Kant, the need for a Transcendental Deduction arose from the apparent possibility that thought and intuitive experience might be disharmonious; for Wittgenstein, the alleged possibility of conflict which must be examined is between inner experience of comprehension and practical ability. Various mental items are canvassed as candidates for providing an explanation of the relation between inner experience and outer use—a mental picture, a method of projection, a formula, a rule—and all are rejected.[20] Surrogates both for the outer use—private mental objects—and for the inner experience—pure behavioral manifestation—are also proposed, only to be found inadequate.[21] The upshot is that an adequate account of language must include both a subjective and an objective aspect. And a question naturally arises as to how these two aspects fit together.

Among the various uses of the word "know," there are two which we characteristically employ when we speak of "knowing the meaning" of an expression: the use which expresses a practical ability, the mastery of a technique; and the use which signals an experience of comprehension: "Now I know!"[22] But when we consider the experience of comprehension and "try and see what makes its appearance here," there seems to be nothing more to be said.[23] From the first person perspective, we are acquainted with the experience of understanding. We should be loath to dismiss this experience as "unreal," but if this is a form of knowing, we should like to know more about it.

One reason Wittgenstein considers the apprehension of mental pictures, formulas, and rules as possible explanations of what knowing the meaning consists in is, I think, that they are all items which can plausibly be grasped in a flash. They would thus serve as a bridge between my inner experience and my practical ability. The same two criticisms continually recur. Viewed from the inside, the experience of understanding does not seem like the apprehension of a picture, formula, or rule. And, of course, none of these items is of any help in explaining the relation between my inner experience and my practical ability, for these items cannot explain how they themselves are to be used over time.

Though my experience of comprehension cannot be analyzed in terms of anything more tangible, it is not therefore to be dismissed. It is considered as one of a family of experiences which resist analysis when looked at "from sideways on."[24] We are tempted to say, for example, that in understanding an order "your mind flew ahead and took all the steps before you physically arrived at this or that one," but we can give no content to this picture.

> "It is as if we could grasp the whole use in a flash." Like what, e.g.?—Can't the use—in a certain sense—be grasped in a flash? And in what sense can it not?—The point is that it is as if we could "grasp it in a flash" in yet another and much more direct sense than that.—But have you a model for this? No. It is just that this expression suggests itself to us. As the result of crossing different pictures.[25]

Wittgenstein is not here impugning our experience of "grasping in a flash." He is criticizing the description of that experience as grasping the whole use in a flash. That is the result of crossing different pictures, a crossing which tempts us (illegitimately, but understandably) to posit an inner mental mechanism which explains our practical ability. This mental model not only promotes a false self-image—of ourselves as guided by some inner mental mechanism; it also suggests a false picture of what understanding an expression consists in.[26] If we forgo the temptation to picture the experience of comprehension as some form of mental encoding, Wittgenstein has no further objection.

> "But I don't mean that what I do now (in grasping a sense) determines the use causally and as a matter of experience, but that in a queer way, the use

itself is in some sense present."—But of course it is, "in some sense"! Really the only thing wrong with what you say is the expression "in a queer way." The rest is all right; and the sentence only seems queer when one imagines a different language-game for it from the one in which we actually use it ...

"It's as if we could grasp the whole use of a word in a flash."—And that is just what we say we do. That is to say we sometimes describe what we do in these words. But there is nothing astonishing, nothing queer about what happens. It becomes queer when we are led to think that the future development must in some way already be present in the act of grasping the use and yet isn't present.—For we say that there isn't any doubt that we understand the word, and on the other hand its meaning lies in its use.[27]

But if we can grasp the meaning in a flash and this grasping cannot be further analyzed, this presents a nonskeptical puzzle about the peculiar relation between inner experience and outer behavior. The sense in which I can be said to grasp a rule in a flash determines no course of action. Thus it cannot serve in an explanation of my practical ability to follow a rule. The distinct sense in which I can be said to grasp a rule, as exhibited in my behavior, seems to be unexplained. And it appears that my "inner" and "outer" graspings of a rule are mutually independent. Certainly their relationship is not what we might initially have expected: that of explanans to explanandum. The conclusion to be drawn, however, is not the Humean one that the "relationship" is a fiction, but the Kantian one that a legitimation is required which could not consist in any empirical explanation.

Wittgenstein has thus far revealed the need for a legitimation of the inner experience of comprehension. Let us call any act of speaking or using a language with understanding a representation. This is not a mere play on words. Representations for Kant were (mental) acts. And, he argued, they were quasi-linguistic performances: one of the intended lessons of the Transcendental Deduction is that intuitive experience is conceptually saturated.[28] Here I am asking that we append the term, by analogy, to explicitly linguistic performances. Wittgenstein argues, roughly, that it must be possible for the "I understand" to accompany each of my representations. That is, for a piece of behavior to be my act of using an expression meaningfully, it must at least be possible to append an "I understand" to it. I must be able to take conscious possession of it for it to be an act of mine. That the "I understand" must be able to accompany each of my representations is an analogue of the analytic unity of apperception. But from this principle, as Kant would say, "many consequences follow."[29] For the "analytic" principles of both Kant and Wittgenstein require a certain synthetic unity among my representations. For Kant, the disparate "I think"s which might be attached to various representations are in themselves diverse: they can express that the various representations are part of a single consciousness only insofar as the representations themselves possess sufficient order to be united in a single consciousness.[30] For Wittgenstein, as we have seen, in the experience of comprehension "nothing manifold is given." The experience becomes contentful only via the representations to which we are inclined to append an "I understand." But this requires that the representations themselves possess a certain synthetic unity:

> To understand a sentence means to understand a language. To understand a language means to be master of a technique.[31]

There is an important analogy between the Kantian "I think" and the Wittgensteinian "I understand," and an important disanalogy. The disanalogy arises from what in the two cases we are willing to call representations. A Kantian ego need not venture out beyond its own experience to determine whether something to which it is inclined to append an "I think" is a representation. A Wittgensteinian representation, by contrast, is an act of using a language with understanding, and whether or not I am doing this may not be fully within my grasp. It must be possible for the "I understand" to accompany each of my representations, but there may also be some nonrepresentations to which I am also inclined to append an "I understand." If language is to be a means of communication, there must, Wittgenstein famously argued, be agreement in judgments, in form of life.[32] Let us say that a person is *minded* in a certain way if he shares the perceptions of salience, routes of interest, feelings of naturalness in following a rule which constitute being part of a form of life. Then if language is to be a means of communication, not only must I be able to attach an "I understand:" to each of my representations, but it must be possible for the "We are so minded:" to accompany each of our representations. Thus our representations stand between two distinct claims: the "I understand" and the "We are so minded:."

That the "We are so minded:" must be able to accompany each of our representations might, from one perspective, look like an analytic principle, defining what it is for something to be a representation of ours. But since it expresses "agreement in form of life" which constitutes our being so minded, it is ultimately synthetic. Language, one might say, is that in the concept of which the (open-ended) manifold of our representations is united.[33] While it is we, to use Kant's dynamic terminology, who unite our representations into a language, we are nevertheless dependent on our language, the unification of our representations, to represent the subject of these representations: ourselves. The "We are so minded:" by itself is empty; it gains content by what we (are so minded as to) place after the colon. Similarly, a concept is that in the concept of which a certain (open-ended) manifold of representations is united. (Or, to eliminate the word "concept" from the explication: a concept is a representation which unites a certain [open-ended] manifold of representations.)

I also said that there is an important analogy between the Kantian "I think" and the Wittgensteinian "I understand": when I append either to a representation, the representation is used and not mentioned. One reason that Kant's analytic principle seems acceptable is that when I think "I think P," I actually think P. Similarly, when I think or say "I understand P," I am not stepping outside of all of our representations and making a claim about one of them from a detached perspective: I am attempting to make another representation. "I understand P" is itself an (attempted) enactment in the form of life: and thus (if successful) it must itself be capable of accepting a "We are so minded:." Properly understood, the "I understand" shows our participation in a form of life; it does not say anything about a representation which is merely mentioned. Thus when someone says the word "cube" to me, my experience of comprehension is not legitimated by any feeling or other inner experience, for example to the whole use coming before my mind. My experience of comprehension is legitimated by my being like-minded with other "cube"-users: sharing certain perceptions of salience, volitions, and practical abilities to continue in certain sorts of ways, seeing the various uses of the concept cube as forming an (open-ended) unity. If the "We are so minded:" must be able to accompany each of our representations, the demand again arises that the representations themselves possess a synthetic unity. If language is to be a means of communication, the technique I must master must be not merely my technique, but our technique. There must be a synthetic unity not only among my representations but also among our representations. The analogue of the analytic unity of apperception—that I be able to attach an "I understand" to each of my representations—seems to demand a synthetic unity among our representations (if language is to be a means of communication).

But what if language isn't to be a means of communication? As far as I can determine, the *Investigations* does not consider this question. (The so-called private language argument is, I think, an examination of an illegitimate model of how language which is used for communication is endowed with meaning.) This silence would be surprising if Wittgenstein were trying to show that the individual considered in isolation cannot mean anything by his utterances. But the silence is to be expected if his inquiry is broadly transcendental: we find ourselves as speakers and understanders of language which is used both as a means of thought and of communication, and ask "What must be the case for this to be possible?"

One answer is that the representations to which I am able to append an "I understand" must also be capable of accepting a "We are so minded:." This is at least a first step in the legitimation of our experience of comprehension. The possibility of language which is used as a means of thought and communication requires that there be a harmony between inner experience and outer behavior. But this harmony does not eliminate the possibility of sour notes: a certain form of skepticism will always be possible. Language mastery consists in an irreducible inner aspect and an outer aspect. Given a speaker's utterance, we can ask "Did he understand what he said?" And of an utterance to which the "I understand" is legitimately applicable as opposed to a mere behavioral surrogate, we can say—as Wittgenstein said of the difference between pain behavior accompanied by pain and pain behavior without any pain—"What greater difference could there be?"[34] Speech behavior may occur even though totally incomprehensible to the being manifesting the behavior; conversely, a being may feel confidently "Now I understand!" and be shown to be wrong by his inability to use the expression correctly. However, if language is to be a means of communication, these cases in which subjective and objective come apart must be exceptional. If language is to be a means of communication, then it is a nontrivial a priori truth that there must be a regular relation between inner experience and outer manifestation. But this regular relation need hold only, as Aristotle would say, for the most part.[35]

A second step in the legitimation derives from a consideration of who, in the broadest of contexts, we are. The synthetic unity of our representations—our being so minded—has no empirical explanation: and thus there is no empirical explanation of who "we" are. In following a rule all I can do, ultimately, is to act blindly; and, similarly, that is all you can do.[36] Each of us acts ultimately without justification; our reasons have given out. Yet if language is to be a means of communication, each of us must follow rules blindly in the same way. (Of course, our acting in the same way is partially constituted by our seeing ourselves as acting in the same way.)

Nor, in this broad context, is there any alternative to the synthetic unity of our representations. Our various representations are an expression of our being so minded—there is a certain synthetic unity they possess—but we cannot make any sense of the possibility of being "other minded." In fact, how we are minded is in part revealed to us by what (we are so minded as to find) does and does not make sense. There can (for us) be no getting a glimpse of what it might be like to be "other minded," for as we try to pass beyond the bounds of our mindedness we lapse into what (for us) must be nonsense: that is, we lapse into nonsense.

One of the ways in which Kant tries to make us aware that the spatiotemporal world is, transcendentally speaking, an expression of mind is by making a series of contrasts. Arguing that space and time are merely forms of our sensible intuition, he is able to contrast the spatiotemporal world with the world as it is in itself. Diagnosing our consciousness as a discursive intelligence whose sensible intuitions are spatiotemporal, he is able to contrast us both with discursive intelligences with alternative forms of sensible intuition and with a nondiscursive intelligence, an intellectual intuition.[37] Wittgenstein, however, is able to awaken us to the possibility that our form of life is partially constituted by our being so minded without making contrasts with "other perspectives."

That the "(for us)" ultimately cancels out is a key to understanding what it is to establish the objective validity of our representations: for we come to see that being one of "our" representations is all that there could be to being a representation. This is an example of what might literally be called a "groundless legitimation": a legitimation which does not consist in providing a foundation, groundwork, or justification of that which is legitimated. Many philosophers today believe that the most that a transcendental argument could show is that any form of life we could recognize must be like ours: that to interpret it as showing that all forms of life must be fundamentally alike is implicitly to assume a form of verificationism. This belief derives from the fact that certain specifically antiskeptical transcendental arguments did implicitly rely on some form of verificationism.[38] It does not follow that transcendental arguments generally must be verificationist: especially if we construe "transcendental arguments" broadly enough to include the investigations of Kant and Wittgenstein. For verificationism to be at play here, the following situation would have to hold: we would have a concept of being "other minded"—say, of constituting a form of life in which $7 + 5 = 13$ and Q does not follow from P and $If\ P,\ Q$—and, on the basis of verificationist scruples, we would dismiss as spurious the apparent possibility of its being satisfied. (Such a strategy notoriously invites skepticism about verificationism.) Wittgenstein's investigation takes a different route: we come to see that there is no concept of being "other minded." The concept of being minded in any way at all is that of being minded as we are.[39] To put it in Kantian terms: language is that in the concept of which the manifold of our representations is united. Wittgenstein's position thus stands to verificationism as transcendental idealism stands to its empirical counterpart.[40]

What emerges from these considerations is not the skeptical conclusion that an individual considered in isolation can mean nothing by his utterances, but rather its post-Kantian inversion: we cannot consider an individual in isolation. But perhaps one ought to distinguish something like an "empirical" and a "transcendental" sense of "considering an individual in isolation." In the "empirical" sense, one considers an individual in isolation when one considers a human being in abstraction from any particular group. It is in this sense that it has been alleged that an individual considered in isolation cannot be said to mean anything by his utterances. In a transcendental investigation, by contrast, one is inquiring into the conditions for the possibility of considering an individual in isolation (in the "empirical" sense). In this inquiry we discover that as soon as we consider an individual at all—select out part of the environment as a being who may or may not be following rules, depending on whether or not we consider him in isolation (in the "empirical" sense)—we are implicitly establishing a relationship between him—the object of our judgment—and ourselves—the subject of judgment.[41] To put it paradoxically: to consider an individual in isolation, we must be treating him as one of us.

But insofar as we can consider an individual in isolation—that is, in the "empirical" sense—Wittgenstein does not argue that it is not possible for him to mean anything by his utterances. He does argue that to obey a rule there must exist a regular use, a custom, a practice; but there is no argument that customs can occur only in communities.[42] Reference to the behavior of other speakers of a language needs to be made only when the question is whether the individual is speaking a particular shared language, say English, correctly or incorrectly. The question of whether a person uses, say, the word "plus" correctly can be treated as a question of whether he uses "plus" as other English speakers do only if we take him to be a (potential) English speaker. It is only when we consider an individual's subjective experience (of comprehension, confidence, grasping of a rule, and so on) in isolation from his practical ability that we can give no content to his meaning anything.[43] When Wittgenstein says that "to think one is obeying a rule is not to obey a rule," he is not saying that the individual considered in isolation cannot follow a rule, but that his thinking does not constitute his obeying: that is what is meant by saying that he cannot obey a rule "privately."[44]

The individual's inner experience cannot endow his practical ability with normative content.[45] But it does not follow from this that we must look to the community for norms: perhaps one could take his practical ability to be endowed with normative content as part of the given which is his form of life.[46] One should not thus equate his practical ability with a mere disposition to respond. So the question whether Robinson Crusoe can be said to speak a language not merely when he is physically isolated but also when he is considered in isolation could, conceivably, be answered affirmatively. The question we could not answer under such conditions is whether the practices and customs which regulate his behavior regulate the behavior of others.

It is only when we switch from an "empirical" to a "transcendental" reading that we discover, not that when considered in isolation he cannot be said to mean anything, but that we cannot consider him in isolation. Kripke, I think, switches between the "empirical" and "transcendental" readings in his discussion of Robinson Crusoe.[47] In setting up the skeptical paradox, Kripke uses the "empirical" reading of "considering an individual in isolation": we can consider an individual in isolation and then allegedly show that he cannot be said to mean anything by his utterances. Of Crusoe, however, he says, "if we think of Crusoe as following rules, we are taking him into our community and applying our criteria for rule following to him." At first, this looks like a valid inference from what has allegedly already been established: if, when considered in isolation, X cannot be said to mean anything, then if X can be said to mean something, he is not being considered in isolation. To see that a switch has occurred, suppose that Crusoe is speaking an invented language in which he uses "plus" according to "quus-like" rules: that is, for any addition where the result is greater than 5, he just says "five." (Perhaps, being on his own, he has no interest in or use for larger numbers of things.) We can't establish whether he is following the rule correctly by reference to the behavior of other speakers, for there aren't any. We must simply observe whether his behavior accords with quus-like rules.

Of course, this requires implicit reference to our own standards of rule-following, but it is not this reference which transforms his behavior into rule-following. It is his practical ability which enables him to follow rules, even ones of his own invention. Reference to our rule-following procedures is needed only (1) when we try to characterize his behavior as a bizarre way of reacting to the training we have all received and then obeying the order "Add 2"; (2) when we try to give our interpretation of the rule he is following.

If, by contrast, one accepts the skeptical paradox, it becomes mysterious how a bunch of non–rule followers (when considered in isolation) can be turned into rule followers simply by considering them together. Although there is an analogy with Hume's treatment of causation—one must look beyond an individual utterance to determine whether it is an act of speaking meaningfully—there is also an important disanalogy.[48] The general regularities in nature allow us to talk of causes, but one must abandon as fictitious the idea that there is agency to be found in them. We cannot similarly treat our meaning something by our utterances as an acceptable *façon de parler*.

Although the concept of a language cannot be fully understood without reference to a judging subject, the actual relation between subject and language remains mysterious. Much of the post-Kantian idealist tradition is devoted to showing that Kant's attempt at a purely formal philosophy was a failure—that the relation between subject and object is far less distinct than Kant thought. In Wittgenstein's philosophy, this issue emerges in a curious way. Before we engaged in philosophical reflection, we were disposed to make various assertions, for example, "7 + 5 must equal 12." As we study the *Investigations*, we come to assert, "We are so minded as to assert: 7 + 5 must equal 12." That is, as transcendental inquirers, we come to be aware that the "We are so minded:" must be able to accompany each of our representations. It is such an insight that, I think, led commentators to think that Wittgenstein denied the objectivity of logical or mathematical necessity.[49] However, after we realize that there is (for us) no alternative possibility of being "other minded"—that is, that there is no alternative possibility—we seem to come back to our original assertion: "7 + 5 must equal 12." Thus the strange case of the disappearing "we." For both Wittgenstein and Kant, the reflective understanding of the contribution of our mindedness to the necessity we find in the world is not meant to undermine the necessity, but to give us insight into it.

But then what position can Wittgenstein's philosophy occupy? If, on the one hand, the "we" does disappear, then it seems we are left investigating the "conditions of thought" or "the way the world must be," having lost the insight of their essential relation to our mindedness: of our routes of interest, perceptions of salience, feelings of naturalness. If, on the other hand, we try to make the "we" vivid, then Wittgenstein's philosophy collapses into philosophical sociology, studying how one tribe among others goes on.

This, I suppose, boils down to the question of whether there is a stable middle position to be occupied between Kantian transcendental philosophy and some form of Hegelianism.[50] Wittgenstein abandoned the attempt to make manifest the structure of thought. Like Hegel, he no doubt would have regarded the Kantian project of providing a purely formal philosophy, of investigating the mind's organization in isolation, an impossible task. Thought, for both Hegel and the later Wittgenstein, should be seen as embedded in activities, projects, customs, and institutions. Hegel was willing to study particular historical and social communities, for he saw them as partial manifestations of *geist*, a relationship which could be appreciated from the absolute standpoint of philosophy. However, if one loses faith in an absolute standpoint, there seems to be nothing left to study but the belief and general goings-on of particular groups. There is no doubt that thinkers inspired by Wittgenstein have drawn just this lesson. But Wittgenstein's own philosophy is remarkably devoid of such inquiry. Occasionally the strange activities of some "tribe" are offered up for our consideration: for example, a people who pile lumber in heaps of arbitrary height and sell it at a price proportionate to the area covered.[51] Such a "group" is not studied in any detail; "it" is presented in abstraction, conjured up at a moment to make us aware, say, that the practice of measuring does not exist in a void, sealed off from the other interests, aims, projects, and practices of a community. Thought may have to be understood in the context of customs, practices, and institutions, but Wittgenstein seems indifferent to the study of any particular community. His thought seems to stand to sociology as Kant's was intended to stand to empirical psychology.

But can it? Some philosophers, encouraged by Wittgenstein's explicit remarks on the point of philosophy, try to turn their backs on this question by treating the request for reflective understanding as an illegitimate

298

appeal for a transcendent viewpoint. Wittgenstein's explicit remarks tend toward the therapeutic: proper philosophical activity cures the disease philosophy.[52] Thus it seems to be all right with him that we in some sense end up back where we started. But in what sense? Wittgenstein was a master in making us aware how philosophical perplexity can arise by asking questions in isolation from the normal contexts in which such questions get asked: it is then that "language goes on holiday."[53] Yet even if we grant that therapy is a valuable approach to certain philosophical problems, it does not follow that there are no legitimate philosophical questions to be asked; in particular, that there is no legitimate question of how we are to understand the therapeutic methods themselves.

Therapy would be useless against a cold: and in getting rid of a sneeze, we really do end up back where we started. Nor is lobotomy a form of therapy: after studying the later Wittgenstein we should not wander around stupefied, oblivious to the existence of any reflective questions. Postneurotic consciousness is fundamentally more complex than a healthy consciousness which has never suffered disease or cure.[54] Further, neurosis isn't just an embarrassing disease which some silly people who call themselves "philosophers" contract, only to be treated and ridiculed by others who also call themselves "philosophers." Neurosis is arguably an important product of civilization; in this case, of civilization's attempt to understand itself.[55] Thus it should not be surprising that both neurosis and cure should demand a fairly complex consciousness. It seems to me that we can both retain an appreciation of the importance of our being so minded to the form of life which we constitute and realize that in this broad context there are no alternative possibilities. How can we do this?

I cannot answer this question in any detail or with confidence. Perhaps a start can be made by pointing out that one ought to expect some such problem as that of the disappearing "we." If establishing the objective validity of our representations consists in showing that they are all there could be to being a representation, then one ought to expect that a certain type of reflective consciousness will have an evanescent quality. I do not yet know how to describe this quality without resorting to spatial metaphors. If our representations have objective validity, then one will not be able to continue looking down upon them: that sort of reflective consciousness must ultimately evaporate. And with it goes the detached perspective on "our" representations. It is not obvious, however, that the "We are so minded:" must therefore disappear. Our ability to append the "We are so minded:" represents a permanent possibility of reflective consciousness. Yet the "We are so minded:" is, like the Kantian "I think," in an important sense empty: we gain insight into who "we" are by considering the representations to which we are willing to append a "We are so minded:"; or by considering which bits of the world we are willing to consider as representations. The "We are so minded:" must thus stand in an analogous "master-slave" relation to our form of life as the Kantian synthetic unity of apperception stands to the object of judgment.

To show how the "We are so minded:" does not disappear would be to describe a form of reflective consciousness which does not consist in looking down upon our representations. It seems impossible to describe such a consciousness, yet it also seems to be the consciousness we have. Perhaps it is impossible to describe; perhaps it can only make itself manifest: perhaps the *Philosophical Investigations* is just such a consciousness making itself manifest. That the "We are so minded:" does not disappear, that we can continue to attach it to each of our representations, makes us reflectively aware that our form of life is not some fixed, frozen entity existing totally independently of us. It is an expression of our routes of interest, perceptions of salience, and so on: it is (our) active mind. But this awareness can occur only from the inside. When we take it to be a way of observing our form of life from a detached perspective, the "We are so minded:" does evaporate. It was Hegel who argued against Kant that ultimately subject could not be separated from object, that there could be no purely formal philosophy, that—to use a phrase with a contemporary ring—there could be no firm distinction between organizing scheme (the mind) and unorganized content.[56] The "We are so minded:" and our form of life both, as Hegel would put it, find themselves in each other. This remains, of course, the barest of metaphors; however, metaphors are not bereft of value, even in philosophy.

NOTES

ACKNOWLEDGMENTS

INDEX

Notes

1. Preface: The King and I

1. See Plato, *Republic* (*Platonis Politeia* [Oxford: Clarendon Press, 1978]) 1.352d: "This discussion is not about any chance question, but about the way one should live." For translations see Plato, *Republic*, trans. G. M. A. Grube, rev. C. D. C. Reeve (Indianapolis: Hackett, 1992); Plato, *Republic*, trans. Paul Shorey (Cambridge, Mass.: Harvard University Press, 1982).

2. Sigmund Freud, "Analysis Terminable and Interminable," in *The Standard Edition of the Complete Psychological Works of Sigmund Freud*, trans. and ed. James E. Strachey (London: Hogarth Press, 1981; cited hereafter as *SE*), 23: 248; and see Janet Malcolm's memorable *Psychoanalysis: The Impossible Profession* (New York: Alfred A. Knopf, 1981).

3. Freud, *Group Psychology and the Analysis of the Ego*, *SE* 18: 91. See also the preface to the fourth edition of *Three Essays on the Theory of Sexuality:* "The enlarged sexuality of psychoanalysis coincides with the eros of the divine Plato"; *SE* 7: 134.

4. Freud, "Resistances to Psychoanalysis," *SE* 19: 218. See also "Why War?" *SE* 22: 218.

5. See, e.g., *Republic* 3.395d, 399e, 401e; 4.421e, 424b–d, 426c–d, 427d, 432d–e; 5.457e, 476c–e.

6. See ibid., 7.514–515.

7. Ibid., 9.571c–d. The translation is from Grube and Reeve.
8. Freud, *Three Essays on the Theory of Sexuality, SE* 7: 168.
9. Ludwig Wittgenstein, "Conversations on Freud," in *Philosophical Essays on Freud,* ed. R. Wollheim and J. Hopkins (Cambridge: Cambridge University Press, 1982), p. 8. See also *Wittgenstein: Lectures and Conversations,* ed. C. Barrett (Oxford: Blackwell, 1966); and *Ludwig Wittgenstein: Lectures in Philosophy, Cambridge 1932–5,* ed. A. Ambrose (Oxford: Blackwell, 1979).
10. Ludwig Wittgenstein, *Philosophical Investigations* (Oxford: Blackwell, 1953), 1.
11. Freud, "Preface to Reik's *Ritual: Psychoanalytic Studies," SE* 17: 261. The *Standard Edition* uses the technical term "phantasy" rather than the familiar English word "fantasy" to draw attention to the unconscious mental activity which may get expressed in our conscious imaginative life, that is, in our fantasies. I discuss the concept of phantasy in Chapter 5.
12. Freud, "Fragment of an Analysis of a Case of Hysteria" ("Dora"), *SE* 7: 77–78 (emphasis added).
13. Freud, *The Interpretation of Dreams, SE* 5: 506–507, n. 2.

2. On Killing Freud (Again)

1. Sophocles, *Oedipus Tyrannus,* ed. and trans. Hugh Lloyd-Jones (Cambridge, Mass.: Harvard University Press, 1994), pp. 390–396.

3. Knowingness and Abandonment

1. There is another fantasy about Asians which is significant: that they are going to engulf us. They will engulf us by sheer numbers—as Secretary of State Dean Rusk intimated in the early 1960s with his classic "a billion Chinese by . . ."—or the Japanese will engulf us by taking over our economy, taking over Hollywood, taking over Rockefeller Center, and so on.
2. For example, on election day A. M. Rosenthal wrote: "Am I better off than I was four years ago? No. In a way important to me I am not only worse off than in 1992, but worse than ever before in my adult life. I have been cheated of the opportunity to make a decision satisfactory to me in the choice of President, the single most important privilege of citizenship . . . For the first time in my voting life neither major party offered us a choice that pays suitable honor to our intelligence and citizenship"; "Am I Better Off?" *New York Times,* November 5, 1996.

   And on the day after the election, Frank Rich wrote:

   "Don't you feel better already? Or as a politician might put it: are you better off today than you were 24 hours ago? Here at last is one question the entire nation can answer in the affirmative. Had the election lasted a single moment longer, the country might have started to get nostalgic about Phil Gramm. . . .

"Whom and what did we not get sick of? Aside from the voters, the only people worthy of sympathy in '96 are the candidates' children . . .

"What could have made election year '96 more exciting? The year is littered with what-ifs. What if Lamar Alexander, the jes-folks millionaire, had switched from red plaid to silver lamé? . . .

"Still those who say the year of campaigning was completely worthless are wrong. If nothing else, I discovered that the year's political rhetoric could be a better cure for insomnia than either counting sheep or playing 'Six Degrees of Kevin Bacon.' Once in bed, eyes shut, the trick is to take the empty yet incessantly repeated candidates' phrases and squeeze as many of them into a single sentence as possible." Frank Rich, *New York Times,* November 6, 1996.

3. Editorial, *New York Times,* July 19, 1996.

4. Or, to take a final example, consider the hoax which NYU professor of physics Alan Sokal played on the editors of the literary-critical journal *Social Text.* What makes this hoax a milestone in the history of academic hoaxes is not that Professor Sokal publicly declared his article to be a hoax the moment it was published, but that the hoax was right there on the surface of the article. *Anyone* who read the article with understanding would have to recognize it as a joke. (Paul Boghossian and Thomas Nagel made this point in a letter to *Lingua Franca.*) The article mentions "the axiom of choice" as though it were part of feminist set theory, when anyone who had taken even the first weeks of an introduction to axiomatic set theory would know that the axiom of choice was simply an elementary axiom concerned with forming sets by selecting members of other sets. It has everything to do with set theory, nothing to do with politics; and that is a flagrantly obvious fact. That is what made this hoax so embarrassing. For the editors, who have long taken a knowing stance with respect to the world, to be able to publish the article, they *could not have known* even the most elementary facts about the areas in which they were publishing articles. The editors were hoist on their own petard of knowingness.

5. For an extended critique of the Freudian reading of *Oedipus Tyrannus,* see Jean-Pierre Vernant and Pierre Vidal-Naquet, *Myth and Tragedy in Ancient Greece* (New York: Zone Books, 1990).

6. Sigmund Freud, *The Interpretation of Dreams, SE* 4: 262–263; Lecture XXI, "The Development of the Libido," *Introductory Lectures on Psychoanalysis, SE* 16: 331. See Letter 71 to Fliess, October 15, 1897, *SE* 1: 265.

7. See Bernard Knox, "Why Is Oedipus Called Tyrannos?" *Classical Journal* 50 (1954).

8. Sophocles, *Oedipus Tyrannus,* ed. and trans. Hugh Lloyd-Jones (Cambridge, Mass.: Harvard University Press, 1994), lines 33–34. All translations in the text are based on this source.

9. See, e.g., Aristotle, *Rhetoric* II.2.1378a31 ff.

10. As Iocaste tells him at 742–743.

11. Note Socrates' demand, at the end of the *Symposium*, that poets ought to be equally good at comedy and tragedy.

12. Thus all such claims of the form "If *only* Oedipus had _____ed, he would have escaped his fate" are either false or empty. See Bernard Williams, *Shame and Necessity* (Berkeley: University of California Press, 1993).

13. He will, of course, expel himself again when he learns of his original abandonment. For Oedipus, "remembering" does not replace, but rather occasions, repetition.

14. I have heard it objected that this is just dramatic license, a device to let the audience know the passage of time. My response: Sophocles is a better poet than that. If all he wanted to do was impart that information, Oedipus could easily have said, "Yes, of course, it's twenty years now since . . ."

15. J. Goux, *Oedipus, Philosopher* (Stanford: Stanford University Press, 1993).

16. To borrow Lacan's ironic reading of the second chorus in Antigone: nothing is impossible for man; what he can't deal with he ignores; Jacques Lacan, *The Seminar of Jacques Lacan*, vol. 7: *The Ethics of Psychoanalysis, 1959–1960*, trans. Dennis Porter (London: Routledge, 1992), p. 275. Cf. the modern descendants: in verificationism, Popperianism, ordinary-language philosophy, these problems are meaningless.

17. See Vernant and Vidal-Naquet, *Myth and Tragedy*, p. 27.

18. Friedrich Nietzsche, *The Gay Science*, trans. W. Kaufmann (New York: Random House, 1974), 125.

4. An Interpretation of Transference

1. At first sight it might appear that nothing could differ more from Socrates' fundamental rule than the fundamental rule of psychoanalysis: try to state whatever comes into your mind without censorship. However, if one believes, as Freud did, that a person's psychic commitments have their own upward thrust—that the contents of the unconscious will tend to get themselves expressed unless they are prevented from doing so by inhibiting psychological forces—then, in trying to state whatever comes into consciousness, one is tending to state one's "beliefs," at least in the extended sense of one's psychic commitments. Freud discovered that if one enlarges the scope of psychological commitments, Socrates' fundamental rule is too narrow to elicit them. Stating only what one believes, in the narrow sense, can be a way of hiding and inhibiting unconscious psychic commitments. But the fundamental rule of psychoanalysis is an emendation and extension of Socrates' fundamental rule, not a reversal. It plays an analogous role in eliciting psychic commitments.

2. Perhaps blame is too easy; and it is certainly controversial: as is almost any serious claim one would wish to make about the ancient world. For a fascinating attempt to recover the historical Socrates as an antidemocrat, see I. F. Stone, *The Trial of Socrates* (Boston: Beacon Press, 1988); and, for a plausible rebuttal, Gregory Vlastos, "On 'The Socrates Story,'" *Political Theory* 7 (1979): 533–536; idem, "The Historical Socrates and Athenian Democracy," *Political Theory* 11 (1983): 495–515.

3. Obviously, a scholarly defense of this interpretation of Plato is beyond the scope of this essay; but I do attempt such a defense in Chapter 10, as well as in "Plato's Politics of Narcissism," in *Virtue, Love and Form: Essays in Memory of Gregory Vlastos*, ed. Terence Irwin and Martha C. Nussbaum (Toronto: Apeiron, 1994). Readers who are interested in textual support for the interpretation offered in this section should consult *Republic* 2.358e, 366e, 376e–377b 378d–e, 381e, 382b–d; 3.395c–e, 401d–e; 4.424c–d, 435c,e; 7.519d–521b; 8.544d–e, 554b–555b; 9.577c–578c, 590e. I discuss the Socratic-Platonic concern with individuation and its relation to psychoanalytic theory in *Love and Its Place in Nature: A Philosophical Interpretation of Freudian Psychoanalysis*, 2d ed. (New Haven: Yale University Press, 1998).

4. This is why, for Socrates, knowledge is sufficient for virtue; bad acts can be commited only out of ignorance, and thus *akrasia* (so-called weakness of will) is impossible.

5. Sigmund Freud, *Studies on Hysteria, SE* 2: 302–303.

6. Freud, "Fragment of an Analysis of a Case of Hysteria," *SE* 7: 116.

7. This passage, as well as the general topic of intrapsychic transference and its relation to transference as an interpsychic relation, is discussed at length in Hans Loewald's "On the Therapeutic Action of Psychoanalysis," to which I am indebted. See his *Papers on Psychoanalysis* (New Haven: Yale University Press, 1980), pp. 221–256. And see Freud, *The Interpretation of Dreams, SE* 5: 562–567.

8. This is in harmony with his conception of the mental molecule as consisting of an idea plus a quantity of energy. (See, e.g., Freud, *Studies on Hysteria, SE* 2: 86, 166–167.) The idea has to stay where it is, so the energy moves. In practice, though, Freud recognized that intrapsychic transference was more than a redistribution of energy. For it also establishes an *energy line* between the unconscious and conscious idea. In the redistribution of energy, transference necessarily preserves its own history. This shows up as the unconscious idea getting itself *covered*.

9. Much psychoanalytic work since Freud has been the elaboration of a theory of unconscious phantasy, which allows more fine-grained analysis among intrapsychic conflicts. As Freud recognized, we regularly find that a conscious or preconscious phantasy serves as a covering for a web of interrelated unconscious phantasies.

10. Freud, *The Interpretation of Dreams, SE* 4–5: 279–305, 595–597, 602.

11. Philosophers have been attuned to the holistic nature of the mental: to the fact that the very content of a given belief or desire depends on its relation to other beliefs and desires. But they have tended to concentrate on the holistic nature of the conscious mental, while Freud's crucial point is that holism must include the unconscious mental. For evidence of Freud's psychological holism, see, e.g., *The Interpretation of Dreams, SE* 4–5: 97–100, 104–105, 179, 218–219, 280–284, 307–308, 330, 350–353, 652–653. For a classic philosophical exposition of the importance of holism for interpretation, see Donald Davidson, *Inquiries into Truth and Interpretation* (Oxford: Clarendon Press, 1984). Elsewhere, however, Davidson ingeniously argues that the repressed should be treated as split off, and thus as functioning almost like another mind; see "Paradoxes of Irrationality," in *Philosophical Essays on Freud,* ed. R. Wollheim and J. Hopkins (Cambridge: Cambridge University Press, 1982), pp. 289–305. In Chapter 5 I argue that this underestimates Freud's insistence on the holistic relations between conscious and unconscious, even taking repression into account.

12. Clifford Geertz has helped us understand the importance of "thick" concepts in the interpretation of cultures; and in those terms one might say that Freud's discovery of intrapsychic transference is a discovery that "thick" concepts tend to be *hyper*thick, though unconsciously so. See Geertz, "Thick Description: Towards an Interpretive Theory of Culture," in *The Interpretation of Culture* (New York: Basic Books, 1973).

13. So although Freud does not explicitly extend the concept of intrapsychic transference to include the structural theory, it is implicit in his account; *The Ego and the Id, SE* 19: 48–49 (emphasis added). See also p. 36: "Whereas the ego is essentially the representative of the external world, of reality, *the super-ego stands in contrast to it as the representative of the internal world, of the id*" (emphasis added).

14. This was pointed out in Loewald, "Therapeutic Action," pp. 247–248; though one should accept that because of projection, externalization, and related psychological activity, this is not a hard-and-fast distinction.

15. Freud, "Remembering, Repeating and Working-through," *SE* 12: 150–151.

16. Winnicott makes a related point when, in speaking of a baby's experience, he says, "As observers we note that everything in the play has been done before, has been smelt before, and where there appear specific symbols of the union of baby and mother (transitional objects) these very objects have been adopted, not created. Yet for the baby (if the mother can supply the right conditions) every detail of the baby's life is an example of creative living. Every object is a 'found' object. Given the chance, the baby begins to live creatively, and to use actual objects to be creative into and with"; "The Location of Cultural Experience," in *Playing and Reality* (New York: Penguin, 1980), p. 119. Of course, once one has grasped the creative-enduring aspect of transference, one can then go back and view it either as a transfer or as a repetition. These

formulations are problematic only insofar as they obscure our understanding of the creative or the enduring aspects of transference.

17. The literal loss of meaning was preceded by a prolonged and widespread cynicism among the citizens about what the true meaning of the Soviet Union was.

18. Interestingly, Freud used the metaphor of a polis to describe the mind and its activity; but because his interest was in capturing the unconscious and infantile mind, he used the image of a *buried* polis. Thus archaeology became, for Freud, an enduring metaphor for psychoanalytic exploration. (See, e.g., "The Aetiology of Hysteria," *SE* 3: 192; and *Civilization and Its Discontents, SE* 21: 69–71.) However, as psychoanalysis has, in theory and technique, tended to move away from deep interpretations toward working with the transference and detailed texture of the analysand's associations, so perhaps the image of a buried polis should be replaced by a living polis (standing above ancient *poleis*). Perhaps, too, the metaphor of archaeology should be replaced by *topological* archaeology: the topological archaeologist inspects the contours of the land, the flow of the rivers and seas, and has faith in the upward momentum of buried artifacts: as the fields are ploughed, there will regularly turn up shards of ancient civilizations. It is by extrapolating from this evidence that the topological archaeologist comes to grasp both what lies buried and its relation to contemporary life. For evidence of Freud's movement in this direction see "Constructions in Analysis," *SE* 23: 259. Interestingly, this movement can be seen both in those influeced by Melanie Klein and in those influenced by Anna Freud: see, e.g., Elizabeth Dott Spillius, "Some Developments from the Work of Melanie Klein," *International Journal of Psychoanalysis* 64 (1983): 321–332; and Paul Gray, *The Ego and the Analysis of Defense* (Northvale, N.J.: Jason Aronson, 1994). See also Warren Polands' thought-provoking description of analytic space, "From Analytic Surface to Analytic Space," *Journal of the American Psychoanalytic Association* 40 (1992): 381–404; and idem, "Transference: An Original Creation," *Psychoanalytic Quarterly* 61 (1992): 185–205.

19. D. W. Winnicott, "Transitional Objects and Transitional Phenomena," in *Through Paediatrics to Psycho-Analysis* (London: Hogarth Press, 1975). Loewald has criticized this use because, as he argues, the developmental path is not from subjective experience to experience of an objective world. Rather the capacity for subjective experience and the capacity for objective experience emerge simultaneously, from a less differentiated state in which there is no firm boundary between subjective and objective. See Hans Loewald, *Sublimation* (New Haven: Yale University Press, 1988).

20. The essence of this idea goes back at least to Freud, *Civilization and Its Discontents, SE* 21: 64–73.

21. When one is trying to make a difficult point, there is an ever-present danger that one will be defeated by one's vocabulary. In the end, though, it matters

less which vocabulary is used then how one understands it. If one wants to say that even the social-cultural world is "transitional," that is fine so long as one does not thereby assume that the boundaries between subjective and objective must be blurred. One should then accept that there may be degrees of transitionality which allow for more or less boundary differentiation. Or, if one wants to use "transitional" only to describe experience in which boundaries are blurred, that is fine too; just so long as one does not thereby assume that "the objective world" is thereby devoid of the psyche's activity. Further, nothing I say in this essay implies that whenever a group agrees it has created something it must be right. There has to be room for the distinction between social reality, on the one hand, and a shared illusion of social reality on the other. Just as analysis is committed to denying the omnipotence of wishes in the individual, so it must be in a position to offer a critique of the omnipotence of certain wishes shared in a culture. Though it is beyond the scope of this chapter to discuss the distinction between reality and illusion at the social level, I shall simply note in passing that certain inadequate interpretations of Wittgenstein make this distinction impossible by assuming that any shared "form of life" has *ipso facto* its own reality. I discuss problems with this interpretation in Chapter 11, "Transcendental Anthropology."

22. Freud, *Introductory Lectures on Psychoanalysis, SE* 15–16: 454.

23. Freud, "Remembering, Repeating and Working-through," *SE* 12: 150.

24. Of course, as Freud recognized, there are exceptions: it is possible to dream that "this is only a dream." See *The Interpretation of Dreams, SE* 5: 338, 488–489. See also Brian O'Shaugnessy, "The Id and the Thinking Process," in Wollheim and Hopkins, *Philosophical Essays on Freud.*

25. See Freud, *Introductory Lectures on Psychoanalysis, SE* 16: 454; and "Remembering, Repeating and Working-through," *SE* 12: 154, in which Freud describes the transference neurosis as an "artificial illness." In his remarkable paper "Notes on Transference: Universal Phenomenon and Hardest Part of Analysis," *Journal of the American Psychoanalytic Association* 20 (1972): 267–301, Brian Bird suggests that in the transference neurosis, the analyst becomes part of the analysand's intrapsychic conflict. It is as though the analyst is being assigned a position inside the analysand's psyche. This insight seems to me both astute and not quite correct. Bird, of course, did not have the concept of an idiopolis which stands in a dynamic relation to the psyche. By contrast, Strachey's classic description of the analyst being brought into the neurotic's vicious circle seems very apt; J. Strachey, "The Nature of the Therapeutic Action of Psychoanalysis," *International Journal of Psychoanalysis* 50 (1934): 275–292. Indeed, one can read this paper as trying to elaborate and explain how a mutative interpretation is possible.

26. Freud, *Introductory Lectures on Psychoanalysis, SE* 15–16: 454.

27. Freud, "Remembering, Repeating and Working-through," *SE* 12: 154.

28. Ibid.

29. There is an interesting analogy in Bernard Williams' discussion of a hypertraditional society in which reflection turns knowledge into belief; see *Ethics and the Limits of Philosophy* (London: Fontana, 1985), pp. 142–148, 158–159.

30. Loewald, "On the Therapeutic Action of Psychoanalysis," p. 249.

5. Restlessness, Phantasy, and the Concept of Mind

1. Plato, *Protagoras* 358.

2. This argument has been elaborated and defended in recent years most prominently by Donald Davidson: see his *Essays on Actions and Events* (Oxford: Clarendon Press, 1980) and *Inquiries into Truth and Interpretation* (Oxford: Clarendon Press, 1984).

3. See Sebastian Gardner, *Irrationality and the Philosophy of Psychoanalysis* (New York: Cambridge University Press, 1993).

4. Here it is important to recognize that this schema is importantly different from such important psychological phenomena as splitting or isolation. So, for example, in splitting there is no presumption that each of the split-off bits of the mind are themselves mindlike structures. Indeed, this schema cannot even account for splitting, for it treats the mind as *already* divided into two mindlike structures, where what we want to understand is the mental activity which splits the mind apart.

5. Aristotle, *Rhetoric* II.2.1378a31 ff. See also II.1.1377b1–1378a21. I discuss this in *Love and Its Place In Nature: A Philosophical Interpretation of Freudian Psychoanalysis*, 2d ed. (New Haven: Yale University Press, 1998), pp. 47–52.

6. This is, of course, a prominent line of thought in the philosophies of Ludwig Wittgenstein (*Philosophical Investigations*, trans. G. E. M. Anscombe [Blackwell: Oxford, 1958]) and Donald Davidson *(Inquiries into Truth and Interpretation)*, even though their respective philosophies themselves differ in important ways.

7. See Donald Davidson, "Paradoxes of Irrationality," in *Philosophical Essays on Freud*, ed. R. Wollheim and J. Hopkins (Cambridge: Cambridge University Press, 1982).

8. For all I know, it is possible to change a person's mental state by subjecting his brain to an electrical volt. Now if that volt were also a belief or desire in one part of the mind, but changed a belief in another part of the mind, not in virtue of its content, but solely as an electrical volt, it would fit the general schema of being a mental item which was not a reason for what it caused, but its mentality would be irrelevant to its nonrational effect.

9. The closest Davidson comes to addressing this issue is in a footnote: "I should perhaps emphasize that phrases like 'partition of the mind,' 'part of the mind,' 'segment' etc. are misleading if they suggest that what belongs to one

division of the mind cannot belong to another. The picture I want is of over-lapping territories"; "Paradoxes of Irrationality," p. 300n. But it is not clear what this picture of overlapping territories is; nor is it clear how such a picture would fit into the general schema of Davidson's solution. For, by hypothesis, each part of the mind is rational—that is the point of the partition—so if this territory is a part of each part it must be rational in both parts.

10. I am not making any claim about there being an interesting a priori science of the mind. Rather, following what I take to be the spirit of the later Wittgenstein, I merely want to say that we live with and among concepts, just as we live in and among many other things. And so, we can inquire not only into minds and what they are like, but also into the concept of mind and what it is like. If "a priori" means "independently of our life with concepts," then this is not an a priori concept. The inquiry is how the concept is used in life, not independently of it. Thus it is that by certain reflection on our empirical discoveries, for example, Freud's discovery that dreams are interpretable, that we can discover not just how our minds work, but also discover something about what it is to be a mind.

11. To take another philosopher's favorite: in self-deception, a wish or desire promotes a certain belief, whose function is to keep me from believing something I have better reason to believe. Again the irrationality is displayed as a structure of propositional attitudes.

12. This is what Gardner, in *Irrationality and the Philosophy of Psychoanalysis,* calls the "special problem of irrationality": why the subject's mental life took an irrational rather than a rational course. This problem will arise whenever irrationality is described and explained by what Gardner calls a "propositionally transparent" structure of propositional attitudes. I discuss Gardner's account at length in "The Heterogeneity of the Mental," *Mind,* 1995.

13. In this context, see Freud's account of the transformations on syntactical structure in the Schreber case, "Psychoanalytic Notes on an Autobiographical Account of a Case of Paranoia (dementia paranoides)," *SE* 12: 62–65. See also the transformations Freud describes in "A Child Is Being Beaten: A Contribution to the Study of the Origin of Sexual Perversion," *SE* 17: 177–204.

14. Freud, *Three Essays on the Theory of Sexuality, SE* 7: 168. I have emended the translation by using "drive" as a translation of *Trieb* rather than the *Standard Edition*'s "instinct." The *Standard Edition* translates both *Trieb* and *Instinkt* as "instinct"; and, for reasons given in the text, it is important to distinguish these concepts. See Jean Laplanche and J.-B. Pontalis, *The Language of Psychoanalysis* (New York: W. W. Norton, 1973), pp. 214–217; and Jean Laplanche, *Life and Death in Psychoanalysis* (Baltimore: Johns Hopkins University Press, 1985), pp. 8–24.

15. See Laplanche, *Life and Death in Psychoanalysis,* pp. 9–11; Bruno Bettelheim, *Freud and Man's Soul* (New York: Alfred A. Knopf, 1983), pp. 103–112; Lear, *Love and Its Place in Nature,* pp. 123–125.

16. Freud, *Three Essays on the Theory of Sexuality, SE* 7: 147–148.

17. Freud, "Notes on a Case of Obsessional Neurosis," *SE* 10: 209.

18. "That from which" is a literal translation of one of the two Greek expressions Aristotle uses for matter. See, e.g., *Physics* II.7.194b24. I use this expression to describe archaic mental states in *Love and Its Place in Nature*, p. 85; and in Chapter 6, "The Introduction of Eros."

19. And so, even an infant's sexual drive is constituted, in part, by representing loved objects in the environment. See Hans Loewald, "On Motivation and Instinct Theory," in *Papers on Psychoanalysis* (New Haven: Yale University Press, 1980). I discuss this point in Chapter 6.

20. So while the liver, say, can be studied as enmattered form—principles of liver functioning in liverish material—if we are studying the entire functioning organism, the liver helps to constitute the matter of the living human being. I discuss this at greater length in *Aristotle: The Desire to Understand* (Cambridge: Cambridge University Press, 1988), chap. 2.

21. Anxiety is of great importance for psychoanalysis not merely because of its prominent role in human suffering, but also because it plays an important conceptual role. Anxiety can occur outside the domain of logos. It makes no claims to be merited, it lacks structure, and thus is capable of bursting forth in rather unformed ways. It lends the Rat Man's cringe affective power without the structural complexity required for fear.

22. See Jean-Paul Sartre, *Being and Nothingness: An Essay on Phenomenological Ontology*, trans. Hazel Barnes (New York: Philosophical Library, 1956).

23. One advantage of an outline is that this account is to a large extent compatible with all the major developments of psychoanalysis since Freud: in particular, those of Melanie Klein, Jacques Lacan, Donald Winnicott, and Hans Loewald, and the ego psychology of Anna Freud and Paul Gray. However incompatible these accounts may be in other ways, the fact that this schema fits them all speaks in its favor.

24. See Hanna Segal, *Introduction to the Work of Melanie Klein* (London: Hogarth Press, 1982); R. D. Hinshelwood, *Clinical Klein* (London: Free Association Books, 1994); Susan Isaacs, "The Nature and Function of Phantasy," in *Developments in Psychoanalysis*, ed. M. Klein, P. Heimann, S. Isaacs, and J. Riviere (London: Karnac, 1989).

25. But being able to form such propositional attitudes is a sophisticated psychological achievement. After watching one show of *Oprah*, a person may *think* he is forming a belief about his inner child; but it is unlikely he is doing any such thing. Rather, he is engaging in the phantasy of forming such a belief.

26. See Freud, "On Negation," *SE* 19: 235–239. This process is plausibly conceived of as projective identification: a phantasy of projecting a bit of oneself into another. (See, e.g., Hinschelwood, *Clinical Klein*.) Here I use the more generic

term "projection" to leave open the question of what precise type of projection was used.

27. Wittgenstein, *Philosophical Investigations*, I.244.

28. See Freud, "Remembering, Repeating and Working-through: Further Recommendations on the Technique of Psychoanalysis, II," *SE* 12: 147–156.

29. I discuss this in greater detail in Chapter 4, "An Interpretation of Transference."

30. For Wittgenstein, philosophy itself is a kind of therapy, and it consists in working through the "bad" philosophy with which one already lives unconsciously. The aim is not to advance any particular theses or information but to help one become aware of and work through certain phantasies one has about mind and meaning. So, for example, Wittgenstein helps us work through a pervasive phantasy of having "private" sensations, but once we have worked through that phantasy, we can go back to calling our sensations private. But we are no longer in the grip of a false picture of what that means. See *Philosophical Investigations*, I.243 ff.

31. Freud, "Notes on a Case of Obsessional Neurosis," *SE* 10: 193.

32. Ibid., 166–167.

33. In this context, I think we can better understand the pleasurable sadistic gratification to be found in the current fad for using the "Valley Girl" expression "Gee, that's a nice jacket you're wearing . . . Not!" Here the person is consciously issuing a contradicting judgment. But the pleasure in doing so is not just that of lulling the interlocutor into thinking he is receiving a compliment, only to take it away. There is also pleasure in the direct expression of aggression. Although this is a contradictory judgment, the activity of making it is drawing on wells of aggressive drive activity. The utterance of the "Not!" is also directly attacking and undoing the previous utterance. In the right mood, it feels good. Thus has the slang taken hold.

34. In this regard, see Wilfrid Bion's classic, "Attacks on Linking," in *Melanie Klein Today*, vol. 1: *Mainly Practice*, ed. Elizabeth Bott Spillius (London: Routledge, 1988).

35. Freud, "Notes on a Case of Obsessional Neurosis," *SE* 10: 166–167; some of the italics are Freud's; I have added others to emphasize my points.

36. See Freud's discussion of intrapsychic transference, *Interpretation of Dreams, SE* 5: 562–564, 589.

37. Freud, "Notes on a Case of Obsessional Neurosis," *SE* 10: 173.

38. See Freud, "The Loss of Reality in Neurosis and Psychosis," *SE* 19: 183–187; and the Schreber case, "Psychoanalytic Notes on an Autobiographical Account of a Case of Paranoia (dementia paranoides)," *SE* 12: 62–65.

39. This is the strategy in Mark Johnston's fascinating essay, "Self-Deception and the Nature of Mind," in *Philosophy of Psychology: Debates on Psychological Explanation*, ed. C. Macdonald and G. Macdonald (Oxford: Blackwell, 1995). One

virtue of this account is that because this activity is subintentional it does not have to satisfy the rationality constraints which Socrates and the subsequent philosophical tradition have shown to be inherent in the concept of intentional mental activity. Thus it is able to do away with the schema of Another Mind as a way of making room for the possibility of the irrational-mental. And it thereby allows for the immanence of irrationality. A second virtue is that it shows how a mental activity which is irrational may nevertheless have a purpose. The mind can be understood as inherently directed towards the relief of its own anxiety.

40. This seems to be Johnston's suggestion; ibid., p. 437. He calls a tropism: "a characteristic, non-accidental and non-rational connection *between desire and belief*—a mental tropism or purpose-serving mental mechanism" (emphasis added).

41. The Rat Man's formation of a wishful belief about his father is of secondary importance. The Rat Man's turn to philosophy enables him above all to stay in some sort of touch, however distorted, with the contents of his own mind. For his father *is* alive in the "next world": only the next world is not heaven, but the internal world of phantasy. And the Rat Man is in some sense correct that if he can pay Lieutenant A., he will protect his father from harm, for this has become the phantasized requirement to ward off an internal attack. What he misunderstands is that this drama is about the goings-on in his own mind, not heaven. The formation of the philosophical belief that, for all we know, his father may be alive in the next world allows his beliefs and desires to stay in some sort of thoughtful contact with the structure of his own mind.

42. Johnston, "Self-Deception," p. 455.

6. The Introduction of Eros

1. See Hans Loewald, "On the Therapeutic Action of Psychoanalysis," in *Papers on Psychoanalysis* (New Haven: Yale University Press, 1980), p. 249.

2. Hans Loewald, "On Internalization," in *Papers*, p. 79. I have made a slight emendation to this and subsequent quotations from Loewald: Where Loewald uses the word "instinct," I have substituted the word "drive." The reason is as follows. When Loewald wrote, he used the vocabulary of the *Standard Edition*, which translates *Trieb* as "instinct." The problem with this translation, as we saw in the preceding chapter, is that it flattens the distinction, which Freud himself made, between a *Trieb* and an *Instinkt*. In order to respect this distinction, I have decided to follow a custom which has developed subsequently to the *Standard Edition* of translating Trieb as "drive" and Instinkt as "instinct." (See, e.g., Jean Laplanche, *Life and Death in Psychoanalysis* [Baltimore: Johns Hopkins University Press, 1985].) One consequence, to put the point in this vocabulary, is that when Loewald says "instinct" he means "drive." That is, he

is writing in a slightly different idiolect from the one employed here. Thus, to quote him accurately I must, in effect, translate him into this idiolect. The only exception I make is to leave the titles of his essays unchanged: for example, "Motivation and Instinct Theory."

3. Hans Loewald, "Review of 'The Regulatory Principles of Mental Functioning' by Max Shur," in *Papers*, p. 62.

4. Freud, *Project for a Scientific Psychology, SE* 1: 353.

5. Freud, *Beyond the Pleasure Principle, SE* 18: 21.

6. Critics argue that psychoanalysis thereby stops taking analysands seriously; in particular, that it becomes insensitive to claims of actual seduction. The lesson ought to be the opposite. Precisely because human life is so permeated with phantasy, one does not need gross sexual abuse in order to be seductive. If adults are insensitive to the phantasy lives of children or, indeed, to their own phantasy lives, they can be "really seductive" though they do not consciously intend to be. Ironically, the effect of abandoning the seduction theory is to widen the scope of actual seductions to include behavior which is often taken to be normal, part of family life.

7. Indeed, although he gives up the belief that each individual neurotic was actually seduced, he retains the seduction theory for the species. He speculates that there was an actual historical occurrence of a primal crime which was phylogenetically preserved—as though the actuality of the occurrence would explain the widespread oedipal phantasies.

8. This is a complex subject about which I hope to say more in future work. For now let this suffice: Because Loewald was a practicing psychoanalyst, writing for other psychoanalysts, he did not highlight the profound influence of the philosophical tradition on his thinking. But it is there. "Philosophy," he says, "has been my first love." And like all first loves, he never left it entirely behind. (Indeed, in five years of meeting with him weekly to discuss psychoanalytic theory and practice, I doubt there was a single conversation in which the work of a great philosopher was not mentioned.) One especially needs to grasp Loewald's place in the Kantian tradition and its aftermath. In particular, Kant argued that the age-old distinction between realism and idealism needed to be made at two levels, the empirical and the transcendental. Roughly speaking, the empirical was the level of space and time; the transcendental concerned the conditions for the possibility of such empirical experience. Freud tried to be both an empirical realist and a transcendental realist (i.e., there is an objective world, and the condition for the experience of such a world is just that world as it is in itself). This is a position which, Kant argues, is ultimately incoherent. In response to Freud's obdurate realism, some psychoanalytic thinkers have lapsed into empirical idealism, treating the objective world just as a person's "psychological world." They may want to be realists, and indeed they may insist that they are realists, but they lack

the conceptual apparatus to make any robust sense of the idea that a person's "reality" is, in fact, *reality*. Kant argued that the only way to succeed at being an *empirical* realist—namely, that there really is an objective world, not of my own making—is to be a *transcendental* idealist—to accept that the mind has organizing conditions which underlie the possibility of there being experience of a genuinely objective world. Loewald, of course, makes no explicit reference to these distinctions in his texts, but the subtlety and originality of his work lie in his ability to make it clear that even objective reality must ultimately be understood as reality for a subject—and this, without collapsing into empirical idealism.

9. Hans Loewald, "The Problem of Defense and the Neurotic Interpretation of Reality," in *Papers*, p. 30.
10. Hans Loewald, "Ego and Reality," in *Papers*, p. 5.
11. This is the perspective required for what I have elsewhere called a science of subjectivity. See Jonathan Lear, *Love and Its Place in Nature: A Philosophical Interpretation of Freudian Psychoanalysis*, 2d ed. (New Haven: Yale University Press, 1998), chap. 1.
12. This theme is prominent in Kant's *Critique of Pure Reason* and flows through the subsequent tradition of German idealism, and of reactions to it.
13. Loewald, "Ego and Reality," p. 6.
14. Ibid., p. 12.
15. *Plato's Symposium*, trans. Alexander Nehamas and Paul Woodruff (Indianapolis: Hackett, 1989), 191d, 192e. I leave *eros* untranslated.
16. Hans Loewald, "The Transference Neurosis: Comments on the Concept and the Phenomenon," in *Papers*, pp. 302–314.
17. Freud, "Fragment of an Analysis of a Case of Hysteria," *SE* 7: 117.
18. Hans Loewald, "Instinct Theory, Object Relations, and Psychic Structure Formation," in *Papers*, pp. 207–209.
19. Nowhere are these disparate roles better portrayed than in the narrator's description of his mother in *Swann's Way*, the first volume of Proust's *In Search of Lost Time*.
20. This is the paradox of psychoanalytic practice: "The unit of a psychoanalytic investigation is the individual human mind or personality . . . The individual's status in this regard, however, is questionable and cannot be taken for granted"; Hans Loewald, "Psychoanalytic Theory and the Psychoanalytic Process," in *Papers*, p. 278.
21. See Hans Loewald, "On Motivation and Instinct Theory," in *Papers*, pp. 115–120; and his review of Max Shur, *Papers*, p. 60.
22. Freud, "Psychoanalysis," *SE* 18: 258. See also "Outline of Psychoanalysis," *SE* 23: 148; *The Ego and the Id, SE* 19: 45.
23. Freud, *Beyond the Pleasure Principle, SE* 18: 30.
24. Loewald, "On Motivation and Instinct Theory," p. 122.

25. Ibid., pp. 127–128.
26. Ibid., pp. 125–126.
27. Plato, *Symposium* 223d.
28. This idea is especially well developed in Richard Wollheim, *The Thread of Life* (Cambridge, Mass.: Harvard University Press, 1984).
29. Here I include in the chorus the instinctually driven *responses* to instincts. So, for example, the cruel superego, repressing the idlike refrains, is part of the chorus. One might say that in neurosis the chorus is singing in three-part disharmony.
30. Loewald, review of Max Shur, *Papers,* pp. 67, 68.
31. Loewald, "The Transference Neurosis," p. 311.
32. Loewald, "On the Therapeutic Action of Psychoanalysis," pp. 244–245.
33. I discuss this in Chapter 4, "An Interpretation of Transference."
34. Loewald, "The Transference Neurosis," pp. 309, 311.
35. Ibid., pp. 309–310. See Freud, "Remembering, Repeating and Working-through," *SE* 12: 154.
36. Loewald, "On the Therapeutic Action of Psychoanalysis," pp. 223–236; and "The Transference Neurosis," p. 311.
37. Loewald, "On the Therapeutic Action of Psychoanalysis," pp. 225–226.
38. Loewald, "Psychoanalytic Theory and the Psychoanalytic Process," p. 278.
39. Ibid., p. 297.
40. Freud, "Two Encyclopedia Articles," *SE* 18: 258.
41. Hans Loewald, "Freud's Conception of the Negative Therapeutic Reaction, with Comments on Instinct Theory," in *Papers,* pp. 317–323.
42. Ibid., p. 319.
43. Ibid., p. 320.
44. Ibid.
45. See Jean-Pierre Vernant and Pierre Vidal-Naquet, *Myth and Tragedy in Ancient Greece* (New York: Zone Books, 1988), chaps. 1–2.

7. Eros and Unknowing

1. Translations are from Plato, *Symposium,* trans. A. Nehamas and P. Woodruff (Indianapolis: Hackett, 1989).
2. Jean-Pierre Vernant and Pierre Vidal-Naquet, *Myth and Tragedy in Ancient Greece* (New York: Zone Books, 1988), p. 27.
3. Cf. Hans Loewald, "The Transference Neurosis: Comments on the Concept and the Phenomenon," in *Papers on Psychoanalysis* (New Haven: Yale University Press, 1980), pp. 302–314. See esp. pp. 310–311.
4. Sigmund Freud, e.g., "The Dynamics of Transference," *SE* 12: 99–108; "Remembering, Repeating and Working-through," *SE* 12: 147–156; and "Observations on Transference-Love," *SE* 12: 159–171. See also *New Introductory Lectures on Psychoanalysis, SE* 22: 153–155.

5. In a paternal transference the analyst need not be treated as as a replica of the analysand's father, even of the father as understood by the analysand. Rather, the analyst may be treated as the wished-for father, the father the analysand never had. The phantasized father is the father-as-missing-half.

6. Freud, "Fragment of an Analysis of a Case of Hysteria," *SE* 7: 117.

7. I discuss this point further in Chapter 4, "An Interpretation of Transference."

8. Compare Achilles' claim that logic will grab the tortoise by the throat and force him to accept the conclusion; Lewis Carroll (Charles Dodgson), "What the Tortoise Said to Achilles," *Mind*, 1895.

9. Freud, "Remembering, Repeating and Working-through."

10. Jacques Lacan, *Le Seminaire de Jacques Lacan*, vol. 8: *Le transfert, 1960–1961*, ed. Jacques-Alain Miller (Paris: Editions du Seuil, 1991).

11. The only exception is the politics outlined in the *Republic*, which is organized to promote the development of the divine principle insofar as it exists in the human realm.

12. Then there is the further issue of how this peculiar phantasy life is embedded in the social world. That too tends to be idiosyncratic; but it is the subject of another essay.

13. See the preface to the fourth edition of *Three Essays on the Theory of Sexuality*, *SE* 7: 134; *Beyond the Pleasure Principle*, *SE* 18: 50; *Group Psychology and the Analysis of the Ego*, *SE* 18: 91; "Resistances to Psychoanalysis," *SE* 19: 218; "Why War?" *SE* 22: 209.

8. Testing the Limits

1. Aristotle, *Politics* 7.1329a2–17, 1332b3–7, b25–29, b41–1333a3, a11–16; 3.1275a22–23, 1277b11–16.

2. Ibid., 1.1253a1–18.

3. Ibid., 1253a7–8.

4. Indeed, the distinction makes sense only from the perspective of explaining psychic pathology or of explaining how a person is educated so as have practical reason in the full sense of becoming a virtuous person. See Sarah Broadie, *Ethics with Aristotle* (New York: Oxford University Press, 1991), pp. 61–72.

5. *Politics* 1.2, 1253a15–18.

6. Ibid., 1.1252a26–34, 1253a29–30.

7. Ibid., 1.1252b27–1253a5.

8. Aristotle, *Poetics* 14.1453b10–22. This and subsequent translations of Aristotle are from *The Complete Works of Aristotle: The Revised Oxford Translation*, ed. J. Barnes (Princeton: Princeton University Press, 1984).

9. Ibid., chap. 15; see also chap. 13.

10. I discuss the claims of this paragraph at length in Chapter 10, "Inside and outside the *Republic*."

11. Plato, *Republic* 9.571b–c.
12. In psychoanalytic terms, these desires resist any form of sublimation. See Hans Loewald, *Sublimation: Inquiries into Theoretical Psychoanalysis* (New Haven: Yale University Press, 1988).
13. See *Republic* 10.605c–d. Thus Plato seems to admit that even in health there will be some, perhaps minimal, degree of intrapsychic conflict.
14. Ibid., 9.571c–d.
15. I am not here concerned with Plato's extreme dualist account in the *Phaedo*, where it is not clear that human nature is embodied at all. I am here concerned with his attempt in the *Republic* to work out the nature of embodied human existence.
16. E.g., *Republic* 4.430e–432b, 441d–444a.
17. Ibid., 7.540d–541b, 546a–547a.
18. Cf. ibid., 9.577d–e: "The tyrannized psyche will do least of all what it wishes."
19. Ibid., 9.573c–579e.
20. Ibid., 10.604e–605d.
21. Ibid., 8.568b.
22. Ibid., 9.547a–c; 8.569b.
23. Ibid., 8.567b–c.
24. *kalon ge . . . katharmon;* ibid., 9.567c.
25. Ibid., 8.546a–547c.
26. Sigmund Freud, *Beyond the Pleasure Principle, SE* 18: 14–15.
27. See ibid., pp. 12–23.
28. Ibid., pp. 37–61; *The Ego and the Id, SE* 19: 40; "Two Encyclopedia Articles," *SE* 18: 258.
29. Freud, "On Narcissism: An Introduction," *SE* 14: 78–79; "The Unconscious," *SE* 14: 174–175; *Three Essays on the Theory of Sexuality, SE* 7: 243.
30. Freud, "Two Encyclopedia Articles," *SE* 18: 258; "An Autobiographical Study," *SE* 20: 57; *An Outline of Psycho-Analysis, SE* 23: 150; *Beyond the Pleasure Principle, SE* 18: 52, 59–60.
31. This is the route I took in *Love and Its Place in Nature: A Philosophical Interpretation of Freudian Psychoanalysis*, 2d ed. (New Haven: Yale University Press, 1998), pp. 13–16.
32. *Republic* 10.607c–d. Cf. *Apology* 22b–c. The idea that the *Poetics* is a response to this Platonic challenge is well canvassed. For one excellent account, see Stephen Halliwell, *Aristotle's Poetics* (Chapel Hill: University of North Carolina Press, 1986).
33. Aristotle, *Nicomachean Ethics* 1094a26–27.
34. *Poetics* 9.1451a37–38; 10.1452a17–21; 15.1454a33–36; 16.1455a16–19; 25.1461b11–12.
35. Ibid., 9.1451a3–4; 10.1452a20–21.
36. Ibid., 13.1453a8–30.
37. Ibid., 13.1452b30–1453a8.

38. Ibid., 15.1454a17–20, b8–13.
39. Jean-Pierre Vernant and Pierre Vidal-Naquet, *Myth and Tragedy in Ancient Greece* (New York: Zone Books, 1988), p. 47.
40. Cf. D. W. Winnicott, "Transitional Objects and Transitional Phenomena," in *Through Paediatrics to Psychoanalysis* (London: Hogarth Press, 1975).
41. *Poetics*, e.g., 13.1452b30–1453a8; 14.1453b10–22.
42. Whatever catharsis happens precisely to be. See Chapter 9.
43. Aristotle, *Rhetoric* II.8.1386a24–27.
44. Ibid., II.5.1382b31; cf. 1382a22–30, 1382b28–1393a12.
45. Ibid., II.8.1386a24–25.
46. Ibid., II.8.1386a 19–23.
47. Vernant and Vidal-Naquet, *Myth and Tragedy*, pp. 26–27, Jean-Pierre Vernant, *The Origins of Greek Thought* (London: Methuen, 1982). Tragedy could thus be viewed not as representing an attack on logos, but as offering a critique of a earlier, flawed attempt at logos.
48. See Bernard Williams' fascinating discussion in *Shame and Necessity* (Berkeley: Univeristy of California Press, 1993), e.g., pp. 16–19, 164–166.

9. Catharsis

1. See Aristotle, *Poetics* 6.1449b22–28.
2. See Baxter Hathaway, *The Age of Criticism: The Late Renaissance in Italy* (Ithaca: Cornell University Press, 1962), pp. 205–300.
3. This is due largely to Jacob Bernays' influential *Zwei Abhandlungen über die aristotelische Theorie des Drama* (1857; reprint, Berlin, 1880). A chapter of this book has been translated as "Aristotle on the Effect of Tragedy" by Jonathan and Jennifer Barnes in *Articles on Aristotle*, vol. 4, ed. J. Barnes, M. Schofield, and R. Sorabji (London: Duckworth, 1979). Bernays' interpretation had a wider influence than on Aristotelian scholarship alone; for Bernays was Freud's wife's uncle, and it seems that Freud and Breuer were aware of the interpretation and relied on it when formulating his conception of catharsis in the early stages of the formation of psychoanalytic theory. (See Bennett Simon, *Mind and Madness in Ancient Greece* [Ithaca: Cornell University Press, 1978], pp. 140–143.) The catharsis-as-purge metaphor is used by Plato in the *Sophist* (230c–231e), where Socrates' elenchic method is represented as purging one of false beliefs.
4. See, e.g., Sigmund Freud, "Notes upon a Case of Obsessional Neurosis," *SE* 10: 233–234; "Formulations on the Two Principles of Mental Functioning," *SE* 12: 218–226; *Totem and Taboo, SE* 13: 78–90; "On Narcissicm: An Introduction," *SE* 14: 73–102; "Negation," *SE* 19: 235–239; Wilfrid Bion, *Learning from Experience* (London: Maresfield, 1984) and *Second Thoughts* (London: Maresfield, 1984); Melanie Klein, *Narrative of a Child Analysis* (London: Hogarth Press, 1961) pp. 31 ff.; *Con-*

tributions to Psycho-Analysis (London: Hogarth Press, 1948), pp. 140–151, 303; *Developments in Psycho-Analysis* (London: Hogarth Press, 1952); W. R. D. Fairburn, "Schizoid Factors in the Personality," in *Psychoanalytic Studies of the Personality* (London: 1984); Richard Wollheim, "The Mind and the Mind's Image of Itself," in *On Art and the Mind* (Cambridge, Mass.: Harvard University Press, 1974); "Wish-Fulfilment," in *Rational Action*, ed. Ross Harrison (Cambridge: Cambridge University Press, 1979); and *The Thread of Life* (Cambridge: Cambridge University Press, 1984).

5. The idea that purgation and purification need not be treated as contraries is argued by Humphry House, *Aristotle's Poetics* (London: R. Hart-Davis, 1956), pp. 104–111; and by Stephen Halliwell, *Aristotle's Poetics* (Chapel Hill: University of North Carolina Press, 1986), pp. 184–201.

6. See, e.g., Aristotle, *Generation of Animals* I.20.728b3, 14; IV.5.773b1, IV.6.775b5; *History of Animals* VI.18.573a2, a7; VI.28.578b18; VII.2.582b7, 30; VII.4.584a8; VIII.11.587b2, b30–33, 588a1. For the use of *katharsis* to describe seminal discharge: *Generation of Animals* II.7.747a19; for the discharge of urine: *History of Animals* VI.18.573a23; for birth discharge: *History of Animals* VI.20.574b4.

7. Aristotle, *Politics* VII.7.1341b37–39.

8. Aristotle uses the word *katharsis* only twice in *Poetics*: once, as we have seen, in the definition of tragedy, and once to refer to the ritual of purification at which Orestes is recognized by his sister, Iphigenia; *Poetics* 17.1455b15.

9. Bernays is explicit that catharsis is a cure for a pathological condition.

10. See *Politics* VIII.5–7. Bernays emphasizes the importance of this passage; though, as we shall see, he is less persuasive in his interpretation of that discussion. G. R. Else and, following him, Leon Golden have argued that one should not look outside the *Poetics* for the meaning of tragic catharsis (G. F. Else, *Aristotle's Poetics: The Argument* [Cambridge, Mass.: Harvard University Press, 1957], pp. 439 ff.; Leon Golden, "Catharsis," *Transactions and Proceedings of the American Philological Association* 93 [1962]: 51–60; and "Mimesis and Catharsis," *Classical Philology* 64 [1969]: 145–153). This, I believe, is a misapplication of a principle from new criticism. The *Poetics* was not meant to be a self-contained universe; it was an integral part of Aristotle's philosophy. If, for example, we were trying to determine what Aristotle meant by art *(techne)* or poetry *(poiesis)* in the *Poetics*, there would be no plausibility to claiming that we should completely restrict ourselves to the *Poetics'* discussion. Of course, Aristotle does use *poiesis* in a special way in the *Poetics:* it is to be translated as "poetry" rather than as a "making," which is the appropriate translation in the *Metaphysics*. However, if we ignore all other Aristotelian works we remain blind to the philosophically important fact that, for Aristotle, poetry is a special type of making. There is no doubt that we must approach other texts with care, for, to return to our current concern, Aristotle's use of "catharsis" when discussing medical purging may be different in significant respects from his

use of the term when discussing tragedy. But such interpretive difficulties are not sufficient grounds for ignoring other texts altogether. (Indeed, Else's and Golden's strictures led them to formulate a highly implausible account of catharsis, in which catharsis is not an effect on the audience of tragedy, but a resolution of the events in the play. This implausible interpretation depends upon an even more implausible translation of Aristotle's definition of tragedy. For an excellent criticism of this interpretation, see Halliwell, *Aristotle's Poetics,* app. 5, esp. pp. 354–356.)

11. *Politics* VIII.7.1341b32–42a18. Here I have made a few changes in the revised Oxford translation: I use "ethical melodies" rather than "melodies of character" for *ta ethika;* I use "catharsis" rather than translating it as "purgation"; I translate *pathos* as "emotion" rather than as "feeling"; and I translate *kouphidzesthai meth' hedones* as "relieved with pleasure" rather than as "lightened and delighted."

12. Bernays makes this point. Halliwell interprets this passage so as to diminish Aristotle's apparent contrast between education and catharsis. For a criticism of this interpretation, see pages 206–213, later in this chapter.

13. See esp. *Politics* VIII.7.1342a4–11. Bernays takes religious ecstasy to be a pathological condition.

14. 1342a11–13: *tauto de touto anagkaion paschein kai tous eleemonas kai tous phobetikous kai tous olos pathetikous.*

15. *Kai pasi gignesthai tina katharsin kai kouphidzesthai meth' hedones:* 1342a14–15 (my translation and emphasis). This statement seems to me to provide absolutely conclusive evidence against House's claim that, for Aristotle, a *phronimos* at the theater would experience no catharsis; *Aristotle's Poetics,* chap. 8.

16. Aristotle, *Problems* 42.864a34.

17. See, e.g., Franz Susemihl and R. D. Hicks, *The Politics of Aristotle* (London, 1894), p. 651, n. 1, who, along with House, *Aristotle's Poetics,* p. 110, quotes Milton's preface to *Samson Agonistes.* Cf. Halliwell, *Aristotle's Poetics,* pp. 192–194.

18. Halliwell is aware of this; *Aristotle's Poetics,* p. 193, n. 37. See *Nicomachean Ethics* 1104b17–18, *Eudemian Ethics* 1220a36.

19. *Rhetoric* II.5, 1382a21 ff.

20. See *Rhetoric* II.1 and II.5. In addition, Aristotle believes there are certain physiological changes which accompany an emotion; *On the Soul* 403a16–19.

21. *Rhetoric* II.5.1382b30 ff.

22. See Hathaway, *The Age of Criticism.*

23. Eduard Muller, *Theorie der Kunst bei den Alten,* 2: 62, 377–388, quoted by Bernays, *Zwei Abhandlung,* p. 156.

24. See, e.g., *Poetics* 13–14, where plots are evaluated on the basis of the type of emotional response they tend to evoke in an audience. Those which do not produce pity and fear but, for example, disgust are rejected as inadequate for tragedy.

25. See House, *Aristotle's Poetics*; Halliwell, *Aristotle's Poetics*; Golden, "Catharsis"; and Martha C. Nussbaum, *The Fragility of Goodness* (Cambridge: Cambridge University Press, 1986). Golden and Nussbaum speak of a "clarification" of the emotions.

26. *Nicomachean Ethics* II.

27. Ibid., II.6.1106b6–28. This is Aristotle's famous doctrine of the mean.

28. Aristotle is clear that one need not actually see a performance onstage in order to experience the effect of tragedy; simply hearing it read out loud is sufficient. See *Poetics* 14.1453b4–7; 6.1450b18–19; 26.1462a11–12. For Aristotle's mention of the peculiar and appropriate pleasure of tragedy, see *Poetics* 14.1453b10–14; 23.1459a17–24; 26.14652b12–14; cf. 1462a15–17.

29. Aristotle, *Metaphysics* I.1.

30. Nor, *contra* Golden and Nussbaum, do his emotions need to be clarified.

31. *Politics* VIII.7.1341b32–1342a18 (quoted above).

32. Halliwell, *Aristotle's Poetics*, pp. 195–196.

33. *Politics* VIII.7.1342a1–2.

34. My translation of 1341b38.

35. This is made clear by 1341b36–38: *ou mias heneken opheleias tei mousikei dein alla kai pleionon charin (kai gar paideias heneken kai katharseos)*. But in case there is any doubt, it is settled by *triton* at 1341b40: clearly, education, catharsis, and intellectual enjoyment are being listed as three distinct benefits obtainable from music.

36. Ibid., 1342b11–15.

37. Ibid., 1342b18–29. This passage is also cited by Bernays as part of his argument that catharsis is not meant by Aristotle to be morally educative.

38. *Ho men eleutheros kai pepaideumenos:* 1342b19. Cf. also *Poetics* 26 (esp. 1461b27–28), which suggests that tragedy will be appreciated by a better sort of audience.

39. *Poetics* 4.1449a10–15.

40. Ibid., 13.1453a33–36.

41. Ibid., 25.1460b13–15.

42. Here I am particularly indebted to Giovanni Ferrari.

43. *Poetics* 4.1448b4–19. I have altered the revised Oxford translation of 1448b14–15: *sullogidzesthai ti hekaston, hoion hoti houtos ekeinos*, which is rendered there as "gathering the meaning of things, e.g. that the man there is so-and-so." My translation is more literal, which I think is important to the interpretation of this passage.

44. *Parts of Animals* I.5.645a4–37.

45. Ibid., 645a8–15.

46. *Poetics* 4.1448b17–19. Such a person, presumably, would not have heard a sufficient description to recognize a mouse: the person Aristotle has in mind, I think, is someone who has no idea of a mouse: so he is in no position to recognize of any painting that it is a painting of a mouse.

47. See, e.g., *Poetics* 9.1451a37–38; 10.1452a17–21; 15.1454a33–36; 16.1455a16–19; 25.1461b11–12.

48. E.g., ibid., 9.1452a3–4; 10.1452a20–21.

49. Ibid., 13.1453a8–30. Nussbaum argues that the point of a *hamartia* is to render the protagonist sufficiently like us that we can identify with him to the extent required to experience the tragic emotions of pity and fear (*The Fragility of Goodness*, pp. 382 ff.). Her reasoning is based on her more general interpretation that, for Aristotle, the point of tragedy is to explore the gap which inevitably exists between being good and living well. I do not think that the general interpretation can be correct. Although Aristotle does accept that being virtuous is not sufficient for happiness and that external misfortune can ruin a thoroughly good man (*Nicomachean Ethics* I.10), it is quite clear that Aristotle does not think that such an event could be the basis for a tragedy. Consider *Poetics* 13.1452b30–36, where Aristotle says that tragedy cannot portray the fall of a good man from good to bad fortune, for such an event does not arouse the tragic emotions of pity and fear but a thoroughly nontragic emotion of disgust. Aristotle does reluctantly admit that a virtuous man can be destroyed for no reason at all, that is, through misfortune, but he denies that this is the stuff of tragedy. Tragic events always occur for a reason.

50. *Poetics* 9.1452a1–6 (my translation except for two phrases from Oxford).

51. Ibid., 6.1449b27–28. Literally, Aristotle says a "catharsis of such emotions" *(ton toiouton pathematon)*, but Bernays has argued convincingly that "such" should be understood demonstratively, as referring exclusively to pity and fear.

52. *Metaphysics* I.982b12–25, 983a12 ff.; *Rhetoric* I.1371a31–b1.

53. *Metaphysics* I.982b12N25. I discuss this at some length in *Aristotle: The Desire to Understand* (Cambridge: Cambridge University Press, 1988).

54. See, e.g., Halliwell, *Aristotle's Poetics*, pp. 70–74.

55. *Poetics* 24.1460a11–17.

56. Ibid., 24.1460a17.

57. Ibid., 26.1462b13–14. See the note on the passage in D. W. Lucas, *Aristotle's Poetics* (Oxford: Clarendon Press, 1968), p. 257.

58. *Poetics* 9.1451b5–11.

59. At *Metaphysics* XIII.10.1087a10–25, Aristotle does qualify his claim that episteme is of universals. See Jonathan Lear, "Active Episteme," in *Mathematics and Metaphysics in Aristotle: Proceedings of the Xth Symposium Aristotelicum*, ed. A. Graeser (Bern, 1986), for an analysis of this passage.

60. Although I am certainly willing to accept that Aristotle thought that tragedy provides deeper insight into the human condition than history does, I don't think that is the immediate point he is making in the passage under discussion.

61. *Poetics* 17.1455b2–13 (Oxford trans.). See also Aristotle's description of the plot of the *Odyssey* at 1455b16–23.

62. Ibid., 17.1455b, 12–13; cf. 9.1451b8–16.

63. Aristotle does not seem to have been familiar with Thucydides. One cannot but wonder how Aristotle would have changed his mind about history if he had carefully read the History of the Peloponnesian War.

64. As we have seen, that is why Aristotle says at the end of chap. 9 that the events in a tragedy should occur unexpectedly but on account of one another.

65. *Poetics* 9.1451a36–38, repeated at 1451b4–5, just before Aristotle claims that poetry is more philosophical than history because it deals with universals (1451b5–7).

66. Among humans, that is.

67. See *Politics* VIII.7.1342b14 and the numerous references in the *Poetics* in which the plot of a good tragedy is distinguished from that which will appeal to a vulgar audience, e.g., 13.1453a30–36 (cf. 9.1451b33–1452a1 and 6.1450b16–19) and chap. 26, in which Aristotle seems to accept the principle that tragedy is a higher art form than epic precisely because it appeals to a better audience.

68. See *Rhetoric* II.5.8; cf. the account of anger as a composite of pain and pleasure; *Rhetoric* II.2.

69. Aristotle, as we have seen, says that everyone undergoes a "certain catharsis and lightening with pleasure"; *Politics* VIII.7.1342b14–15.

70. *Poetics* 6.1449b24–28.

71. *Physics* III.3.

72. I say "ultimately" because there is a two-step process involved: the poet's creating the plot and writing the play, and the performance of the play before an audience. I am using the word "performance" widely to cover both the enactment of the play onstage by actors and the simple reading or recital of the play out loud. Aristotle is explicit that a tragedy can have its proper effect even when it is not acted out on stage: a person who merely hears the tragedy read out loud will experience pity and fear. See *Poetics* 14.1453b3–7; 6.1450b18–19; 26.62a11–12, a17–18.

73. Ibid., 13.1452b30–1453a8 (Oxford trans. except that I use "disgusting" for *miaron* rather than Oxford's "odious").

74. Ibid., 13.1453a4–6.

75. See ibid., 15.1454b8–13.

76. Ibid., 13.1453a8–17.

77. Ibid., 14.1453b10–22 (my translation).

78. Ibid., 11.1452b10–11. For other objective uses of *pathos* in the *Poetics,* see, e.g., 13.1453b18, b19–20, b39, 1454a13. See also *Rhetoric* II.5.1382b30; *Metaphysics* V.21.1022b20–21; *Nicomachean Ethics* I.11.1101a31.

79. It is tempting to speculate that, for Aristotle, there is an objective as well as a subjective catharsis. For the catharsis referred to in the definition of tragedy is clearly subjective—i.e., something which goes on within the souls of the members of the audience; while the catharsis at which Orestes is saved (*Poet-*

ics 17.1455b14–15) is clearly objective: viz. a ritual sacrifice. It goes beyond the evidence of the texts to construct a theory of the relation of objective to subjective catharsis. But it is worth noting in passing that if Aristotle believed that a subjective catharsis occurs in response to an objective catharsis, then the entire debate over where the catharsis is occurring, within the play itself or in the audience, would be idle. It would be occurring in both places (albeit in different forms).

80. Ibid., 13, esp. 1453a17–22; 14.1454a9–13.

81. *Rhetoric* II.5.1382a22–30.

82. Ibid., 1382a28–30.

83. Ibid., 1382b31–31; cf. b28–1383a12.

84. Ibid., 1383a5–8. Those who have lost all hope of escape grow resigned and callous.

85. *Poetics* 13,1453a5; *Rhetoric* II.8.1385b14 ff.

86. *Rhetoric* II.8.1386a24–27.

87. *Poetics* 13.1453a5–6.

88. *Rhetoric* II.8.1386a24–25.

89. Ibid., 1385b19 ff.

90. Ibid., 1385b23–27. Cf. *Politics* VIII.7.1342b19, where an educated audience *(hoi pepaideumenoi)* is contrasted with a vulgar one.

91. Since it is an incredibly complicated subject, I would like to reserve for another occasion a discussion of the general conditions required for emotional identification.

92. *Poetics* 13.1453a5–6; *Rhetoric* II.5.1383a10–13.

93. One might lamely try to keep the objection alive by saying that when we feel pity we are identifying with the chorus. But then the question arises: why should we identify with the chorus? The only plausible answer is that the chorus is in some way expressing our views. And if that is so, we are again led back to the conclusion that we believe that what happened to Oedipus could happen to us.

94. *Rhetoric* II.5.1383a7–12.

95. E.g., *Poetics* 9.1452a36–38, b5–7, b15–19.

96. I use "outside the theater" in the widest possible way: even the oral recitation of a tragedy counts for the purposes of this essay as going on "inside the theater."

97. If I may for a moment indulge my desire to be droll, let me put this in the language of modal semantics: In the virtuous man's opinion (and thus: in truth) the worlds in which he kills his mother, is killed by his mother, etc. are possible worlds and thus stand in an accessibility relation to the real world. All tragic worlds are possible worlds. However, all such tragic worlds are sufficiently removed from the actual work of a virtuous person (in ordinary circumstances) that they do not fall within the set of legitimately feared worlds.

98. *Rhetoric* II.8.1386a32–35. Of course, Aristotle is here talking within the context of rhetorical persuasion, but his point obviously carries over to the theater.

99. See Thompson Clarke, "The Legacy of Skepticism," *Journal of Philosophy* 69 (1972): 754–769.

100. *Psychagogei:* cf. *Poetics* 6.1450a33–36.

101. *Poetics* 13.1453a7–17; 15.1454b8–13.

102. Which was, of course, Hegel's choice.

103. See W. R. D. Fairbairn's account of "the moral defense" in "The Repression and the Return of Bad Objects," in *Psychoanalytic Studies of the Personality* (London, 1984).

104. Aristotle makes a related (though different) point at *Nicomachean Ethics* I.10: he reluctantly admits that even a virtuous person can suffer great misfortune; however, he offers the consolation that the virtuous person will at least bear his misfortunes nobly and with greatness of soul.

105. *Rhetoric* II.5.1383a3–5.

106. For another treatment of skepticism and its relationship to tragedy see, of course, Stanley Cavell, *The Claim of Reason* (Oxford: Clarendon Press, 1979).

10. Inside and outside the *Republic*

1. In the parlance of contemporary psychoanalysis, it leaves out Plato's object-relations theory. Indeed, it leaves out the possibility of object-relations theory's being an element of Plato's psychology. Freud, of course, understood that a person's ego and superego are formed around internalizations of parental figures. In the analytic situation, he concentrated on the intrapsychic configurations of the analysand, but he recognized that these configurations are due in part to interpsychic relations. See, e.g., Freud, "Mourning and Melancholia," *SE* 14: 249–250; *The Ego and the Id, SE* 19: 29–31; and Jonathan Lear, *Love and Its Place in Nature: A Philosophical Interpretation of Freudian Psychoanalysis,* 2d ed. (New Haven: Yale University Press, 1998), chap. 6. For an introduction to post-Freudian object-relations theory, see, e.g., Melanie Klein, *Love, Guilt and Reparation* (London: Hogarth Press, 1981) and *Envy and Gratitude* (London: Hogarth Press, 1984); D. W. Winnicott, *Through Paediatrics to Psycho-Analysis* (London: Hogarth Press, 1975) and *The Maturational Process and the Facilitating Environment* (London: Hogarth Press, 1982); W. R. D. Fairbairn, *Psychoanalytic Studies of the Personality* (London: Routledge and Kegan Paul, 1984); Margaret Mahler, *On Human Symbiosis and the Vicissitudes of Individuation* (New York: International Universities Press, 1967); Otto Kernberg, *Internal World and External Reality* (Northvale, N.J.: Jason Aronson, 1980).

2. See, e.g., Iris Murdoch, *The Fire and the Sun: Why Plato Banished the Artists* (Oxford: Clarendon Press, 1977); G. R. F. Ferrari, "Plato and Poetry," in *The Cambridge History of Literary Criticism,* vol. 1, ed. G. Kennedy (Cambridge: Cam-

bridge University Press, 1989); D. Halliwell, *Plato: Republic 10* (Wiltshire: Aris & Philips, 1988).

3. Plato, *Republic* (*Platonis Politeia* [Oxford: Clarendon Press, 1978]) 2.358b; cf. 366e. For translations see, e.g., Plato, *Republic,* trans. G. M. A. Grube, rev. C. D. C. Reeve (Indianapolis: Hackett, 1992); Plato, *Republic,* trans. Paul Shorey (Cambridge, Mass.: Harvard University Press, 1982). For notes and commentary: Plato, *Republic,* ed. James Adams (Cambridge: Cambridge University Press, 1965).

4. Ibid., 3.368d–e; 4.434d.

5. Ibid., 2.378d–e. Cf. 5.449d, where Plato says that the constitution of the community of women and children makes all the difference to the constitution of the state.

6. Ibid., 3.386a; 4.424e.

7. Ibid., 3.411e–412a; 4.424c–d.

8. Ibid., 4.420d–422d; cf. 430a–c, 441e–442c; 5.465d–466d.

9. Ibid., 2.366c–d; 4.424e; 6.492a–493a, 495a–b, 496c, 499b–c.

10. Ibid., 8.553c–d; cf. 9.581c.

11. Ibid., 8.554c–d. I do not believe that Plato's conception of "forcible restraint" should be equated with Freud's concept of repression, though there are of course similarities. For Freud, repression is itself unconscious, it is dynamically motivated, and the repressed is unconscious but continues to exercise influence in hidden ways. Plato does not suggest that the "forcibly restrained" is thereby rendered unconscious or that these intrapsychic struggles must, by nature of the process, occur unconsciously.

12. Similarly, just as the democratic polis lets a hundred flowers bloom (ibid., 8.557b–c), so democratic man is "manifold" (561e). The timocratic man is a compromise formation: an attempted solution to the conflicting demands of reason and appetite (550a–b). However, that the compromise fails is attested by the emergence of oligarchic man in the next generation. The tyrant is just a mess. (I shall discuss the democrat and tyrant in the section titled "Poetic Justice.") For Plato, a human being, looked at from the outside, is only apparently a unity (9.588c–e); whether each forms a genuine unity depends on the integration of the (potentially) disparate bits of the psyche.

13. Plato says (ibid., 4.433d) that in the just polis each person, in performing the task which suits his nature, will be not a multiplicity, but a unity. (See also 443e.) This suggests that a healthy polis encourages the development of healthy psyches: people who achieve the degree of psychic unity of which their character types are capable. Injustice, by contrast, is a kind of civil war both in polis and psyche (444a–b).

14. Ibid., 3.401b–c. Cf. 401c–d.

15. I here stipulate "internalization" to mean the process, whatever it is, which Plato thought grounded cultural influence. For an introduction to the concept

of internalization as it occurs in the modern psychoanalytic tradition, see, e.g., Roy Schafer, *Aspects of Internalization* (Madison, Conn.: International Universities Press, 1990); Hans Loewald, "On Internalization" and "Internalization, Separation, Mourning, and the Superego," in *Papers on Psychoanalysis* (New Haven: Yale University Press, 1980); Jean LaPlanche and J.-B. Pontalis, *The Language of Psychoanalysis* (New York: W. W. Norton, 1985), pp. 205–208, 211–212, 226–227, 229–231; B. Moore and B. Fine, eds., *Psychoanalytic Terms and Concepts* (New Haven: Yale University Press, 1990), pp. 102–103, 109–110; R. D. Hinshelwood, *A Dictionary of Kleinian Thought* (London: Free Association Press, 1991), pp. 68–83, 319–321, 330–334; Arnold Model, *Object Love and Reality* (Madison, Conn.: International Universities Press, 1985).

16. *Republic* 3.402d. Cf. 401a; 6.535b; 9.577a.

17. Ibid., 4.435e–436a; see also 441c.

18. Ibid., 6.500c. Cf. 484c: "They have a paradigm of the reality of things in their psyche." See also 490b.

19. Ibid., 6.484c, 490b. Some such internalization is necessary, Plato thinks, for a person with a philosophical nature to achieve excellence (492a). This may be through a proper education, but with poor upbringing even a philosophical nature is destroyed and corrupted (495a–b). Such a person is then capable of the greatest evils, and his only hope is divine inspiration. That is why a person of philosophical nature ought to shun political life in a pathological polis: he must take care of the "constitution inside himself" and not allow cultural influences to "undo the state of his psyche."

20. Socrates argues that education is not, as the sophists think, a matter of putting knowledge into a psyche, but rather more like turning the eye from the dark (world of becoming) to the light (world of realities); ibid., 7.518b–e. This metaphor may have impeded understanding of Plato's psychology. For Plato is not here saying that internalization does not take place in education; he is rather explaining how internalization comes about. It is more, he thinks, than learning a few sophistical speeches. The point of turning one's gaze toward reality is not just to gawp at it like a bewildered tourist; it is to take reality in, to be educated by it.

21. Ibid., 6.485d. For the economic model in psychoanalysis, see, e.g., Freud, "The Unconscious," *SE* 14: 181; *Studies on Hysteria*, *SE* 2: 17, 86, 166–167; "The Neuro-Psychoses of Defense," *SE* 3: 48–49.

22. Bernard Williams, "The Analogy of City and Soul in Plato's *Republic*," in *Exegesis and Argument: Studies in Greek Philosophy Presented to Gregory Vlastos*, ed. E. N. Lee, A. P. D. Mourelatos, and R. M. Rorty, *Phronesis:* suppl. vol. 1 (1973). This essay has influenced a generation of philosophers, myself included. I turn to it here because I have come to believe, first, that the argument is unsuccessful; second, that in coming to understand why it is unsuccessful we will better understand our own tendency to misread Plato's psychology.

23. Williams derives this from 435e. See "Analogy," pp. 196–197.

24. Ibid., p. 197.

25. Terence Irwin argues that the whole-part rule does not play a role in the argument of book 4, and focuses instead on Macrocosm-Microcosm rule (MM): the structure of the state is analogous to the structure of the psyche; *Plato's Moral Theory: The Early and Middle Dialogues* (Oxford: Clarendon Press, 1977), p. 331, n. 29. The MM is true, but it does not give us the psychological principles which ensure its truth. John Cooper also provides criticism of the whole-part rule in "The Psychology of Justice in Plato," *American Philosophical Quarterly* 14 (1977).

26. Williams, "Analogy," p. 198; cf. "the ineliminable tension," pp. 200 ff.

27. This is the strongest version of the whole-part rule we are legitimately entitled to attribute to Plato.

28. Williams comes close to accepting this when he later adopts the "predominant section rule," which I shall discuss later in this chapter.

29. Williams, "Analogy," p. 199.

30. Since we have substituted (a''') for (a'), there is no longer reason to believe that everyone in a just polis is just. We therefore look at the psyche of an appetitive-type person.

31. Essentially the same problem occurs in Freud's discussion of the id. Freud often describes the id as not listening to reason. But he is so describing it in the context of trying to make clear the dynamic structure of neurotic pathology. There is another conception of the id, manifest in his dictum "Where it was there I shall become," which allows the possibility of the appetites' harkening to reason. See Lear, *Love and Its Place in Nature,* chap. 6.

32. Of course, there is truth in the claim that money is a means to satisfy bodily appetites (*Republic* 9.580e–581a), but that is not the whole truth. The oligarchic man, for example, is not using money just as a means to satisfy his bodily appetites: indeed, he keeps these appetites under control precisely because he has developed an appetite for money and property (8.553c–554c).

33. Ibid., 10.580d–581e; cf. 8.553c–554e.

34. In fact the variation can be much more fine-grained than I have indicated. See the explication by C. D. C. Reeve in *Philosopher-Kings* (Princeton: Princeton University Press, 1988), pp. 5–9, 135–153, a book which I found inspiring and to which I am indebted. See also John Cooper, "Plato's Theory of Human Motivation," *History of Philosophy Quarterly* 1 (1984); and Richard Kraut's account of normative rule, "Reason and Justice in Plato's Republic," in Lee, Mourelatos, and Rorty, *Exegesis and Argument.*

35. *Republic* 4.433e–434a. See Reeve, *Philosopher-Kings,* pp. 246–247.

36. Plato, as we have seen, believes a change in musical modes will ultimately upset constitutional laws: it is precisely because lawlessness is internalized with the music that it is subsequently externalized in attacks on established

business relations, on the laws and the constitution (*Republic* 4.424c–e). I shall discuss this further in the section titled "Poetic Justice."

37. Ibid., 8.560. Plato's account of faction vs. counterfaction struggling within the psyche bears some similarity to Freud's account of cathexis and counter-cathexis in a neurotic struggle—although there is no evidence that Plato thought this intrapsychic and interpsychic struggle was unconscious. Cf., e.g., "Further Remarks on the Neuro-Psychoses of Defense," *SE* 3: 169–170.

38. *Republic* 8.557c; quoted by Williams, "Analogy," p. 201.

39. Williams, "Analogy," p. 201. By now Williams has put, in place of the whole-part rule, another which he calls the predominant section rule: A city is *F* if and only if the leading, most influential, or predominant citizens are *F*.

40. Plato does make an exception for those who have been divinely inspired; *Republic* 6.492a, 496c–497a, 499b–c.

41. Williams, "Analogy," p. 204.

42. I suspect that Williams' formal objections to the analogy are fueled by a democrat's suspicion of Plato's conservative political theory: in particular by what he takes to be an ultimately repressive relation between ruling class and ruled. From a democratic perspective the means and organization of society ought to be transparent to all, while Plato advocates feeding the appetitive class a diet of noble falsehoods. It is, of course, beyond the scope of this chapter to respond to this type of objection. But I would like to note in passing: (1) Such an objection does not itself constitute an objection to the idea of an isomorphism between polis and psyche. (2) Plato himself issues a challenge to the idea of transparency. One of the motivations for the "noble falsehood" is that one cannot just assume that, say, the Freedom of Information Act guarantees freedom of information: one has to take into account what the subjective meaning of this (external) information will be. And once one does so, Plato thinks, one can get this information across only if one presents it in certain mythic forms, which, strictly speaking, are not true. Each side will think the other is restricting information, one because of the alteration in form, the other because the idea of subjective understanding is being ignored.

43. The phrase is from Thomas Mann's description of psychoanalysis. See "Freud and the Future," in *Freud, Goethe, Wagner* (New York: Alfred A. Knopf, 1937).

44. See, e.g., *Republic* 6.488a–489b, 496c–d, 497a–b, 499b–c.

45. Virtue or excellence, Plato says, is a certain sort of health; ibid., 4.444d.

46. In a sense Plato has again to recapitulate the poet, only at a philosophical level. Socrates must tell a tale in which the just man is stripped of all the outer trappings, and the glittering prizes—which from a conventional perspective are all the rewards there are—are given to the unjust man (ibid., 2.360e–361d). This, in effect, is what the poets have already done (362e–366a). They have shaped a culture which values only the appearance of justice. By showing that it is nevertheless better to be just, Plato is doing more than

showing that justice will triumph even in the worst possible dialectical circumstances. He is trying to show that it will triumph in (what he took to be)
the actual situation. From Plato's perspective, his argument has to take this
shape if it is to be persuasive, for the worst-case scenario is the way things
are. Plato thus starts out with poetic appearance in order to work through to
a (nonpoetical) conclusion which penetrates beyond surface appearances.

47. So for any pathological structure F*, one should not expect that an F* polis is
an immediate and simple externalization of F* citizens. Nor should one think
that F* citizens are shaped by a simple internalization of the structure of the
F* polis. The whole point of F*'s being pathological is that no such simple
mirroring relation can occur. So, for example, the democratic polis is shaped
not only by the degenerate son of oligarchy, but also by the rebellious poor
(ibid., 8.556c–557a). However, the rebellious poor also had their psyches
shaped via internalizations of previous externalizations of the oligarchical
rulers. And both they and democratic man—the metaphorical and literal sons
of oligarchy—help to shape the democratic polis via externalization of structures in their psyches.

48. And this is built up by what Plato calls a "circle of growth," which seems to be
the opposite of the tale of degeneration: "a sound nurture and education if
kept up creates good natures in the state, and sound natures in turn receiving
an education of this sort develop into better persons than their predecessors"
(ibid., 4.424a–b). Although, of course, Plato thinks that even the ideal polis is
subject to eventual decay (8.546a–547a).

49. Ibid., 4.441d–e. See, e.g., 5.462c–d, 463c, 464a.

50. And thus I think the psychological principles of internalization and external-
ization can help us to address a long-standing interpretive problem: why did
Plato think there was a relation between justice as a condition of the psy-
che—psychic justice—and conventionally recognized justice? See, e.g.,
Gregory Vlastos, "Justice and Happiness in Plato's Republic," in *Platonic Studies*
(Princeton: Princeton University Press, 1981); David Sachs, "A Fallacy in Plato's
Republic," *Philosophical Review* 72 (1963); Irwin, *Plato's Moral Theory*, pp.
205–206, 331. I address this problem in "Plato's Politics of Narcissism," in *Virtue,
Love and Form: Essays in Memory of Gregory Vlastos*, ed. Terence Irwin and
Martha C. Nussbaum (Toronto: Apeiron, 1994).

51. In fact Plato never uses the word "analogy" to describe the relation between
polis and psyche, though he is sometimes translated as though he did. See,
e.g., Paul Shorey's translation of *Republic* 2.368e in the Loeb edition (Cambridge, Mass.: Harvard University Press, 1982).

52. The contradictory arguments of book 1 bear a significant resemblance to the
problems which Plato says are provocative of thought; *Republic* 7.523–524.

53. Ibid., 3.411; cf., e.g., 395c–d, 401b–d, 413c.

54. See, e.g., Ferrari, "Plato and Poetry."

55. *Republic* 3.395c–396e, 378d, 398a–b, 401b–402a; 10.605–606.
56. Ibid., 10.598b: *phantasma;* cf. 599a. In fact Plato says that imitation gives us a phantasy of a phantasy—a second-order phantasy, but this depends on his metaphysical conception of ordinary empirical objects themselves being removed from reality. There are, obviously, important metaphysical objections to tragic poetry and art, but here I am restricting my focus to the primarily psychological objections.
57. Ibid., 10.603a–b; cf. 605a–b.
58. Ibid., 10.604b; cf. 603d.
59. Ibid., 7.559e–560. See above, pages 235–236.
60. Ibid., 3.399e. The purgation is supposed to have occurred as an unconscious by-product of banishing the poets.
61. Ibid., 9.573d; cf. 573b.
62. Compare Freud on the omnipotence of archaic mind, e.g., *Totem and Taboo, SE* 13: 83–91, 186, 188; "The Uncanny," *SE* 17: 240–244.
63. Freud noticed that the superego often speaks with an iddish accent: it tends to take on a harsh, vindictive tone which testifies to some sort of commerce with the id. (See, e.g., *The Ego and the Id, SE* 19: 36, 48–49, 52; "Neurosis and Psychosis," *SE* 19: 151–152; *Inhibitions, Symptoms and Anxiety, SE* 20: 115–116.) This was puzzling both because the superego's function is to help keep the id in place and because it is unclear how this commerce takes place. Plato in fact provides a satisfying explanation of how commerce between id and superego can occur via commerce between inside and outside. This is superior to simply saying that the superego becomes fused with aggression, because it explains how this fusion comes about.
64. *Republic* 2.382b: often translated as "veritable lie" or "truthful lie."
65. Ibid., 577–579. This, I think, provides one of the deeper reasons why book 10 comes where it does. It is not just that it has to follow the entire psychology and metaphysics of the *Republic* but that it has to follow book 9.
66. Nor has the theory of technique. See, e.g., Paul Gray, "'Developmental Lag' in the Evolution of Technique of Psychoanalysis of Neurotic Conflict," *Journal of the American Psychoanalytical Association,* 1982; reprinted in *Ego and the Analysis of Defense* (Northvale, N.J.: Jason Aronson, 1995).

11. Transcendental Anthropology

1. Ludwig Wittgenstein, *Philosophical Investigations,* trans. G. E. M. Anscombe (Blackwell: Oxford, 1978) (hereafter cited as *PI*), p. vii.
2. *PI* I.7.
3. *PI* I.23.
4. *PI* I.415.
5. *PI* I.97, 116, 120, 121.

6. This perspective is well described by Stanley Cavell, "The Availability of the Later Wittgenstein," in *Must We Mean What We Say?* (New York: Scribner's, 1969).

7. *PI* I.497.

8. In a previous incarnation, the chief was a tortoise. See Lewis Carroll (Charles Dodgson), "What the Tortoise Said to Achilles," *Mind*, 1895.

9. They are not, as Bernard Williams says, "alternatives to us, they are alternatives *for us*." See his fascinating essay "Wittgenstein and Idealism," in *Moral Luck* (New York: Cambridge University Press, 1981). I am indebted to Williams' formulation of the problem; this chapter is, in effect, an attempt to formulate a response.

10. Ludwig Wittgenstein, *On Certainty*, ed. G. E. M. Anscombe and G. H. von Wright, trans. D. Paul (Oxford: Blackwell, 1979), 97.

11. Immanuel Kant, *Kritik der reinen Vernunft* (Berlin: de Gruyter, 1968), B25. See *Critique of Pure Reason*, trans. Norman Kemp Smith (London: Macmillan, 1929).

12. See, e.g., *PI* I.109, 126.

13. *PI* I.124, 133.

14. See, e.g., G. W. F. Hegel, *Encyclopaedia of the Philosophical Sciences*, vol. 1, trans. W. Wallace (Oxford: Clarendon Press, 1975), 40–60; and Robert Pippin, *Kant's Theory of Form* (New Haven: Yale University Press, 1982).

15. Kant, *Critique of Pure Reason*, B129–138.

16. *PI* I.193–195. See Saul Kripke, *Wittgenstein on Rules and Private Language* (Oxford: Blackwell, 1982), pp. 23–37.

17. *PI* I.1, 208, 211 *(bis)*, 217, 219.

18. *PI* I.139–141, 152–153.

19. *PI* I.201.

20. Ludwig Wittgenstein, *Remarks on the Foundations of Mathematics*, ed. G. H. von Wright, R. Rhees, and G. E. M. Anscombe, trans. Anscombe (Oxford: Blackwell, 1967), I.5, 148–149, 118.

21. *PI* II.230.

22. Wittgenstein does recognize the possibility of shifts in interests and practices. See *On Certainty*, 63.

23. *PI* II.226.

24. See Gerold Prauss, *Erscheinung bei Kant* (Berlin: de Gruyter, 1971) and *Kant und das Problem der Dinge an sich* (Bonn: Bouvier Verlag H. Grundmann, 1974); Henry Allison, *Kant's Transcendental Idealism* (New Haven: Yale University Press, 1983).

25. *PI* I.175–177.

26. Kant, *Critique of Pure Reason*, B132. See also Pierre Lachieze-Rey, *L'idéalisme Kantien* (Paris: Librairie Philosophique J. Vrin, 1950).

27. See Thomas Nagel, "What Is It Like to Be a Bat?" in *Mortal Questions* (Cambridge: Cambridge University Press, 1979).

28. *PI* I.69, 208, 210.
29. Here I am indebted to Richard Wollheim's fascinating discussion of psychotherapy in *The Thread of Life* (Cambridge: Cambridge University Press, 1984).
30. See Donald Davidson, *Inquiries into Truth and Interpretation* (Oxford: Clarendon Press, 1984), esp. essays 9, 10, 13–16; *Essays on Actions and Events* (Oxford: Clarendon Press, 1980), esp. essay 11.
31. This dilemma is posed by Bernard Williams in "Wittgenstein and Idealism."
32. *PI* I.242.
33. *PI* I.81.
34. *PI* I.89.
35. *PI* I.94, 89.
36. *PI* I.81, Wittgenstin, *Remarks on the Foundations of Mathematics,* V.40, 48.
37. *PI* I.108.
38. Cf. Manley Thompson, "On A Priori Truth," *Journal of Philosophy* 78 (1981).

12. The Disappearing "We"

1. Immanuel Kant, *Critique of Pure Reason,* trans. Norman Kemp Smith (London: Macmillan, 1929) (hereafter cited as *CPR*); *Kritik der reinen Vernunft* (Berlin: de Gruyter, 1968). Cf., e.g., B167–168.
2. The most eloquent exponent of the antiskeptical interpretation is, I think, Barry Stroud. See, e.g., "Transcendental Arguments and Epistemological Naturalism," *Philosophical Studies* 31 (1977), esp. pp. 108, 109, 113; "Transcendental Arguments," *Journal of Philosophy* 65 (1968), esp. pp. 242, 252, 256.
3. *CPR* B147, B166, B218.
4. See, e.g., *CPR* B147.
5. See, e.g., *CPR* B137.
6. *CPR* A90/B122.
7. *CPR* A93/B125–B126. Cf. also A89/B122 ff., B137–140, B142, B165–168.
8. *CPR* B137. Cf. B158.
9. *CPR* B167–168.
10. See, e.g., *CPR* A94/B127, A89/B122–A92/B124, B168.
11. *CPR* B138.
12. *CPR* B138.
13. I cannot here discuss Kant's use of such expressions as "intelligible object" (noumenon), "transcendental object," or "thing in itself," but I do not think that the concept of an object is legitimately applicable to such "things." These expressions are *façons de parler,* which discursive intelligences find helpful when discussing that of which a different type of consciousness (an intellectual intuition) is conscious or that of which we discursive intelligences are considered independently of our modes of experience or thought.

14. The literature on the transcendental deduction is enormous, so I will confine myself to mentioning a few works which I think are helpful: Henry E. Allison, "Kant's Refutation of Realism," *Dialectica* 30 (1976); Karl Amariks, "Kant's Transcendental Argument as a Regressive Argument," *Kant-Studien* 69 (1978); Robert B. Pippen, *Kant's Theory of Form* (New Haven: Yale University Press, 1982); Gerold Prauss, *Erscheinung bei Kant* (Berlin: de Gruyter, 1971) and *Kant und das Problem der Dinge an sich* (Bonn: Bouvier Verlag H. Grundmann, 1974); and Wilfred Sellars, "Some Remarks on Kant's Theory of Experience," *Journal of Philosophy* 64 (1967).

15. Saul A. Kripke, *Wittgenstein on Rules and Private Language* (Oxford: Blackwell, 1982). In working out an alternative interpretation, I find myself much indebted to the depth and clarity of Kripke's work. He is not alone in suggesting that the *Investigations* can be read as a response to skepticism. See, e.g., Rogers Albritton, "Wittgenstein's Use of the Term 'Criterion,'" *Journal of Philosophy* 61 (1959); reprinted with postscript in *Wittgenstein: The Philosophical Investigations*, ed. C. Pitcher (London: Macmillan, 1970); Stanley Cavell, *The Claim of Reason* (Oxford: Clarendon Press, 1979). Of course, none of these interpretations agree as to what the challenge of or Wittgenstein's response to skepticism is.

16. That there are affinities between Kant and Wittgenstein is hardly news. See esp. Bernard Williams, "Wittgenstein and Idealism," in *Moral Luck* (Cambridge: Cambridge University Press, 1982). Cf., e.g., David Pears, *Wittgenstein* (London: Fontana, 1971); and P. M. S. Hacker, *Insight and Illusion* (Oxford: Clarendon Press, 1972).

17. See, of course, Donald Davidson, "Radical Interpretation," in *Inquiries into Truth and Interpretation* (Oxford: Clarendon Press, 1982).

18. *PI* I.138.

19. *PI* I.197.

20. *PI* I.139; Cf. 141, 146, 152–154, 185–190.

21. See, e.g., *PI* I.243 ff., 159–165.

22. *PI* I.151–152.

23. *PI* I.151; cf. 155.

24. See the discussion of the experience of being guided, *PI* I.171–178.

25. *PI* I.191.

26. See, e.g., *PI* I.193–195 and 156.

27. *PI* I.195, 197.

28. See Wilfrid Sellars, "Some Remarks on Kant's Philosophical Theory of Experience," in *Science and Metaphysics* (London: Routledge, 1968). This insight pervades much of Sellars' work.

29. *CPR* B133.

30. *CPR* B131–130.

31. *PI* I.199.

32. *PI* I.241–242.

33. Cf. *CPR* B137.
34. *PI* I.304.
35. Kripke says: "It should then be clear that the demand for 'outward criteria' is no verificationist or behaviourist premise that Wittgenstein takes for granted in his 'private language argument.' If anything it is deduced in the sense of a deduction akin to Kant's. A skeptical problem is posed, and a skeptical solution is given"; *Wittgenstein on Rules and Private Language,* pp. 100–101. I agree with his claim that there is no verificationist premise, but disagree (1) with his interpretation of what a deduction is; (2) with his claim that it is the need for outward criteria rather than the "inner process" which is deduced. See also Albritton, "Wittgenstein's Use of the Term 'Criterion'"; Cavell, *The Claim of Reason;* Crispin Wright, "Anti-realist Semantics: The Role of Criteria," in *Idealism Past and Present,* ed. G. Vesey (Cambridge: Cambridge University Press, 1982); Hacker, *Insight and Illusion,* chap. 10; Gordon Baker, "Criteria: A New Foundation for Semantics Ratio," *Ratio,* 1974.
36. Cf., e.g., *PI* I.211, 219.
37. Cf., e.g., *CPR* Bxl, A27/B43, B68, B71–72, B135, B138–139, B148–150, B161, A230/B283–A231/B284, B307, B309–311, A286/B342.
38. See, e.g., Stroud, "Transcendental Arguments."
39. Cf. Norman Malcolm, "Wittgenstein and Idealism," in Vesey, *Idealism Past and Present,* which is an extended critique of Bernard Williams' essay of the same name. Malcolm's central criticism does not, I think, succeed. Malcolm notes correctly that Wittgenstein regularly uses "we" to pick out one group among others: e.g., when he asks what we would say in response to the peculiar goings-on of some tribe. However, the issue is not whether Wittgenstein makes such contrasts, which he undoubtedly does, but what is the point of such contrasts. Williams' argument, which Malcolm's paper does not impugn, is that the point is to discover reflectively more about what our form of life is like. That the "common behaviour of mankind is the system of reference by means of which we interpret an unknown language" means, *pace* Malcolm, that ultimately "they" are part of us.
40. See John McDowell, "Anti-realism and the Epistemology of Understanding," in *Meaning and Understanding,* ed. H. Parret and J. Bouveresse (Berlin: de Gruyter, 1981).
41. This is why the skeptical paradox gets more complex when I am asked to consider myself as opposed to an arbitrary individual, in isolation. In such a case I am both subject and object of judgment. And, to paraphrase Kant, I can know myself only as I appear to myself. I may appear to myself to be following rules even though I am not. This does not imply that I cannot follow rules when considered in isolation, but that my appearance to myself of rule-following is not a sufficient condition of rule-following.
42. Cf. *PI* I.198, 199, 202.

43. I do not think that the remarks at, e.g., *PI* I.258–265 impugn this claim, for these are part of an investigation into the possibility of a language which essentially depends on reference to private mental objects.

44. See *PI* I.202 and Wittgenstein's characterization of a "private" language at I.243.

45. See Kripke, *Wittgenstein on Rules and Private Language*, pp. 22–37.

46. See *PI* II.226.

47. Kripke, *Wittgenstein on Rules and Private Language*, p. 110.

48. Ibid., pp. 68–70.

49. Cf., e.g., Michael Dummett, "Wittgenstein's Philosophy of Mathematics," in *Truth and Other Enigmas* (London: Duckworth, 1978); Crispin Wright, *Wittgenstein on the Foundations of Mathematics* (London: Duckworth, 1980). I discuss this in more detail in "Leaving the World Alone."

50. Derek Bolton argues that a philosophy like Wittgenstein's, which bases itself in life forms, cannot be idealistic; "Lifeform and Idealism," in Vesey, *Idealism Past and Present*. Insofar as his argument succeeds, it does so, I think, by construing "idealistic" too narrowly. He assumes that all forms of idealism are characterized by a tendency toward a transcendent viewpoint and by immaterialism (pp. 269–275). If so, then of course Wittgenstein's later philosophy will not be "idealistic." (By these criteria Hegel's philosophy will not be "idealistic.") Bolton says that in Wittgenstein's life forms "what is taken as fundamental is . . . human action, and this being so there is no reason for calling this philosophy a kind of idealism" (p. 272). But if it is human action, not behavior, which is fundamental, and if action is the expression of beliefs, desires, interests, concerns, then there is reason for calling this philosophy a kind of idealism. See Williams, "Wittgenstein and Idealism," pp. 152–153.

51. Cf. Ludwig Wittgenstein, *Remarks on the Foundations of Mathematics* (Oxford: Blackwell, 1956), I.148.

52. See, e.g., *PI* I.133, 119, 254–255, 309, 593.

53. *PI* I.138.

54. Thus, *pace* Thompson Clarke, either we are not just left back "in the plain" or "the plain" is much too complex to have C. E. Moore as its paradigm representative. See Clarke's marvelous article "The Legacy of Scepticism," *Journal of Philosophy* 69 (1972).

55. See Sigmund Freud, *Civilization and Its Discontents*, *SE* 21: 64–145.

56. Donald Davidson, "On the Very Idea of a Conceptual Scheme," *Proceedings and Addresses of the American Philosophical Association* 67 (1973–74). Cf. G. W. F. Hegel, *Encyclopaedia of the Philosophical Sciences*, vol. 1, trans. W. Wallace (Oxford: Clarendon Press, 1975), e.g., pp. 40–47.

Acknowledgments

I should like to thank Bernard Williams, the late Hans Loewald, and Irad Kimhi for helping me to think through central themes of this book. Whatever open-mindedness is actually manifest in these pages would not be there had Sam Ritvo not patiently sat by me and steadfastly refused to get in the way. Philosophy and psychoanalysis are, each in their own way, extended conversations, and as I think of the people from whom I have learned over the two decades in which these essays were written, I find that, paradoxically, the list gets embarrassingly long and embarrassingly incomplete at the same time. On three occasions I have been blessed to be surrounded by remarkable individuals who collectively made an institution come alive as a center for humane thinking. The first was as a Fellow of Clare College and Lecturer in the Faculty of Philosophy at the University of Cambridge: my friends and colleagues were examples of how an imaginative life and one committed to intellectual inquiry might be of a piece. The second is as a member of the Western New England Institute for Psychoanalysis: my colleagues have shown me how a life which looks at the complexity and depth of human life, even its darkness, hatred, and envy, might nevertheless be one full of creativity and joy. The third is as a member of the Committee on Social Thought at the University of Chicago, my current intellectual home: here my colleagues have provided the ideal environment in which to think independently. I should like to thank my editors at Harvard, Lindsay Waters and Ann Hawthorne, as well as Anne Gamboa, Regina Starolis, and Michael Harrold, who helped in the production of this book; and Suzy Pafka, who rescued it from countless computer crashes.

I thank Special Rider Music for permission to reprint the lines in the epigraph from Bob Dylan's "Love minus Zero/No Limit," copyright © 1965 by Warner Bros. Inc. Copyright renewed 1993 by Special Rider Music.

Several of the essays in this volume were initially published elsewhere. I thank the various journals for permission to use them here in somewhat different form.

CHAPTER 2: "The Shrink Is In," *New Republic,* December 1995

CHAPTER 4: "An Interpretation of Transference," *International Journal of Psychoanalysis* 74 (1993)

CHAPTER 6: "The Introduction of Eros: Reflections on the Work of Hans Loewald," *Journal of the American Psychoanalytic Association* 44, no. 3 (1996)

CHAPTER 8: "Testing the Limits: The Place of Tragedy in Aristotle's Ethics," in *Aristotle and Moral Realism,* ed. Robert Heinaman (London: University College Press, 1995)

CHAPTER 9: "Katharsis," *Phronesis* 33 (1988)

CHAPTER 10: "Inside and outside the *Republic,*" *Phronesis* 37 (1992)

CHAPTER 11: "Transcendental Anthropology," in *Subject, Context and Thought,* ed. John McDowell and Philip Pettit (Oxford: Clarendon Press, 1986)

CHAPTER 12: "The Disappearing 'We,'" *Proceedings of the Aristotelian Society* suppl. vol. 58 (1984); reprinted by courtesy of the Editor of the Aristotelian Society © 1984

Index